Tobias Churton is Britain's leading scholar of Western Esotericism, a subject that encompasses Blake's deepest influences. Appointed Honorary Fellow, School of Humanities and Social Sciences, Exeter University, in 2005, Tobias holds a Master's degree in Theology from Brasenose College, Oxford. Apart from his influential contribution to religious television, and his achievements as a composer and lecturer, Tobias's many books include: a biography of Elias Ashmole (1617–1692), the great man who gave us the Ashmolean Museum, Oxford; and *Aleister Crowley: The Biography* (Watkins, 2nd edition September 2012), the definitive work on this controversial figure. He can be contacted via his website at www.tobiaschurton.com

By the same author:

*Aleister Crowley, THE BEAST IN BERLIN: Art, Sex and Magick in the
    Weimar Republic*
The Mysteries of John the Baptist
The Babylon Gene (novel)
Aleister Crowley: The Biography
The Missing Family of Jesus
The Invisible History of the Rosicrucians
Freemasonry: The Reality
Kiss of Death: The True History of the Gospel of Judas
The Magus of Freemasonry: The Mysterious Life of Elias Ashmole
Gnostic Philosophy
The Golden Builders: Alchemists, Rosicrucians and the First Free Masons
The Fear of Vision (poetry)
Miraval: A Quest (novel)
The Gnostics
Why I am still an Anglican (ed.)

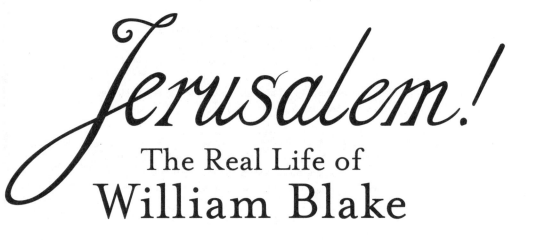

Jerusalem!

The Real Life of
William Blake

TOBIAS CHURTON

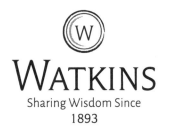

WATKINS

Sharing Wisdom Since
1893

This edition published in the UK and USA 2015 by
Watkins, an imprint of Watkins Media Limited
19 Cecil Court
London WC2N 4HE

enquiries@watkinspublishing.co.uk

1 3 5 7 9 10 8 6 4 2

Designer: Manisha Patel
Managing editor: Deborah Hercun
Project editor: Rebecca Sheppard
Production: Abigail Pukaniuk

Printed and bound in Europe

A CIP record for this book is available from the British Library

ISBN: 978-1-78028-750-8

www.watkinspublishing.com

I dedicate this book to the memory
of Kathleen Raine CBE (1908–2003)

Contents

List of plates

Foreword

Tobias Churton's work and research in *Jerusalem!* are truly astonishing in their detail. He has revealed to me so much. This must be one of the most illuminating and enlightening biographies of Blake to date. I would very much like him to speak at Glastonbury 2015 and read some extracts from *Jerusalem!*

William Blake has always been very close to my heart. Perhaps it is the rebel in him that appeals, or indeed our shared love of Methodism. To me the fundamental attraction to William Blake is, of course, the magical words of the hymn *Jerusalem*. Is there any piece of English literature that is half as well known as these wonderful words? Then there's poetry and prose that have challenging and searching intentions for us all. I've used so many quotes from Blake in my efforts to portray what exactly Glastonbury is all about – the mysticism and the hope that there is a force of nature that not only created us but sustains us daily in our pursuit of pleasure and meaning in our lives.

Blake might have been slightly barmy by today's definition of sanity but his incredible visions and childlike beliefs in God drove his energy and created the heroic genius that he really was.

Michael Eavis CBE
Founder of the Glastonbury Festival

From a Dorsetshire family, **Michael Eavis** (b.1935), dairy farmer of Pilton, Somerset, is best known as the founder of the Glastonbury Festival. The son of a Methodist preacher and a schoolteacher, Michael was educated at Wells Cathedral School and the Thames Nautical Training College, whence he entered the Merchant Navy as a Midshipman. Inheriting Worthy Farm, Pilton, in 1958, he returned to the land, combining his commitment to agriculture with an interest in 1960s politics and pop culture, deeply informed by the practical spirituality of Methodism (he attends Pilton Methodist Church every Sunday). Aware of the needs of young people for freedom and space, Michael hosted the Pilton (Free) Pop Festival on Worthy Farm in 1970, launching the Glastonbury Festival the following year, with its longstanding commitment to charitable causes, local, national and international.

Holding honorary degrees from the universities of Bath and Bristol (Master of Arts, *honoris causa*, 2006), Michael Eavis was awarded the CBE in 2007. Now a major part of the British cultural landscape, and much loved by musicians and festival visitors alike, *Time* magazine listed him as one of the most influential people in the world in 2009.

Foreword

In *Genesis* 1: 26–27, God decides to make man 'after his image': a qualification with far-reaching implications. How good, omniscient, eternal or infinite, is man? At first sight, the image is rather deformed. Can the image be restored?

Answers to this question have been formulated in terms of mirror metaphors. William Blake found inspiration in Jacob Böhme's theosophical system wherein the original Adam reflects God's gaze in passive contemplation. Adam is God's imagination until distracted, whereupon he falls into created substance. A second fall occurs in the earthly paradise (Eden): the mirror image is clouded. Adam longs for the light. What makes Adam human is a sense of loss, of melancholy. Eventually, however, Jesus, the mediator and saviour, will return to restore the original image; hence Blake referred to Jesus as 'Jesus the Imagination'. Blake intended, through Art, to restore the original image of Man.

Blake lived at a time when Immanuel Kant was searching for the boundaries of reason: that which was ungraspable had to fit within this scope or else be excluded as nonsense. Kant realized that not everything could be understood through the faculty of reason alone. The sense of the vastness of a mountain landscape, for example, has an unsettling effect on our reasonable perception. Something happens which transcends the boundaries. Kant referred to this phenomenon as *the sublime*. For Blake such an experience was anything but exceptional: he saw infinity in things.

In a way, this is where modern art begins. Perspectivist construction is gradually abandoned, as a result of which the difference between the foreground and the background is blurred. Things lose their confines, and the mathematical model makes way for vision and gesture.

Blake was absolutely *unzeitgemäss:* he literally did not fit the measure of his times: an untimely stranger, an anachronism. Before Blake it was unthinkable that the graphic arts were judged in terms of their expressive abilities: the brush was more flexible than the burin. Moreover, graphic artists, etchers and engravers were in the first place craftsmen, who simply copied the work of another artist. Blake succeeded in fusing verbal and pictorial expression in a completely new way, producing a modern emblem capable of providing insight to those susceptible to its meaning. He was a visionary extraordinarily aware of a spiritual dimension in our perception. To him, perception was a faculty that served 'poetic genius', by which he meant not the romantic ego, but Mind, the Maker, himself. The Maker himself beheld him, he felt, as in a mirror.

Few documents on the life of William Blake have survived. His image was already distorted shortly after his death. Tobias Churton has stripped his biography of numerous *idées reçues* that clouded that image, allowing Blake to emerge from his work against the backdrop of an age marked by revolutions and modernization. It is a brilliant and illuminating book with a personal touch that invites further reading, as Churton generously shares with his readers his pansophical grasp of rejected knowledge.

Frank van Lamoen

Frank van Lamoen (b.1959) is Assistant Curator of Visual Arts at Amsterdam's Stedelijk Museum. Together with Geurt Imanse and curator Frits Keers, he organized the exhibition 'Kazimir Malevich: drawings from the collection of the Khardzhiev–Chaga Art Foundation' (1997). Frank is co-author (with Geurt Imanse) of the remarkable *Russian Avant-Garde:The Khardzhiev Collection* (*nai010*, 2014). Described by the Stedelijk's Director, Ann Goldstein, as 'an incomparable document', it was published in 2013 by the Stedelijk Museum.

He has published articles on alchemy, Hermetic philosophy, and Jacob Böhme's followers in Holland, and has compiled the first Dutch selection from the work of Giordano Bruno. He has contributed to a quarter of a century of prestigious publications of the *Bibliotheca Philosophica Hermetica,* Amsterdam, concerning the Hermetic textual tradition and the works of Jacob Böhme, including *Jacob Böhmes Weg in die Welt* (Amsterdam, In de Pelikaan, 2007).

The Golden String

It was a girl called Val who introduced me to William Blake. That was back in 1979. She was in the Brasenose College Christian Union and I was a fellow Theology student struggling with unorthodox ideas and a desire to be lauded as a poet. Val thought I should have a look at Mona Wilson's 1927 Blake biography, as the things I was saying reminded her of things she'd read in the book. I think Val was as concerned for Blake's salvation as she was for mine. I remember picking up the paperback and being quite struck by the cover image: the Thomas Phillips portrait of Blake aged about 50. The modestly attired artist-poet had large wide eyes that focused on something elevated beyond the frame. Whatever compelled his gaze rendered an honest face alive with inspiration. I flicked through the pages, packed with long extracts of verses, and put it down again. It looked like hard work.

Some time during the next 18 months I bought the book and read it. Val had been right; there was kinship of idea, and some disturbing messages. The one that struck me most came with a literary creation of Blake's: the blind pseudo-deity called Urizen, the 'jealous God' who knows no God beyond him. As the main villain of Blake's mythic universe, Urizen was instantly recognizable among Blake's artworks as the magnificent 'Ancient of Days'. You must have seen him, famously bounding, and bonding, his universe with a compass-hand. As his epic frame crouches amid brazen clouds on the edge of an infinite sea of time and space, he shoots limits into the infinite, rendering it measurable, accountable, solid, material and, one might say, intelligible – that is, within the circumference of Reason.

This Blake had big ideas; obviously a man of vision! But I could see something else too. I could see 'Urizen' all around us and in 1981 wrote a poem, 'The Return of Urizen', to that effect.

Urizen personifies the human faculty of Reason abstracted from every other psychological faculty. Blake, like Jung considerably later, believed there were four principal categories of mind-function. Reason was one of these four faculties of the psyche; the others being Feeling, Intuition and Sensation. Back in the 18th century, Blake had been playing with the Biggest Idea of his times, times commonly known, or disguised, as the 'Age of Reason'.

Fearing past 'superstition', many thinking people of Blake's parents' generation – and his own – took complacent refuge amid the cold comforts of Reason: very good for some tasks, but not all. Antichristian Pierre-Gaspard Chaumette would erect a 'Goddess Reason' in Nôtre Dame, Paris, in 1793 during the French Revolution – the logical end to a cult that had been gaining pace for a century: Reason had apparently outrun the Catholic Church. Reason appeared supreme as the stable guide to thought and action: man's sole hope in the darkness of unknowing lay in his rationality. Partisans to the principle identified the spark of God within the human breast as Reason, a power of discernment, and therefore, it was thought, of creation.

Blake took this apparently comforting idea and turned it on its head. Far from abstracted reason being a source of stability, Blake demonstrated Reason to be as stable as a devoted husband whose wife has just quit him for a clown. Imagining himself sole lord of the universe, Blake's Urizen alienates himself from his female 'emanation', named 'Ahania'. He abstracts or separates himself, just as reason 'analyses', which means to 'break apart'. As Urizen's rejected consort, Ahania personifies both Wisdom and Pleasure. Both of these essential qualities are abandoned when Reason goes it alone. Ego-enveloped, ruptured both from her and his three fellow faculties, Urizen is blind and chained, dwelling alone in a self-created hell. He is a fallen power, and the perceptible universe displays the mounting wreckage of his infinite yobbery.

Yes, I certainly knew what Blake was getting at with his dynamic, daemonic mythology. I'd heard enough of Urizen's followers as a student (haven't we all?): the smart-alecks and 'objective' evangelists of science, oiled by smooth talk and an answer for everything, contemptuous of spiritual existence, insulated from the effects of their folly by all-consuming pride and safety in numbers:

arrogant, sneering, mocking, cynical ... empty. I had seen 'Urizen' aged 16 when I wrote a poem about two comic knights who, getting lost in a forest, nevertheless eschew the succour of a fine building that springs out of the tangled nature about them: 'Reason was the portal above its gates secure,/ but the knights yielded not to its feminine allure.'

It was difficult to escape the world of Urizen as we grew up in the Western technocracy that could so calmly contemplate its own destruction, along with a pervading and persistent cult of 'security' that seems to know no bounds, save the ones it places on everyone else.

Not long after a considerate girlfriend bought me *Blake's Dante* – Blake's last project – for my 21st birthday, I was introduced to BBC Producer Ed Goldwyn at a café in Farringdon Road, London. Ed was planning a documentary series on possible 'Futures' for Britain and Europe. Over coffee I regaled him enthusiastically with Blake's myth of Urizen – now representing 'the new Europe and its Media' – challenged by 'Orc', the Child of freedom and rebellion, who emerges from the tortured depths of anguished love when psychic balance is fundamentally disturbed. Orc was – and is – quite a character! In 1969 he insinuated himself into Jim Morrison and The Doors' song that began 'Wild Child, full of grace: saviour of the human race – your cruel face!'

If Urizen is the furious 'Bill Sykes' of his universe, then Orc is a rampant Artful Dodger who has broken free from Fagin's grip to let rip in a riot of libertarian frenzy. Blake expert Kathleen Raine once told me how she saw fiery Orc 'in the little punk children on the King's Road'. I asked the BBC Producer to see him in the movement of German 'Alternativen' that had sprung up in Berlin, Frankfurt and elsewhere in the wake of Germany's oh-so-rational 'economic miracle' and *Sicherheit* (= Security) superstructure in the late 60s and 70s. I introduced the BBC Producer to the burgeoning German 'Green Party' (*Die Grünen*), about which neither he nor the British people had heard anything at all (this was 1982). The German Greens challenged the prevailing Logic of the System, a system that always declares 'There is no alternative' while stigmatizing alternatives as 'New Age' fantasies to be kept neatly bottled up at Glastonbury and in English Literature courses: far from power.

It was perhaps politics that ensured that deeper knowledge of events in West Germany never came to grace the TV screen. The 'Alternativen' movement was bound up with socialist individuals and groups opposed to imminent NATO missile deployments in a country widely tipped as the first battleground of any war between the West and the Soviet Union: not surprisingly, there was little relish for the prospect of a peaceful West Germany blown into a wasteland and its inhabitants to premature ashes in the event of miscalculation of Soviet intentions. This was the period of the 'Iron Lady' and the Mrs Thatcher-Ronald Reagan mutual admiration club. Anyhow, I don't think Britain's Broadcasting Company was ready to take on the dreams and aspirations of young Germans as a viable 'alternative future', however sympathetic, in a political climate still fissured by the government's 1980 publication of pamphlets telling every British household what to do to survive a nuclear attack (stay indoors!).

Shortly before Michael Caine uttered playwright Willy Russell's words 'Blake is a dead poet!' while 'educating Rita' in the 1983 movie of that name, I was finding there was still life in the old dog, dead as Blake may have appeared to the world. I was in the village of Rodenhausen, Hessen, a guest of German friends (two musicians, a painter and an industrial psychologist) who had taken me to heart during a research visit with BBC money for my *Futures* proposal. There I recorded my first 'Song of Innocence', an original melody that adapted its lyric from the 'Introduction' to Blake's *Songs of Innocence and Experience*, an illuminated book project Blake launched in 1789 (a date famous in French history) and, as far as I was concerned, still running. Blake and revolutionary hopes always seem to go together, though Blake's revolution was not of the banal 'smash and grab' kind. I sang about 'piping down the valleys wild' in a wild, German valley, accompanying myself on guitar, full of wide-eyed innocence-recovered, and a spiritual vocation the Church of England could not handle. *T'was bliss to be alive!* as Wordsworth would have said in the rosy dawn that precedes the leaden slap of reality.

Upon returning to England, between Channel 4 and BBC TV research assignments, I began to develop a music and film project alongside a bigger documentary series project. The 'film with music' concept was called *LOVE IS ON FIRE! William Blake 1757–1827*. The documentary project was called *The Gnostics*, of which more in a moment.

In 1983 I met an artist whose parents owned a beautiful Steinway grand. I had never heard such a tone! Faery-like, the music redounded in its soulful echo: tunes from another world, known before I heard them. Innocence of approach paid off wonderfully. Open yourself to the Higher and 'it' just might come, though I do think '*it*' comes to the prepared mind, which is to say, the mind freed from dominance – or consciousness of dominance – of any particular faculty. All four faculties must work together. When they do, it might *feel* as if the mind is empty, but if it is integrated – that is, ready to listen – then you can get beyond the vegetable world and the beyond can, as it were, get to you. This is what Blake meant by 'Fourfold Vision' as opposed to what he called, with disdain: 'Single vision and Newton's sleep'. That is *Isaac* Newton, of course, who never succeeded in becoming an artist; Newton took alchemy literally. It was Pink Floyd and their album cover designers *HipGnosis* who realized the artistic potential of Newton's prism, even when taking it to the moon's darker side. In Blake's view, for all Newton's work on 'Opticks', the scientist remained blind to the spiritual universe he sought so assiduously to understand by numbers. He sought too hard, perhaps. As Blake said: 'God is not a mathematical diagram.' Newton got his greatest ideas without trying. 'Unless ye die and be born again, ye cannot enter the kingdom.' But Blake did not know everything about the real Newton: he might have been surprised if he had.

Over three years the score to my Blake movie grew as my girlfriend at the time encouraged and listened to the enterprise with a patience akin to that which Blake's wife Kate lavished on her husband's nocturnal bursts of writing and vision. *Do good ideas come from heaven?* asked Mao Zedong. 'No!' he asserted, 'They come from correct revolutionary practice!' Mao was wrong about this, as he was about most things that matter. Good ideas come from heaven. In 1986 I met the irreplaceable, the great Kathleen Raine CBE (1908–2003), poet and Blake expert, and she told me what Blake meant by heaven. She began with a Blake quote:

'Poetry, painting and music: the three powers for conversing with Paradise that the Flood did not sweep away' – by 'the Flood', Blake meant the *Flood of Time and Space*.

'Conversing with Paradise', of course, goes back to the Gospel, in which it is said that 'The kingdom of heaven is within you.' *That* is Paradise. Paradise is the inner life of every man. We can all converse with Paradise.

That was Blake's firm belief. We can all converse with Paradise. But, of course, you've got to want to, and many do not. And many of *them* work in films and art and publishing and television, the very places where you might imagine belief in such things could convey real bounties, to the public. So long as the arts have social status, and there is money to be made, these places will attract the worst as well as the best, and it only takes one bad apple for things to fall back to earth, as the mythic Newton knew well enough.

How did I get to meet Kathleen Raine? At the end of 1985 I began work on *The Gnostics*, a four-part Channel 4 series, the like of which had never been seen before and has never been seen since (you can't get to see it for love nor money) – no accident, I'm sure. The series covered the history of what Kathleen called 'the excluded tradition', the tradition of independent spiritual experience and thought, taking the 1945 discovery of the famous 'Gnostic Gospels' in Egypt as a starting point, then tracing kindred ideas to that of the Christian Gnostics through time. We investigated, in a thoroughly historical and reassuringly scholarly manner – the conservative *Daily Telegraph* approved strongly – the Cathars of 12th- and 13th-century Languedoc, the Hermetic tradition that served as the little-known 'manifesto' of the Renaissance and early scientific movement, and the modern world, focusing on Carl Jung, neo-Gnosticism in the US, and a remarkable Dutch businessman who has become a philanthropist of Gnostic and related studies with a special library in Amsterdam, the *Bibliotheca Philosophica Hermetica*. The founder, Joost Ritman, was raised in the Dutch Rosicrucian tradition. We had truly linked the ancient and the modern.

It had not escaped my notice that William Blake could well be described as a 'Gnostic' if we define that term precisely enough. I wanted to feature Blake in some detail in the series. Unfortunately, the sea of time and space, being limited by old Urizen, you might say, did not permit this inclusion. However, I had interviewed Kathleen Raine and knew I would come back to her on the issue as soon as possible. In the meantime, I put a special chapter on Blake in the series's accompanying book *The Gnostics,* which was a national bestseller, introducing many thousands of people to the tradition in the UK as well as in Europe and in America; it made me a lot of good friends, and I dare say, some enemies too.

My reward for being a good boy on the *Gnostics* series was – at last – to direct my film on Blake, a 'composed film' for which I had had the pleasure of taking friendly advice from Michael Powell, not long before that visionary of the cinema screen left this world for the ultimate Picture Palace.

The idea was to show Blake's life *as he saw it in his own mind*. Commissioning Editor John Ranelagh secured £20,000 of development money. I found a Producer, Karla Ehrlich, and a production company, and secured the agreement of Brian Blessed to play Blake (minus beard; Michael Powell had suggested Wayne Sleep, a surprising, but in retrospect, intriguing choice). Dennis Rich, storyboard artist – he had planned out the James Bond film *Never Say Never Again* – produced an absolutely exquisite storyboard, a real work of art in its own right, declaring he was so pleased at last to work on a movie for which he did not have to draw a helicopter! I researched the locations and wrote the script and recorded a test track of my opening theme ('London 1769'), played and arranged with brilliance by ex-Genesis member, Anthony Phillips. All looked fair. And then, John Ranelagh left Channel 4 in late 1987, an event followed by one of the severest storms to hit London in its entire history (15–16 October). Strangely, nothing was quite the same after that.

The new commissioning editor came in. He was a very different kettle of fish, and despite assurances offered to his predecessor, the project was dropped. I was informed the British public was not ready for immersion baptism into the mind of William Blake. Well, it never would be, would it? But a child does not know what Christmas is, until he or she has experienced it. Was it blind Urizen, 'back again; back again in fear again'? As compensation – or was it the 'kiss-off'? – I was commissioned to make a film about Doctrine in the Church of England. Yes, the irony of this seems harder and more vivid 27 years later!

I had a friend in Holland, a spiritual friend of William Blake: the founder of the Hermetic Philosophy Library, Joost Ritman. Thanks to him, I was able to make a film to run as a new fourth part of *The Gnostics* when that series was shown on Dutch TV. I set up my own company this time and *The New Age and the New Man* was born, in 1989, while nobody was looking. I interviewed Kathleen Raine for the third time (I made sure she made an appearance in the Church of England Doctrine film, *No Man Hath Seen God,* Channel 4, 1988), and devoted a good third of the film to William Blake. The Technicolor show-print is sitting in my shed, its can rusting away. I took it to Channel 4 and they would not show it: no one was interested in 'the excluded tradition'.

The televisual door slammed shut, and, as far as I am concerned, has remained shut ever since; there's no vision in the *tele*.

However, life must go on. And Blake has been with me through it all. In 1993 I was about to travel to Uppsala to train as a priest in the Church of Sweden – I wish I had space to tell you *that* story! Shortly before, as a parting gift, my girlfriend's mother bought me a fine copy of Blake's complete work *Jerusalem,* consisting of over 100 illuminated plates. And what was Blake's conclusion? It was this: that 'Jerusalem' meant *spiritual liberty*. Did this, I wonder, influence my sudden decision to turn back from the airport, and return to engage in years of productive work on what is now called 'Western Esotericism'?

Twenty years, to be precise. It seems astonishing to me. Where has all the time gone? And what is this 'time thing' anyway?

Now, who is the 'real Blake'? There is a Blake I've got to know through some shared experience, gifts and temperamental, spiritual and intellectual affinities, but is he the same one that will emerge from the fire of objective – yes, objective – investigation?

Looking for the historical Blake is a bit like looking for the 'historical Jesus', or the historical *anything*, for that matter. He has become a legend (as befits a Gnostic saint) and lately, far worse, a 'national treasure'. The person we know inwardly recedes as we objectify them. Aha! Isn't that always true? Things always seem very different in court, where the aim is to arrive at the 'facts' and the 'proof' of statements made, events recalled. A passionate love affair looks very different before judge and jury!

But circumstances have conspired, and conspired strangely, to make this biography happen at this time. Indeed, it is a splendid thing that I was not asked to write a full biography 30 years ago. I would have accepted the offer, but I was not, as I realize clearly now, prepared for such a task. I can only assert my belief that the intervening years of study of that 'excluded tradition' that Blake also took as his own have at last made me a candidate for the effort. And I also remember something Kathleen Raine said to me. When I called her out of her comfort in Paultons Square, Chelsea, for a third interview (filmed) she sighed, 'I suppose I'm the only one who can do it!' I think she was right. Then, when I began researching this biography, I found in my attic – honestly! – a bag of lost micro-cassettes of interviews with great Gnostic scholars such as Hans Jonas, Gilles Quispel, Elaine Pagels and, of course, Kathleen Raine. Playing the Raine tape again I was astonished. As we got further into a long and magical conversation, she suddenly announced: 'You, Toby! You are the future! You will carry on the torch!' That was a bit strong! No adventurous young man likes having his future carved out for him; but it is beginning to look like Kathleen shared in her guru's (that is, Blake's) prophetic powers. For here we are.

My thanks go in the first instance to my commissioning editor at Watkins, Michael Mann, who seized on the idea of a Blake biography that really delivered the substance of what Blake himself was driven by (and which has been so often ignored, downgraded, garbled or lost). Michael will not mind sharing honours with the late Kathleen Raine, without whose insight I should have been the poorer reader and viewer of Blake. I would also like to thank Frank van Lamoen, Assistant Curator at Amsterdam's Stedelijk Museum, and the staff of Joost Ritman's *Bibliotheca Philosophica Hermetica*, Amsterdam, especially José Bouman and Cis van Heertum, for access to first editions of Blake's *Job* engravings and his version of Young's *Night Thoughts*.

I also wish to thank the graphic artist, Jean Luke Epstein, for undertaking research on my behalf with the very kind assistance of the Museum and Library of Freemasonry, Great Queen Street, opposite the building where young Blake spent seven years of his life as an apprentice engraver. Archivist and Records Manager, Susan A Snell of the Library and Museum of Freemasonry, Freemasons Hall, was most helpful with information about Blake's mostly tenuous links with Freemasonry.

I should also like to offer belated thanks to my late mother and father, Victor and Patricia Churton, who introduced me to little-known or remembered circles of the 18th and 19th centuries 40 years ago as they embarked on a truly remarkable chronicle of family history that almost brought me to Blake's front door, as we shall see.

Tobias Churton
Staffordshire

A Note on Blake's Punctuation

William Blake was not university educated. Indeed, he would not tolerate the discipline of 18th-century schooling at any level. His linguistic education, where not governed by his mother, and possibly a nurse, was mostly self-taught. It is likely that Blake inherited his idiosyncratic grammar and punctuation in part from his mother's limited abilities in writing English. However, Blake read widely and, as he grew up, he familiarized himself with the classics of English literature, as well as the works of antiquarians, spiritual writers and philosophers. Nevertheless, despite his gift for producing beautifully crafted, inspired poetry and didactic prose, his punctuation – or lack of it – may surprise some readers. What may appear to be typographical errors in transcribing Blake's writings can be laid at the door of Blake's 'free-form', perhaps even cavalier, employment – or non-employment – of full stops, commas, possessive apostrophes and capital letters, combined with occasional peculiarities of spelling. While the English language was not strictly standardized to the degree it is today, Blake's punctuation, grammar and spelling were objectionable to some observers even in his own day, his faults being regarded as signs of poor education, or the want of a gentleman's education. Blake himself, however, was proud of his knowledge, acquired through hard work. He was deliberately anti-conformist with regard to literary creativity. Blake's linguistic peculiarities may, therefore, be ascribed more to willfulness and habit than to ignorance.

Jerusalem!

I give you the end of a golden string
Only wind it into a ball:
It will lead you in at Heaven's gate,
Built in Jerusalem's wall.

(Introduction to Chapter 4, *Jerusalem;* dated 1804)

Every weekend of every week in England you can be sure a gang of revellers somewhere will launch into a spontaneous rendition of William Blake's 'Jerusalem' – whether it be a wedding, pub-party or rugby carouse. Few of the voices raised in song will either have visited, or heard about, Tate Britain's William Blake retrospective of 2009, or know that on 6 May 2013, Tate Britain re-launched designated Blake galleries to house examples from a collection that has toured the States, Spain and Russia. It doesn't matter; *Blake* has reached them already.

On BBC Radio 3 in April 2013, a call was issued for a specifically English anthem. Top of the list came 'Jerusalem'; it touches the parts other anthems can't reach, including the National Anthem. Needless to say, it inspired Jez Butterworth's 2009 Royal Court Theatre hit play *Jerusalem*, starring Mark Rylance, who first played William Blake (in the nude) in a fascinating BBC production back in 1993.

'Jerusalem' transcends the National Anthem because it is not a nationalistic anthem; it expresses a universal yearning in the English soul, something vital and appreciable by people across the Seven Seas. Americans need no reminding that William Blake inspired Ralph Waldo Emerson and US visionary Walt Whitman. Though Blake called himself 'English Blake', he would have been a poor poet and prophet if his message spoke only to one country. Some of his most insightful commentators have come from India. Blake addressed Man – and what had gone wrong with Man – and how to put it right.

Many people today yearn deeply for some kind of spiritual revival, not in the 'Billy Graham' sense, but a renewal of the faculty of vision, a re-embodying liberation of ourselves and of our narrowing culture. We look, mostly in vain, to television and cinema, finding confusion, superficiality and exploitation. Many of us feel lost among our own objects – and feel objects ourselves, numbered and taxed. The universe, for all its scale, has begun to feel closed, our lives imprisoning, our best thoughts and feelings closed in. Grand opportunities are thrown away, day in and day out, in the ceaseless media mayhem.

William Blake addressed our predicament at the dawn of the materialism that has enveloped us. He did so in poetry, painting and music (sadly his tunes, if not his verses, are lost to us). Blake can put us back in touch with paradise while on earth, as Kathleen Raine stated in the conversation quoted in the Preface to this book. Toward the end of Kathleen's life, she would say simply: 'Blake is my guru. He taught me everything.' It was clear when you met her, that Blake – who could never afford a university education – knew everything worth knowing.

But Blake the guru has been lost under a myriad of inadequate biographies, college dissertations and arts commentaries, too frequently written by people who have not found the luminescent keys to Blake's symbolism and liberating spirit. Too often, commentators strain at gnats and swallow camel-loads of trite or obscure, overly literary interpretation. Appropriate words appear – like 'spiritual' – but only in rare cases do you feel the writer really *knows* (as you would know a person) what he or she is talking about.

It was long ago observed that had Blake been born in Germany, he would have been as famous as Beethoven, with statues of him in the cities and his books required reading for the cultivated. It took a century after his death in 1827 for Blake to be appreciated at practically any level beyond a tiny coterie of supporters (*viz*: Samuel Palmer, John Linnell, Dante Gabriel Rossetti). The star that rose to bring the poet, engraver, painter and philosopher to 'national treasure' status rose steeply in the late 1960s when the efforts of poet-prophets like Adrian Mitchell (1932–2008) and free political experimentation let loose a visionary, youthful energy, formerly suppressed by party orthodoxies. Suddenly, with LSD, Pink Floyd, Yoga and Sufism in the air it became possible to join Blake in seeing, *really seeing*, 'a heaven in a wild flower, a world in a grain of sand, and eternity in an hour'. Even science seemed to be on the side of the visionaries: Jacob Bronowski, presenter and writer of the 1973 BBC documentary series, *The Ascent of Man*, was one of Blake's biggest fans.

Aldous Huxley took to heart Blake's line, 'When the doors of perception are cleans'd, then we shall see all things as they are: infinite,' and he took the concept to his influential book on expanded consciousness, *The Doors of Perception* (1954). Jim Morrison took those same 'doors' as the name for his revolutionary poetic/theatrical band, The Doors – who lit the fire of everyone who was listening after they burst onto the crowded scene to 'Break On Through to the Other Side' in that year of so many 'Songs of Innocence', 1967. Innocence soon became Experience – with Jimi Hendrix – and William Blake was there too with comfort and guidance through the darkening years that followed the first brief opening of perceptual doors in the late 1960s. Everyone now realizes that something happened in that time, though few are sure what exactly.

Blake wrote for us because he perceived, so far ahead of his time, that the philosophy of materialism would dominate the world, but not defeat 'the Ancient Man', 'the Poetic Genius', the 'Divine Imagination'. He was 'not a number'; he was 'a free man'. Through fires of rebellion and cataclysmic change, the 'Child of Freedom and Rebellion' would rise again, challenge the dominance of abstracted Reason, and its baleful Law, and break the dams on the infinite worlds within. The spiritually Free Man and Woman would rise again and re-integrate the Broken Man, living in darkness, into the heart and centre of his or her own true being. Eternal Life would mean something to the objects of the Western world once more.

Blake's titanic spiritual effort has been obscured and variegated by numerous academics and specialists who, in my judgement, have often not seen the wood for the trees, missing the essence. Thus, for some, Blake is a 'romantic poet' with some prescient ideas about poetic form. To others, he is a proto-socialist revolutionary, an angry Cockney 'Digger' with some ideas about free love – 'one of the lads' whose 'visionary side' is a bit of an aberration: allegedly too obscure for 'modern people'. Chief among exceptions to prevailing misapprehensions stand, in my opinion, commentaries by WB Yeats and Kathleen Raine: they make sense of the man.

Blake was concerned with a total spiritual revival. If you had asked him to paint the church at Felpham, Sussex (where he lived 1800–03), he would not think you meant a portrait or landscape. Having little time for either genre, he would want to *paint the church*! From top to bottom, inside and out, restoring the colour of a popular church of a lost Middle Ages, before human beings became, in the words of Orson Welles, paraphrasing Blake, a 'poor, forked radish', cut adrift from immortality.

So how does the popular love for 'Jerusalem' fit into all of this? In many ways, and at first sight, there is little connection between enthusiasm for the 'hymn' and the biography of the person who wrote it. When I have asked singers of the song if they knew who wrote it, they have oft expressed surprise at the question. *What does it matter?* We shall see, however, that to understand the writer is to understand the hymn. If we care about the hymn, we shall want to learn about its author.

Misunderstanding of the man – and therefore of the hymn – was plain, nay, was stark, from the moment in 1916 when 'Jerusalem' first entered popular consciousness, more than a century after the composition of the lyrics.

As many readers will already know, 'Jerusalem' was not even a hymn, nor can the stirring verses accurately be described as a 'poem'. And 'its' name is not really 'Jerusalem'; the verses that we know, which have been subtly changed, did not *have* a name because they were part of something else. The lines beginning 'And did those feet in ancient time…' come from the preface to Blake's epic poem *Milton*, which he began writing around 1803–4 but which he did not complete for a decade or so; at least, he did not complete the etching of it in an illuminated book that could be purchased at his home in South Molton Street, Mayfair, around the time of Waterloo.

A century later, Poet Laureate Robert Bridges included the verses 'Jerusalem' in a 1916 anthology with patriotic intentions called *The Spirit of Man*. This is odd, because the first edition of the *Oxford Book of English Verse* (1900; edited by Arthur Quiller-Couch), to which Bridges contributed, included ten poems by Blake, but no 'Jerusalem'. Somebody introduced the lines to Bridges who, encouraged to use his position to raise morale in a war feared too costly and potentially endless, decided the lines could inculcate the right spirit of national self-sacrifice to a higher cause ('building Jerusalem', or the New Jerusalem – a vision from the Book of Revelation, familiar to the scripturally aware people of the time).

Bridges wanted Blake's words set to music for a rousing 'Fight for Right' campaign meeting to be held in London's Queen's Hall, so he approached composer Sir Charles Hubert Hastings Parry (1848–1918), who had composed the beautiful melody 'Repton' to the popular hymn 'Dear Lord and Father of Mankind'. Bridges thought the so-called 'Jerusalem' stanzas, as lyrics, would remind people of what was at stake in the war, along with a vision of what could be made out of the long struggle: 'nor shall my sword sleep in my hand until we have built Jerusalem in England's green and pleasant land.' The 'sword' could easily be taken as a crusading equivalent for a rifle and bayonet. People were fighting for a better future, a Godly future vouchsafed by Christ's favour for the land that the Lamb of God – willing to be sacrificed – was happy to be identified with. There was not only a 'green hill far away' where the 'Lamb' was crucified, but also a green and pleasant land threatened by Germans in their collective devilry.

Personally averse to the possible 'jingoism' of the 'Fight for Right' campaign, Parry was uncomfortable with the use of his melody and arrangement when he presented the finished work on 10 March 1916. Nevertheless, 18 days later, Queen's Hall saw it performed with organ and choir to rapturous appreciation. Parry's doubts, however, were not allayed by such red-blooded popularity. In May 1917, he withdrew his musical support from the 'Fight for Right' campaign. The song was in danger of disappearing from the repertoire when Millicent Garrett Fawcett of the National Union of Women's Suffrage Societies requested Parry to permit its use on 13 March 1918 at a Suffrage Demonstration Concert, and subsequently, as a women's voters' hymn. Women saw another aspect of the beauty of the work. Thanks to them, we know it still. They were not alone in their approval.

When King George V heard the orchestrated version prepared by Parry for the Suffrage concert, he declared a preference for 'Jerusalem' over 'God Save the King' – an irony Blake would surely have appreciated. The combination of poetry and music cast a spell over listeners akin to that which Sir Edward Elgar's 'Nimrod' held over Winston Churchill. 'Jerusalem' spoke of spiritual struggle as the highest purpose of existence, that inner struggle which gave life its essential and transcending dignity and to which the world was blind. Parry himself was pleased that 'Jerusalem' would, in the women's hands, bring a sense of joy, of something good being done that would brighten lives. He understood that 'building Jerusalem' was not something to be achieved with bombs and bullets that knocked people and things out of existence: it must be *built* with the inner commitment of lives devoted to a life higher than ordinary selves. What artist could wish for more? England's greatest composer, Sir Edward Elgar, would write his own arrangement of Parry's mysterious melody.

Inevitably, socialists got on the bandwagon and loaded the 'new Jerusalem' with a politically oriented social-welfare meaning that was definitely earth-bound, but which kidded many people that the Labour Party was a Godly influence. In the critical 1945 General Election, aspiring PM Clement Attlee declared the Labour Party would build a 'New Jerusalem'; in this dream at least, socialists could all sing from the same hymnbook. But there would be no jewelled buildings or golden spires in the new flats, estates and tenements of post-war Britain. The New Jerusalem would be constructed in a hurry with a lot of reinforced concrete, enforced austerity and social-architecture theory – the Luftwaffe's preparatory demolition completed by 'Hell-Drivers' in trucks storming about the country like Valkyries high on diesel fumes.

And it must be said that Blake would have found little to admire in the philosophy of either state-controlled, or liberal, socialism. He was against its principles at the most fundamental level. First, the idea of 'equality' would have repelled him. As he wrote in his explosive work *The Marriage of Heaven and Hell*: 'One law for the lion and the ox is repression.' Individuals are absolutes; by our own thoughts and actions we become either 'sheep' or 'goats'. Man desires to be a free agent and every human being is different, while all share in the 'Divine Humanity' to such degrees as individuals may experience.

Man's highest state is 'spiritual liberty' and this is realized minutely and particularly in individuals, not collectively. Man's liberty increases as he discovers his spiritual dignity. Where lies this dignity? It lies in the realization that Man is a spiritual being, a spiritual being of infinite, not rationally predictable, potential. Contrary to Thomas Paine's *Rights of Man* and the

Rousseau-Voltaire faction, Blake did not believe Man was basically 'good', but basically *God*. And God, as the German 'mystic' Jacob Böhme (1575–1624) had taught him, had two apparently contrary aspects, and Man was caught in the outflow of these until he woke up. In the dual aspects of God's nature could be found the only 'historical dialectic' that caught Blake's attention. He was not interested in any alleged 'class struggle': such would be a chimaera, a tale of jealousy and envy for the embittered. True wealth resided in the spirit. Man does not 'belong' to society; we are all, Blake believed, members of the Divine Body, co-existent with God. Blake's 'Albion' is not another word for 'Society'. Politics boils down to convenience; society in general is a frightened gang, full of 'accusers' and the spirit of accusation against anyone who 'breaks ranks' – such as Jesus, whom Blake did not identify with the 'workers', but with the Imagination.

All this explains the emphasis in 'Jerusalem' on the 'Mental Fight'. Every person can hear the voice of 'Satan' or false ego (attached to the world of nature) and the voice of the angel – that is, the spiritual being. The 'prince of this world' is *Self*: 'self first, self last, self all the bloody time!' as my mother used to say. This false self hides the true God.

Blake had read in the Bible and in the Hermetica, as well as in the works of Neo-Platonists, Gnostics and 'Rosicrucians', a consistent message confirmed by his chosen teachers Paracelsus and Jacob Böhme. Primal Man had fallen from his spiritual dignity as a result of what esoteric spiritual Tradition has called the 'love of the body': a fatal and narcissistic fascination with the reflection of Man's eternal form in nature.

Blake found his inner conceptions truer to spiritual reality than what his 'vegetable eye' could see of what was apparently 'outside of himself'. The rule of Nature divorced from God was a cruel and tyrannical rule, and the 'Satan' of the material creation was effectively the 'false ego' of the universe: strutting about arrogantly with his 'rules and regs'. Blake – and this is important to grasp – believed the philosophy and science of his time was pushing Man further and further into this 'desert' of abstracted time and space.

Well, here we are. We've arrived. We're deep into the sand and do not perceive eternity in its grains. Blake would not be at all surprised to see what the Hubble telescope has brought to our vegetable eyes: an endless ocean of exploding and imploding forces that expand or contract as the current leading theory supposes, all done with numbers and spectroscopes. If we could smell the 'grandeur of the cosmos' (as presently seen), it would largely stink, of methane and worse, clouded with gaseous abortions: sole oases of escaping light in an endless desert pocked with 'black holes'. Blake called the 'guv'nor' of the natural universe 'a very cruel being', awesome in his Goliath-like way, but cruel, and blind. And that cruelty dwelt in ourselves. Dealing with it, grappling with the forces of our inner nature, was the *Mental Fight* that 'Jerusalem' was all about. You cannot build the New Jerusalem with brick or stone; it is built with love and tears and the sacrifice of the false self that hides the Real. The masons of the Great City are the men and women of Imagination fed on spiritual truth.

As to what Blake precisely meant by 'these dark Satanic mills' (changed, pointedly, to *those* dark Satanic mills, in the popular hymn), we shall discover in due course. But one thing I can tell you: the dark Satanic mills of Blake's vision were definitely *not* the smoky, clattering, banging and hammering manufactories, foundries, extrusion presses and cotton mills of sweated labour and techno-supremacy that, as the royal steam engine roared up the iron road through the Midlands' 'Black Country', so alarmed Queen Victoria that she insisted on having the carriage curtains closed, lest the sooty vapour of filthy, empire-building lucre-in-the-making spoilt her day.

Regardless of the distortion of Blake's words into some patriotic heaven on earth, the 'hymn' ploughs on to work its expressive magic and, to no one's surprise, was heard and sung at the wedding in Westminster Abbey of Catherine Middleton and Prince William – now a song for a 'new age' of democratic, rational, emotional monarchy, or perhaps, a yearning for something better than what we think we 'have' now.

I have no doubt that Blake would have been flattered by the attention: he had spent the larger part of his creative career ridiculed and suppressed. Nevertheless, it is hard to imagine Blake could have stomached for a minute the use of his words to promote recruitment and enthusiasm for the First World War. He would have noted, I suspect, that the 'sword' that did not 'sleep in the hand' line was preceded, as we have observed, by a glaring emphasis on the '*mental* fight'. Blake made explicit a few lines earlier in his Preface to *Milton* that the 'Mental Fight' was the proper, Christian alternative to 'Corporeal War':

> Rouse up, O Young Men of the New Age! Set your foreheads against
>   the ignorant Hirelings!
> For we have Hirelings in the camp, the Court and the University, who
>   would, if they could, for ever depress Mental and prolong Corporeal War.

A 'hireling' is a mercenary, someone unconcerned with the essence of the conflict, someone who profits from the fight itself. Blake was advocating a kind of interior, personal 'jihad' or struggle against the forces of the material world; a struggle that could only be fought with spiritual, not material, weapons, for there was ultimately nothing to be gained from the material world as such: 'the kingdom of heaven is within you.' The Great Powers were, from the standpoint of the highest plane, fighting over precisely Nothing.

Furthermore, the patriotic emphasis of 'Jerusalem', as we know it, would require considerable qualification in order to secure the author's approval for the use of his work. Blake regarded his country as one that had fallen from a primitive grace, an epic simplicity. The country's primary goal should be to rediscover its magical, spiritual science, secreted like a fugitive in the land, to restore itself to full 'manhood' – that is, to re-integrate its energies as you would a broken Man. That 'Man' he called 'Albion': the spiritual idea enfleshed in the British Isles. Every Briton was spiritually a part of him and shared in his catastrophic Fall, the diminution of his powers, and his division into lesser potencies. To reduce Blake's vision of the Primal Man to a tune and sentiment about nationalist 'victory' would have appalled him while confirming his conviction that everything that tumbles into the material world is fatally distorted both in substance and in meaning.

> My mother groan'd! my father wept.
> Into the dangerous world I leapt.
> Helpless, naked, piping loud;
> Like a fiend hid in a cloud.

> ('Infant Sorrow'; from *Songs of Experience*)

Blake's vision is really too big, too fundamentally disturbing for many today who have, in my experience, inherited not the 'excluded tradition' that Blake embraced, but a philosophy or philosophies the very opposite of what Blake was advocating in poetry and painting and music. Matter is king; Man is matter: organism gene-driven.

There is in the Western, and especially European, artistic, scientific and political establishment, a seething well of outright hostility to anything whatsoever smacking of 'Western esotericism', all of which is consigned to a dustbin of outmoded beliefs, a haven for eccentrics and Luddites. Smirking and sneering at spiritual ideas is prevalent and encouraged. Who dare put his or her head above the parapet? It was so in Blake's own time, not so very long ago, and it is so today. More surprising is it then that Blake has become a 'national treasure' (ugly phrase) of the exportable British Art Industry while becoming accepted as the author of a popular, arguably nationalistic, hymn of pride: something to keep the English happy. Nevertheless, Blake has somehow 'got in', and while some of the captions at his permanent exhibition at Tate Britain, for example, read awkwardly, as though the curators were not quite sure how to present Blake to the general public (he is, on one wall currently, mysteriously and ludicrously associated with the development of British landscape art), he is there to see, though curiously 'cut off' from the main galleries, at least for the present.

As this book demonstrates, an historical understanding of William Blake is impossible without a good knowledge of the cultural forces prevailing in his lifetime. In many respects, Blake failed to meet his prime audience, the English nation – a failure that I think made him more eager to assert in the last decade of his life that he considered 'publication' of his works accomplished when the letters 'flew all about' his room to be read by the 'spirits' who would convey the works, as we might say today, into the collective unconscious. In the spiritual worlds, Blake believed he enjoyed a big fan club, whereas in the England of George III, the Regency and George IV, significant members of the ruling establishment targeted Blake as an enemy. You don't have to lock a man up or hang or transport him to render his voice un-hearable. Poverty would ensure that only brave, more searching spirits would approach his door.

I do not think the greater *Sitz im Leben*, or life-setting, of Blake has been adequately dealt with or persuasively understood in previous biographies. To help establish this greater perspective, I have been blessed with having inherited a large body of never-before-published records – letters, diaries, pamphlets and books – that I will employ to cast light and perspective on Blake's life and times (the *Churton Papers*). Archdeacon Ralph Churton (1754–1831) was an almost exact contemporary of Blake, and, like Blake, did not emerge from pecuniary wealth. Their paths in life, however, took them in different directions even while their essential interests, the spiritual destiny of their country, remained, fascinatingly, the same.

> *The Thing I have most at heart – more than life, or all that seems to make life comfortable without – Is the Interest of True Religion and Science…*

> (Letter from William Blake to Thomas Butts, 1802)

While Blake, unschooled, developed an idiosyncratic system of Christian belief, Ralph Churton went to Brasenose College, Oxford, distinguishing himself subsequently as a theologian and pillar of the English religious establishment. He was also a famous biographer, a correspondent of Boswell and Gilbert White, and a leading antiquarian.

It is one of my contentions that Blake owes far more than has been recognized to the development of British antiquarianism in the 18th century, both in thought and deed. To take one key example, it was not Blake alone who came to value the treasury of art to be found in the country's 'Gothic' churches – Westminster Abbey in particular – while apprenticed to James Basire's engraving firm in Great Queen Street, opposite the Freemasons' Hall and Tavern. The work at the Abbey was done at the behest of Churton's friend and correspondent, Richard Gough (1735–1809), godfather to Churton's daughter, Mary. Gough, like Churton, was a Fellow of the Society of Antiquaries of London, founded by royal charter in 1751, six years before Blake's birth. Society director from 1771 to 1791, Gough spent the period of Blake's apprenticeship and career up to Blake's 42nd year compiling his mighty two-volume *Sepulchral Monuments* and an English translation of Camden's *Britannia* (1789), the greatest contemporary work on ancient English topography and history. *Britannia* seems to have informed Blake's epic visionary poem *Jerusalem*. It was Gough's work that took the teenage Blake into Westminster Abbey and to his famous and influential realization that 'Gothic form is living form'.

Churton used the Basire firm to execute engravings for his *Life of Alexander Nowell, Dean of St Paul's* (Oxford, 1809) at Gough's suggestion. He was also a regular correspondent of antiquarian Thomas Dunham Whitaker (1759–1821), a friend of fellow antiquarian Charles Townley (1737–1805) whose collection of Roman and Greek art would form a large part of the British Museum's holding of sculptured antiquities. Royal Academy member Townley knew both Blake and one of Blake's three closest friends, sculptor John Flaxman (1755–1826). Flaxman was also a correspondent of Blake's patron (1800–04), William Hayley. Churton also knew Flaxman and personally organized a monumental job for him at the Radcliffe Library, Oxford, in 1805–06.

Churton was closely aware of developments in religion that grieved him. He prayed for the return of those who had absented themselves from the Church of England. Was Blake one of them? We shall see that, in the circles that controlled much of the artistic and intellectual world Blake needed to belong to in order to secure a reputation, established opinions and loyalties counted a great deal. We shall find Archdeacon Churton and his friends, we might say, on the 'winning side' and Blake, 'poor Blake' as *his* friends so often called him, on the losing side. However, we shall also see that matters were never quite that simple in this extraordinarily volatile and deeply surprising period of political, religious and intellectual ferment.

Perhaps the greatest surprise to Blake aficionados of the last decade has been delivered by the extensive research of Dr Keri Davies, Visiting Fellow in the School of Arts and Humanities, Nottingham Trent University, and Atlanta-based Dr Marsha Keith Schuchard, author of *William Blake's Sexual Path to Spiritual Vision* (Inner Traditions, 2008). In 2004 Schuchard collaborated with Davies on the seminal article 'Recovering the lost Moravian history of William Blake's family',[1] following Schuchard's astonishing discovery in 2002 of records concerning William Blake's mother Catherine and her first husband, Thomas Armitage, at the Moravian Church Library and Archive at Muswell Hill, London.

Davies's and Schuchard's illuminating work on Blake's mother and his mother's first husband knocks on the head at a stroke the long-held belief that Blake came from a family of Dissenters (Muggletonians, Baptists or some other group), a supposition that has encouraged the idea of a religiously dissenting

Blake 'naturally' moving into dissenting 'left-wing' political radicalism. This is the first published biography to take in the new knowledge about the authentic spiritual background of Blake's Nottinghamshire-born (not 'Cockney') mother and the spiritual influences available to his upbringing. This knowledge – and I bow to Davies and Schuchard in this respect – has enormous implications for understanding the real Blake, helping us to see him in a far richer, broader context than hitherto, while scotching once and for all the persistent notion of Blake as a startling peculiarity, a kind of curiosity or blip in the history of art and letters, to be explained away by psychological, vaguely religious or even psychiatric jargon.

In the process of investigation, we shall have to overcome much of the romanticism that has enveloped Blake's reputation from the time of Alexander Gilchrist's beautifully written biography (1861; 1880) and we shall find some painful surprises and the puncturing of a few perhaps cherished illusions on the way. I am sure we shall find Blake as challenging as he was to his contemporaries, and while distance of time will doubtless lessen the shock value that might have brought tremors to Gilchrist's Victorian audience, I have no doubt that Blake's continued relevance to our predicaments will still induce as much dismissive (if veiled) hostility, as it will generate joy for the open-minded – for Blake was a saint. And the miracle is, that we have heard of him.

Tobias Churton
Staffordshire, November 2014

ONE

The Only Way to Die

1827

England in 1827 was a dangerous place to be King. In February, after fifteen stormy years in office, Prime Minister Lord Liverpool suffered a paralytic stroke. Torn between hardline Tory Duke of Wellington and moderate George Canning as successor, George IV felt vulnerable. He quit his 'Kremlin by the Sea', Brighton Pavilion, for Windsor Castle on 7 March. Exposed to an assassin's wiles by Brighton's expansion, the Pavilion would never see the King again.

Ever since Lord Liverpool's Importation Act of 1815, the King's government had endured widespread resentment for high grain prices. Intended, like so many painful political poultices, as a temporary measure, the so-called Corn Laws' prohibition on foreign wheat imports protected landowners from low prices but caused misery and starvation across the country, even where bread was not scarce. Crippled economically by Napoleonic war debts, the government raised taxes consistently. In a bid to ease popular concerns, the King chose former Foreign Secretary of brilliance, George Canning, as Prime Minister in April. Hopes in Canning's liberality were dashed by his sudden death on 8 August: unsettling news to a very poorly artist called William Blake who, in his seventieth year, was himself dying by inches at 3 Fountain Court, just off the Strand.

Earlier in the year, a physically enfeebled Blake had annotated Robert John Thornton MD's latest book, *The Lord's Prayer, Newly Translated* (1827) with vigorous fulminations against what Blake saw as its 'Tory' translation in curious league with tyrannical taxation. Blake, strong in spirit, even added a vicious parody of the Lord's Prayer in terms he envisioned as lying surreptitiously behind Dr Thornton's pieties:

Our Father Augustus Caesar [that is, King George Augustus Frederick] who art in these thy Substantial Astronomical Telescopic Heavens, Holiness to thy name, or Title & reverence to thy Shadow; Thy Kingship come upon Earth first, & thence in Heaven. Give us day by day our Real Taxed Substantial Money-bought Bread, deliver from the Holy Ghost, so we call Nature whatever cannot be Taxed, for all is debts & Taxes between Caesar & us & one another. Lead us not to read the Bible, but let our Bible be Virgil and Shakespeare, and deliver us from Poverty in Jesus that Evil one. For thine is the Kingship or Allegoric Godship & the Power or War, & the Glory or Law Ages after Ages in thy Descendents, for God is only an Allegory of Kings & nothing Else. Amen.[1]

Blistering stuff, nowise intended for publication: giving the lie to any notion of a Blake chastened by poverty from expressing his prophetic ferocity in old age. In himself, he was himself to the last. And the last came four days after Canning's death, on Sunday 12 August 1827.

Fate had chosen an interesting place for Blake to depart this world. Kept by Blake's brother-in-law, Mr Banes, Fountain Court was a three-storey red-brick house on the west side of a narrow, insignificant court that ran down to the Thames, close to Beaufort Buildings, Somerset House (on the Strand) and the Savoy (on the Thames's bank). Holding its own within the parish of St Clement Danes, the densely populated area had been notorious for much of the previous century for poverty, child mortality and crime. Known as 'radical Westminster', its extremities attracted the practical ministrations of philanthropists, workhouses and other social controls.

By 1821, when Mr and Mrs Blake moved in, the parish was largely of middling levels of income, while the Strand itself, after serious improvements around 1810, was quite a colourful, old-fashioned street of ludicrous but contentedly varied structures, politely jostling one another on every side for attention. Most were of brick, rendered and not rendered, with squared and rounded tall sash windows, while gabled protuberances of eccentric character lurched over latticed 'Old Curiosity' shop-panes, mounted by large, framed painted signs. The street was paved with loaf-like cobbles that bubbled their way east to Wren's magnificent St Mary le Strand and west to the Royal Academy at Charing Cross (Trafalgar Square and Nelson's Column did not exist). Men and women of all classes spilled over the pavements into the street, while women on stools with high bonnets sold lavender and shop boys in smocks took deliveries. Gentlemen in frock coats and tall top hats accompanied wives in long, stiff, tasselled dresses, wearing shawls over broad lace collars with ribbons binding bonnets broad and small. Offices for publishing books, newspapers and magazines punctuated the thoroughfare down to Fleet Street and Middle Temple Lane. There was still good business in radical, utopian and reactionary publishing, though little business found its way to Fountain Court.

If we ascend a flight of stairs, bounded by graceful Queen Anne balustrades and wainscoting to the first landing of No. 3 Fountain Court, we shall see two doors, lit by a window overlooking the backyard. The door on the left gives entry to the back room where Blake works, his wife cooks, and the loving couple sleeps. The right door brings the visitor to the somewhat gloomy 'reception room' where Blake's watercolours, prints and temperas are hung. This room has a window that looks out onto Fountain Court itself, while a door to the left of the entrance brings the visitor to the *inner sanctum*.

A broad-panelled room considered by the artist's handful of devoted young admirers as a veritable Holy of Holies and place of enchantment is but twelve by just under fourteen feet in width and length. Entering, the visitor finds he is standing to the left of a bed, beyond which is a fireplace for cooking in the right-hand corner. Beside the bed is a cupboard. Looking to the left, the room is lit by a pleasant sash window. Beneath its sill is spread Blake's engraving table and a chair, to the right of which is a cupboard where the master keeps his tools. Through the window we can, through a gap in the backyard, see a slice of the River Thames, its muddy banks and the hills of Kent and Surrey beyond.

A drawing and a watercolour by Blake's devoted admirer Frederic Shields (1833–1911) show the room as Shields saw it when, as illustrator to Gilchrist's 1863 biography of Blake, he paid homage to his master by visiting Blake's 'death-room'. Such was the impact of Shield's work on Dante Gabriel Rossetti that the Pre-Raphaelite luminary was moved to poetry, inspired by what now appeared little less than a shrine. Such emotion did not deter the building's demolition subsequently. Curiously, Shield's drawing shows three Blakean souls ascending, arms upraised, possibly angels. They appear to have been painted on the panel to the left of the sacred window. One would love to think they were Blake's work: bright spiritual graffiti. But they are absent from Shield's watercolour: one feels some artistic license has been exercised in response to rooms which, when inhabited by Mr and Mrs Blake, inspired a 'sensation of FREEDOM' that was 'very seldom felt elsewhere' in another of Blake's younger admirers.[2]

Already we sense we have entered a land of legend: saints inspire legends but saints do not write them. The legend of Blake's saintly death at 3 Fountain Court began almost immediately in the words of 18-year-old Royal Academy student, George Richmond (1809–1896):

> He died on Sunday night at 6 o'clock in a most glorious manner. He said He was going to that Country he had all His life wished to see & expressed Himself Happy, hoping for Salvation through Jesus Christ – Just before he died His Countenance became fair. His eyes Brighten'd and He burst out into Singing of the things he saw in Heaven. In truth He Died like a Saint as a person who was standing by Him Observed – He is to be Buryed on Friday at 12 in morning. Should you like to go to the Funeral – If you should there there [sic] will be Room in the Coach.[3]

The 'Dear Friend' invited to the funeral by Richmond was 22-year-old painter, Samuel Palmer, a Baptist minister's son from London's East End. Palmer was one of the select few to have provided our vision of Blake (through Gilchrist), but Richmond and Palmer's saint is a Blake in old age; Palmer only met Blake in October 1824, three years before the end. The legend of Blake's good death was assembled with gathering romanticizing from the reminiscences of Palmer, Palmer's friends, and acquaintances of his friends.

Anecdotes about Blake's death appeared within a year of his demise in the second volume of *Nollekens and his Times* (London, Henry Colburn, 1828) by Blake's friend, John Thomas Smith. Joseph Nollekens (1737–1823) was arguably the greatest British sculptor of the 18th century and Smith was this highly successful Royal Academician's executor.

Smith preferred Blake to Nollekens:

During his [Blake's] last illness, which was occasioned by the gall mixing with his blood, he was frequently bolstered-up in his bed to complete his drawings, for his intended illustration of Dante; an author so great a favourite with him, that though he agreed with Fuseli and Flaxman, in thinking Carey's translation superior to all others, yet, at the age of sixty-three years, he learned the Italian language purposely to enjoy Dante in the highest possible way. For this intended work, he produced seven engraved plates of an imperial quarto size, and nearly one hundred finished drawings of a size considerably larger; which will do equal justice to his wonderful mind, and the liberal heart of their possessor, who engaged him upon so delightful a task at a time when few persons would venture to give him employment, and whose kindness softened, for the remainder of his life, his lingering bodily sufferings, which he was seen to support with the utmost Christian fortitude.

On the day of his death, August 12, 1827, he composed and uttered songs to his Maker so sweetly to the ear of his Catherine, that when she stood to hear him, he, looking upon her most affectionately, said, 'My beloved, they are not mine – no – they are not mine.'[4]

This latter, luminous detail was attributed 'to the widow' by Gilchrist some 32 years later. Since the widow (Catherine Blake) was long dead, he may have acquired the story from Frederick Tatham (1805–1878), a painter and extreme dissenter whose sister Julia married George Richmond, and who claimed Blake's widow had appointed him charge-hand of Blake's artistic legacy.

Lawyer and critic Henry Crabb Robinson visited the widow in January 1828. Visibly affected by his thoughtfulness, she told him that Mr Blake had 'died like an Angel'. This, Robinson confided to his diary; it represents the sole certain, first-hand account of Blake's death.

The next layer of the legend arrived in print two years after Smith's account. Allan Cunningham's *Lives of the Most Eminent British Painters, Sculptors and Architects* (6 vols, John Murray, 'The Family Library', 1830) relied heavily on Smith's account and still got important facts wrong, including the year of Blake's death (only three years after the event). Cunningham's second edition was more sympathetic, correcting earlier suggestions that Blake could not distinguish between what he imagined and what his ordinary eye saw.

He [Blake] had now reached his seventy-first year [incorrect], and the strength of nature was fast yielding. Yet he was to the last cheerful and contented. 'I glory,' he said, 'in dying, and have no grief but in leaving you, Katherine [misspelt]; we have lived happy, and we have lived long; we have been ever together, but we shall be divided soon. Why should I fear death? Nor do I fear it. I have endeavoured to live as Christ commands, and have sought to worship God truly – in my own house, when I was not seen of men.' He grew weaker and weaker – he could no longer sit upright; and was laid in his bed, with no one to watch over him, save his wife, who, feeble and old herself, required help in such a touching duty.

The Ancient of Days [Blake's painting] was such a favourite with Blake that three days before his death, he sat bolstered up in bed, and tinted it with his choicest colours and in his happiest style. He touched and retouched it – held it at arm's length, and then threw it from him, exclaiming, 'There! That will do! I cannot mend it.' He saw his wife in tears – she felt this was to be the last of his works – 'Stay, Kate! (cried Blake) keep just as you are – I will draw your portrait – for you have ever been an angel to me' – she obeyed, and the dying man made a fine likeness [the work, if it existed, has disappeared].

The very joyfulness with which this singular man welcomed the coming of death, made his dying moments intensely mournful. He lay chaunting songs, and the verses and the music were both the offspring of the moment. He lamented that he could no longer commit those inspirations, as he called them, to paper. 'Kate,' he said, 'I am a changing man – I always rose and wrote down my thoughts, whether it rained, snowed, or shone, and you arose too and sat beside me – this can be no longer.' He died on the 12th of August, 1828 [*sic*], without any visible pain – his wife, who sat watching him, did not perceive when he had ceased breathing.[5]

If this is clearly a heart-warming hack job, the next account of Blake's death comes from a more peculiar, positively sickly source. Frederick Tatham undertook to exploit Blake's legacy while at the same time repudiating much of its substance. Having become a follower of Scots clergyman Edward Irving's sect, the Catholic Apostolic Church, Tatham was, he claimed, persuaded by the convictions of fellow sectarians to burn much of the inheritance, or rather, alleged inheritance, of Blake's work.

Tatham had received written accounts of Blake from four of his friends. He destroyed them as well, and produced his own, putting himself at the centre of the Golgotha of Blake's transition from this world to the next. He stuffed his 1832 account into sales copy for Blake's personal print of his enormous and technically elaborate *Jerusalem* poem, presumably as 'added value' in hope of a sale.

Take a listen to Tatham's gory prose:

> Life however like a dying flame flashed once more, gave one more burst of animation, during which he [Blake] was cheerful, & free from the tortures of his approaching end. He thought he was better, and as he was sure to do, asked to look at the Work over which he was occupied when seized with his last attack: it was a coloured print of the ancient of Days, striking the first circle of the Earth [?], done expressly by commission for the writer of this. After he had worked upon it he exclaimed 'There I have done all I can it is the best I have ever finished I hope Mr Thatham will like it. [Tatham's punctuation was weak] He threw it suddenly down & said Kate you have been a good Wife, I will draw your portrait. She sat near his Bed & he made a Drawing, which though not a likeness is finely touched and expressed. He then threw that down, after having drawn for an hour & began to sing Hallelujahs & songs of joy and Triumph which Mrs Blake described as being truly sublime in music & in Verse. He sang loudly & with true extatic energy and seemed too happy that he had finished his course, that he had ran his race, & that he was shortly to arrive at the Goal, to receive the prize of his high and eternal calling. After having answered a few questions concerning his Wifes means of living after his decease [from whom?], & after having spoken of the writer of this, as a likely person to become the manager of her affairs, his spirit departed like the sighing of a gentle breeze, & he slept in company with the mighty ancestors he had formerly depicted. He passed from Death to an Immortal life on the 12th of August 1827 being in his 69th Year [incorrect; Blake was

in his 70th] Such was the Entertainment of the last Hour of his life
His bursts of gladness made the room peal again. The Walls rang &
resounded with the beatific Symphony. It was a Prelude to the Hymns
of Saints. It was an overture to the Choir of Heaven. It was a chaunt for
the response of Angels.[6]

I trust readers will see right through this nauseating, pseudo-pious, slippery
drivel and see the 'Uriah Heap' behind the pretence. This was no more than
an individual on the make, attempting to profit from a perceived advantage in
controlling the works of an artist whose value was likely to rise when there
was no more work to be had and the irritation of his presence on earth could
no longer stimulate offence or objection. Tatham is, as the evidence suggests,
the classic Victorian weeper at the bedside of future profit. Even the semi-
divine underlined '*He's*' appear lifted from Richmond's devotional use of the
capital 'H' for the dying man's pronoun. It is extraordinary that this evident
imposture of classic hypocritical evangelicalism has gone unexamined for so
long, though John Linnell, artist friend and patron of Blake's last years, never
trusted Tatham's account, to say the least, and Palmer could not be brought
to speak to Gilchrist of his old 'friend' Tatham: fear of a libel case, perhaps, or
simply a cartload of trouble from a highly unstable character.

Tatham was a swine of the stamp that good men and women in their
innocence can never quite believe really exist; but they do. The very idea that
Blake would leave it to his last breath to make arrangements for his wife's
welfare without him! In this detail, furthermore, we may in all probability
discern a conscious reference to the image of Christ on the cross leaving care
of his mother to 'the beloved disciple' (John 19:27, with Jesus giving up the
'ghost' three verses later); in this case, Tatham is presenting himself, and himself
alone, as that 'beloved disciple'.

Incidentally, Tatham's grandfather Ralph was an adventurer, while his
father's architectural career (Charles Heathcote Tatham, 1772–1842) has
something of the manipulative adventurer about it as well. Charles Tatham
had a talent for regularly saving himself from imminent financial collapse by
attaching himself to the talented and the wealthy at the critical moment: his
life reads like a name-dropping exercise. Frederick Tatham, Charles's eldest son,
a 22-year-old sculptor at the time of Blake's death, was as opportunistic as his

paternal relations; his art was unoriginal as well.

Tatham's self-serving 'biography' relied on stolen goods. It was a marketing tool, and like many a medieval legend of the saint, tailored to extract coin from the relics of the silent witness. What Tatham couldn't flog of Blake's, he burnt.

Anyone imagining Tatham was himself a witness to Blake's death should read the account carefully and note that John Thomas Smith's 1828 account includes the detail, likely as not from Tatham himself, that the latter travelled 90 miles, even though ill, to attend Blake's funeral on the Friday (17 August) at Bunhill Fields, such was his 'esteem' for Blake, an esteem matched, Tatham insisted, only by feelings for his own family.

Tatham established himself with 'rights' over Blake even up to the 1850s, when Gilchrist researched Blake's life. Gilchrist's account relies heavily on Tatham's, as well as Smith's; Gilchrist's artful concoction of sources has been accepted by biographers ever since, because he appeared to be in closest touch with Blake himself, through Blake's 'disciples' and friends.

Gilchrist's saintly death narrative adds only one detail, which itself seems to be an extrapolation from Richmond's moving letter to Palmer: 'He Died like a Saint as a person who was standing by Him Observed.' Gilchrist writes: 'A humble female neighbour, her [Kate's] only other companion, said afterwards: 'I have been at the death, not of a man, but of a blessed angel.' While this undoubtedly smacks of John Wayne's pious ejaculation as the Centurion witnessing Christ's Crucifixion in *The Greatest Story Ever Told* (George Stevens, 1965), it contradicts Gilchrist's earlier, pathetic statement regarding the deathbed scene: 'August, 1827, he lies, in failing strength, in the quiet room overlooking the river, yet but a few yards removed from the roaring Strand: she [Kate] beside his bed, she alone. He has no other servant, nor nurse, and wants no other.' Extras gather at the bedside like witnesses to the Resurrection. Imagine Gilchrist's crepuscular prose on the lips of Peter Cook (in Bryan Forbes's radical satire *The Wrong Box*, 1966, for example), and you get some idea of the 'working' the record of Blake's death – and life – has been subjected to. Legends tend to be built about a spiritual core, or need, but in the end they strangle the reality before entering the universal field of mythology where anyone can read anything they like into the material.

For the biographer, it is a distinct challenge to realize that the Legend of William Blake began within a week of his death, at the end of a life already laden with calumnies by those who exploited him, opposed him, or possibly knew him all too well.

Religion was the cause of much of the distortion of Blake's life; more particularly, the romanticization and sentimentalization of the Bible which by 1827 was a cultural norm in England and in America: a necessity of respectability, a required component of polite discourse that inevitably sank into acceptable modes of unspoken hypocrisy. The dénouement of the death scenes described above almost begs for the following conclusion:

> When Jesus therefore had received the vinegar, he said, It is finished: and he bowed his head, and gave up the ghost. [...] Then the disciples went away again to their own home. But Mary stood without at the sepulchre weeping: and as she wept, she stooped down, and looked into the sepulchre, And seeth two angels in white sitting, the one at the head, and the other at the feet, where the body of Jesus was lain.
>
> (John 19:30; 20:11–12)

Angels had played quite a role in Blake's life. During the period when Blake died, the attendance in some manner of angels, or imminent meeting with the same, was a vital feature of the 'good death'. The good death was an evangelical staple; children were brought to the demise of the dying so that they might see and believe, and be edified by the fading of life and the soul's passing into the Saviour's loving care.

Of course, it was not always so simple. There was *another way to die*. Sometimes, God forbid, a 'bad death' occurred, and it could be very unsettling to faithful brethren. To understand the disturbing alternative to the good death, we need only examine the real life of Blake's mother, Catherine, a life unknown to Gilchrist or to subsequent biographies.

TWO

The Canvas Prepared

1727–1752

In April 1751, André François le Breton published volume one of the French *Encyclopédie*, with contributions from Voltaire and Rousseau. It offered rational explanations, and the expectation of rational explanations, for every facet of existence.

Seven months later, Peter Böhler (1712–1775), Bishop of the Moravian Churches in Britain and America, ministering to the Moravian Brethren's Meeting House in Fetter Lane, off Fleet Street, City of London, was perturbed by the spiritual condition of one of the Brethren's inner core members: 38-year-old Thomas Armitage, a hosier, born in Royston, Yorkshire, now trading at 28 Broad Street (today's Broadwick St), Soho.

Surviving Moravian Church records show that on 20 November 1751 Brother Böhler was anxious about the effect on his congregation of Brother Armitage's 'not being in so good Condition in his heart'. Armitage was dying of consumption (tuberculosis), but Böhler did not mean Armitage's physical heart organ; what he meant by 'heart' was the hosier's deepest emotional centre through which Brethren were expected to enjoy spiritual intercourse with Jesus. It was through God's love that salvation came to the believer. God's love was mediated through the heart, and the expected response to that love was the commitment of the heart. The Moravian Brethren's religion was a 'religion of the heart', not of reason. Facing the prospect of death, Armitage's heart was not 'warm' enough. He was dying badly.

Böhler hastily instructed members of the 'Congregation of the Lamb', the inner group of the Moravian fellowship, to be more careful in future as to who was admitted into the community's heart, and to the 'Lord's Supper'. There were problems with Armitage's estate, vexatious to Armitage's wife and perhaps other Brethren. Böhler felt that he or one of his fellow 'Labourers' should have exercised a guiding hand in the matter. As a result, Böhler felt he could not mention Brother Armitage in the 'Liturgy'. Böhler further lamented the absence of a Congregation-approved *Nurse*. A Brother or Sister ready to give account to the Congregation of the state of the sick Brother's heart should have attended Armitage night and day. Böhler insisted such a provision was part of the Congregation of the Lamb's established Constitution: a rule to be applied strictly in future.[1]

Three days later, the Congregation recorded the burial in Bloomsbury-Ground of the body of married Brother Thomas Armitage who had been received into the Congregation of the Lamb on 26 November 1750 and partook of the Holy Sacrament on his sick-bed on 28 September 1751. He had died 'last Tuesday Morning', but not before 'a little Fretfulness' that 'clouded his Love, which he otherwise always bore to his nearest Hearts'. This was a matter of real importance to Böhler: those on the inside of Jesus's love, *who took refuge in His wounds*, were supposed to be secure from the stain of purely worldly concerns that interrupted communication with God, especially at the end. Brethren were supposed to be different to outsiders to faith, those for whom death was 'the king of terrors'.

At the last, however, the record noted that the night before Armitage's departure, he desired the forgiveness of those he had upset, afterwards taking 'a cordial Leave' of his wife.[2]

This Thomas Armitage, hosier, with his last-minute worries about his estate, and his life, was none other than the first husband of William Blake's mother, Catherine, *née* Wright. Indeed, it was Catherine who first sought membership in the Congregation of the Lamb at Fetter Lane.

The discovery and analysis of the Moravian Brethren's records at Muswell Hill by Dr Marsha Keith Schuchard and Dr Keri Davies between 2002 and 2004, while of immense significance for understanding William Blake, was not the first intimation that Blake's parents were not, as the common biographical record maintains, 'dissenters'.

On 5 April 1797, along with 18 other engravers, William Blake signed a testimonial to the effectiveness of a forged banknote detector invented by

Alexander Tilloch (1759–1825). Tilloch, who knew Blake personally, was great great uncle to William Muir, a Blake facsimilist. In the 1920s, Muir informed the largely forgotten Blake biographer Thomas Wright that the Blake family attended the Fetter Lane Moravian Church. Wright published Muir's information, possibly derived through Tilloch-Muir familial memories from Blake or Blake's relatives, in *The Life of William Blake* (2 vols, Olney, T Wright, 1929).

Muir's anecdote led both Wright and critic Margaret Ruth Lowery to consider whether some of Blake's 'Poetical Sketches' (1783) and *Songs of Innocence and Experience* might reflect Moravian spiritual priorities, hymnody and imagery.[3] Curiously, however, it was not this clue that led Marsha Shuchard to the Moravian Church Archives, but her interest in relations enjoyed with the Fetter Lane community by Swedish scientist and religious visionary Emanuel Swedenborg. These relations, she suspected, influenced controversial sexual doctrines associated with Swedenborg.

Some of Blake's most extraordinary ideas have been considered as developments in tension with Swedenborg's recommendations and experiences. There did exist in the 18th century a spiritual sensibility that could accommodate Swedenborgian and Moravian spirituality *in tandem*. Did Blake enjoy such a sensibility?

When we realize young William Blake was educated not at school, but at home by his mother, we see why knowing about the Moravian Brethren and Blake's mother's part in that community is so important to Blake's biography.

Catherine and the Moravians

Count Nikolaus Ludwig von Zinzendorf und Pottendorf (1700–1760) was a descendant of imperial counts from Lower Austria who had converted to Lutheranism and moved to Protestant Saxony. In 1722, 35 years before Blake's birth, Count Zinzendorf opened his heart to the needs of wandering members of the *Unitas Fratrum*. The 'Unified Fraternity' represented the surviving community of the Protesting reformist movement of Jan Hus (1369–1415). Jan Hus has been called the 'first Protestant'. In the year of Agincourt, Hus was burned at the stake for doctrines the Roman Catholic Church deemed heretical. After Hus's death, followers in Czech-speaking lands Bohemia and Moravia resisted violent oppression, carrying their founder's example into the Reformation period and beyond. Hideously persecuted during the Thirty Years' War (1618–1648), the Bohemian, or Moravian Brethren, as they were known, were scattered, while maintaining community contacts through appointed ministers. Czech genius Johann Amos Comensky, or 'Comenius' (1592–1670), was one of those ministers. Comenius not only influenced some of the founders of London's Royal Society, but also revolutionized ideas about education in Holland, Scandinavia, Britain and Germany (he has been called the father of UNICEF) – and, significantly, among the Moravian Brethren themselves. Comenius was a deep spiritual thinker.

People who appreciated Comenius in the 18th century, such as literate members of the *Unitas Fratrum*, often found themselves in sympathy with spiritual-alchemical Rosicrucianist works, and with the theosophy of Jacob Böhme (1575–1624). Böhme saw the 'heart' as the engine or *locus* of alchemical transformation of matter into spirit, separating the base aspect of man (chaff) into the God-man, Jesus: the Bread of Life. The Brethren held to a deep, medieval-style personal mysticism with an intensity of mystical prayer and spiritual visualization. Christ was to be encountered in the everyday: an everyday transformed by the heart.

Count Zinzendorf's spirituality had been much affected by the Pietist movement that dominated the University of Halle where Zinzendorf undertook his schooling before university at Wittenburg. His godfather Philipp Jakob Spener, a leading Pietist, opened Zinzendorf's eyes to the inner spiritual life of a humanity divine that enabled him to feel himself in ecumenical sympathy with different Churches (each he believed had something to offer), while being conscious of a spiritual vocation, unusual in his aristocratic family.

Count Zinzendorf permitted *Unitas Fratrum* members and others – including followers of the evangelical knight Caspar Schwenckfeld (1490–1561) who held to a doctrine of communion with the 'inner Christ' – to settle freely on his lands at Berthelsdorf, Saxony. The Moravians built a village called Herrnhut, which became the movement's radix.

After some early conflicts, Zinzendorf imposed a discipline and established a focus that on 13 August 1727 led to a kind of collective spiritual experience, an awakening. The upshot involved the Brethren in embracing the idea of a global preaching mission, not, where Churches existed, to supplant existing Churches, but to revitalize the body of Christ on earth.

The system was based not on monastic principles, but on the family and individual experience shared. Missionaries travelled to America – they had to leave from English ports and so came to London – thence establishing bases from Bethlehem, Pennsylvania, to as far away as Greenland, the West Indies, South Africa, Algiers, Suriname and South America. Brethren went to the Copts of Egypt and to the Inuit of Labrador. A radical spiritual equality brought nobles into the same accommodation as black slaves, North American Indians and Inuit. It seemed the religion of the heart did indeed have universal application. Zinzendorf said that in Jesus, God had at last found an image people could fully and intimately approach: 'He became as we are that we may become as he is.' He showed those who had received the grace to see a 'Humanity Divine'. Zinzendorf spoke of the 'humanation' of the 'divine essence'. The 'Divine Humanity' would, of course, become a cornerstone of William Blake's visionary experience, the depth of whose meaning was obvious to him, but his use of which has been much misunderstood.

In 1736, exiled from Saxony over doctrinal differences with Lutheran authorities, Brethren consecrated Zinzendorf a Bishop in Berlin in 1737. Accused by opponents of abandoning his missionaries, he demonstrated his faith in 1739 by carrying the mission to St Thomas (now US Virgin Islands), not knowing if he would ever return.

Three years after Zinzendorf granted the *Unitas Fratrum* asylum on his lands, Catherine Wright, seventh child of yeoman farmer Gervase Wright and his wife Mary, was christened at the church of St Mary Magdalene, Walkeringham, Nottinghamshire, on 21 November 1725.[4] How, why or when Catherine came to London is still unknown, but now we know her origins, the idea of an entirely 'Cockney Blake' can be dispensed with: Blake had the country in his soul.

Catherine Wright was 12 when a group of four Moravian Brethren from Germany arrived in London to secure a convenient passage to Georgia. One of them was Peter Böhler. Böhler encountered a London of flourishing Anglican religious societies, some of which were friendly with the Oxford 'Holy Club', run by Charles and John Wesley for young clergy, establishing themselves as a group at the house of bookselling tradesman James Hutton in Little Wild Street, north of the Strand.

Fate introduced Wesley to Böhler, and Wesley's heart was, famously, 'strangely warmed'. Impressed by Moravian spirituality, Wesley was, in the idiom of our times, 'turned on' by the Brethren. He formed with Böhler what Zinzendorf called a 'banden', consisting of eight members in Christian fellowship.

By the end of 1738, the group had mushroomed to over 50 members, so a room in a court off Fetter Lane was hired, between the Strand and Lincoln's Inn Fields. Leading Moravian theologian August Gottlieb Spangenberg (1704–1792) visited the group in 1739, encouraging a sense of mission to the American colonies.

Wesley had already made an unsuccessful voyage to Savannah, Georgia, in 1736. By July 1740, however, Wesley felt frustrated with the Moravians. Finding intolerable the Moravian practice of restricting active community participation until after a period of 'stillness' or 'waiting on grace' had passed, Wesley left the group. Many joined him, the majority being women who found Wesley charismatic and his arguments persuasive.

In 1741, remaining members appealed to Zinzendorf to save the London community from decline. Zinzendorf, however, was fully engaged in Pennsylvania, meeting Benjamin Franklin and arranging with Iroquois leaders for free movement of Moravian missionaries. Nevertheless, he dispatched Bishop Spangenberg and a party of 'Labourers' (full-time Moravians) to the rescue. So successful was this rescue that the following year James Hutton had to lease a long-empty, former Independent Dissenters' Meeting House, with a pulpit, to accommodate new members. This became the Brethren's Chapel, Fetter Lane.

Records from 1743 show that in that year a Mr and Mrs Blake were Society members: could they have been William Blake's paternal grandparents? The speculation might be entertained on the basis that Catherine may have met her second husband through Moravian contacts. The year 1743 also saw the establishment of The Congregation of the Lamb – the inner society of 72 members 'within the Church of England in union with the Moravian Brethren'[5] – to which Catherine Armitage, Blake's mother to-be, would seek closer association in 1750. Three months after Bonnie Prince Charlie's 'romantic' escape from Scotland to France, Catherine Wright and Thomas Armitage were married. It was 14 December 1746 and the Rev. Mr Alexander Keith performed a quick, economy wedding with no banns at St George's Chapel, Mayfair.

Born at Cudworth in the parish of Royston, Yorkshire in May 1722, Catherine's new husband was a hosier and an Anglican; he was 24, she 21. In 1748 the couple moved into a smart four-storey house on the corner end of Broad Street and Marshall Street, Soho.

Perhaps it was the exciting arrival of the 'Pilgrim Count' Zinzendorf in London in 1749 that sparked Catherine Armitage's interest in the Fetter Lane Chapel; perhaps she or she and her husband were 'hearers' already (that is, not full members but attenders of preaching services) – the Meeting House supported some 70 different meetings a week. Zinzendorf leased Lindsey House in Chelsea for the next six years, adorning it with striking paintings, intended for study and meditation.

Visualization of the God-man Jesus and his wounds was vital to Zinzendorf's spiritual practice and doctrine. Zinzendorf also agreed with Comenius's extensive use of emblem and educational picture books to explain to adults and children the human crafts and divine links that bound the world, often invisibly – that is, to the blind, but clear to those who could see. The spirit of God granted vision, as well as reason. Elaborate 'emblematical' and 'hieroglyphical' paintings and transparencies were discussed on the occasion of Zinzendorf's birthday.[6]

The 17th century had been a golden age for engraved emblem books. Emblem books showed peculiar pictures that contained an allegorical or moral message, like a parable literally expressed. Metaphors such as 'the anchor of the soul' were depicted as such. Alchemical emblem books were popular and intriguing: meaning was not always apparent, but strangeness could be very attractive. Usually accompanied by verses or a statement, often paradoxical, emblems were laden with double meanings. Hence they were to be 'entered into' before essential meaning 'came out'.

Nature could be seen as a vast cryptogram in which God had secreted his spirit as in a 'signature' or style discernible to the initiated. Blake was very familiar with the art and pleasure of emblem books that addressed, we might say, unconscious levels of meaning, sometimes in a logical, sometimes in an alogical way.

Brethren were encouraged to visualize to the point of vision the divine body of the wounded Jesus. Such vision expressed the 'humanation' of the divine essence. Likewise, gazing at a spiritual emblem could create an intermediate visionary plane where the spiritual substance of the message could become vividly real, or super-real.

The heart had to be progressively detached from the devil's world that influenced or ruled the soul by the attraction of earthly enticements. Attraction to Jesus raised perception levels to the vision of another, higher world. The divine was, as it were, *secreted* in the image of the world. One can usefully compare these ideas with Blake's remarkable 'song of innocence', 'The Divine Image':

> And all must love the human form,
> In heathen, turk or jew.
> Where Mercy, Love & Pity dwell,
> There God is dwelling too.

Note that the 'human form' that is to be loved is '*in*', not *of*, the apparent identity, or image, of the 'heathen, turk or jew'; this realization provided the basis for Moravian ecumenism: humanity divined. The Moravian message addressed the *divine image*. Spiritually regenerated Brethren were to regard the sexual organs as restored from the taint of former sinfulness and directed to their divinely intended functions in which no shame existed, Christian marriage being a true sacrament: the 'divine body' was given back to partakers of the sacrament: 'This is my body which I give to you.'

Zinzendorf pronounced that the first of the 'Lamb's' redeeming wounds was at His circumcision. The blood-wound indicated the holiness of redeemed sexuality, of the genitals, combined with a perfect image of childlike innocence. As far as the Christian was spiritualized, he or she was free of the devil of the lower nature. Divinity, you might say, was a state of mind, a state of mind resulting from reorientation of the heart. This was no vulgar sexual revolution, though the vulgar might take it as such.

With the advantage of personal and familial relations with the Protestant court of Denmark, Zinzendorf cultivated influential men of differing confessions. John Potter, Archbishop of Canterbury (1737–47), joined

Zinzendorf's Order of the Grain of Mustard Seed, as did the Catholic Archbishop of Paris. Zinzendorf sought the English Primate's help in having the Moravian Church recognized in England as 'an antient Protestant Episcopal Church'. In 1749 the Moravians' sister status with the Church of England was recognized by Act of Parliament, even though, for technical reasons, Moravians had to register places of worship in conformity with the Toleration Acts. Accession to ecclesiastical sisterhood was perhaps the event that made Catherine and Thomas Armitage embark on their Moravian journey. It may also explain why in JT Smith's 1828 account of Blake's death a year previously, Smith records that Mrs Blake allegedly asked her husband where he wished to be buried and whether he wanted an Anglican minister or a 'Dissenting Minister' to read the service. Blake expressed personal indifference to where his body might be placed, but thought it might as well be put close to his immediate family in Bunhill-row. As to the service, he expressly desired Church of England.

It might be that Mrs Blake, or the writer, did not understand that Moravians were not 'dissenters': a common error. On the other hand, it is also possible that Blake's thorough ecumenism, itself necessitating a rejection of sectarianism, had led him to friendly terms with a dissenting clergyman of Mrs Blake's acquaintance – Blake had been on good terms with several in his lifetime, and perhaps Mrs Blake was a little confused given Blake's sometimes ambiguous, sometimes inflammatory views regarding organized religion.

Managed by the City of London Corporation, Bunhill-row was popular as a burial place for Nonconformists (being unattached to consecrated Church of England ground), but was open to anyone who paid the modest fee. It was therefore suitable for any Anglican who did not attend Anglican services regularly, or, as in Blake's case, at all. Blake believed religion was *all* practice and perception, without ceremony or pious public display. The Church was the Body of God, giving and receiving forgiveness. A Church of England minister, incidentally, would not have entered an enclosure reserved for Dissenters, or managed by them, to conduct sacred service. This principle, observed by an Anglican minister, probably also guided Blake's parents and aunt, who died, as far as we know, as they were baptised, within the Church of England. For the Blakes, Bunhill-row was not a Dissenter's burial-place, but a Christian cemetery.

Certainly Catherine Armitage was a baptised Anglican when she was approached, at her own request, for counselling by members of a Moravian 'Choir'. The Choirs were sub-groups of the 'band', organized as helpers according to marital status, gender and age. Moravian Church records for 12 March 1750 show a married woman of the name Armitage on a list of 13 other women to be visited for one-to-one counseling.[7] The 'circumstances' of her 'heart' would then be reported back to the Congregation. On 30 July, Böhler organized a 'Class' of eight 'visited' persons so they could get better acquainted. Mr Armitage was now included.

On 13 August it was recorded that Thomas Armitage expressed a desire to 'come nearer' to the Brethren.[8] This expression of 'desire' was deemed very important in the Pietist tradition, for it was held that the principal and most profound *desire* of the soul was union with Jesus, and this purified *love* was the substance of the desire the Choirs were listening out for. Note also Blake's famous 'arrows of desire' from his 'bow of burning gold' in the hymn 'Jerusalem': many rush to the idea that Blake meant carnal desires as such. While the word 'desire' has been romanticized and, of course, eroticized, this was not its primary meaning in cultivated discourse in Blake's day. Desire expresses the *will*.

Having been introduced to members of the Congregation, it now fell on Catherine and Thomas Armitage to make formal applications to join the inner circle by means of letters. Their contents would be assessed according to the state of the heart revealed. Amazingly, Blake's mother's letter of application has survived, as has that of her husband, Thomas Armitage. Note how Catherine's letter ends with the second verse from a Moravian hymn by James Hutton, printed in 1742, beginning: 'Stream through the bottom of my heart.'

> I have very littell to say of my self for I am a pore crature [sic] and full of wants but my Dear Saviour will satisfy them all I should be glad if I could allways lay at the Cross full as I do know thanks be to him last friday at the love feast Our Savour was pleased to make me Suck his wounds and hug the Cross more then Ever and I trust will more and more till my fraile nature can hould no more at your request I have rit but I am not worthy of the blessing it is desird for I do not Love our

Dear Savour halfe enough but if it is his will to bring me among his hapy flock in closer conection I shall be very thankful I would tell you more of my self but itt is nothing thats good so now I will rite [write] of my Savour that is all Love.

> Here let me drink for ever drink
> nor never once depart
> for what I tast[e] makes me to cry
> fix at this Spring My heart
> Dear Savour thou has seen how oft
> I've turnd away from thee
> O let thy work renewd to day
> Remain eternally.[9]

The reference to the 'love feast' derives from primitive Christian practice of the 'agapē', meaning spiritual love. Congregation members gathered to share simple food while intimately, and in a childlike way, speaking of their joy in faith with prayers and hymns. The rather startling references to 'sucking his wounds' and 'hugging' the Cross reflect Zinzendorf's extraordinary emphasis on the blood and wounds of the Saviour: the cost of salvation, vivid signs of the love of Christ. Zinzendorf wanted members to get as close as possible to the 'divine image' in which God brought his essence to the knowledge of humanity.

Members were encouraged to envision themselves climbing inside the 'hole' in Christ's side, and also tasting the 'gory' blood of the wounds and finding sweetness therein. Commentators have understandably criticized this aspect of Zinzendorf's teachings for encouraging a sublimated, or even manifest, eroticism. In fact, Zinzendorf's son Christian Renatus did take the imagery to extreme lengths with his own band in Germany. At Herrnhaag ('God's Grove'), near Büdingen, homosexual acts allegedly performed in a Christian 'loving' spirit caused a scandal. Zinzendorf always endeavoured to get members to channel their physical desires into a purely spiritual phase by confronting the body rather than ignoring it. Members who 'strayed' – say by 'chatting up' other members – were dismissed from the Congregation. Christian Renatus's behavior resulted in his being dismissed by his father from

Church offices. Trying to hold such a highly charged form of mutual love service without evoking euphoric ideas of 'free love' was never going to be easy, but by and large the community coped, even though individuals might slip from professed ideals.

Thomas Armitage's letter (dated 14 November 1750) makes it clear that the couple had been 'hearers' at the Fetter Lane chapel for some time before desiring to join the Congregation.

> My Dear Saviour has maid me Love you in Such a degree, as I never did Experience before to any Set of of People; and I believe it is his will that I should come amongst you; because he has done it himself, for I could not bear the Doctrine of his Bloody Corps, till; very lately, till non but my D[ear]r Saviour could show me; perfectly, & he over came me so sweetly that I shall never forget, when I only went out of curiosity to hear Bro[the]r Cennick, which was to be the last Time I thought I wo[ul]d care in hearing any of the Brethren; & my Jesus Show'd me that I had been seeking something else besides him, nor could I then bear the thought of hearing anything Else; but of him being Crucified & of his Bleeding wounds, which I Experienced very Sweet & the only food for my Soul then; I am but very poor in my Self & weak and find my Love very cool sometime toward him, for all hes done for me so much, but when my Loveing Saviour comes again and kindles that Spark, then I feel I can love him dearly; so he makes me love him or Else I should not love him at all − ; & I can feel my Saviour, forgive me all my base acctions [*sic*] from time to time; for all that my D[ea]r Lords Love is such, as bad as I am I know he Loves me with that ever lasting Love, that nothing shall separate us, as St Paul sais, from Your Unworthy Brother in the Suffering Jesus.[10]

The mention by the self-described 'base' and 'unworthy' Armitage of going out of curiosity to hear 'Brother Cennick' is interesting. An Anglican from Reading, John Cennick (1788–1755) was a very popular preacher who personally founded Moravian communities from Yorkshire to Wiltshire, composing hymns and living a preaching, travelling life not unlike the more famous Wesley.

From 1748 to 1755 Cennick was based in Dublin. Wesley, who detested Cennick, met him both there and at Fetter Lane.

Having received his first invitation to Ballymeena in August 1746, Cennick was afterwards tirelessly involved in preaching and community-founding work throughout the Irish mainland. In Dublin he became a figure of fun and butt of ribald song to some Catholics while suffering dismissal as a 'Papist' from some Protestants. At the time of the Armitage letters we know from Cennick's journal that he had spent October 1750 preaching at Balinderry in the north, before walking a considerable distance back to Dublin, then back to Balinderry. In December he preached in the hall of Pontmore Castle by invitation and was still preaching in the Pontmore vicinity in the spring of 1751. One wonders if it was at Dublin, Fetter Lane, or during Cennick's English missionary travels that Armitage first encountered the extraordinary Brother Cennick.

One thing is clear from all of these accounts. This was not really the Age of Reason. There was warmth in religion if you knew where to go.

After a casting of lots by Church Elders, Catherine and Thomas Armitage were admitted to the Congregation of the Lamb on 26 November 1750. Four months later, the couple suffered the loss of an only son, Thomas. The Moravian Archive records the baby's burial on 1 March 1751 at the cemetery in Lamb's Conduit Fields, Bloomsbury.[11] This was William Blake's little half-brother. Did he ever know it?

Little Lamb, who made thee?

Brother Armitage was finding things a strain in his Broad Street shop. On 14 August he said he'd be glad if the Brethren recommended someone to help him. The record states that Brother Lehman would speak to Brother Page about it. Things got worse. On 12 September 1751 Armitage asked the Brethren if 'someone' could stump up £20 for him to settle a promissory note due the previous year, 'but as the Brethren were scanty of money it was thought he might propose the Person to give him another [note] for the Payment thereof'.[12]

By the end of September, Catherine's husband was seriously ill. On 28 September, 'Br[other] Armitage, being sick, & having long desired it, had the H[oly]. Communion administered to him privately. At 1 o'clock was Sabb[ath]. Love F[east] at Bloomsbury.'[13]

We know the dénouement. On 19 November, a fortnight after Britons were cheered by news of 26-year-old Robert Clive leading a brilliant defence against a superior French army at Arcot, India, Thomas Armitage died: an unedifying death followed by unedifying events.

It was a controversial feature of Moravian Church practice that Elders oversaw marriages of unmarried members. The idea of 'falling' in love simply echoed the fall of man into material bondage. Couples must be prepared to rise to the high calling of the Lord, as befitted a sacrament. If the widowed Catherine intended to remarry, she could expect the Elders to advise closely. If she intended staying in the Congregation of the Lamb, she would be expected to take their advice.

At first, Catherine's problem seemed to be money. On 4 December, Böhler requested Brothers Mason and Syms to look into her financial affairs, as her late husband's will was very 'unequitable'. Its terms required she pay £80 to Armitage's brothers if she married again. Such a sum would exhaust any inheritance at all, leaving her destitute, unless, of course, she married again for money: a course the Elders would disown. Annoyed, Böhler insisted that when wills were made in future, Brethren must accept advice from the 'Elders' Conference'.[14]

After closer examination of Catherine's affairs by Brethren, it was concluded on 18 December that once her debts were paid she would have about £150 in stock as well as household goods.[15]

What happened next we cannot precisely tell. The Church Book of the Brethren states simply that Catherine Armitage 'Became a widow and left the Congregation'.[16] That means that she left the Congregation of the Lamb: it does not mean she ceased attending services at Fetter Lane as a 'hearer'. The likelihood seems to be that it was her marriage, 10 months later, to James Blake, father-to-be of William, that caused her to leave, or was the occasion of her leaving the Congregation, especially if there was any hint at all of impropriety or worldly motive.

According to Dr Keri Davies's close analysis of the Moravian archives, Elders and 'Choir House Labourers' sincerely attempted to protect unmarried persons from harmful outsiders and to find partners spiritually compatible with the ideals of the Brethren and the personalities of members. It is possible that Catherine's choice of James Blake was for some reason unacceptable to

Elders (perhaps it came too soon in widowhood after a suspiciously short grieving period); as Keri Davies has observed, 'Even if James Blake were himself a Moravian, marriage without the agreement of the elders would have led to exclusion from the Congregation.'[17] It might simply have appeared that James Blake was a journeyman hosier looking for a leg-up in business and here was a young widow who had inherited a hosier's shop and needed a man to provide an income – and a family. Such a 'bond', at least on the outside, would not have been edifying for members of the Congregation, especially if it was projected in defiance of Elders' advice, or in secret. We might also wonder if Böhler's conscience was entirely at ease about having accepted the Armitages into the Congregation in the first place, given all that had passed: we do not know for certain.

What we do know is that on 15 October 1752, Catherine Armitage returned to St George's Chapel, just off Hanover Square, and married James Blake, hosier and haberdasher. There were 15 other quick marriages that day; theirs cost a guinea. Meanwhile, some 4,000 miles to the west of them, at the very moment the couple entered 28 Broad Street as a married couple, Bishop August Gottlieb Spangenberg and a party of five Moravians from Bethlehem, Pennsylvania, accompanied surveyor and cartographer William Churton (1710–1767), my ancestor, to survey for the first time tracts totalling 98,925 acres beyond Virginia's Blue Ridge Mountains for the Moravians.

Zinzendorf's work was paying off, and a new world was coming to birth.

THREE

Of such is the Kingdom of Heaven

1806–1863

Suffer little children, and forbid them not,
to come unto me: for of such is the kingdom
of heaven.

(Matthew 19:14)

Investigation of William Blake's life has to contend with the frustrating fact that there remains little reliable first-hand biographical information about him. Past biographers have side-stepped this thorn by producing a 'Diatessaron' – the Diatessaron being a 2nd-century 'harmony' of the four canonical gospels into one. You just add bits from one or another of the sources that the principal source in hand for any narrative element does not have, then smooth it all over, adding extraneous detail to fill out the picture like a good art director on a movie. You avoid many of the nasty questions of authenticity, authorship and reliability. The result in my experience is that reading a Blake biography tends to leave you confused as to just where you are in the narrative. Years pass by unnoticed, historical context vanishes, critical comments about paintings or poems get mixed up with disparate quotations as if 'Blake' held the same ideas at all times throughout his life, the biographer cherry-picking the ones that suit the narrative, even where anachronistic. You are seldom sure how old or young the main character is.

The reason for the frequent mess is that the essential template for biographies derives from the approach of Alexander Gilchrist, whose account of Blake's life appeared posthumously in two volumes in 1863. Gilchrist relied principally on five brief reminiscences of Blake's life written between 1806 and 1832; only those of writer Benjamin Heath Malkin (1806) and Unitarian lawyer and critic Henry Crabb Robinson (1811 and 1825–7) were written while Blake lived. Much of Gilchrist's information derived from hearsay and from enquiries among a handful of people who knew Blake in their youth – that is, in Blake's old age. Gilchrist's work justly earned authority from its invaluable reminiscences of men who had actually met Blake and with whom Gilchrist had made contact. These men were George Richmond, Samuel Palmer, Frederick Tatham, John Linnell and Edward Calvert: all of them artists. Maria Denman, sister to sculptor John Flaxman's wife, also contributed anecdotes, as did John Linnell's children. Written sources and anecdotal evidence from people who had known Blake came from Malkin, Robinson, antiquarian John Thomas Smith and landscape artist and astrologer John Varley, of whom only Crabb Robinson was still living when Gilchrist wrote his biography.

So far, so good. Now the bad news: among William Blake's surviving works we have no diaries, no journals, no self-written accounts of his life and, surprisingly, not many letters. Of these, while a number are revealing of Blake's philosophy and attitudes, not one of them is truly intimate. The earliest letter is dated October 1791, a few lines from Blake's *thirty-third* year, then ... nothing for over four years. It was Blake's sometime patron, the poet and biographer of Milton, Cowper and Romney, William Hayley (1745–1820) who preserved the majority of surviving letters. These, however, cover only the years of their collaboration (1800–05). Blake does not appear to have kept many letters from others and he was habitually tardy or lax in replying, to his friends' annoyance.

We have no accounts by Blake of his childhood, his education, his family background, or even his father and mother – and nothing from *them* either (save his mother's petition to enter the Moravian Congregation). Personal matters only entered Blake's work when there was a critical, spiritual dimension at stake into which human relationships had become entwined, and then only abstractly. He seems to have had little interest in, or awareness of, *time*. His sense of history was strong, but his wide knowledge served mostly internal, ideal and spiritual priorities. One might conclude that he did not wish to be seen as a creature of space and time, but an inhabitant of heaven cast for a season into our darkness.

Writings and drawings in his famous 'Notebook' (preserved in the British Library) are undated, sometimes undateable. Indeed, the two principal editors of his collected writings, Geoffrey Keynes and David V Erdman, were severely tested to match works to dates at all. Often the watermark on the paper had to suffice for a rough guide. It is therefore frequently impossible to match writings to specific events in Blake's life with certainty.

We have no loving poems dedicated to his wife (and only one, arguably two, surviving portraits by him of her), no words, dutiful or otherwise, for mother or father; no panegyric exists on the places or people of his youth. If he ever wrote such things, they have been lost or destroyed. We do not even know if he ever travelled beyond London, Surrey or Kent before his forties; had the 'Mental Traveller' ever seen Glastonbury, in the flesh, so to speak?

What we have, by and large, in terms of first-person biographical materials, are snapshots, and with them we must seek out their proper setting and meaning.

It has been tempting for past biographers to present Blake's life and work in thematic and even mystical phases, but Blake was not Picasso: we don't have convenient blue or white periods. Blake's work unfolded often over many years. He seldom regarded work as finished; he leapt back across years of 'new' projects to re-touch or resurrect 'old' works. Time meant little to him; eternity was all. Even his life was not finished; it simply ended, though to him, it had just begun again.

Vision of Angels

We can see the effects of the biographical confusion when we look into the truth-value of a well-known 'event' and image of Blake's early years.

In 1993 the Dulwich Festival commissioned artist Stan Peskett to paint a mural for the side of a house by Goose Green, East Dulwich. Peskett's wonderful 'Vision of Angels', executed with local schoolchildren's help, may now be seen by one and all. The colourful painting of an oak tree radiating with angelic presences represents a sight widely believed to have first been seen by the boy, William Blake, wandering out of the market gardens of Dulwich into the fields of Peckham Rye. It is one of the strongest images to encapsulate the popular myth of William Blake, visionary and child of heaven. Unfortunately, the story seems, like so much else, to have been given the 'Diatessaron' treatment.

Benjamin Heath Malkin (1769–1842), author of the earliest contemporary account of Blake's career, doubtless consulted him for the biographical introduction on the artist to his book *A Father's Memoirs of His Child* (1806). Blake contributed an engraving of Malkin's brilliant son who had died tragically young.

Malkin's account begins with Blake as a lad frequenting auction rooms and seeing paintings in the fine houses of his social superiors. There is nothing about angels on Peckham Rye. Such an omission, however, might have been made to protect Blake's reputation from doubts regarding his sanity or religious soundness.

Leaning on Malkin's account, Crabb Robinson's article for the German journal *Vaterländisches Museum* (II, pp107–131, 1811) again launches Blake as the precociously young connoisseur: no angels on Peckham Rye. Blake's interest for Robinson lay in Blake's alleged combination of 'genius' and 'madness' in one man, a view Robinson would modify after he met Blake in 1825. Robinson was, however, aware of angels in Blake's life: 'Our author lives,' Robinson wrote, 'like Swedenborg, in communication with the angels.'

Robinson tells a story, heard directly from one who claimed Blake's confidence, of how Blake was one day carrying home a picture 'for a lady of rank' (possibly *The Last Judgement*, painted for Lady Egremont) and wanted to rest in an inn. There, the angel Gabriel touched him on the shoulder: 'Blake why are you tarrying here? Walk on, thou shouldst not be tired;' whereupon Blake 'arose, unwearied'. As far as Robinson was concerned at this time (1811), it was Blake's concourse with angels that rendered him deaf to criticism (Blake was in fact highly sensitive to criticism). Robinson attributed the following to Blake without a source: 'I know that it [a painted image] is as it should be, since it is an exact reproduction of what I saw in a vision and must therefore be beautiful.' Blake's paintings were mostly illustrations of his visions.

The subject of Blake's childhood must have been partially broached after Crabb Robinson called on Blake at Fountain Court on 17 December 1825 following a first encounter a week earlier at the home of wealthy art collectors Mr and Mrs Aders in Euston Square – there was no railway station there in those days, and the fields by Rhodes Farm were only two streets to the north.

Robinson recorded packets of Blake's conversation: 'His faculty of vision, he says, he has had from early infancy. He thinks all men partake of it, but it is lost for want of being cultivated.'[1] Blake was not hallucinating unwillingly like a mad person, as Robinson had believed formerly (on Robert Southey's insistence, incidentally): Blake exercised a faculty open to all. The means might have been taught him. In a letter about Blake sent to Dorothy Wordsworth two months later (February 1826), Robinson concluded, significantly: 'He is not so much a disciple of Jacob Böhme and Swedenborg as a fellow-visionary.'[2] Clearly, by citing such distinguished visionary company, Robinson was prepared to accept that Blake had cultivated the faculty to an exceptional level.

The Peckham Rye angels story, complete with 'bright angelic wings bespangling every bough like stars', is first told in its fullness by Gilchrist, over 30 years after Blake's death. Gilchrist has a similar story to tell in chapter 35:

At one of Mr Aders's parties – at which Flaxman, [Sir Thomas] Lawrence, and other leading artists were present – Blake was talking to a little group gathered round him, within hearing of a lady whose children had just come home from boarding school for the holidays. 'The other evening,' said Blake, in his usual quiet way, 'taking a walk, I came to a meadow and, at the farther corner of it, I saw a fold of lambs. Coming nearer, the ground blushed with flowers; and the wattled cote and its woolly tenants were of an exquisite pastoral beauty. But I looked again, and it proved to be no living flock, but beautiful sculpture.' The lady, thinking this a capital holiday show for her children, eagerly interposed: 'I beg pardon, Mr Blake, but *may* I ask *where* you saw this?' '*Here*, madam,' answered Blake, touching his forehead.[3]

Quite a memory to relate all that after 30 years! Nevertheless, the Aders party setting may be accurate. Crabb Robinson maintained his first meeting with Blake took place over dinner at Charles and Elizabeth Aders's house on 10 December 1825. Blake's friend John Linnell, as well as another painter and engraver, possibly John Thomas Smith, were also present. Robinson noted in his diary: 'In the Evening came Miss Denman and Miss Flaxman [probably Flaxman's sister].' Since John Flaxman's wife's younger sister, Maria Denman, corresponded with Gilchrist, she may have been the story's source, though it may have come from Linnell. Anyhow, we have here what appears to be a genuine anecdote concerning a vision in a meadow, albeit not set in Blake's childhood.

A year after Blake's death, John Thomas Smith's book about sculptor Joseph Nollekens appeared. Smith dismissed any suspicion of Blake being of 'deranged intellect'[4] – but there was nothing about angels in a tree. The same may be said of Allan Cunningham's account of Blake from 1830: *Lives of the Most Eminent British Painters, Sculptors, and Architects*[5] – no angels in a tree there either.

We may come closer to reliable sources when we turn to Frederick Tatham's self-serving manuscript 'Life of Blake', written in about 1832, five years or so after Blake's death. However, three things about Tatham's account must be noted. First, George Richmond told art collector John Clark Strange, while Strange was researching an abortive Blake biography during 1859–61, that four friends of Blake had entrusted extensive written accounts of Blake to Tatham, and that Tatham destroyed them. Second, Blake's widow, Catherine, had died in October 1831 and was in no position to add to, or contradict, anything in Tatham's suspiciously timed account. Third, Tatham's story not only borrows from Malkin's and Smith's but is also peppered with inaccuracies, where, that is, inaccuracies may be detected.

Though Tatham's has become an established source, we can never be certain if any story unique to him is true. And much of Blake's established 'biography' relies on Tatham's writing. Tatham claims some of the stories came from the lips of the widow herself, but we have no way of knowing: Mrs Blake wrote no account of her own. Tatham employed Blake's elderly widow as a housekeeper to his young family. He implies that Mrs Blake doted on him; we may wonder. We know nothing of Mrs Blake's psychological state after losing the lamp of her life, but we do know that Tatham's former friends considered *him* half mad with sectarian religious zeal – Richmond had married Tatham's sister Julia in 1831, so Richmond had inside information on his brother-in-law. Tatham was only 22 when Blake died, hardly an age capable of understanding the needs of an elderly woman, even if Tatham had been a perfectly normal character, which he was not. The rule of thumb in judging Tatham's manuscript must be: he included what suited his purposes. His purpose was to sell Blake's work, with himself as the 'authoritative' source as regards both information about Blake and sellable 'product'. If a story increased sales potential in a religiously conservative market, it was in.

Anyhow, Tatham's account knows nothing of angels in a tree, though he does recount something intriguingly similar: 'even when a Child his [Blake's] mother beat him for running in and saying that he saw the Prophet Ezekiel under a Tree in the fields.'

We have fields, and a tree this time, and the prophet Ezekiel, who, of course, was famous for his vision of heavenly creatures whose wings made a noise 'like great waters' (Ezekiel 1:24). Why his mother should have beaten him, as Tatham asserts, we do not know; the detail may be an error. Tellingly, Gilchrist has a kind of reverse version of the beating story. In Gilchrist, after the alleged vision of angels in a tree on Peckham Rye, Blake's mother *saves* Blake from a beating by his 'honest father' who believed his son was lying, and lying about a sacred thing too. Again, how can we be certain which of the parents was sympathetic? One of them? Both? Neither? The question is important, but is not treated as such in the sources.

Perhaps we come closer to an answer when we consult notes concerning Blake made by John Clark Strange. A Quaker from Streatly, near Reading, Strange had bought some of Blake's pictures at Thomas Butts Junior's auction at Foster's on 29 June 1853 – Butt's father had kept Blake going by regular purchases and commissions of Blake's work. Strange's gathering fascination culminated in a series of research trips with a biography of the obscure artist in mind. Strange met the possessor of Blake's *Notebook*, artist and poet Dante Gabriel Rossetti, in London. He also met Samuel Palmer and Palmer's brother William who was working in the British Museum as an attendant. Strange patiently attended on George Richmond's convenience, and, in 1861, met Alexander Gilchrist, only to hear the latter had nearly finished his own Blake biography. They had covered the same ground.

On Tuesday 10 May 1859 Strange paid a second call on successful portrait painter George Richmond. Richmond was busy with visitors and gave hurried answers to Strange's questions.

Richmond remarked that 'none of his [Blake's] relatives could feel any interest about him [Blake]', then added a rare detail, unique to Strange's manuscript:

Blake spoke most tenderly of an old nurse. T'was to her he related his first vision – when a lad out walking at harvest time he saw some reapers in the field & amongst them angels he came home & told his friends but all of them laughed at him – excepting his old nurse, who believed what he told her – He always spoke of her with great affection.[6]

No beating here. One can only speculate as to whether this kindly nurse – reminiscent of young Winston Churchill's famously sympathetic 'Womany' – was one of the nurses that Moravian Bishop Böhler had believed vital for keeping a spiritual eye on the hearts of sick Brethren.

This engaging snippet shows just how much we have missed by not having Blake's own testimony of youth. However, we do have something close to the famous angels and tree image – without the beating or threat of beating this time. Nevertheless, confidence that we may at last have got to the root of the famous story is swiftly unsettled by Strange's visit to artist, Samuel Palmer, in Kensington, on Wednesday 11 May 1859. Palmer's story appears to be the root of Gilchrist's anecdote set at the Aders's party in Euston Square where Blake described a flock of sheep that turned into sculptures. Or is it simply a variant telling? In its favour, it lacks the intricate dialogue that seems such an unlikely feature of Gilchrist's 'version'. In his account, Strange relates how:

At a lady's home (whom P[almer]. named [probably Mrs Elizabeth Aders]) where several were met amongst whom Blake & [Samuel Taylor] Coleridge – Blake was telling the company that when passing over Dulwich fields the other evening he saw a most lovely scene which he described in glowing language – and in a corner of the field were several beautiful angels wandering about – A Lady present was so struck with the description that she begged Mr Blake to tell her where the particular spot was as she would like to take her little son. When Blake remained silent & pointed mysteriously to his forehead in reply. – The scene had been in his brain.[7]

Again the story of angels is told by Palmer to Strange in terms of a recent event of Blake's experience, and not a memory of childhood. The 'beautiful angels' in Blake's way of speaking may simply have meant people who were a little pompous. Blake could take a dim view of angels: he asserted – after having read Swedenborg's accounts of angels – that 'angels' had a tendency to think themselves always right! Alternatively, he could talk of his friends as 'angels' when doing something he considered divine. An angel is a being who brings something from God, an intermediary. As Blake's widow said to Crabb Robinson in January 1828: 'he died like an Angel'. Do angels die?

Palmer had another angel story up his sleeve to impart to Strange, and this one seems to be the clincher for Gilchrist's famous account:

> When very young Blake used to go out for walks in the country & would frequently come home & describe the angels he had seen in the trees – His father was so angry at first with his accounts that he treated them as falsehoods & severely whipped him several times.[8]

Now we have angels in trees – not *a* tree, but trees – and on more than one occasion too. There is no 'Peckham Rye', just 'walks in the country'. We also have the idea of Blake giving a description of what he saw (which I suspect Gilchrist provided with his pretty phrase about angels bespangling the boughs). His father is angry but, note, only 'at first'. Nevertheless, young Blake has to suffer several 'whippings'. There is neither nurse nor mother to sympathize or intervene in this account. Did James Blake come to tolerate his son's descriptions, or even believe in them in some way? We shall see in the next chapter what might have made little Will see angels in the first place.

What is clear from all these accounts is that Blake's special way of seeing the world around him, when combined with ordinary states of mind, was likely to generate legends, because Blake always made his primary appeal to the imagination, and hearing him, we can enter an imaginative realm, an intermediate zone somewhere between the world we know, or think we know, and a higher realm, the 'kingdom of heaven' within.

More prosaically speaking, the story of the tree full of angels is most likely to have come about as a conflation of several accounts of fields, a tree, trees, and angels, woven over some three decades through the memories of a small circle of people whose minds Blake had touched.

We may safely conclude that the story of Blake's seeing a particular tree full of angels in Peckham Rye is a myth, popular and potent because it encapsulates the idea of an innocent child's mind, full of imagination and open to spiritual worlds visible through a translucent, glorious veil of nature. We like the myth because, deep down, we feel the want of the vision. As Blake said to Crabb Robinson, we are all born with this visionary faculty, but it is soon clogged up by the cares and delusions of the world. In Blake, the faculty grew.

Was there something in his upbringing that encouraged this to happen?

FOUR

Childhood

1752–1767

It is time we caught up with Catherine and James Blake. We left them shortly after their marriage in October 1752, entering their home at 28 Broad Street, Soho, in the parish of St James's, Piccadilly. Had the couple come out again and walked briskly 10 minutes to the north, they would have found themselves soft underfoot in green fields on Green Lane, heading for Bilson's Farm on the New Turnpike Road, running east-west. Had they covered the same territory a century earlier, their walk would have begun in open fields by a windmill.

The Earl of Craven bought Soho Field during the Great Plague of 1665 to bury thousands of the dead and to provide 36 small dwellings for the poorest souls. Development of the West End lumbered on after the Great Fire of 1666. Architect Sir Christopher Wren wanted handsome houses of brick and stone with good sewers and polite trades. Builders ('freemasons') did their best, no doubt. Construction between Broad Street and Golden Square was well under way at the beginning of the 18th century, with fine town houses for aristocrats and services for the well-to-do.

Establishing their new family in shouting distance of Carnaby Market, the Blakes inhabited a respectable area that had come down only a little as aristocrats moved southwest towards the palaces of St James's and Westminster. For William Blake's father, James, it was a step up in the world.

According to GE Bentley, Jr, the James Blake born on 12 April 1722, baptised by Rev. John Peirson at St Mary's, Rotherhithe, Surrey, was almost certainly Blake's father: son to James and Elizabeth (probably *née* Baker) who married at St Olave, Southwark on 30 April 1721.[1] James's birth coincided with the arrival of the *Unitas Fratrum* to the estates of Count Zinzendorf in Saxony.

On 14 July 1737, at the Company of Drapers' great hall, Throgmorton Street, in the east of the City, 15-year-old James Blake was apprenticed by his father to draper Francis Smith, for £60. Smith would become Master of the Worshipful Company of Drapers in 1778.

In 1743, with seven years of apprenticeship completed, hosier and haberdasher James Blake entered 5 Glasshouse Street, near Great Jermyn Street, Westminster. While Catherine's first husband Thomas Armitage was making his will in 1751, James Blake was paying 'Watch Rates' (to pay for the employment of night watchmen) for Glasshouse St with a co-resident called 'Butcher' – possibly a relative, for when William Blake was suffering from a broken love affair in 1781, he went, according to Gilchrist, to stay in Battersea at the home of a market gardener called 'Boutcher' (Gilchrist traced James Blake's relatives to Battersea).

When, in late 1752, hosier and haberdasher Sarah Adams took over James Blake's lease, 5 Glasshouse St was valued at £18 whereas Broad Street was valued at £21. Aged 30, James Blake's life had risen a notch.

The arrival of William Blake's elder brother, christened James after his grandfather at St James's Piccadilly on 15 July 1753, coincided not only with riots in Bury against John Kay, inventor of the job-cutting 'Flying Shuttle' – Kay had to flee to France – but with a scandal-generating series of publications promoted by an enemy of the Moravian Church (or 'Herrnhutters', as he called them), one Henry Rimius.

Henry Rimius versus the Moravians

Rimius took advantage of a near-ruinous financial crisis in London's Moravian Church caused by the sudden death of a moneylender. For us, Rimius's short work *A Candid Narrative of the Rise and Progress of the Herrnhutters* (London, A Linde, 1753) offers some insight, if twisted, into the teaching philosophy of Count Zinzendorf. For Moravians, the effect of the publications was to stigmatize the community, in hostile minds, with the brand of 'fanaticism'. This accusation was reinforced by Rimius's publication in London the same year of *A Pastoral letter against Fanaticism, Addressed to the Mennonites of Friesland, by Mr John Stinstra* ('Printed for A. Linde, Stationer to His Majesty', 1753).

Stinstra opens his work thus: 'Fanaticism, and the spirit of *Domineering*, are the two most dangerous Enemies of Religion.'

Johann Stinstra (1708–1790) was a Dutch Mennonite preacher who, when accused of denigrating the Trinity by Frisian authorities in 1742, defended himself by recourse to English ideas of liberty and toleration found in works such as John Locke's *The Reasonableness of Christianity* (1695), and in other 'Enlightenment' writers and theologians. Stinstra's critique of the emotional religiosity of the Moravians came from his conviction that God gave us reason as a guide to discern what was good in religion, and that passions, therefore, should be subject to reason.

Moravians in Germany and Holland stood accused of denigrating reason in favour of 'enthusiasm' and 'fanaticism', by which was understood the tendency for domination, contrary to liberty. We see at once the lineaments of the great contest of Blake's spiritual and philosophical life, laid out four years before his birth. Rival claims of Reason and Enthusiasm (based on alleged duplicitous trickery of the *Imagination*) would shape the perception of Blake and his work for much of his life and beyond, even into our own time.

Translated by Rimius, Stinstra's work included a translator's Preface in which he accused Zinzendorf of trying to absorb failing Dutch Mennonite communities to bolster ailing finances. Rimius wrote scurrilously of a Dutch sect in Guelders, United Provinces, who responded to excessive preaching with bodily convulsions, groans and vain crying – 'O give me Jesus, I must have Jesus, Jesus' – while previously uninstructed children 'said fine things on the Corruption of Man and the Mystery of Redemption'. He then tarred the Moravians or 'Herrnhutters' with the same brush, alerting Englishmen to flee their 'illusions' in 'these realms'.

The German Rimius had witnessed the deviant activities of Zinzendorf's son Christian Renatus at Herrenhut, Saxony. Much chastened, Christian Renatus had died, to his father's sorrow, in London in 1752. Indifferent to the personal effects of his attacks, Rimius followed up his 1753 onslaught with a *Solemn Call to Count Zinzendorf* in 1754. The 'Solemn Call' consisted of further 'revelations', such as the shameless use of the word *pudenda* in Moravian hymns (the Latin 'pudenda' for the female genitals actually means 'that whereof one ought to feel shame'; Zinzendorf believed this was no longer the case for the spiritually regenerated Christian).

Rimius's was a vituperative scare story, sold on the streets and, employing a canny marketing ploy, put into the hands of every MP that entered the Commons.

Zinzendorf took advice from senior establishment figures, including Commons Speaker, Sir Arthur Onslow. Zinzendorf was advised this sort of thing was just a fact of life in George II's London; surely friends would defend him. The government was more concerned with French hostilities on the Continent and in America: on 12 December 1753, General George Washington of the British army issued an ultimatum to French forces at Fort le Boeuf, Lake Erie; Washington told them the British (including himself) claimed the Ohio Valley, and that was that.

For his part, Zinzendorf was reluctant for uninformed people to come out defending the Moravian Church, so, under pressure, in May 1754, he himself wrote *An Exposition, or the True State, of matters objected in England, of the People known by the Name of Unitas Fratrum.*

Points 68 and 69 in the work would have been familiar, if vexatious, principles to William Blake's mother:

68. Regularly no Marriage must be concluded without the Knowledge of the Directors of the respective Choirs. And a Promise given without their Knowledge, would be deemed a rash Action, tho' not absolutely made void. 69. None of the Brethren or Sisters marry, properly speaking, of their own Accord; as the Fathers of the first Century advise; but if Persons should agree honestly to marry one another, then they should not be hindered to do so by any Means. Marrying people against their Inclination, may be the case of worldly Families, but never in our Communion.[2]

Zinzendorf's sober, detailed response to accusations of fraud and fanaticism was not published until 1755, when Zinzendorf left Lindsey House, Chelsea, to care for the Dutch and German communities; much damage had been done to the reputation of the Church in the meantime. One can only wonder what effect the attack had on Mrs Blake, whose marriage to James Blake, an outsider to the Congregation of the Lamb, doubtless displeased Bishop Böhler; or, for that matter, what effect did it have on Catherine's new husband, trying to maintain a business reliant on social respect? Would his pride not have been affected by spiritual objections to his marrying Catherine? Might he not have seen a case for thinking the Elders somewhat 'domineering', himself preferring 'liberty' – a catchword of the day? The sole support to the idea that the Blakes attended the Moravian Chapel after their marriage is that of Muir, referred to in Chapter Two; by itself, I should not build *too* much on it.

In 1756, the first regular passenger ship service between Britain and the American colonies was established. In London, the Blakes' second son, John, was baptised at St James's on 1 June. A year later, Robert Clive won a decisive victory at Plassey, 100 miles up the Hooghly River from Calcutta, making Clive the ruler of Bengal. The battle (22 June 1757) marked a watershed in Britain's growing ascendancy in India. Five months later, on 28 November, William Blake entered this world. He was christened at St James's Piccadilly on 11 December, five days after Frederick II's Prussian army defeated the Austrians at the Battle of Leuthen, in Prussian Silesia. Which event has proved to be the more significant?

Sometime between 1755 and 1759, baby John died, so when a fourth son was born to the Blakes in 1760, he also was christened John, on 31 March. Little William was two years old, and little John would grow into the bane of his brother Will's youth.

Blake was four when he acquired another little brother, Robert. Robert, by contrast, he would grow to love. 'Bob' was baptised in Piccadilly on 11 July 1762, while in Paris, Rousseau's *Concerning the Social Contract* was published. Rousseau argued that the whole population constituted the State's sovereign power, as distinct from its government. The idea was food for revolution, if revolution was what you wanted; few did at the time.

The arrival of little sister Catherine Elizabeth on 7 January 1764 when Blake was six completed Blake's immediate family. It is worth observing that William was, to all intents and purposes, the middle brother, a situation exacerbated by the fact that his parents doted on younger brother John, unjustifiably in William's view. Was the parents' special consideration because John was a lost child 'returned', at least in name? Or was it because they could identify more with him in some way? Whatever the reason, we may note that the middle brother is frequently frustrated by the question, uttered or held in silence: 'What about *ME*?' There is something of the partially aggrieved-yet-spoilt personality lurking in William Blake's adult psyche, which, as you get closer to him, becomes less attractive, though he could gently charm when so inclined. Furthermore, it is plain from all the records that William Blake was a 'hyper-child', precociously intelligent and hyper-conscious, extremely sensitive and 'different' from his fellows. Was there something in his education that brought this forth?

Education

According to Count Zinzendorf, Moravian children were brought up differently from most other children: 'We do not presume to require of a son that he should follow the same maxims of his father,' he wrote, adding: 'we allow the greatest freedom with the hearts of our children.'[3] The Moravians established their own boarding schools and clearly saw the spiritual destiny of the individual child in community with the Church, and in harmony with God's universal creation, as the primary end of education: spiritual welfare was all. Comenius had taught that knowledge of science, properly integrated, brought children to an awareness of divine intelligence, presence and providence. Blake did not attend a Moravian school but his mother had probably absorbed something of Zinzendorf's spiritual liberality.

In 1811, on whose authority it is unknown, Crabb Robinson wrote how Blake, being born of 'not very well off parents', was early on 'given up to his own guidance, or misguidance'. Robinson implied his parents could not afford schooling, a suggestion in tune with the cynicism of his opening paragraphs for the German journal he was writing for, 14 years before he met the man he calumniated as 'mad'.

However, since his mother could read and write, she was in a perfect position to teach him the basics, and even, perhaps, a few Moravian hymns, prayers and childlike intimacies to settle into his unconscious. The Moravians had a ready supply of children's teaching books, religious emblem books, and practical guides based on, or including, Czech educator Comenius's *Orbis Sensualium Pictus* ('The Visible World in Pictures', Nuremberg, 1658) first published in English in 1659. Using charming woodcuts and captions, it introduced children to practically every trade and useful activity, including writing, drama and some sports, showing how they were all part of a world of experience that led to wisdom and 'pansophy' – all-knowledge. 'I will show you everything,' the book promised. It even included an easy-to-learn visual alphabet based on phonic images.

Allan Cunningham has some very interesting things to say, though whence he acquired his information is a mystery: 'The boy, it seems, was privately encouraged by his mother.' Neglecting arithmetic, 'he desired anxiously to be an artist.' Young Blake 'drew designs on the backs of all the shop bills, made sketches on the counter.' Most interestingly, Cunningham states that Blake's chief delight (no age is given for this) was to 'retire to the Solitude of his room, and there make drawings, and illustrate these with verses, to be hung up together in his mother's chamber.' Again, the impetus in his early education comes from his mother. The combination of pictures illustrated by verses not only suggests Blake's adult productions of course, but the emblem books noted earlier, in particular one which Moravian preacher John Cennick found of great value and which he discussed with the Congregation.[4] That book was the perennially popular 17th-century children's devotional work, *Pia Desideria* ('Pious Desires'), written in Latin by Jesuit military chaplain Herman Hugo (1588–1629), containing remarkable engravings by Boëce van Bolsvert (1580–1633). An English translation by Edmund Arwaker with 47 copper plates was published as *PIA DESIDERIA or Divine Addresses* in London in 1690.[5]

Reading through it is like entering the forming mind of the child, William Blake. The book opens its visual feast on page 3 with a quite literal treatment of 'arrows of desire'. Opposite the engraving is a bold title:

TO THE DESIRE OF THE Eternal Habitations, JESUS CHRIST, Whom the Angels desire to pry into

By no discov'ry did I e'er impart
The secret paintings of my love-sick Heart;
Whose close recesses to no other eye
But that great Pow'rs that fram'd them, open lie ...

To the left of the poem is an engraving of exceptional graphic power, showing a man opening his shirt. From out of his heart fly firm arrows that shoot straight up to the literal all-seeing eye and literal ears of God, surrounded by clouds above ('O clouds unfold!'). The quote beneath from Psalm 38:9 rams the message home: 'Lord, thou knowest all my desire...' Beside the man is an actor's mask (he has stripped away his social self); next to this a quiver of arrows: his ordinary desires. His true arrows of desire come from within when he shows the spiritual truth of himself to his God.

The next engraving illustrates Isaiah 26:9: 'With my Soul I have desired thee in the Night.' The image shows a winged head, lit by a lantern, wandering through an exquisite starry night. It is unmistakably reminiscent of several of Blake's mature works, especially 'I want! I want!' in his *For Children: the Gates of Paradise* (1793), and many a Blakean 'wanderer' – a recurrent visual motif.

The emblematic art of Boëce van Bolsvert had, I believe, a profound effect on Blake's imagination and even style, most evident in his smaller commercial engraving designs – for *Blair's Grave*, for example, as well as minor work illustrating William Hayley's verses, where a story needed telling in a single image. Anybody who has seen Blake's engravings of souls chained to earth, unable to rise heavenwards, for *Young's Night Thoughts* will be astonished to see van Bolsvert's image of the winged Soul trying to soar to heaven in *Pia Desideria*. However, where *Pia Desideria*'s Catholicism insists the soul is impeded by a globe of sin or self-love, Blake attributes frustration to Nature's cruelty. Within van Bolsvert's image is a secondary image where the main action is compared to a boy attached by a string to his bird-like kite that he can, not being chained to it, release. The demands of God are not the stuff of earthbound games: something of the earth has to be released for the Soul to reach its Desire.

How can we avoid noticing Hugo's and his illustrator's use of youthful guardian angels, and child-angels, as companions to penitent souls? The angels observe the action and, in some cases, 'stand in' for us, the viewers, identifying us with the angelic vision. They come straight into us. When the psalm 'Lord thou knowest my foolishness' is illustrated, we see a cherubic guardian angel covering his eyes to avoid seeing the folly of the fool. The guardian angel and the soul are frequently shown as children – images very much in tune with the Moravian emphasis on childlike spiritual states of love and receptiveness, reminding us also of Coleridge's comment on some of the *Songs of Innocence* showed to him by Crabb Robinson, that the poems and their author might suffer from the want of innocence in their readers: a true prophecy.

It is also suggestive that *Pia Desideria* was the title chosen for an important book by Count Zinzendorf's Pietist godfather, Philip Jacob Spener (1635–

1705). Published in 1675, Spener's *Pia Desideria* alerted readers to spiritual corruption in the Lutheran Church. It explained how, by better preaching and spiritual understanding, the corruption could be addressed. Originally intended as a preface to a work by Johann Arndt (1555–1621), the book's 'Pious Desires' for a spiritually regenerated Church were shared by this father of Pietism and author of the classic *True Christianity* with Spener himself, and with Arndt's friend, Lutheran theologian Johann Valentin Andreae (1586–1654), who first created the mythology of the Rosicrucian Fraternity. From them the pious desires entered Count Zinzendorf, and, after him, William Blake.

We may add that the question '*What constitutes a PIOUS DESIRE?*' would become a theme of Blake's life and work.

Henry Rimius's merciless attack on the 'Herrnhutters' grabbed anything it could to bring them down. In his 1753 *Candid Narrative of the Rise and Progress of the Herrnhutters*, Rimius quoted from Zinzendorf's writings to show him as a fanatic, an enemy of reason, a destroyer of true religion. However, viewed sympathetically, Zinzendorf's thought reveals something liberal in the kindly sense, something about how hard logic and rationality can divorce a person's mind from intuition, feeling, understanding, and even common sense. Zinzendorf's following observation could have been uttered by William Blake at practically any time in his career: 'Feeling is ascertained by Experience; Reasoning is hurtful, as makes us lose ourselves.'

It is hard not to think that Catherine Blake had not, to some extent at least, Moravian priorities in mind where William's upbringing was concerned. It was Zinzendorf who saw painting, art and music as roads to God, and it was Blake who would say, more poetically, that painting, poetry and music constituted 'the three powers in Man for conversing with Paradise that the Flood did not sweep away'. This assertion constituted an advanced view of education in an era when acquaintance with the Roman and Greek classics was often, if tacitly, deemed superior to knowledge of the Bible, never mind vocational or scientific studies. However, there would have been plenty of hostile critics ready to declare that the idea of creative arts as a centerpiece of education was a retarded system for the retarded.

Blake, thankfully, was not, in his childhood, subject to such critics. We ought not to forget the telling story Richmond related to Strange: that Blake remembered with great fondness his 'old Nurse', the person he could tell his visions to who did not scold him, or doubt him. *Who was this marvellous woman?* We may owe her more than we know.

It is remarkable that when Blake, in later life, described the figures who had had the greatest influence upon his thinking, he never mentioned a teacher or intimate guide likely to have entered his father's premises. Sometimes he gave the impression he owed the formation of his mind to astral or heaven-translated beings encountered in a state of pre-existence: beings who could be summoned in his imagination from inner worlds. At their first encounter, Blake offered Crabb Robinson the image of his having been conversationally intimate with Socrates and with Jesus Christ, dimly, vaguely, as though in another time or on another plane of being. In his maturity he would undoubtedly claim to have formed bonds with the thought of Paracelsus (1493–1541), with Jacob Böhme, and with Emanuel Swedenborg (1688–1772): a Swiss, a German and a Swede, only the latter of whom ever trod England's green and pleasant land. However, it is impossible to point to a precise time when he first read their works, though we know he annotated a 1784 edition of Swedenborg's *Heaven and Hell*, published in London when Blake was 26. Swedenborg's religious books had been available in Latin since the 1760s, but Blake was not a Latin reader, at least not as a youth.

It would be fair to say that Blake did not entirely *learn* Böhme's, Paracelsus's and Swedenborg's points of view – though he valued phrases and aphorisms, he *shared* their points of view. It was written of a great admirer of Paracelsus, Dr Tobias Hess of Tübingen (1558–1614), that 'Hess listens to God, and no one else.' And I think we can, broadly, say the same of Blake.

In 1852, Crabb Robinson compiled a manuscript of 'Reminiscences'. He copied out old diary entries, and added passages to them as they came to him. Transcribing his diary covering his meeting with Blake at Fountain Court on 17 December 1825, he added a detail that came to him which had not been recorded on the day:

> It is quite certain that she [Blake's wife] believed in all his visions And on one occasion, not this day, speaking of his Visions she said – 'You know, dear, the first time you saw God was when You were four years old And he put his head to the window and set you ascreaming['] –[6]

John Lennon's Aunt Mimi recorded something similar of her nephew when he was eight or nine. John entered her kitchen to announce that he had just seen God. Mimi asked what He (God) was doing, to which John replied that he was just sitting by the fire. Mimi nodded: 'I expect he was feeling a bit chilly.'[7] In an interview conducted in 1980, the adult Lennon stated that 'psychedelic vision' had been an accessible reality to him, indeed reality itself, since he was a child, and it was what made him a 'genius', if such a thing really existed (genius, that is).[8]

Like any young poet, William would have developed an ear for words, music, cadences, but at what age he developed specific literary tastes is unknown. We may presume some precocity here. We know at some time he came to be inspired by Chaucer, as well as by Elizabethan poets including Shakespeare and Spenser. And there was John Milton, of course, and Andrew Marvell, and much English history.

There is little doubt that some of the curious names we find in his more 'prophetic' works partly owe their origin stylistically to the alleged fragments of ancient Gaelic poetry woven together by James Macpherson and published under the name of *Ossian* in 1760, when Blake was three. We may doubt if he was exposed to them at that time. In later life he would declare that it was of no interest to him whether Macpherson could be shown to have put the verses together from his own imagination (that is, fraudulently as is generally accepted): as far as Blake was concerned, Macpherson had, through his imagination, accessed ancient truth; Blake's heart told him so. The supposedly antique Bard named 'Ossian' was, to Blake, essentially *real*. Blake knew what it was to touch ancient worlds to the point of feeling strongly that he had inhabited them. History for him was a case of *déjà vu*.

Blake fully accepted the idea that there had once been a civilization that, even if it had fallen from spiritual realms into time and space, still enjoyed sufficient links with heaven to render it an indestructible, permanent ideal whose lineaments could be discerned through entering inner worlds, the paradise of the Imagination. It had existed in the British Isles and could be expressed in terms of a single figure: ALBION.

For Blake, Imagination was not simply a faculty, a kind of creative tool, a department of brain. Still less was the essential imagination a snare for the reason, though reason could be 'shown up' by it. Imagination was divine life itself. Imagination retained the link between earth and heaven, matter and spirit. Its fruits: intuition, poetry, painting and music. Blake, with staggering idiosyncratic audacity, would refer to 'Jesus the Imagination' because traditionally Jesus had opened that link, descending and ascending with the angels, and in His being constituted that link ('I am the Way'), that 'golden string' Blake would come to celebrate in his epic *Jerusalem*. Having opened the heavens to the vision of Man – that is, to simple folk, not intellectuals – he could say: 'the kingdom of heaven is within you.' And so, Blake could say that Jesus was indeed the offspring of God – 'and so am I, and so are you,' as he informed a perplexed Crabb Robinson in 1826. There seems little reason to doubt that Blake realized this identification at some level from his infancy, even if he had not the intellectual or technical tools yet to express it. Certainly, his earliest extant poems, gathered as *Poetical Sketches* in 1783, were written from the age of 12; they give little hint of the beauties and phantasmagorias to come.

Tatham offers information about Blake's upbringing, but how much confidence we may place in it is questionable. GE Bentley, Jr asserted the disconcerting caveat: 'Tatham is not very trustworthy, but it is probably best to trust him until we have cause not to.'[9] If untrustworthiness is not a cause for mistrust, what is? Tatham even gets Blake's birthday wrong and refers to James Blake's eldest son as 'John'.

Tatham tells us that James Blake was 'lenient and affectionate'. All evidence supports this, except, perhaps, for the uncertain 'beating' story. Blake's younger brother John was, according to Tatham, 'the favourite of his mother and father'. He would be apprenticed to a gingerbread maker and while in the end he came to no good, Blake's parents dismissed Will's remonstrations with the rebuke that one day he would beg at John's door – that is, that Will (Blake's familiar name) would never make any money. John would die in reduced circumstances sometime between 1793 and 1802. Blake was the better prophet, but it availed him little. Blake would write to his elder brother James, trying to reassure him his pecuniary boat was about to come in, but James found it hard to approve of his artistic interests, offering him 'bread and cheese' advice.

Tatham indicates a passivity in Blake that would annoy Blake himself in times to come, and which, with benefit of hindsight, can annoy mature commentators on his conduct: 'Although easily persuaded,' says Tatham, 'he despised restraints and rules, so much that his father dare not send him to school.' The reason Tatham gives for a reticence Robinson attributed to lack of means is that Blake 'hated a blow'. There were plenty of masters in 18th-century London who could have handled such resistance with impunity. Breaking a child's will was a staple of ordinary education: to 'whip out the offending Adam' from the recalcitrant soul was the justification for regular whippings of boys. Perhaps Blake's parents did not regard their son as having within him 'an offending Adam' that wanted whipping out. Perhaps they believed in the boy and recognized something special about him that required careful handling. Are we to imagine they did not love him? Did Blake imagine this?

Surviving accounts suggest a growing independence in the boy before the age of 10. Malkin, who probably got his account from Blake himself, describes the lad attending sales at Christie's, Langfords and other auctioneers. According to Malkin, Blake's father was 'indulgent' of Blake's artistic interests. With money from his father, Blake bought prints and began a collection. While auctioneer Abraham Langford (1711–74) called the 11 to 13-year-old Blake his 'little connoisseur' and kindly knocked down the occasional lot for the youngster's sake, another dealer got sick of Blake's obsession with Michelangelo, as if no one else existed.

The development of a keen aesthetic sense, especially if directed to ideal forms of art was, I believe, likely to set him at some, perhaps even great, distance from his mother. It is noteworthy that where the encouragement of Blake into contemporary arts was concerned, his father made the running. I strongly suspect that if Catherine Blake had stayed inwardly close to a Moravian or Moravian-like spirituality, she would have advocated in some way or another the idea that her son should be grateful to the wounds of the Lamb, and that he ought to think deeply about his salvation, won at the price of the shedding of Christ's blood. She herself had 'sucked the wounds' and embraced the Cross. One thing that is absolutely notable from the very many religious paintings that Blake wrought over his career is that he did not, would not, associate blood with Jesus. His Jesus is not of this world. Blake's iconography is thoroughly on a par with Gnostic sensibilities, rather in the manner of Dali's *St John of the Cross*: there is a Cross, there are hands outstretched, but to the regret doubtless of the evangelical, neither artistic nor symbolic significance is given to blood itself as salvation's currency. This is no mere speculation of mine.

On 7 December 1826, Crabb Robinson enjoyed one of his final conversations with Blake.

> And this day he spoke of the Old Testament as if it were the Evil Element. Christ, he said, took much after his Mother & in so far he was one of the worst of men.[10]

Blake was referring to the conception of God that he associated with parts of the Old Testament. Blake sensed a bullying, inferior conception of the divine that, like so many others before and since, he found at variance with the gospel of repentance, love and forgiveness. Blake could be very cynical about the idea, opining that it was as though God came in the Old Testament with a stick to hit the head, returning in the New with a balm to heal it.

Most interesting is Blake's use of the word 'Mother', by which he surely meant the Jewish faith ('Old Testament') in which Jesus had been nurtured. What Blake thought Jesus might have held against his actual mother would make an interesting discussion, though passages of the gospels show a Jesus fairly indifferent to members of his family.[11] Jesus did not take his mother's advice. However, the force of the use of the word 'Mother' in this context cannot go unremarked. Was Blake determined not to take after his mother?

Robinson took up the challenge of Blake's words and asked him what he meant by Jesus behaving like the 'worst of men'. Blake gave the example of the casting out of the moneychangers from the Temple; Jesus, he believed, should not have involved himself with political issues of government: that was not his world. Jesus as a man had, said Blake, no right to sit in judgement on the moneychangers. He had taught, 'Judge not, lest ye be judged.' Why should he do what he had told others was wrong?

Robinson then recorded the clincher: 'Speaking of the Atonement in the ordinary Calvinistic sense, he [Blake] said, "It is a horrible doctrine; if another pay your debt, I do not forgive it."'[12] This is a straightforward denial of the forensic doctrine of the atonement – that God wanted blood as the Epistle to the Hebrews directed: 'And almost all things are by the law purged by blood; and without shedding of blood, there is no remission [of sins]' (9:22). This doctrine (based on Leviticus 17:11) went deeply against Blake's aesthetic and ethical sense. It is extremely telling that he linked the doctrine to the figure of the 'Mother'. We do not know why Blake had nothing to say of his mother, at least in surviving documents, but it may be, given his artistic development, that he associated her with a conflict over the meaning of religion in which they found themselves opposed. She wanted blood; he didn't.

And yet, of course, there was a great deal more to the Moravian spiritual universe than the emphasis on Christ's wounds. The distinction of spiritual and earthly life, the primacy of the former, with a corresponding emphasis on the spiritual value of art: these had doubtless become essential to Blake's inner life.

Nevertheless, Blake's discussion with Robinson shows categorically that Blake, at least in maturity, simply denied the forensic atonement – which is to say, that Christ took on our sins and paid a redemption-price in blood on behalf of all slaves to sin, and that this signal act constitutes the meaning of the Crucifixion, being the crux of Christian salvation: God was angry with man and would destroy us but for Jesus's paying our debts in advance to the Lord – something for which we could never thank him enough, nor account for. It was a free, undeserved gift that cost Jesus his human life. One could only have faith that atonement had been achieved. The Devil was outwitted because the Devil did not know the crucifixion-atonement had been planned all along and had been kept a secret through all time. In the end, the Devil provided the means for his own downfall. The redeemed Christian could be freed from the Devil. Such was St Paul's interpretation of the atonement. It derived from the sacrifice of lambs that attended the deliverance of Israel from the bondage of Egypt, and this was the 'type' established for the ultimate release from bondage: the bondage of sin.

If we fail to see that Blake had no use for this doctrine in its evangelical or as Robinson called it 'Calvinistic' sense, we shall become very confused about what constituted Blake's sincere Christian belief.

Henry Pars's Drawing School

In 1754, three years before Blake was born, the Society for the Encouragement of Arts, Manufacture and Commerce (The Royal Society of Arts) was established. Benjamin Franklin was one notable member of this useful and wholly successful society founded by Maidstone-born drawing master from Northampton, William Shipley (1715–1803).

Shipley began his London career with a drawing school on the east corner of Beaufort Buildings – very close to Blake's last home in Fountain Court – on the Strand. To it came distinguished pupils including Richard Cosway (1742–1821) and William Pars (1742–1782).

Landscape artist William Pars was chosen by the Dilettanti Society in 1764 to accompany Richard Chandler and Nicholas Revett to Greece, as illustrator. The epoch-marking tour, which took Asia Minor in its stride, occupied four volumes of 'Ionian Antiquities' published in 1769, dedicated by the Society of Dilettanti to King George III. George had become first patron of the Royal Academy of Arts, formed from the ranks of the Dilettanti, the previous December.

William Pars's elder brother was Henry Pars (1734–1806). In 1767, Henry Pars was Principal of Shipley's Drawing School, and to him James Blake brought his 9-year-old son William for instruction in drawing. Blake was attending Pars's drawing school at the time his teacher's younger brother returned from Asia Minor to make such a hit with his paintings and drawings of Ionian Antiquities.

James Blake had certainly chosen the right place to give his son a proper start in a life of Art. It shows in James a great sense of pride as well as intelligent application of opportunities. According to Malkin, the generous Mr Blake bought young Will casts of Hercules, Venus de' Medici, a Gladiator and 'various heads, hands, and feet'. Casts were expensive. Blake copied copies of Raphael, Michelangelo, the Flemish Master Hemskerck, Albrecht Dürer, Julio Romano and what Malkin called 'the rest of the historic class', while Blake's youthful companions laughed at his 'mechanical taste', restricted to works many regarded as *passé*, but which Blake loved regardless. We can see elements of many of Blake's distinctive human forms in all of these works.

Where Simpson's Restaurant now stands on the Strand, Blake had the opportunity to meet the next generation of artists, and to make a little impression on a world of art that was growing in influence, even as it would suffer from its success by the perils of princely patronage.

And all would be well, until Blake made the worst decision of his life.

FIVE

Lines and Chains

1767–1772

I will arise and go to my father, and will say unto him,
Father, I have sinned against heaven, and before thee,
And am no more worthy to be called thy son: make me
as one of thy hired servants. And he arose, and came to
his father. But when he was yet a great way off,
his father saw him, and had compassion, and ran, and
fell on his neck, and kissed him. And the son said unto him,
Father, I have sinned against heaven, and in thy sight, and
am no more worthy to be called thy son.

('The Prodigal Son'; Luke 15:18–21)

Art is a view that is shared. The artist is always viewing. In the process of creation, the artist shares his view with him or herself, afterwards with those who see or read the view. The art is in the point of view. Whose views did Blake share when he entered Henry Pars's drawing school in 1767? His parents? His teacher? His brothers? His friends? Past Masters? Himself?

Before Henry Pars's younger brother William joined Richard Chandler and Nicholas Revett on their taste-creating, culture-quenching tour of Greece and Asia Minor in 1764, Suffolk gentleman, artist and architect Revett had already impacted upon what would seem by the 1780s an unstoppable Greek Revival; Blake, at its epicentre, would be heavily immersed in it.

Setting out in 1748, Revett, James Stuart (1713–1788), fellow artist Gavin

Hamilton and architect Matthew Brettingham the Younger studied *in situ* the classical ruins of Naples, Pula in the Balkans, and ancient sites in Salonica and Athens. Returning in 1755, Stuart and Revett shared their elegant, enticing view of Athens with over 500 subscribers to their masterwork of antiquarianism, *The Antiquities of Athens and Other Monuments* (1762). It quickly became an indispensable guide to authentic Neo-classical taste in painting, architecture and ceramics.

The task of engraving Stuart and Revett's drawings and paintings fell to James Basire (1730–1802) of 31 Great Queen Street, a few minutes' walk north from the Strand. Basire had known Revett and Stuart when he studied in Italy after 1749 and was well placed to contribute engravings to Pars, Chandler and Revett's *Ionian Antiquities* (1769) as well as obtaining prestigious commissions from the Society of Antiquaries and the Royal Society, while Blake persisted at drawing school.[1]

It is significant that William and Henry Pars's father was a metal engraver. Artists relied on engravers for bringing their designs to a larger audience. In this period, art and antiquarianism were inseparable; culture largely consisted of the acquisition and presentation of past glories to render the present glorious by association. Novelty could be dangerous. Like everybody else, Blake looked to the past for inspiration.

This cultural tendency, with its gathering shades of romantic nostalgia, was offset, among those less involved with artistic circles, by the priorities of trade. Where *that* was concerned there was a great deal happening that ought to have fixed political minds more securely on the present and the future.

When Blake was five, the demise of French power in America and India was sealed by the nonetheless costly terms of the 1763 Treaty of Paris. Agitation against London's rule in the American colonies began shortly after; some colonists disliked paying taxes for defence against a defeated foe. James Otis's famous denunciation of 'taxation without representation' was voiced on 24 May 1764, little over a year after the Paris Treaty. Boycotts of British luxury goods followed. Against the judgement of William Pitt (the Elder), unfortunately out of power in 1765, Lord Bute's administration secured the passing of a Stamp Act: taxing stamps that were fixed to printed matter in America. Pitt knew the measure would damage trade and spoke eloquently against it, warning the government to manage the colonies with more sense and less pride. Bute, concerned with failing finances and debts from the war with France, imposed a Quartering Act, requiring colonists to shelter soldiers and horses. This sparked riots and protests in New York in July, which, incidentally, was roughly the time Gilchrist dated the Peckham Rye 'angels in the tree' story.

Returning to power with Lord Grafton in 1766, Pitt secured the Stamp Act's repeal in March, but the Quartering Act remained, leading to British troops' closure of New York's Assembly in December for refusing to comply.

While in 1767 young Blake entered his second year of making copies from casts, impressing his teacher with his drawing skills, the British government was hit by strident cries for 'liberty' at home and abroad. In May 1768, when John 'Liberty' Wilkes failed to get re-elected as an MP in London on an anti-government platform and was arrested as an outlaw, troops fired on his supporters for chanting 'No Liberty, no King!' Five were killed. Three months before, far away in what Englishmen called the 'Provinces', Samuel Adams denied Parliamentary authority over the colonies. Adams's call for united action provoked the arrival of two regiments in Boston, dispatched by the Secretary of State for the Colonies, Lord Hillsborough. Colonial Tories, fearing anarchy in the states, greeted them. Unfortunately, Pitt resigned in October, incapacitated by gout and some mental disorder that alienated him from serious affairs.

The year 1768 ended with the establishment of the first Wesleyan Chapel in the States (in New York) and the founding in London of the Royal Academy of Arts. Under Dilettanti Society member Joshua Reynolds, its first President, the Academy planned for a school in Somerset House, next door to Pars's drawing school. Meanwhile, in Nottingham, Blake's mother's home county, pioneer industrialist Richard Arkwright set up a mill for a horse-powered spinning frame, while Captain James Cook set sail for unchartered territory in the *Endeavour*, taking with him brilliant botanist Joseph Banks, a member of Shipley's Society of Arts and Manufactures since 1761.

The latter Society exhibited George Stubbs's famous painting *The Tiger* in Somerset Street, right by Pars's drawing school, in 1769. It is hard to imagine the 12-year-old Blake not seeing it, but whether it influenced his remarkable poem 'The Tyger' we shall never know, though his own etching of a tiger to illuminate his poem some 20 years later had nothing of Stubbs's finesse or observational skill about it; animals were never Blake's strongpoint.

In November 1769, North Carolina joined South Carolina in adopting the Virginia Association's ban on British trade until the Chancellor of the Exchequer Charles Townshend repealed his 1767 tax measures to provide independent governors and judges in the colonies. Freethinking scientist Thomas Jefferson, elected to the colonial House of Burgesses, called for emancipation of slaves; while in France, Denis Diderot published *D'Alembert's Dream*, advocating a materialist conception of the universe. The following year, Diderot's ally Paul-Henri Dietrich, baron of Holbach, published his godless, mechanistic world system, *The System of Nature*, portraying Man simply as a physical being organized to feel and think. While scandalizing the religious and political establishment of 1769, it would have garnered a horde of supporters today.

On 19 January 1770, New Yorkers calling themselves 'Sons of Liberty' fought British troops over the Quartering Act. Two months later in Boston, government troops shot five demonstrators (the so-called 'Boston Massacre'), while in London, still condemning government policy in America, 'Liberty Wilkes' was released from prison and appointed sheriff of London, becoming mayor in 1774. On 12 April, Lord North's new administration repealed all the Townshend legislation but for the tax on tea. A week later, Captain Cook sighted Australia for the first time.

Things seemed quieter in the American colonies in 1771 as governors attempted to enforce order amid sporadic local rebelliousness. William Tryon, Governor of North Carolina, spent May suppressing so-called 'Regulators', a group that since 1764 had rebelled against Carolina élites' fiscal control of property transactions. At new town Hillsborough, North Carolina, laid out by Lord Granville's late surveyor and cartographer William Churton (who had surveyed lands west of the Blue Ridge in 1752–3 for Bishop Spangenberg and the Moravian Church), the house Churton had bequeathed to Tory loyalist, now William Tryon's private secretary, Edmund Fanning, was burnt to the ground by angry 'Regulators'.

As Captain Cook returned, having claimed Australia for Great Britain, Swedish scientist and mystic Emanuel Swedenborg also returned to London, from Amsterdam, where he had just published his swansong, *The True Christian*

Religion. Swedenborg wrote to John Wesley, saying the world of spirits desired contact with him. Wesley replied that he had first to make a journey but would meet on returning, to which Swedenborg replied that he would be making *his* last journey to the spiritual world on 29 March 1772 and could therefore not oblige Wesley's schedule. Following a stroke, Emanuel Swedenborg died in London – on 29 March 1772. Servant Elizabeth Reynolds upheld the truth of Swedenborg's prediction; he had spoken of dying as of going on a holiday or to some merrymaking.

Now 14, William Blake approached a watershed in his life. On 4 August 1772, at Stationers' Hall, between Ludgate Hill and St Paul's, Blake stood before liveried officers of the Court of Assistants while his father, hosier and haberdasher James Blake, exchanged indentures with leading engraver, James Basire. Basire received 50 guineas. For this sum he would take young Blake into his premises at 31 Great Queen Street, to live for seven years, on condition the apprentice abstain from gambling, taverns and theatres.

This was no way to become an artist.

James Basire and the Awful Truth

Accounts of how young Will became an apprentice boy differ. The 1828 account by Blake's old friend John Thomas Smith points out that Will was 'totally destitute of the dexterity of a London shopman'. He was 'sent away from the counter as a booby'. At the time Blake was indentured, his elder brother James was himself apprenticed as a hosier and haberdasher. Did his father want Will out from under his feet, as he was a liability to trade? Did Blake feel such a thing, even if it wasn't entirely true?

A telling story Samuel Palmer told Gilchrist of Blake's old age depicts Palmer hearing Blake reading the parable of the Prodigal Son – which opens this chapter – with great emotion. When Blake came to the lines about the son seeing the father 'a great way off', he could not speak, but wept. Like Dr Johnson, Blake felt guilty about his relations with his father. Father and son appear to have suffered a breach of understanding, perhaps around the time his father relinquished him to Basire's care and discipline.

Cunningham, on the other hand, has James Blake at least trying to put his son under the tutelage of 'an eminent artist' whom he consulted. The artist, however, 'asked so large a sum for instruction, that the prudent shopkeeper hesitated' – whereupon Will spoke up: 'young Blake', writes Cunningham, 'declared he would prefer being an engraver'.[2] Cunningham points out that such would at least 'bring bread' and was, at least, connected to painting: a fairly worthless statement. A successful artist could also expect to bring bread, lots of it. Most of the great or at least successful British artists of Blake's time came from relatively humble backgrounds (relative to the people and property they painted, that is), but they had to attend recognized places of instruction, such as the club-like 'Second St Martin's Lane Academy', established by Hogarth in 1735, several of whose members were, incidentally, engravers. Unfortunately, that academy, moved by George Michael Moser and Francis Hayman to Pall Mall in 1767, had just closed when the issue of Blake's future became critical. Its closure occurred in 1771 when Moser was appointed first keeper of the Royal Academy, which itself moved from Pall Mall to temporary accommodation at Old Somerset House, on the Strand.

The question then is: *why didn't Blake attend the new schools run by the Royal Academy?* His (later) friend John Flaxman did, and just missed winning a gold medal there in 1772 when RA President Joshua Reynolds pipped him to it. Could it have been that Reynolds was the 'eminent artist' Blake's father had consulted? Blake held a lifelong loathing for Reynolds, apparently based on variant assessments of the role of imagination in art. Could the seed have been sown in an imagined humiliation of his father? Blake was given to sudden outbursts when passions were high; they could cost him dear. It is interesting that after his apprenticeship, Blake would come to Moser as a pupil at the Royal Academy, as if trying to make up for lost time, and find himself almost uncontrollably incensed by a comment of Sir Joshua's on his sense of style. Flaxman would, so to speak, steal seven years on Blake, establishing himself with the Academy while Blake donned an artisan's apron.

Akin to Cunningham's, Tatham's 1832 account refers to a 'huge premium' required by a 'painter of Eminence' for training Blake. According to Tatham, Blake 'requested with his characteristic generosity that his Father would not on any account spend so much money upon him, as he thought it would be an injustice to his brothers & sisters [*sic*]; he therefore himself proposed Engraving as being less expensive & sufficiently eligible for his future avocations.'[3]

Blake, if we trust this account, asked for it. To satisfy his son's alleged insistence, James Blake sought a suitable engraving master. According to

Samuel Palmer, in conversation with JC Strange in 1859, James Blake took his son to an engraver in Broad Street, but Blake was so horrified by the engraver's face he would not be bound to him. As proof of Blake's knowledge of physiognomy, Palmer related to Strange that Blake declared the man would come to be hanged, 'which was actually his end'.[4]

The indefatigable Blake researcher and biographer GE Bentley Jr discovered that there were two engravers living in Broad Street in 1772: Royal Academician and 'Engraver to the King' Francesco Bartolozzi (1725–1815) and Pierre Étienne Falconet (1741–1791). However, while Falconet did execute a small number of engravings, he was known chiefly as a portrait painter, of eminent artists especially, having studied under Joshua Reynolds's direction – Reynolds was a friend of Falconet's father.

Falconet himself could well have been the 'eminent artist' who asked for too much, though he did not come to be hanged. Taking the latter detail as the most significant, Bentley, following Gilchrist, reckoned Blake's father had taken him to see engraver and artist William Wynne Ryland, who did indeed come to be hanged, but who in 1772 lived at the Royal Exchange, Cornhill, and in Queen's Row, Knightsbridge, not Broad Street, as Palmer maintained to Strange in his hanging anecdote.[5]

I should like to advance the hypothesis that Blake met Ryland at Falconet's home on Broad Street, or, at the least, that Falconet directed James Blake to Ryland personally: an hypothesis based on the following evidence.

The Royal Academy of Arts collection holds a 'crayon manner' engraving of miniaturist Ozias Humphry (1742–1810; later a friend of Blake) by DP Pariset. Beneath it is written: 'Sold by P. Falconet at the Corner of Panton Street [a tradesmen's street], Hay Market by Ryland & Bryer, Cornhill'; it is dated 1768. In fact it is one of a series of prints published by Falconet, Ryland & Bryer. *Falconet had recently been in business with Ryland*, the engraver who would come to be hanged.

Indeed, the National Portrait Gallery holds DP Pariset's engraving (dated 1768–9) of William Wynne Ryland himself 'after Pierre Étienne Falconet'. It is one of 34 portraits painted by Falconet of prominent members of the London art scene, engraved by Pariset (1740–*post* 1783), the majority having been published by Falconet with Ryland & Bryer. A two-shilling print of Joshua Reynolds from 1768 even gives a familiar publisher's address: 'Sold by

P. Falconet Broad Street Carnaby Market, & Ryland & Bryer Cornhill.' If you wanted knowledge of eminent painters, Falconet was the place to go; he could also put you in touch with engravers. And he lived practically next door to the Blakes.

Ryland (1738–1783) became 'Engraver to the King' after engraving portraits of King George III and Queen Charlotte after other artists. He was admitted as a member of the Incorporated Society of Artists in 1766 and went into the print business with his pupil Henry Bryer. The business went bust in December 1771, a very recent event at the time of Blake's apprenticeship. Ryland's urgent need for capital would explain why associate Falconet might have pointed Blake in Ryland's direction. One cannot imagine young Blake wishing to be put into the hands of someone whose primary need was money. One can well imagine, however, a scenario in which Falconet called on his sometime business associate to come to Broad Street to investigate a nice 'opportunity': James Blake was willing to pay a tidy sum.

Ryland would be hanged at Tyburn on 29 August 1783 for forging two bills for £714 with intent to defraud the East India Company. Providence at least saved Blake from apprenticeship to a desperate character, but proved powerless against Blake's own willfulness.

Undoubtedly, apprenticeship to James Basire was a far better bet than getting involved with the uncertain business of Falconet or Ryland. As we have seen, Basire was a man whose work was respected highly by the antiquarians of Great Britain, and that meant the educated gentility of the country. Basire enjoyed excellent relations with the Society of Antiquaries, the Royal Society and the Society of Dilettanti. This may have 'swung it' as far as young Blake was concerned, with his passion for history and antiquity, and a need for familiar securities. More viscerally, he may simply have wanted to get out of the family house and away from his elder brother's likely complaints that he was not contributing to the family's coffers: if an apprenticeship was good enough for the father and the elder son, then why not for William Blake? What made *him* so different? Such arguments would certainly have screwed into Blake's sensitive soul. Besides, engravers were to be found in the Royal Academy and Blake undoubtedly recognized engraving as a *bona fide* art in its own right. He held the great Albrecht Dürer in high esteem and owned a print of Dürer's remarkable engraving *Melencolia I* whose theme of highest inspiration deriving from the shadows of Saturnian introspection would haunt his thoughts, for he found it true.

Smith assures us Blake shared with Basire an admiration for Italian engraver Marcantonio Raimondi (*c*.1480–1534), while emblematic engravings had been part of Blake's education and first visual awareness of spiritual things. It might have been a convincing argument that in engraving, Blake could combine his artistic passions with a future financial security, combined with a shared commitment to his family that did not look like he was 'getting above himself' in their eyes.

It is noteworthy that in the Royal Academy collections today, James Basire has but two works of art attributed to him. *Christ and the two Disciples at Emmaus* is an etching and engraving 'after Raphael' – a favourite artist of Blake's – published in 1753 by Richard Dalton (*c*.1715–1791) after Basire's return from Italy. *Pylades and Orestes*, 'after Benjamin West' (1738–1820), was a recent publication by John Boydell (July 1771) when Blake was apprenticed to the eldest son of celebrated printmaker Isaac Basire (1704–1768).

But note those simple words 'after Raphael' and 'after Benjamin West'. The engraver came 'after' ... the artist. Who was the artist? Obviously not the engraver! Artists could expect more than engravers. Take Benjamin West, for example. Born in Pennsylvania, a close friend of Benjamin Franklin, West would become second Royal Academy President in 1792: *that* was security. In the year of Blake's apprenticeship, George III appointed West 'historical painter to the court' on an annual stipend of £1000. Now that was *real* security. After that, came the engraver.

The Royal Academy did not teach engraving. It saw itself as promoting, above all, excellence in 'design' as well as painterly and sculptural accomplishment. Roles in art were becoming formalized, and Blake entered the art scene at precisely the time this process was occurring systematically. Something very similar had occurred in the case of 'architecture' during the previous half-century. When Christopher Wren was born in 1632, building in stone was the work of 'freemasons', workers in 'free stone': stone suitable for carving. After completing an apprenticeship, promising freemasons who were trained further, found capable of running a business, drawing designs and supervising their execution, became master masons. The King's architect was called Master Mason to the King.

When gentlemen began to take an interest in building, as a classical discipline (*viz: De Architectura* by Vitruvius) and as an extension of the liberal art Geometry, they called themselves, grandly, *architects*, distinguishing themselves from men who had undergone the apprenticeship and had hands-on building experience. They directed 'masons' to do the work. The Art, they wished to believe, was in the *Design*. Masons were understood as tradesmen. If they wanted to be 'architects', they had better get rich, appeal to new tastes, especially in classicism, and keep their hands clean.

The awful truth was that engraving was experienced fundamentally as a *service industry* to artists, writers and publishers. An artist might dabble at engraving to broaden his 'pallette', so to speak, but it would be an encroachment for an engraver to claim to be an Artist as an engraver. Of course, the whole nomenclature was bound up with class distinctions. An aristocrat did not expect to be painted by a gentleman of rank, but he certainly did not expect to hold himself poised before a *tradesman*. People did not pose for engravers. Ladies did not reveal their décolletage for engravers.

A seven-year apprenticeship as an engraver was the wrong footing for Blake altogether. It was the worst and most fundamentally damaging decision of his life, and he made it, or was forced into it, when he was just 14. To give just one example of why it was so damaging to him, just look at what Blake's *friend* Flaxman had to write to Blake's patron, William Hayley, at the time Blake left to work for Hayley at Felpham, Sussex in 1800. Royal Academician Flaxman explicitly advised Hayley that Blake was *not to be encouraged to attempt large paintings*, something for which he was 'not fitted either by training or capacity'.

Few doubted Blake's 'genius', but that was not enough.

SIX

The Golden Cage

1772–1778

With sweet May dews my wings were wet,
And Phoebus fir'd my vocal rage
He caught me in his silken net,
And shut me in his golden cage.

He loves to sit and hear me sing,
Then, laughing, sports and plays with me;
Then stretches out my golden wing,
And mocks my loss of liberty.

(from *Poetical Sketches*, printed 1783)

It might have seemed to Blake by the end of 1772 that the whole world was crying out for liberty, and he was the only one chained to his burin, his ink, his wax, his mordant acid, his copper plates, and his master. On 2 November, to promulgate their claims to rights, radicals in America set up 'Committees of Correspondence'. More unrest was brewing across the Atlantic. Blake could only write to himself.

Some time during his apprenticeship Blake acquired Abbé Winckelmann's *Painting and Sculpture of the Greeks* (1765). Inscribing his name, Blake gave his address as 'Lincoln's Inn' as if he were a lawyer in his chambers, but his chambers were Basire's. Blake's master had married Isabella Turner in August 1768, though Basire could hardly do otherwise, because only four months later, the Basires had a son, christened James. We may imagine Blake would have heard quite a lot from young James. Whether the infant's mother was kind to the new apprentice we know not. There was another apprentice, but only for another two weeks: Thomas Ryder completed his apprenticeship on 16 August 1772.[1]

It must have seemed a little odd to find his family's names following him to Great Queen Street: two Jameses, father and son, with himself stuck in the middle again, just like home.

It is likely Blake wrote the following lines (included in *Poetical Sketches*) during his apprenticeship:

Heavenly Goddess! I am wrapped in mortality, my flesh is a prison, my bones the bars of death. Misery builds over our cottage roofs, and Discontent runs like a brook. Even in childhood, Sorrow slept with me in my cradle; he followed me up and down in the house when I grew up; he was my school-fellow: thus he was in my steps and in my play, till he became to me as my brother. I walked through dreary places with him, and in church-yards; and I oft found myself sitting by Sorrow on a tomb-stone![2]

He would soon be finding his comfort on many a cold tombstone.

Richard Gough (1735–1809) was the brilliant son of a wealthy Member of Parliament and director of the East India Company. Since 1771 this precocious graduate of Corpus Christi College, Cambridge had been Director of the Society of Antiquaries of London. Gough's interests covered the entire history of Great Britain and as such served as a vital counterweight to the burgeoning Neo-classical consensus. Gough was particularly keen on ancient British history, and no less concerned with the art of the Middle Ages, that art and architecture that had come to be called 'Gothick'.

Gough did not share Scottish clergyman, and Free-Mason, Rev. James Anderson's dismissal of 'Gothick' as 'rubbish', and wrote in his *Constitutions of Free-Masons, viz*.: 'the polite Nations began to discover the Confusion and Impropriety of the Gothick Buildings; and in the Fifteenth and Sixteenth Centuries the AUGUSTAN STILE [*sic*] was rais'd from its Rubbish in Italy' (*Constitutions*, 1723, p.39). If he did not already, Blake would come to share Gough's partiality and speak up for the neglected art and building of medieval

Britain as 'living form'. For Blake, 'Gothick' was grounded in instinctive, and inspired, spiritual feeling, not rationalism, which Blake associated with Greek and Roman styles of art and thought.

So it must have been music to Blake's ears when in 1773 he was called to make his contribution, even while still an apprentice, to what would 13 years later be published as the first volume of Gough's magnificent *Sepulchral Monuments of Great Britain, applied to illustrate the history of families, manners, habits and arts at the different periods from the Norman Conquest to the Seventeenth Century.* It would be followed in 1796 by a second volume covering the 15th century.

In 1806, Malkin first published the story of two new apprentices who turned up two years into Blake's apprenticeship and 'completely destroyed its harmony', whereat 'Blake, not chusing [*sic*] to take part with his master against his fellow apprentices, was sent out to make drawings,' adding that Blake 'always mentions [this circumstance] with gratitude to Basire, who said that he was too simple and they too cunning.'[3]

Somebody's memory seems to be at fault here for GE Bentley Jr examined Company of Stationers records and found only one new apprentice after Blake (in Blake's apprenticeship term that is), and that was James Parker (1750–1805), son of Paul Parker, a corn chandler of St Mary le Strand who was apprenticed on 3 August 1773: a year after Blake.[4] So, either the story is legendary or Blake fell out with Parker, at least temporarily, for the two apprentices, Blake and Parker, would go into business with one another after they had both left Basire's.

Tatham also mentions Blake falling out with 'fellow apprentices' over 'matters of intellectual argument', but Tatham was following Malkin. It is possible that Basire might have found reason to borrow somebody else's apprentices for a while on account of workload, but the motivation seems unlikely. The story is told to get Blake out into Westminster Abbey for solitary drawing and even mystical enlightenment: Blake's time is fairly romanticized in all biographies. However, Gough insisted that drawings be taken for his work from ecclesiastical structures all over the country, and if Blake personally engraved few of the finished works himself, he certainly was a skilled draughtsman, as the many surviving drawings of sepulchral monuments attributed to his hand demonstrate. Gough paid Basire for drawings to be taken from anything that took his antiquarian fancy. Blake would simply have had to get out of 31 Great Queen Street to get on with the job as directed by the will of Gough, the man of means.

Tatham asserts that while Blake was working on one of the Westminster Abbey monuments, a Westminster schoolboy thought it fun to rag him, and Blake, furious, pushed him bodily off the scaffolding before complaining to the Dean. The Dean then allegedly banned boys from the Abbey. Well, the Westminster boys were a rowdy lot, forever fighting among themselves and their masters, and threatening anyone who got in their way as they played football in the cloisters. That Blake had a scrap or two seems consistent with all reports of the boys' attested demeanour in the abbey, but the school has no record of any disciplinary action and since its boys went to the Abbey daily for its service, they could hardly have been banned. Perhaps there was a warning of some kind, but it would have had to be extraordinarily stiff to have any effect. If Blake himself gave a boy or boys a decent thrashing, he would have established protection enough, I should think. After such a scrape, one could imagine them protecting *him*.

Gilchrist relates that Blake envisioned scenes of the past taking place before his eyes in the Abbey. Who would not, after spending hours in concentrated effort, poring over the faces of Richard II, Edward III, his Queen, Philippa, and the exquisitely sober monument to the knight Aymer de Valence, at sundry times, dawn, dusk and candle-lit, as the voices of excited boys faded and the stones surrendered their record? Palmer wrote a moving letter to Gilchrist, dated 23 August 1855, indicating the power the Abbey experience exercised on Blake's imagination:

In Westminster Abbey were his earliest and most sacred recollections. I asked him how he would like to paint on glass, for the great west window, his 'Sons of God shouting for Joy,' from his designs in the Job. He said, after a pause, 'I could do it!' kindling at the thought.[5]

Contrast between old and new could hardly have reached more profound intensity as it did in the hours spent in the abbey and churches of London and perhaps beyond. As Blake marvelled at the Gothic 'architects' (Master Masons), 1773 saw construction on the world's first cast-iron bridge: 'Ironbridge' at Coalbrookdale Gorge in Shropshire; while brothers Robert and James Adam published their manifesto of the Neo-classical movement, *Works of Architecture,* in a wholly different cast of mind.

First Work

Blake's classical age was not that of Greece and Rome. His true sympathies are clearly evident in what scholars consider his first, or one of his first, engravings: *Joseph of Arimathea among the Rocks of Albion*. In its first state, it is dated 1773, when, one might have thought, Blake's skill at engraving would be slight. He was either a very speedy learner (which in general he was) or he has dated it that way for some other reason. It depicts he who provided Jesus with a tomb, or temporary respite, the man English legends held had once brought the boy Jesus himself to the shores of Britain. Blake would make a revised engraving, adding that Joseph was 'one of the Gothic Artists who built the Cathedrals in what we call the Dark Ages.' Clearly, they were not dark to Blake, and we must presume that he believed that Joseph, at least, had walked on England's mountains green. Blake has taken the muscular form from Michaelangelo's *Crucifixion of St Peter* but has placed Michelangelo's classical proportions in a Gothic setting, as he would do many times.

The figure has another resonance too. At some unknown date, Blake became familiar with the work of Gough's predecessor at the Society of Antiquaries, William Stukeley (1687–1765). The fascinating engravings that illustrate Stukeley's *Stonehenge, a Temple Restor'd* (1740) were executed by Gerard van der Gucht (1696/7–1776), a member of the Society for the Arts situated next to Shipley's Drawing Academy. Blake almost certainly consulted Stukeley's work for his late illuminated poem *Jerusalem*, and it is likely that Stukeley's work was in his mind when he conceived his design for Joseph of Arimathea.

One of van der Gucht's engravings depicts 'A British Druid'. Stukeley believed the Druids had built Stonehenge, a view that Gough himself did not accept. History and science have gone with Gough in this, but Blake accepted the idea of an original, pristine religion, centred in the British Isles, that, in his view, had been corrupted by the failings of the Druids. The figure of the British Druid and of Joseph of Arimathea warrant comparison, for Blake would have known that Joseph's legendary visit to Britain would have roughly coincided with the defeat of the Druids by the Romans. In Blake's imagination there was a curious explosion when these stories were combined, for Joseph was bringing back to Albion the descendant of the patriarchs, and Blake believed the patriarchal period had flourished *in Britain*. These were Holy Isles – and look what had happened to them! And look what *was* happening to them!

Telling and understanding the story or myth of the ancient corruption of a pristine science and religion was something that drove Blake all of his adult life, and it happens that the same thing can be said of William Stukeley.

In 1998 I was delighted as editor of *Freemasonry Today* magazine to publish a scoop by Stukeley expert David Haycock, telling of his discovery of a rare illustrated document by Stukeley in the archives of the Wellcome Institute in London: *Paleographia Sacra – or Discourses on Monuments of Antiquity that relate to Sacred History, 11*.[6] Its contents complement Stukeley's work on Stonehenge in subtle and direct ways.

Around the edge of van der Gucht's portrait of Stukeley in *Stonehenge* is Stukeley's nickname, 'Chyndonnax', supposedly the name of a Gaulish Druid. The name 'Chyndonax' appears on a rock or stone in front of the 'British Druid', also in Stonehenge. The morphology of the left arms of Blake's 'Joseph of Arimathea' and of the 'British Druid' is identical. In fact, both arms form a square, as in a builder's square. Remember that Blake insisted Joseph was one of the builders of the Gothic cathedrals in what Blake saw as a *Light*, not a Dark Age, compared with his own. And Stukeley believed the Druids had been not only the builders of Stonehenge, but also the lineal predecessors of the Freemasons. That is in part what the document Haycock discovered was about.

Freemasonry and Blake

Stukeley is one of the many famous Freemasons of the 18th century, and one of the first to record his experience of the new 'Grand Lodge' system established between *c*.1716 and 1723 out of an earlier 'Acception' system run within the London Company of Masons and freemasons' fraternities about the country, now obscured to us. Stukeley was initiated on 6 January 1721 at the Salutation Tavern, Tavistock Street, London. A new lodge was established with Stukeley as Master in December that year at the 'Fountain Tavern', the Strand, presumably the origin of the Fountain Court in which Blake lived and died a century later. Stukeley's friends included Isaac Newton and John, 2nd Duke of Montagu (elected Grand Master of London's Grand Lodge on St John Baptist's Day, 24 June, 1721). In 1723, the Rev. James Anderson, working for the Duke, maintained in his *Constitutions of the Free-masons* that 'Celtic Edifices' evinced the spread of the 'Craft of Masonry' from the East.

In 1753, Stukeley's account of his own life reveals that he suspected Masonry represented the 'remains of the mysterys of the antients'. The background to the statement was discovered by Haycock. The ambition of Stukeley's previously unknown essay of 1735 was to discover 'a scheme of the first, the antient, & patriarchal religion that had first existed before the birth of Moses and Christ'.

At first the patriarchs enjoyed 'the most excellent gift from heaven' but 'its native charms were miserably defac'd, obscur'd and perverted into superstition and idolatry'. The teachings of Moses and of Jesus were intended to restore the original religion. This would be Blake's precise view as well, and the seed of it was well planted, or so at least it would appear, by 1773. Indeed, we may call Blake's later mythic figures battling it out for the psyche of Albion, *patriarchetypes* without demur.

Stukeley recognized in the first written Masonic documents (the 'Old Charges' and their prototypes that go back to the end of the 14th century) the analogous view of the original and primal knowledge being inscribed on pillars or tablets, attributed to Enoch and discovered by Hermes Trismegistus, and built to survive deluges of flood and fire. Blake understood, or would come to understand, that access to this primal, antediluvian knowledge was through painting, poetry and music: the arts of the divine imagination, which reason abstracted suppressed. Blake was a spokesman for the original art that was the original science. It is curious he should have stood against Newton, for Newton also was seeking the original science that was the original religion!

The job of the antiquarian, as Stukeley saw it, was primarily to bring back to light that which ignorance had left to decay: 'The origin of the mysterys (as we hinted before) is no other than the first corruption of true religion, when they [first] began to deviate from the patriarchal religion, into idolatry and superstition, and this was as nigh as early as the renovation of mankind, after the Noachian [of Noah] deluge.' Thus we see the signal importance of antiquarianism in Blake's career, and the seed was early planted.

According to Haycock, 'The mysteries, therefore, had existed throughout the ancient world, and it was this secret religion – a fragment of the primeval patriarchal religion – which Stukeley believed the Druids had possessed, and which he [Stukeley] had hoped to discover in the secrets of Freemasonry.'

Blake's poem *Jerusalem* could be called a very protracted comment on this line of Stukeley's in the once lost manuscript: 'such was the craft of the evil power that perverted true religion ...' Masonry existed because of loss of knowledge through past corruption of an ancient, pristine and patriarchal religion. Blake's understanding is practically identical. Beneath his engraving of Joseph, he shows that his ancient patriarchs were not grand figures but Good Men: 'Wandering about in sheep skins and goat skins of whom the World was not worthy such were the Christians in all Ages.' *Yes*, those feet had walked on England's mountains green – but it was damned hard to imagine it *now*. The 'Satanic mills' had taken over.

So, was Blake a Freemason? In short, we do not know. His place of work and lodging, 31 Great Queen Street, was in fact directly opposite the old Freemasons' Hall and Tavern, London Freemasonry's epicentre. He might well have been fascinated by what was going on, daily, opposite. He would have seen plenty of men in aprons making their way into both tavern and hall for ritualized meetings, and out again. However, at age 15 and 16 (as he was in 1773) he was definitely not eligible for the fraternity, not just because of age but because he was bound, and bound men cannot be Freemasons.

The name 'James Blake' has been found on a list of members of an 'Antient' Lodge, Lodge No. 38, from 1757–1759.[7] It is not out of the question that Blake's father had joined the rival organization to the Grand Lodge, the 'Antients', founded in 1751.

What is rather extraordinary is that deeds relating to the Basire family's occupation of premises opposite Freemasons' Hall came into the collection of the Royal Masonic Institution for Girls (RMIG), as this Masonic charity redeveloped this and adjoining properties to form their administrative offices at the turn of the 20th century. The numbers are now 30, 31 and 32 but were formerly numbers 19, 20 and 21 Great Queen Street. The documents are now part of the archive of the Library and Museum of Freemasonry, Freemasons' Hall, Great Queen Street.

The documents include a copy of the marriage certificate of James Basire and Isabella Turner, married by licence on 26 August 1768 by Richard Southgate, curate, in the presence of Joseph Holman and Joseph George Holman at St Giles in the Fields, Middlesex; the baptism certificate of their son, James Basire II (1769–1822), baptised at St Giles in the Fields, Middlesex, 8 December 1769; and the deeds relating to the sale of the house and garden at Great Queen Street when Basire's grandson James (1796–1869) moved to Quality Court, Chancery Lane to produce printed forms for legal firms.

It is a realistic possibility that Blake's master joined the Fraternity, along with his son perhaps. There might have been social advantages to consider in terms of broadening the circle of potential commissions. Otherwise it is difficult to see how a Masonic charitable organization should have come by family documents of such intimate significance. However, we simply do not know enough about the thinking of mid to late 18th-century English Freemasons in general to ascertain whether Blake would have felt spiritually at home in the Fraternity as it was after his twenty-first year.

We know there were spiritually minded Masons but whether the organization as a whole was worthy of the respect due to the mythologized history and spiritual ideals which upheld its mystique is far from certain. The fact is that Blake's perception of history and religion did not require Masonic initiation to sustain it. Masons had more to learn from him, in due time, than he from them. Furthermore, the Masonic emphasis on geometry, classicism, the seven liberal arts, Whig politics in the sense of Newtonian philosophy and aristocratic privilege, as well as the notion of the framer of the universe as a Great Architect or Grand Geometrician would have repelled rather than attracted him. However, individual lodges and brethren of the 'old school' may have sustained sympathetic cultural priorities. There were Masons interested in the 'Noachite', patriarchal idea, and in Hermetic philosophy. There were also serious charitable activities, social idealism and welfare structures that attracted Masonic interest and funding. Campaigners against slavery would find London's Masonic Lodges generous providers of accommodation for lectures. Masonic culture, anyway, was part of the culture around Blake and cannot be discounted from a consideration of his world view. In addition, Masonry was undergoing a transformation on the Continent into more philosophical, spiritual, chivalric and esoteric forms, influenced to a great degree by thinkers with whom Blake empathized

(Swedenborg, Böhme and Paracelsus), and it is difficult to imagine Blake did not pick up much that was in the air: air very different to that we now inhale, though I have not had cause to mention the open sewers of Blake's time.

In March 1773, Irish writer Oliver Goldsmith's play *She Stoops to Conquer* was performed in Covent Garden, a minute's walk from Basire's front door. Was Blake allowed to see it? Gilchrist recounts a story of Goldsmith himself entering Basire's premises, admired by Blake for his 'finely marked' head, the kind of head he himself would like when he grew to be a man. Goldsmith would die shortly after, on 4 April 1774.

Blake was just 16 when he heard about the 'Boston Tea Party'. This blatant act of rebellion occurred on 16 December 1773 when about 1,000 Boston agitators divested three British ships of their tea cargo. On 20 May 1774 Parliament passed acts to close Boston's harbour and to reduce Massachusetts's legislative power. A fortnight later, the Quartering Act was reactivated. Pitt did his utmost to counsel restraint and concession but complacency, strictness and outraged pride won the day.

Outside of Westminster Abbey's ancient confines, 1774 was quite a year. In Austria, Franz Mesmer used hypnotism for therapy, while William Herschel built an enormous telescope unlike anything ever seen. And while James Watt sold his first steam engine to industrialist John Wilkinson, a wave of suicides shocked the German states, after the publication of Johann Wolfgang Goethe's *The Sorrows of Young Werther* lit a new touchpaper of collective romanticism. An Ossian reader (like Blake), Goethe presented Werther as an artist at odds with society, while a mystical force of nature was glorified. Goethe's message of a natural salvation all about us, unseen by the earthbound, would not appear in English for another five years, but the news of sympathetic suicides crossed linguistic boundaries, and youngsters took to dressing in Werther's colours.

On 1 December George Washington signed the Fairfax resolves, banning slave imports and exports to Britain. A fortnight later, lawyer John Sullivan led rebels to capture powder and shot at Fort William & Mary. The 'Sons of Liberty' prepared for war.

On 9 February 1775, Parliament declared Massachusetts a state in rebellion, while English agitator Tom Paine, fresh to the American states, founded a radical magazine in Pennsylvania. In March, Edmund Burke in London urged reconciliation, but Lord North demanded restriction of New England trade to Britain and Ireland in retaliation for outrageous rebelliousness.

Science was gaining pace, stimulated by a feeling of burgeoning liberty and imminent revelation. Henri Lavoisier overturned millennia of traditional science by proving that water was not a fundamental element, but reducible to two gases. Natural philosopher Joseph Priestley, at his laboratory at Bowood House, Wiltshire, identified seven gases, and discovered oxygen, or 'dephlogistated air' as he called it.

And Scottish explorer James Bruce returned from an epic journey of exploration up the Blue Nile from Egypt into Ethiopia. He carried back with him the 'Bruce Codex' of Christian Gnostic writings, the like of which had only ever been read of in early Church references to heresy; he had bought the codices in Upper Egypt in 1769. A work entitled *The great Logos* [Word] *corresponding to Mysteries* was just one surprising esoteric Christian text in Bruce's collection. Carl Gottfried Woide, a Pole who was expert in Coptic and Sahidic languages, made copies of this and of the lost Book of Enoch in the Ge'ez language of Ethiopia. In 1782 he would become the British Museum's Assistant Librarian. He did not translate the works (that was not accomplished until 1933!) but Indian scholar Piloo Nanavutti was of the opinion that Woide would have communicated his discoveries to circles Blake and his friends frequented, especially Swedenborgian circles.[8] It is not unlikely that Blake's own poetic myths owe structural debts to Gnostic creation and fall myths, including concepts of emanations in pairs of divine beings, male and female, and the idea of 'Aeons' derived from absolute spirit and de-forming into matter and conflict under internal metaphysical pressures.

Metaphysical pressures were nothing new to Benjamin Franklin and Dr Benjamin Rush. On 14 April 1775 they formed the first colonial anti-slavery group: the *Society for the Relief of Free Negroes Unlawfully Held in Bondage.* While Franklin and Rush strove to abolish slavery, there was outright fighting at Lexington and Concord, Massachusetts. One look at some of the names involved and you can see the contradictions and agonies of the American situation. While the evidence is disputed, it is possible that independence was first declared at Charlotte, County of Mecklenburg, North Carolina. Charlotte and the County of Mecklenburg were named after the Queen, Charlotte of

Mecklenburg-Strelitz. Carolina was named after King Charles II, the 'merry monarch' welcomed back to Britain after popular disenchantment with the Cromwellian republic. Republicanism was nothing new, but suddenly it *felt* new.

On 17 June, rebels suffered defeat at Bunker Hill. Six days later, Virginia's George Washington took command of what would be called the 'continental army'. Failing to realize what Pitt foresaw – that is, that the war could not be won without satisfaction being achieved by the majority of rebels – George III rejected a peace offer, unable to see the rebellion in terms other than another open rebellion against the Crown, such as the last Jacobite Rebellion, 30 years earlier. That rebellion had been quashed with a victory that had proved absolute. But this was very different.

On 13 October, Congress barred negroes from the continental army, so Governor Dunmore offered freedom to slaves prepared to fight the rebels. This move upset planters who regarded slaves as indispensable to their economy. On New Year's Eve, Washington declared that free slaves could join the army.

It was 1776, and William Blake was 18 years old, still tied to Basire's, dreaming of summer's days in the countryside across the Thames and girls who could ensnare his heart.

On 9 January, Tom Paine, full of his ideas of 'The Rights of Man', published a pamphlet called 'Common Sense'. Everyone likes to think they possess this increasingly rare commodity and 120,000 copies were printed for those who wanted to know what common sense was. Paine described King George III as cruel, which, by the standards of the time, he was not. 'Let the names of Whig and Tory be extinct,' Paine declared, and he was supported or rejected by either Whigs or Tories.

On 28 March Blake would doubtless have joined in the family celebration that his elder brother James was now returned to his father's business, the late apprentice to Gideon Boitoult, citizen and Needlemaker of London, 'made Free by Servitude'. James was 'admitted upon Livery' and 'cloathed accordingly'. He was a Haberdasher. On 4 July, across the Sea, another group of men declared they were free from servitude: that is to say, they signed a Declaration of American Independence. Meanwhile, in Birmingham, England, the industrial revolution cranked forwards another ratchet as Watt's new steam engine, engineered with business partner Matthew Boulton, underwent crucial technological advances. The result would be money, lots and lots of it, and in case the pioneers were not sure what this might mean philosophically, Adam Smith obliged with the publication of his *Inquiry into the Nature and Causes of the Wealth of Nations*. It all had to do with self-interest, profit, capital and jobs; William Blake, in due course, would see there was more to it than that. The first volume of Gibbon's *Decline and Fall of the Roman Empire* was also published. Gibbon blamed Christianity: apparently, it weakened resolve.

And on New Year's Eve, Benjamin Franklin found himself in Paris, negotiating French aid for the rebels. George III was thunderstruck by what he considered King Louis XVI's treachery to sound principle. The French King would eventually have to face the consequences of encouraging rebellion against a lawful monarch, though Louis would doubtless have defended his fatal inconsistency in the name of 'national interest'.

In 1777, Washington won a significant victory at Princeton, followed, on 17 October, by a humiliating defeat for the King when General Burgoyne's British army from Canada surrendered to Horatio Gates at Saratoga.

William Blake was now 20 years old. On 17 December 1777, Louis XVI of France recognized the American states' independence, agreeing to negotiate with them as a sovereign body.

The colonial war's cost was depressing England, and the states too. On 6 February 1778, France and the 'United States' signed a trade agreement. As France joined the war, the French Enlightenment suffered. On 30 May, Voltaire died, aged 84. A month later, Rousseau died insane, swiftly pursued to the grave by Denis Diderot, who died of apoplexy.

And then, after seven long years, William Blake achieved his twenty-first year. He was free of his apprenticeship, a son of liberty, at last!

It was time to catch up.

SEVEN

Sex and the Single Genius

1779–1782

And the eyes of them both were opened,
and they knew that they were naked;
and they sewed themselves fig leaves together,
and made themselves aprons.

(Genesis 3:7)

Beneath the apprentice's apron beat the heart of a romantic. That heart was now set free. Blake at 21 was sure to get into trouble.

Comparing Berlin in the 1930s to Paris in the 1920s, poet Aleister Crowley opined that at least in Paris license was never allowed to descend into liberty. The problem for the sexually eager in 1780s London was that there was no license at all. A leap into liberty could be catastrophic. The sole license was a marriage license. Blake's poem 'London', possibly composed during the decade, speaks of the 'marriage hearse': a strong image requiring no elucidation. The Church, conformist and Nonconformist, maintained the tried-and-trusted, millennia-old doctrine that those desiring salvation had best abstain from lustful urges or channel them into legitimate heirs, lest urge become vice and so corrupt the host into Satan's progeny, fit for damnation. Death was ubiquitous and as each soul dropped from the stage of the world, the Devil, knowing his own, could take his pick. Filth went into the sewer, and everybody could see, and smell, what that was like.

The result was a society characterized by exemplary holiness, personal torment and widespread hypocrisy. Sinners tried to keep their liberties a secret, but among the close quarters of London, truth would ever out. The Prince of Wales's affairs were common knowledge, to the despair of a King who believed in the Church and decorum and tried to impose both.

Apart from illicit literature, there were two fields in which sexual thoughts could be legitimately transposed. The first was science; the second, art. Both were preserves of the upper classes, though that was changing, and the upper classes, on the whole, did not like it.

In the north of England, dissenting scientist Joseph Priestley (1733–1804), a cloth finisher's son, had moved from educational books and natural philosophical studies on the 'current state of electricity' to radical reasoning on government and religion, evinced in works such as his *Institutes of Natural and Revealed Religion* (1772–74), a three-volume ejaculation that would annoy Blake possibly even more than it annoyed the government.

Even as Blake left Basire's tutelage for the last time, Scottish pioneer sexologist Dr James Graham (1745–1794) was in Europe, garnering the patronage of Lady Spencer, mother of 'Foxite' radical Georgiana, Duchess of Devonshire. Graham had shot to fame in 1778 when his 21-year-old brother William Graham entered into a scandalous marriage with a widow more than twice his age. Catharine Macaulay (1731–1791) was a Republican historian and friend of the American anti-slavery reformer, Benjamin West.

Dr Graham returned from the Continent in 1781 to establish his 'Temple of Health' at the Adelphi, a grand construction of the Brothers Adam. To further public comprehension of the health benefits of his 'pneumatic chemistry', visitors were treated to the sight of a succession of exemplary 'Goddesses of Health', one of whom was the young Emy, or Emma Lyon, who would become muse to obsessed artist George Romney, wife to Sir William Hamilton in 1791, and Lord Nelson's mistress a few years later: clearly a rejuvenating goddess of health in all but name.

Dr Graham had notions in keeping with the soaring columns of classical architecture. Having studied electro-magnetism in America with Ben Franklin's friend and colleague Franklin Ebenezer Kinnersley, while absorbing thought-emanations, so to speak, from hypnosis expert and 'magnetizer' Franz Mesmer, Graham became convinced that the essential life-force in the human body was semen. Its free flow through the male and female systems was, literally, vital, and should not be cast away in masturbation or prostitution. It should be celebrated and glorified in the conjugal bed. Taking literal vitality beyond metaphor, Dr Graham instituted the 'Celestial Bed' at Schomberg House, Pall Mall, in 1781. For £50, married couples could find a night's heavenly joy and scientific rejuvenation at a switch of the great mechanical joy-boat, as it and the couple stirred into action with cantilevers to angle the bed into positions conducive to bliss, while celestial music circulated through pipes responding to vibrations with additional volume, while the whole glass-pillared colossus was electro-magnetically charged to perk up the spirits and get the body in tune with the pearly essence of the cosmos. From the dome above, oriental perfumes were emitted to keep things sweet and deliciously mysterious. A biblical quote served both as the bed's rubric and to keep moral guardians at bay: 'Be fruitful, multiply, and replenish the earth!' (Genesis 9:1)

Favoured by the Prince of Wales's courtesan Mary Darby Robinson (called 'Perdita'), national hero Admiral Keppel, pro-liberty politicians Charles James Fox and John 'Liberty' Wilkes, along with much of Whig society, Graham's overt showmanship in the cause of safe sexual enlightenment was only one of the more colourful and accessible aspects of a frustrated sexual revolution stirring beneath the periwigs, breeches and petticoats of a London that was hot for 'action'.

In July 1779, William Blake submitted a drawing and a testimonial from a respected artist to the Royal Academy's Keeper, George Michael Moser (1706–1783). Blake was admitted as a probationer for three months to the Academy's Antique School in Somerset House, the Strand, where he was expected to make outline drawings of an anatomical figure two feet high and to list and copy muscles and tendons. As is evident in many of his works, Blake attended closely to the lessons. At the end of the probationary period he had to submit another drawing with his application for full student status. On 8 October 1779, Blake, with six others, was admitted. He received admission tickets, signed by President Joshua Reynolds and his Secretary, FM Newton. Blake was now entitled to draw in the Academy galleries and to attend lectures and exhibitions for six years. He had access to professors of anatomy, painting, architecture and perspective. The professors were required to give six lectures each per year. Engraving was not included.

The Swiss Moser had taught George III to draw when the King was a boy. Moser was a highly skilled gold chaser, enameller, engraver and artist. Unfortunately, Blake's view of him has been conditioned by an anecdote he inscribed as an annotation after 1798 to *The Works of Sir Joshua Reynolds* (edited by Edward Malone). Concerned that young Blake was too obsessed with what he called the 'Hard Stiff & Dry Unfinished Works' of Raphael and Michelangelo, Moser offered for Blake's perusal copies of the works of Elisabeth Vigée Le Brun and of the Baroque artist Peter Paul Rubens. Well! Blake had no time for Rubens, while Elisabeth Vigée Le Brun was a fashionable French portrait painter. Being French was no crime, but being a fashionable portrait painter was a kind of Judas-kiss betrayal of artistic integrity as far as Blake's spiritual aesthetic was concerned: flattery by deceit. Blake became practically unbalanced on the issue as his own work was ignored and, where not ignored, ridiculed.

In fact, Moser was simply trying to open Blake's prejudiced mind: a tough task at the best of times with insecure students. Moser was trying to show Blake something really *new*.

Admitted to the French Academy in 1783, Elisabeth Vigée Le Brun had secured the appreciation of Queen Marie Antoinette. Aged just 24 in 1779, Elizabeth was inspired by Rubens's work, developing her own style in the process. Moser may have wished young Blake might similarly be inspired and make a worthy living for himself. And how did Blake react? He 'secretly raged', then spoke his mind. Whatever he recorded of his mind, he cut away from his annotations to *The Works of Sir Joshua Reynolds*, leaving the following stern lecture for his teacher: 'These things that you [Moser] call Finishd [*sic*] are not Even Begun how can they then, be Finishd? The Man who does not know The Beginning, never can know the End of Art.' One wonders if those were his actual words at the time. Anyhow, Moser might have thought less of the student after being the butt of such instruction. Blake did himself no favours by advertising his cleverness, but he would go on doing it. His rationale: *Would you tell a prophet of God to tone it down?* Like the freethinking Mr Emerson in EM Forster's *A Room with a View,* Blake believed there was a time for being polite and 'a time for speaking out!'

One cannot help thinking that if Tatham's comment about Blake 'hating a blow' were true, then it would be little wonder if every time he felt himself in the presence of a rebuke or even criticism *as regards his perception,* his soul imagined the whip-hand of his father raised above him, and he struggled to control himself, while longing for a Nurse who would understand and comfort him.

While Blake the belated student continued his austere and self-insulating devotions to the Quattrocento, contemptuous of public taste or fashion, many other strands of interest and excitement whirled around the Royal Academy. He may have been less blind to these than he insisted he was to the beauties of Rubens and Elisabeth Vigée Le Brun.

The Royal Academy was not an isolated institution. Founded thanks to the efforts of the Society of Dilettanti, society members, such as Joshua Reynolds, exerted considerable influence. The Dilettanti were closely associated with Brook's Club, which had recently moved from Pall Mall into grand premises in St James's Street, a move imitated in 1782 by Boodle's Club, founded by the Earl of Shelburne (Prime Minister 1782–3), across the street.

As Blake got into his stride at the Academy in 1780, Dilettanti Society member Richard Payne Knight (1750–1824) took his seat in the Commons as an MP. Tending to observe rather than cast his views into the fire of parliamentary debate, Payne Knight did not expect popular approbation of his interests. He was a collector of classical bronzes, coins, drawings and engravings, particularly with regard to his great interest: Priapism. His *Account of the remains of the worship of Priapus* would be published in 1786 and would include many engravings of *priapi*.

Priapus was, of course, the god sacred to the rustic gardener and was carved or depicted with an exaggerated penis. Knight took the phallic imagery as a universal principle of divine creation and generative genius. In other words, he took what the Christian religion frequently regarded as an instrument of shame and raised it into a religious symbol, which, Knight believed, it had once been. In doing so, he recognized how artistic sensibility and aesthetic appreciation were stimulated by physical sensation, whose drive need not be to debasement, but to elevation of consciousness. Unwittingly, Payne Knight had created the prime principle of neo-paganism. Blake was not immune to this message.

The obvious often passes us by. An art gallery was a place where people could see naked genitals in the context of art and beauty (though that has never stopped schoolchildren giggling): the idea of the 'human form divine' was almost a cliché of the art world of the time, and they were not referring to the Son of God, at least not as the Moravians conceived that expression. Art could prove an excellent cover for sensual stimulation that might otherwise be sought in a brothel or love affair. Indeed, Art would provide set and setting to the intrigues of the rich and the romances of the romantic – that is, where rude Nature Herself did not suffice. But what would a classical landscape be without a statue, mythical figure or ruined temple? Hard-core 'new romantics', of course, would shortly remove the antique garden furniture in place of a conception of Nature as the rude temple itself, and Man the perceiver as the object of worship, phallus and all.

The discreet crossover between art and high-quality pornography was most evident in a number of the elaborate works of French art dealer Pierre-François Hugues, self-styled 'Baron d'Hancarville' (1719–1805), particularly his notorious *Monumens de la vie privée des XII Césars d'après une suite de pierres et médailles gravées sous leur règne* (place of publication given as 'Capree [Capri], chez Sabellus'; Rome, 1785). The 'Mounments from the private lives of the 12 Ceasars' practically established a new genre of 'rare' publication whose relation of physical stimulus to elevation would be forever ambiguous.

D'Hancarville knew his market very well. In 1780, he introduced Britain's Ambassador to Naples, Sir William Hamilton, to the Porcinari family, from whom Hamilton purchased a considerable collection of antiquities, one of enormous interest to the Royal Academy. Hamilton and Hugues decided to capitalize on the acquisitions by producing one of the most striking art books of all time, the 'Collection Of Etruscan, Greek And Roman Antiquities From The Cabinet Of The Honourable William Hamilton' (*Antiquités Etrusques, Grècques Et Romains, Du Cabinet De M. Hamilton*; 4 vols, Naples, 1766–7).

D'Hancarville's *Recherches Sur L'Origine, L'Esprit Et Les Progrès Des Arts De La Grèce; Sur Leur Connections Avec Les Arts Et La Réligion Des Plus Anciens Peuples Connus* (3 vols, Londres, 1785) was a financial disaster whose uninhibited illustrations of classical genitalia and sexual activity caused such a scandal that the art dealer had to flee England for France. Despite the scandal, d'Hancarville's original work with Hamilton was enormously influential. The illustrations of vases were copied by Josiah Wedgwood at his manufactory at Etruria in Staffordshire and drove a new pottery market, while John Flaxman (1755–1826), now a friend of Blake, was influenced in his drawing style by the freshness of the Greek and Etruscan lines. Flaxman worked for Wedgwood from 1775, modelling reliefs for jasperware and basaltware. He would find employment for Blake with Wedgwood in years to come.

Blake himself was not unmoved by d'Hancarville. Two works by Blake's hand are copies of engravings from volumes 2 and 3 of d'Hancarville and Hamilton's 1766–7 work.[1] Tatham wrongly attributed the designs to Blake copying painter and classical *intaglio* collector George Cumberland (Cumberland was ardent for priapic classicism). Blake's first pencil and wash drawing depicts an 'apotheosis' of Bacchus, with Ariadne holding a horn of abundance while Iris offers him ambrosia, her dress covered with eyes, while Silenus strums his lyre. The second pen and pencil drawing depicts Bacchus in a fury, in the form of a bull and led by a winged Genius, possibly Ariadne, towards an altar. Equally furious male attendants dance about them, some bearing torches. A small tripod indicates the scene as a place of oracles (that is, divine inspiration), while a skull between one of the attendant's feet suggests a place of sacrifice. All of these Bacchic Mystery themes would have appealed to Blake. It is likely, but not certain, that the works were copied during Blake's time at the Academy. All the penises are flaccid. One would have to wait until the next decade for an erect priapus to appear boldly in Blake's own work.

Another significant figure in the world surrounding the Academy was Charles Townley (1737–1805). Townley joined the Society of Dilettanti in 1786, after a youth spent travelling in Italy collecting antiquities. His friend, Scots artist and Rome-based art dealer Gavin Hamilton, participated in the 1748 Italian tour with James Stuart, Matthew Brettingham Jr and Nicholas Revett that encouraged the Dilettanti to fund further explorations to Greece and Asia Minor.

In Johann Zoffany's 1782 painting of *Charles Townley in the Park St Gallery*, we can see Townley in conversation with the Baron d'Hancarville, surrounded by a collection of marbles and Greek and Roman vases that would form, in the next century, the basis of the British Museum's classical collection, overshadowed since by the Elgin Marbles. If the Elgin Marbles should ever be re-sited to Athens, the British Library might consider re-elevating Townley's collection, which, during Blake's time at the Academy, could be seen in Park Street where it had been placed in a purpose-built house since 1778.

Richard Cosway (1742–1821) had, before Blake's time, been a pupil at Shipley's Drawing Academy on the Strand. When Blake was copying the work of Masters at the Academy, Cosway was earning a handsome crust as a miniaturist. A full member of the Royal Academy since 1771, he painted the Prince of Wales in 1780 and made a good impression. In January 1781, Cosway would marry the Anglo-Italian composer Maria Hadfield. Maria hosted a fashionable salon at Schomberg House, Pall Mall, the couple's home from 1784 – the Celestial Bed having been dismantled, replaced by a slightly more conventional boudoir. Two years later, when Thomas Jefferson was serving as United States ambassador to Paris, Jefferson fell in love with Maria Cosway, keeping Cosway's miniature of his wife close to him. Cosway himself was a libertine, willing to try anything, and in London in the 1780s that left a lot of scope. There was Mesmerism, magnetic treatments, mystical kabbalistic and messianic Judaism, visionary theatrical shows, High Grade Freemasonry and Cagliostro's white magic to indulge the senses and the spirit, if you could afford the frantic trip. The Celestial Bed would in due course appear somewhat tame.

Had young William Blake been a man of real means, might he have been tempted?

Early Works

Blake would develop a patent aversion to the art of classical antiquity that would alienate him from much of the taste of his period, though not all by any means. In about 1820, when over 60 years old, he would write, memorably, on a single copper plate entitled *On Homer's Poetry and on Vergil*: 'Grecian is Mathematic Form: Gothic is Living Form. Mathematic Form is eternal in the Reasoning Memory: Living Form is Eternal Existence.' Existence beats Reason. Life beats Memory. Feeling beats Geometry. Nature beats Maths. This famous dichotomy may well have been a swipe at Flaxman, with whom, as he did with antique art, Blake also indulged in a kind of love-hate relationship. Flaxman's design for Wedgwood, 'The Apotheosis of Homer' (1778), was famous, and so was Flaxman. Blake wanted an 'Apotheosis' of things *he* believed in. He believed Christianity was losing its sap by being classicized. He didn't like the new churches built like Roman temples (such as St Paul's Cathedral). Blake liked things to be vivid, natural, hearty and direct (we might say 'organic'): his art would be too much 'in your face' for many. His directness could embarrass people.

In short, the classics were cold; Gothic was hot, like the Bible, properly understood as a geyser of poetry, rising from the spirit. In the battle of head and heart, Blake was a true Moravian (if unconsciously so): heart was the closest to God. English history, for Blake, was like an extension of the Bible, but written by historians unaware of the spiritual continuity.

Not surprisingly then, Blake's earliest known pictorial inventions are dominated by English historical subjects, usually in pen and watercolour. Subjects from his Academy period include *Lear and Cordelia in Prison; The Landing of Brutus in England; St Augustine Converting King Ethelbert of Kent; The Making of Magna Carta; The Keys of Calais; The Penance of Jane Shore; Joseph of Arimathea Preaching to the Inhabitants of Britain*. He also did vignettes from Shakespeare: *Cordelia and the Sleeping Lear; Juliet Asleep; Falstaff and Prince Hal; Prospero and Miranda; Lear Grasping his Sword; Macbeth and Lady Macbeth; Othello and Desdemona*. He would rework several of these subjects in the 1790s, vastly improving them.

One early design he would perfect considerably later is known severally as *Glad Day, Albion Rose* and, as Geoffrey Keynes called it, *The Dance of Albion*. The finished painting (*c*.1794) shows a figure on a mountain, surrounded by radiant coloured beams, principally red and gold, his arms outstretched as if he has been given a vivifying electric shock, while one leg extends to his right. It has become very popular and the title *Glad Day* has been extended to 'Glad Day, Love and Duty' as the motto of visionary educationalist Cecil Reddie's Abbotsholme private school in Staffordshire (founded in 1889), linked through the international Round Square Association with schools inspired by German educationalist Kurt Hahn, such as Gordonstoun in Scotland.

The two pencil sketches from around 1780 show variant positions, one of them revealing that Blake was not sure, to begin with, what to do with the legs of his figure. One can just see a tentative outline of both legs wide apart, like the figure of the Magus in Agrippa's *Three Books of Occult Philosophy* (English version, 1651) where a 'Vitruvian Man' stretches out arms and legs whose four points form a square (another shows the proportions forming a pentagram). But the strongest of Blake's lines put the legs demurely together with, apparently (the drawing is obscure), one foot behind the other like a ballet dancer about to bow or curtsey. The other sketch shows the figure in reverse, with the left leg plainly at an angle, precisely as Blake would depict Albion worshipping the crucified Christ in the illuminated poem *Jerusalem* (completed 1815–1820 but begun in 1804). I should think the geometrical conceit of the 'Vitruvian Man' whose form is the architectural measure of all things (squares, circles, right angles), whose proportions establish the proportions of creation – being made 'in the image of God' – was not entirely to Blake's taste.

While Blake was content with the Paracelsian idea of Man as a Microcosm, a little Universe, he would not like the 'squaring' of the 'human form divine'. His Albion is the True Man, but as *Living Form*, not Mathematic Form. And Albion, like Blake, will not con-form. It is also worth noting that in the famous painted version of the design, the figure looks forwards, with wide-eyed innocence and newly realized joy. In the older sketch his eyes are directed above, to his Desire, and his head is cocked back. This makes the gesture one of complete self-offering, utter openheartedness: Man, as it were, as God loves to see him as-He-sees-Himself: his hands open, hiding nothing, naked, honest and true.

This, I believe, is nothing less than the Apotheosis of William Blake: the inner man whose 'garment' (body) has been utterly transformed by the breaking through into time and space of the real Man, resurrect and shining, radiant as a star. Like all the best, most personal art, it immediately becomes universal in import. As Blake insisted: we are all members of the body of God.

Blake was prepared to take from the classical, but he would not be bound by it; he wanted to do something new, but clearly, he was not ready yet.

Meanwhile, in the world of time and space, Britain was finding it could not gain a decisive victory against General Washington's grinding strategies. Besides, there was no hatred for the 'enemy': little, or no, will to kill; only, occasionally, to punish. But now that France had taken sides, and the rebels had taken on France and Spain as allies, and the war was costing the country dear, there was certainly a will to win. England's traditional enemies were attacking England by proxy.

In early 1780, Britain's colonies were removed from the Secretary of State for the Colonies' authority and put under the Secretary of State for War. This meant a military administration replaced a civilian and trade-oriented structure. On 12 May came news of victory. Around 5,000 troops under US Major Benjamin Lincoln surrendered to Lt General Henry Clinton. At the same time, in London, Blake exhibited his pen and watercolour picture 'The Death of Earl Godwin' at the twelfth Royal Academy exhibition. It was a conventional historical subject, approached with verve and a strong sense of effective figure placement. On 27 May, when *The Morning Chronicle* and *London Advertizer* published the fourth part of George Cumberland's survey of the exhibition, Blake got the thumbs up from Cumberland: 'though there is nothing to be said of the colouring' – there wasn't much colour in it – 'a good design and much character'.

George Cumberland (1754–1848) was an artist himself. He'd attended the Royal Academy Schools in 1772 but would later fall out with the Academy. Cumberland had become Blake's friend, joining him, Thomas Stothard (1755–1834), Flaxman, and, on occasions, engraver William Sharp (1749–1824), in good times together, holding forth and sharing ideas. Cumberland and Sharp held radical social and sexual ideas, some of which Blake liked, some he did not. Flaxman and Sharp would share with Blake their enthusiasm for Swedenborg in the late 1780s.

More conservative in nature, Stothard had been studying at the Academy since 1778. He would become an Associate in 1792 and a full academician in 1794 with a portfolio of popular designs for mainstream publications.

Blake and the Gordon Riots
In June, Blake caught his first taste of what radical politics could mean on the streets. Lord George Gordon, 29-year-old godson of George II, was incensed by minor concessions made to Roman Catholics in 1778. Encouraging the mob to believe it had all been a scam to get Catholics into army officer positions to go to America to kill Gordon's brother Protestants, Lord Gordon stoked up the old 'No Popery, No Slavery!' fires and unleashed his 'Protestant Association' on London. The Association was in fact little more than a mob high on gin and extreme oratory.

On 6 June, William Blake got caught up at the front of rampaging rioters. Having already burned down Catholic 'Mass-houses', they were now attacking Lord Justice Hyde's townhouse in Leicester Fields, whence they headed, pushing Blake along with them, through Great Queen Street, past Basire's quiet house, to Newgate Prison, freeing 300 prisoners and threatening passersby to join them in an orgy of drunken violence and misplaced euphoria. Over 300 people were killed and London faced its biggest fire since 1666.

Magistrates seemed paralysed with indecision, as was the Lord Chancellor. The King jumped to it, called a meeting with the Privy Council and with the Attorney General, secured a ruling that rioters could be fired on without hearing the Riot Act first. George offered to lead the Guards himself: 'I lament the conduct of the magistrates, but I can answer for *one, one* who will do his duty,' he said, meaning every word. The King's actions saved the capital from worse than it suffered. The rioters had gone insane: they even attempted a frontal assault on the military in Fleet Street.

Marsha Schuchard's *William Blake's Sexual Path to Spiritual Vision* (2008) suggests that the Gordon Riots marked the time Blake was inspired to produce *Glad Day*, the work of a visionary caught up, not so much by rioters, but in a vision of Albion rising up against alleged monarchical oppression and government fudging. Apart from the fact that *Glad Day* did not exist as an engraving or as a painting at this time, it is hard to imagine lower-middle-class Blake supporting hate-filled anarchy from the denizens of London's lowest quarters. Blake shows no visible signs of being a radical Protestant in the political sense: all the evidence suggests a tolerant, ecumenical approach to Catholicism. We don't know what Blake thought of the horrifying spectacle, but we do know what his friend, George Cumberland, thought about it – and Cumberland was himself more politically radical than Blake:

> ... near the greatest part of Sunday night [4 June] on a wall near the Romish Chapel in Moor fields witnessing scenes which made my heart bleed, without being able to prevent them – it was the most singular and unhappy sight in the world – the Mob encouraged by *Magistrates* and protected by *troops* – with the most *orderly injustice* destroying the property of innocent individuals – Next to Lord Gordon, for whom no punishment could be too great, the magistrates of this City deserve an ample share of vengeance from a basely deserted people [...] grown bold by sufferance they yesterday burnt Sir G. Saville and a Chandlers who had taken one of them besides two schools and many private Masses – today they burnt Lord Peters Furniture Mr Hydes &c and

armed with clubs to the amount I am informed of 5000 are at this instant going to the Duke of Richmonds Lord Shelburns &c they have broken open Newgate and the prisoners at large and at this moment it is in flames [...] the soldiers its said laid down their arms today on being ordered to fire ...[2]

About 70 years later, Stothard's daughter-in-law Mrs AE Bray described a curious event, supposed to have occurred in September 1780, that links Blake to radicalism once more, though again only by mistaken association. In her biography of Stothard, Mrs Bray described Blake in the company of Stothard and the latter's friend Mr Ogleby being arrested as spies by the military while out sketching on the River Medway. On being informed by the Royal Academy of their prisoners' innocent intentions, the commanding officer of Upnor Castle near Chatham had a merry time with the young men. Ogleby said it was an experience he cared never to repeat.

It must have been the place. Originally built in Elizabethan times, the castle had been rebuilt in 1718 to house artillery, with a barracks for 64 soldiers and two officers. It would have felt very salutary for young, sensitive artists, armed only with pencils and brushes. Perhaps they had to drink more than they were used to, as well. Blake probably felt he'd seen enough of soldiers for a lifetime after the events of 1780. The way of the world, however, would not oblige.

On 20 November, Britain declared war on Holland after the Dutch joined Czarina Catherine II's League of Armed Neutrality. Neutrality consisted of giving weapons to US rebels through a Dutch base in the West Indies. Meanwhile, Washington ordered the devastation of the Iroquois peoples of the valleys around the Mohawk River, while his friend the Marquis of Lafayette returned to America, having secured Louis XVI's agreement to send troops and ships to help Washington.

Britain was not standing still. On 3 February 1781, the Dutch island of St Eustatius in the West Indies was captured, while in Paris the Marquis of Condorcet contributed to a growing debate by publishing his *Reflections on Negro Slavery*. About 100,000 slaves were imported annually from Africa into the Indies and the Americas.

In Königsberg, philosopher Immanuel Kant (1724–1804) asserted that in the formation of will, intuition and sense experience preceded reason. While at first sight Kant's philosophy might have been claimed here on Blake's side, the philosophy had a sting in its tail: convictions based on intuition and the senses could be seen to be devoid of rational content. A religion that could make no firm appeal to reason could be dismissed as the product of imagination. The question remained: which faculty had greater authority? The matter would deeply trouble Blake in the 1790s, not least because it had such a bearing on the conduct of pictorial art.

As if to rub in the point, in 1782 Blake's acquaintance Zürich-born Henry Fuseli (1741–1825), having returned to London from the Continent in 1779, exhibited his unforgettable 'Gothic horror' painting, *The Nightmare*. The painting shows a creature of imagination, a little demonic fellow crouching on the vulnerable body of a young woman in a nightgown, apparently asleep or dead on a bed, her head falling to the ground while the creature's lightless eyes stare at the viewer. Is this real? Surely not: it's a nightmare, like the title says. What are we to make of it? Is there reason in a nightmare? No? Then why do nightmares happen? What do they mean? What are we afraid of? The scene is undoubtedly sexual, erotic, menacing, and yet oddly comic, with shades of a *Midsummer Night's Dream* (Fuseli was working on Alderman Boydell's Shakespeare Gallery at the time). It was one in the eye for the rationalists, forced to dismiss it because they couldn't think of anything else to do with it – least of all, enjoy it.

It wasn't philosophy that was going to decide what was going to happen in America, it was cost. On 27 February 1782, in a body-blow to Lord North's ministry, Parliament voted against taking the war any further. Lord Rockingham became Prime Minister: a temporary triumph for the Whigs. Sometime radical and libertine Charles James Fox became Foreign Secretary and pursued a policy of ending the war in America. The administration also oversaw the Relief of the Poor Act that created workhouses: an advantage, as it turned out, to Blake's father, who would gain by providing clothing for the poor.

Around this time William Blake's mind was probably less concerned with Britain's future than it was preoccupied with how to marry his fiancé, Catherine Sophia Boucher (or 'Boutcher'). He had got himself tied up again. It was probably in 1781, the previous year, when a girl called Clara had broken his romantic heart, in what seems to have been the latest in a string of romantic disappointments. So upset was Will that the family sent him away from Broad Street to a market-gardening relative of James Blake Senior's in Battersea. Was Blake ready to play Priapus in this leafy enclave? During the stay, Blake met Catherine, last daughter of William Butcher (the spelling of the surname varies) of the parish of St Mary Lambeth, who had married Mary Davis of Wandsworth in 1738. Catherine 'Boucher' was born on 25 April 1762, and baptised on 16 May in St Mary's, Battersea.

Catherine plumped for Blake the moment she saw him: her heart leapt and she just knew he was the one. She waited for a chance. It came when Blake opened his heart to her about how desperately sad he was to have lost his past love. Catherine is supposed to have said: 'I pity you from my heart,' to which Blake replied: 'Do you pity me? Then I love you for that.' And that was that: off on the rebound.

There is a drawing of young Blake in profile attributed to Catherine and drawn after his death. She drew Blake as she remembered him, with large eyes, noble forehead and dome-like crown, ablaze with wavy, yellow-brown hair. He was like a creature from another world.

On 18 August 1782, the Rev. J Gardnor married Will and Kate in the presence of Thomas Monger, James Blake (presumably Will's father) and Robert Munday, Parish Clerk. Gilchrist and Tatham shared the notion that Blake's father did not favour the marriage. He may not have done, but he turned up anyway. James Blake had experienced the discomfiture of entering into a marriage other men considered unacceptable, but in the case of his son he probably felt he had ample reason to disapprove of the match. Could the young man really afford it? What was Miss Boucher bringing to the feast? Both questions invited doubtful answers, but in its favour, the marriage might have been considered an emollient to settle Will's heart and mind while providing an incentive to earning a living. It was not likely, in any case, that Will was going to let go of the very pretty Kate: he was over 21 and big enough to look after himself. Catherine signed her name with an 'X': either she could not write or did not feel like it. Blake recorded his home parish as Battersea. Perhaps his father had told him they weren't coming back to Broad Street; perhaps Blake had told his father the same.

The couple went to live at 23 Green Street, Leicester Fields (now Leicester Square). The Prince of Wales had lived in Leicester Fields. It was a good area, even though the Prince had moved to Carlton House, Piccadilly, courted by radical Whig opportunists.

Blake was trying to get commercial engraving work to keep a roof over his and his wife's heads. He needed a publisher. It was probably around this time that he became acquainted with Joseph Johnson. Johnson ran a bookshop and weekly literary dinner of modest provision at 72 St Paul's Churchyard. The most famous publisher of radical books in England, Johnson had occasional work for journeyman engravers like Blake. Johnson knew William Godwin, Mary Wollstonecraft, Erasmus Darwin, Henry Fuseli and Joseph Priestley.

Apart from job opportunities, it was probably through Johnson that Blake acquired knowledge of the Gnostics ('knowers'), the esoteric and theosophical resistance to early orthodox Christianity whose thoughts and literary myths split opinion in the Christian Church of the 2nd and 3rd centuries CE.

Johnson published the famous Unitarian preacher Joseph Priestley's new book, *An History of the Corruptions of Christianity*, in two volumes, printed in Birmingham. Page 9 of this work uses the word 'emanation', perhaps seen here by Blake for the first time. The context was that of Christ's soul being an emanation from the divine mind. The word 'emanation' would characterize the archetypal figures of Blake's analogous philo-theosophical system. It means a kind of 'birth by thought': a being spiritually or psychologically created, linked inherently to source. In Gnostic systems, emanations usually came in pairs: 'male and female created he them.'

Priestley's book quotes from de Beausobre's French work on the history of Manichaeism (a 3rd-century Gnostic religion, based in Iran), from Irenaeus's *Opera* (an anti-Gnostic collection by Church Father Irenaeus, *c.*180 CE), from JL Mosheim's six-volume *Ecclesiastical History Ancient & Modern,* translated by Presbyterian Archibald Maclaine (London, T Cadell, 1782), and from Presbyterian minister Nathaniel Lardner's *The History of the Heretics of the two first centuries after Christ* (published in 1780; Lardner, 1684–1768). There was a rash of Gnosticism about in bookshops in the early 1780s. So Blake did not have to have read James Bruce's Codex of Gnostic manuscripts under Woide's care at the British Museum to learn about Gnostic systems. It was hot stuff already.

Priestley's book on 'Corruptions of Christianity' was intended as the fourth part of his *Institutes of Natural and Revealed Religion*. Blake's first major philosophical publication was *There is no Natural Religion* (1788): in blatant contradiction to Priestley and a bevy of 'natural religionists' going back to the previous century.

Thomas Jefferson himself rested on Priestley's *Institutes* as, as Jefferson put it, 'the basis of my own faith'. Its principle being: the only revealed religious truths that can be accepted are those that conform to the natural world. For Blake, this was devilish error. For Jefferson, it was his religion. Jefferson wrote to Priestley in 1803 when compiling a Deist version of the New Testament. This Jefferson did by taking out all references to miracles and the supernatural. Calling it 'The Philosophy of Jesus of Nazareth', Jefferson asked Priestley to complete it (Priestley had fled Birmingham in 1791 before migrating to Pennsylvania).

Needless to say, Priestley's somewhat controversial point was that the primitive Christian Church was Unitarian: if you followed Jesus, you would follow Priestley. And to show how tight all these circles were, consider this: the portrait of Priestley commissioned by Joseph Johnson was painted by Henry Fuseli.

On 19 October 1782, General Cornwallis's representative surrendered to General Washington's representative at Yorktown, Virginia. It was the effective end of the war. King George lamented: 'America is *Lost!*' All those beautiful hills, and rivers, and plains, and valleys, farms, forests and grand estates, all LOST! Thomas Jefferson gloated prematurely, writing in 'Notes on Virginia concerning the British Empire': 'The sun of her [Britain's] glory is fast descending the horizon.' He was not the last to write off Old Blighty. Great Britain had 174 ships of the line and 294 smaller vessels at her disposal. And she had William Blake. She wasn't finished yet.

And there were other conquests to be made. Frederick William Herschel was appointed King's Astronomer, having discovered Uranus (called originally 'the Georgian star' but the French wouldn't accept the reference to George III). An 'evil generation' looks to the heavens for a sign, warned Jesus. There were signs of things to come much closer to home. In November, US troops brought utter devastation to British-backed Shawnee Indians. A thousand Kentucky rifles fired unceasingly on the Indians and destroyed their food supply. Where did they bury their heart?

EIGHT

A Ticket to Rise

1783–1785

John Flaxman's famous self-portrait in red chalk depicts an earnest, even solemn young man in 1779.[1] He has large, penetrating eyes, a face mature before its years, full, rather stern lips, and hollow cheeks flanked by long, curly dark hair. It is the face of a critic, as well as an artist, the sympathetic face of a sensitive man who takes himself seriously. A more worldly soul, Stothard, first introduced Flaxman to Blake. Flaxman, in his turn, would perform many signal services to a man he never ceased to admire; it was doubtless Flaxman who first introduced Blake to the esteemed polite drawing room salon of the Rev. AS Mathew and his wife Harriet at 27 Rathbone Place. Flaxman would also introduce John Thomas Smith (author of *Nollekens and his Times*) to the Mathews' circle, in 1784. Smith describes hearing a 26-year-old Blake singing and reading his poems there. His melodies were 'singularly beautiful', wrote Smith, who heard them. Blake's 'original and extraordinary merit' was recognized. Music professors admired Blake's original melodies, committing the tunes to notation – something, to our great regret, Blake himself was unable to do.

Cunningham, possibly building on Smith's anecdote, wrote of Blake 'writing songs, and composing music', even describing the process:

As he drew the figure he meditated the song which was to accompany it, and the music to which the verse was to be sung, was the offspring too of the same moment. Of his music there are no specimens – he wanted the art of noting it down – if it equaled many of his drawings, and some of his songs, we have lost melodies of real value.[2]

Indeed. The idea of combining verse, image and melody was a feature of some of the finest emblem books, such as the extraordinary *Atalanta Fugiens* by Count Michael Maier (Johann Theodor de Bry, 1617). *Songs of Innocence* might have had a wider sale had Blake recovered his melodies from the anonymous music professors and included them – and one can only wonder if Blake himself had a tune for the words that have come to us as the hymn 'Jerusalem'. It would take the invention of cinema before the full exposition of Blake's inner idea could reach fruition, especially in what Michael Powell would call 'the composed film', where image, music and dramatic development were poetically integrated.[3]

Around April 1783, Blake engraved the frontispiece 'after Dunker' for Thomas Henry's translation of *Memoirs of Albert de Haller,* published by Joseph Johnson for a series on botany and chemistry. Blake's circular portrait of the Swiss natural philosopher de Haller bears the simple name 'Blake' at its edge. Executed in Basire's stipple style, it has a warm, old-fashioned, antiquarian character, unrefined in comparison to later work. Johnson commissioned nine further plates from Blake.

Things seemed to be going Blake's way. On 18 June 1783 Flaxman wrote to his wife Nancy that he had been called upon by traveler, collector, geologist and dilettante John Hawkins (?1748–1841), son of the MP for Grampound, Cornwall, Thomas Hawkins, a Fellow of the Royal Society. Perhaps conversation between Hawkins and Flaxman included de Haller's own fellowship of the RS and thereby of Blake's portrait engraving. Like Blake, Hawkins appreciated the Flemish masters. Flaxman suggested Blake do a 'capital drawing' for John Hawkins, which Hawkins commissioned. Hearing the news, Nancy replied: 'I rejoice for Blake.'[4]

Determined to help Blake on his way, Flaxman discussed combining resources with the Mathews to print a selection of Blake's poetry, prose and drama to promote the prodigy. While Mozart completed his Symphony in C major in Austria, in London Blake gathered work from ages 12 to 20 to produce *Poetical Sketches* (1783), his first collection of printed poetry. Printed, yes, but published, no. The intention was to give Blake something he could distribute to friends, acquaintances and possible publishers.

Poetical Sketches

The fairly slim collection repays return visits and soon its apparent modesty is swept aside to reveal the haunting ambition that vaults across its pages declaring: 'Look at Me! I can write!' One feels that had youthful Wordsworth or Coleridge committed like verses to print, they would have received fulsome praise (if not sales) from the booksellers of Bristol, as well as that censure that sniffs out genius and automatically hacks at it.

Opening 'nicely', to use the word in its contemporary sense, with odes to every season, to the Evening Star, and to 'Morning' – all redolent of 17th-century English verse of high order with more modern, carefree touches and strokes superimposed – we enter a world of 'Song' (eight in all) that looks forward gently to the word-scape of the *Songs of Innocence*. Sadly, no tunes appear to make us appreciate that these are *songs,* not poems as we think of them. Printing lyrics on album covers was a good way of advertising artistry in the 1960s and 70s, but without the music within, to whom would Sgt Pepper have sung?

Most of the lyrics betray their sources and influences. This author was always very keen on that 'Song' that began 'How sweet I roam'd from field to field,/ And tasted all the summer's pride', until I later discovered that that marvellous 'summer's pride' had been tasted previously in Shakespeare's fifteenth sonnet:

> To me, fair friend, you never can be old;
> For as you were when first your eye I eyed,
> Such seems your beauty still. Three Winters cold
> Have from the forests shook three Summers' pride

The underlying feeling is one of melancholy, lost love and pure English nostalgia, for sometimes it seems the English soul is made of fallen leaves. Griefs come to the poet as he retires to bed and the cold outside is echoed in his head, and he sleeps and dreams of ladies fair, and moments lost in lightened air, till the sleep he sleeps scarce ever ends, and he in time must join his absent friends. *That sort of thing ...*

O should she e'er prove false, his limbs I'd tear,
And throw all pity on the burning air;
I'd curse bright fortune for my mixed lot,
And then I'd die in peace, and be forgot.

('Song')

We have portents of Neo-Platonic mysteries to come. 'Mad Song' reveals that 'fiend in a cloud': a flame from heaven encased in flesh. We have a penchant for Nordic legend in 'Gwin, King of Norway' and a love for Spenser exhibited in an honest 'Imitation' of him. Blake's short play *King Edward the Third* is a clear *hommage* to *Henry V*, with Creçy standing in for Agincourt. Compare Blake's 'Prologue' intended for an unfinished *King Edward the Fourth* with Chorus's opening words in the prologue to Shakespeare's *Henry V*. This is Blake:

O For a voice like thunder, and a tongue
To drown the throat of war! – when the senses
Are shaken, and the soul is driven to madness,
Who can stand? When the souls of the oppressed
Fight in the troubled air that rages, who can stand?

Shakespeare:

O! For a muse of fire, that would ascend
The brightest heaven of invention!
A kingdom for a stage, princes to act
And monarchs to behold the swelling scene!
Then should the warlike Harry, like himself,
Assume the port of Mars ...

Blake had the 'muse of fire' all right and the wit between his teeth, and all might have been well had not the Rev. Anthony Stephen Mathew bizarrely pre-empted the ubiquitous Hostile Critic by printing the following 'Advertisement' to introduce Blake to a new audience:

The following sketches were the production of untutored youth, commenced in his twelfth, and occasionally resumed by the author till his twentieth year; since which time, his talents have been wholly directed to the attainment of excellence in his profession, he has been deprived of the leisure requisite to such a revisal of these sheets, as might have rendered them less unfit to meet the public eye.

Conscious of the irregularities and defects to be found in almost every page, his critics have still believed that they possessed a poetic originality, which merited some respite from oblivion. These their opinions remain, however, to be now reproved or confirmed by a less partial public.[5]

With friends like that, who needs hostile critics? Not surprisingly perhaps, Blake himself seems to have done little, if anything, with the eleven quarto pages of *Poetical Sketches* presented to him as an encouragement. He never seems to have been interested in them, possibly because he saw defects himself and wished to 'do better next time' or possibly because the deprecatory words of Mathew incensed and depressed him: they would most poets in the intemperate flush of youth. A perennial stumbling-block for youth in every age is that youthful genius feels, and knows, the full force of *potential*, combined with a presentiment of 'things to come', without the realization and fulfilment of that potential in works *achieved*. Even great artists waste years reacting to early knocks, twisting their virtues with bitterness.

On 26 April 1784, Flaxman informed established poet William Hayley, then living at Eartham Hall, Sussex, that he had left Blake's *Poetical Sketches* with a mutual friend to convey to him. Having spoken of Blake before, Flaxman wished Hayley to advance Blake's cause. However, Flaxman practically repeated the censorious caveats of the Rev. Mathew in a manner likely to dilute any initial interest: 'his [Blake's] education will plead sufficient excuse to your [Hayley's] liberal mind for the defects of his work & there are few so able to distinguish & set a right value on the beauties as yourself.'

Mindful of his *own* reputation, Flaxman was doing Blake no great favour when he added this to what Hayley would already have to read in the poems' 'Advertisement'. Told to forgive a defect, it is hard to avoid looking for it.

Nevertheless, Flaxman did his best to 'puff up' Blake by informing Hayley that his admired painter George Romney considered Blake's historical drawings to rank with Michelangelo's, while 'a Cornish Gentleman has shewn his taste & liberality in ordering Blake to make several drawings for him, & is so convinced of his uncommon talents that he is now endeavouring to raise a subscription to send him to finish studies in Rome; if this can be done at all it will be determined on before the 10th May next at which time Mr Hawkins is going out of England – his generosity is such he would bear the whole charge of Blake's travels – but he is only a younger brother, & can therefore only bear a large proportion of the expense.'[6]

Flaxman clearly implied that Hayley should consider supplying the balance before 10 May: rather short notice. Presumably unable to commit the whole amount himself, Hawkins left England without launching Blake on what would have been a career-maker. Again, it would not have helped Blake's case when Flaxman informed Hayley that Blake was 'presently employed as an engraver, in which his encouragement is not extraordinary'. So the man wasn't even a successful engraver! Hayley must have been slightly confused: just what *was* this uneducated man: poet, sketch-artist or engraver? – why should Hayley stump up for a man in whom even his friend found fault? Faint praise ne'er won fair maiden. Hayley would not offer a helping hand to the engraver for another 16 years.

Mrs Mathew and Flaxman continued to advertise Blake at the Rathbone Place salon where, according to Smith, 'most of the literary and talented people of the day' regularly met. Smith is our only source indicating why Blake's visits became 'not so frequent'. According to Smith, it was Blake's 'unbending deportment' or 'manly firmness of opinion' that was 'not at all times pleasing to everyone'. Smith wanted no criticism of Blake to come from this information; the weakness of others was at fault, and playing up to their sensibilities was not in the young man's gift – nor would it ever be. Blake was himself, and you could take him or leave him; most preferred the latter. As Blake would lament of the Royal Academy, it suffered from the vices of society. It was more important to be a held a good fellow of perfect manners, a genial ever-tolerant companion of unremarkable opinion, than it was to be an inspirational genius of true value to a world whose politenesses covered what St Paul would call a 'whitewashed sepulchre'. Prophets were not welcome, unless they were foreign and offered novelty, and even then ... Having said that, there was no prophecy in Blake's early poetry; we should therefore not expect it in the drawing-room. It may simply have been that Blake was too outspoken for established norms of polite discourse.

Having suffered the disappointment of not being funded to study in Italy, whither Flaxman himself would in due season repair, Blake had once more to content himself with scraps from Joseph Johnson and whatever crumbs Flaxman could gather for him.

On 5 February 1784, Flaxman wrote to Josiah Wedgwood the elder who was decorating Etruria Hall, near Stoke-on-Trent, close to his pottery. Wedgwood was a member of Birmingham's informal 'Lunar Society', whose 'Lunaticks', during their 1780s heyday, gathered at Matthew Boulton's Soho House. Members included Joseph Priestley and Erasmus Darwin, both closely connected to Joseph Johnson.

Perhaps attempting to bring Blake to the notice of figures beyond London, Flaxman tried to slip him in while designing the heads of classical deities to adorn Wedgwood's hall ceiling at Etruria. References in the hall account book show a 'Blake' as a painter of Flaxman's designs. A reply of 20 February from Wedgwood to Flaxman was not encouraging: 'I have hastily looked them over [two heads of gods and an allegory for the centre], but am obliged to put them by for the present.'[7]

Experimental science, encouraged by the 'Lunaticks', was going from strength to strength as Blake lamented a corresponding etiolation of poetry. Technology had little use for Art, and Art had little use for either technology or William Blake.

While the French Academy of Sciences dismissed Mesmer's 'Animal Magnetism' as imagination – something in its favour from Blake's point of view – Englishman Henry Cort, the inventor of 'puddling' to refine pig iron with coal, lost control of his patents, allowing industry to stride ahead in the wake of the formal end to the American war sealed by the Treaty of Paris (3 September 1783).

On 18 May 1784, 24-year-old William Pitt the Younger (PM since December 1783) was returned with an increased majority after having dissolved Parliament in March over his bill to bring the East India Company – and with it, much of India – under government control. Governor General

Warren Hastings was recalled from India with the passing of the India Act. That same month, Blake exhibited two paintings at the Royal Academy exhibition: 'War unchained by an Angel – Fire, Pestilence and Famine following' and 'A Breach in the City – The Morning after the Battle'. Perhaps Blake, hoping the son would promote peace, reflected concern that Pitt's father had been most successful as a war leader. On 27 May, *The Morning Chronicle* demeaned Blake's work: 'it ['A Breach in the City' etc] outdoes most of the strange flights in our memory.' Its anonymous critic declared it was 'like Fuseli but with an additional aggravation of an infuriating bend sinister.'[8] The critic objected to Blake's individuality of style; he might as well have objected to his walk.

At the end of June, Blake's father died. He was buried at Bunhill Fields on 4 July for 13 shillings and sixpence. Blake's eldest brother assumed the business, while brother John moved across the road to 29 Broad Street where he worked as a baker and perhaps coal merchant until 1793 when he ran away, possibly to join the army.

Blake himself now made another of what hindsight shows was one of his singularly bad decisions. He moved in next door to the family hosiery business and set himself up at 27 Broad Street in partnership with his old fellow apprentice James Parker. They would sell prints. Earlier in the year, Blake had provided an engraving 'after Stothard' for *The Wit's Magazine*. In December 1784 'Parker & Blake No 27 Broad St Golden Square' engraved, printed and coloured 'Callisto' and 'Zephyrus and Flora', also 'after Stothard'. Blake was effectively putting himself down again, but since he was not being 'put up' or raised in esteem, one might ask what else he could do. The money probably came from his father as an inheritance. Smith's account suggests Mrs Harriet Mathew might have contributed to putting Blake on his feet.

Ten years later a print shop might have done better business, but it was not a good time for prints, and the shop was not situated advantageously for the trade. They might have made a success of it on the Strand or in Piccadilly, or even Golden Square itself, but Broad Street was no artistic mecca, and Blake was no businessman.

Like many others at the time, Blake's imagination was drawn skyward. An English translation of Emanuel Swedenborg's *Heaven and Hell* was published in London in 1784, though we don't know if Blake first read it that year. His personal copy features few annotations and nothing to help us fix when he was first impressed by the book. Unlike other commentators, Blake did not dismiss Swedenborg's visions of the heavenly and infernal worlds as unreal because they were imaginative. Swedenborg's account of the landscape of the hells being 'convexities' elicits an annotation appropriate for one versed in Jacob Böhme's theosophy: 'under every *Good* is a hell i.e. hell is the outward or external of heaven. & is of the body of the lord. for nothing is destroyd.'

On 15 September, Londoners came a little closer to the external celestial regions when the Prince of Wales and a staggering 150,000 onlookers beheld the rising of Vincent Lunardi, England's first hot air balloonist, together with a cat, a dog and a picnic hamper. That the Montgolfier brothers in Paris had performed a like feat in June was no inhibition to London's astonishment as the population gazed stupefied at a canvas globe filled with inflammable gas derived from burning straw. Ten minutes in the air, the balloon rose to a height of 950 metres. Afterward exhibited at the Pantheon on Oxford Street, just round the corner from Blake's home, it attracted as much attention earth-bound as it had in heavenward trajectory. Blake watched and wondered where heaven was best found, and by what means. As he wrote, *beneath every Good is a hell.* It strikes this author as curious that the balloon flight occurred in the same year that English astronomer John Michell worked out mathematically that a star as dense as the sun but 500 times greater in radius would exert enough gravity to stop light particles travelling through space. That is to say, Michell had hypothesized the existence of black holes, or stars. Without leaving the earth (except in imagination), Michell and Blake had separately reached analogous conclusions about the inhibition of 'light' in the universe. For Blake, true illumination did not come from the world of the senses; rather, the world of the senses was illuminated by the light of imagination. Dense matter restrained the light. When blind to the spirit, the unaided senses registered quantities of dense matter, generating a view that was literally 'unenlightened'. Blake was operating in a culture that considered 'enlightenment' a fruit of Reason alone.

On 27 April the Royal Academy exhibition opened. Aged 27, Blake exhibited four watercolours. As far as we know, *Joseph's Brothers bowing before him*, *Joseph making himself known to his Brethren* and *Joseph ordering Simeon to be bound* attracted little comment. *The Bard, from Gray*, however, elicited the following anonymous review on 23 May from the *Daily Universal Register*: 'W. Blake, appears like some lunatic, just escaped from the incurable cell of Bedlam; in respect of his other works, we assure this designer, that grace does not consist in the sprawling of legs and arms.'[9] The comments calumniated their subject. The Joseph designs are graceful and modest, and while *The Bard, from Gray* is a demanding design, looking in the direction of Blake's more famous work, it hardly merited the insult aimed at its creator.

GE Bentley Jr was of the view that Gilchrist's account of a reproof given to Blake from Joshua Reynolds should be dated to Blake's first year or two at the Academy, but it might have come at the opening dinner for the exhibition of 1785. Gilchrist's source said Reynolds advised Blake to draw with 'less extravagance and more simplicity'. Blake was 'very indignant when he spoke of it.' 'Extravagance' not being identical with lunacy, Reynolds's words may to us seem mild criticism; for Blake, however, the comment constituted a direct attack, indirectly expressed, on the authenticity of imaginative creation. For Blake, the sin of Reynolds was to impose rules over the faculty of vision.

Blake's annotations of a work published in Dublin in 1785 show us where his head was at the time. *A Translation of the Inferno in English Verse … Historical Notes on Dante. A COMPARITIVE VIEW OF THE INFERNO. With some other POEMS relative to the ORIGINAL PRINCIPLES OF HUMAN NATURE* by Henry Boyd elicited comment after comment that revealed young Blake as a romantic. In literature, for example, feeling and passion matter most; moral virtue is dull. The 'Perfect characters' are villains. Blake believes 'the grandest Poetry is Immoral the Grandest characters Wicked. Very Satan. Capanius. Othello a murderer. Prometheus. Jupiter. Jehovah. Jesus a wine bibber. Cunning and Morality are not Poetry but Philosophy the Poet is Independent and Wicked the Philosopher is Dependent & Good.' Among the further comments: 'Poetry is to excuse Vice & shew its reason and necessary purgation', 'Nature teaches nothing of Spiritual Life but only of Natural Life', 'What is Liberty without Universal Toleration'? [10]

To restrain Blake is to clip the wings of a child before he has taken off.

We don't know precisely why in autumn 1785 Blake moved from Broad Street to 28 Poland Street, round the corner towards Oxford Street, other than that the print shop was evidently a failure; perhaps living within shouting distance of his eldest and most irritating brother proved too much for Mr and Mrs Blake.

Leaving James Parker and his wife next door to James Blake, they found themselves in a narrow house with a back garden behind which was a timber yard, rather than the St James Infirmary burial ground that backed on to Broad Street. The King's Arms pub occupied number 22. Twenty years later it was a meeting place for artists and people of many nationalities; perhaps it was so in 1785.

On Blake's birthday – 28 November 1781 – the Ancient Order of Druids had been revived at the King's Arms. Druidism would play a significant role in Blake's imaginative conception of Ancient British history (*King Edward III* in his *Poetical Sketches* included an account in song of the arrival of the Trojan Brutus, or 'Brut', to British shores, the supposed origin of 'Britain' in Geoffrey of Monmouth's medieval history).

The St James 'School of Industry' and the Workhouse were also in Poland Street. 'Schools' or 'Houses' of Industry were state-ordered institutions where numbers of very poor people of all ages were gathered from homes of appalling filth, given work clothes and food and set to work making things, a small percentage of profits from sales being given back to them. Health facilities were supposed to be provided for. Conditions in poorly run Houses of Industry became a national scandal on account of the deaths of many children in badly ventilated premises. In fact, child mortality was as bad, or worse, outside of the houses, but official statistics made conditions inside the houses appear especially alarming because concentrations of people were counted together, whereas outside, spread amongst the general population, the worst afflicted became statistically obscure.

The parish of St James's took a responsible approach. In September 1782 a 'Parish School of Industry' was opened in King Street, Golden Square, to get 6 to 14-year-olds out of the sight of vice and profligacy in the Workhouse and train them as housemaids and apprentices. King Street stood two streets west of Broad Street's western end, running parallel to Carnaby Street. James Blake, father and son, supplied much of the school's haberdashery during the 1780s.

The government was constantly under pressure to deal with poverty and crime as the industrial and agricultural revolutions, exacerbated by conflict with France, changed the country: steam, coal and iron were all big business. New canals shifted coal and new products from the North to the Midlands and from the Midlands to the South. Windmills were disappearing. The largest windmill could generate 30 horsepower; a steam engine, 300 horsepower. As for manpower, there was now a distressing surplus. With prisons full and conditions often atrocious, the government sought to capitalize quickly on Captain Cook's discoveries. In September 1786, English naval officer Captain Arthur Philip was appointed commodore of a fleet that in May 1787 sailed, at the Home Secretary Lord Sydney's behest, with over 700 convicts to Botany Bay to establish a penal settlement in Australia. Captain Philip's bait: the governorship of New South Wales, a state that did not as yet exist. They might as well have sent him to the moon.

NINE

An Island in the Moon

1786–1787

Liberty shall stand upon the cliffs of Albion,
Casting her blue eyes over the green ocean;
Or, tow'ring, stand upon the roaring waves,
Stretching her mighty spear o'er distant lands;
While, with her eagle wings, she covereth
Fair Albion's shore, and all her families.

(from 'Warriors' Song', *King Edward III*, scene 6)

Blake's ticket was up. It was now six years since Royal Academy President Joshua Reynolds had signed his student entry permit. Blake's friend George Cumberland, who had attended the RA Schools in the 1770s, had hoped for election as an Associate Member in 1784; disappointed, he criticized the Academy in essays. Completing his term at the end of 1785, Blake was not elected an Associate either, though he was at liberty to enter paintings for the annual exhibition. It is not difficult to see why Blake was passed over.

In January 1786, Blake was 28 years old. He had not produced a single recognized masterpiece; his only good review had come from Cumberland's pen. He was at sharp variance with Reynolds, and it is likely Reynolds knew it. It is unusual for great artists not to demonstrate prodigious, if unrefined, feats in their twenties, or even earlier. Blake's poetry and song had received praise in certain circles, but it remained unpublished, and he had not broken through as a designer in the visual arts. In fact, it is surprising to appreciate how little Blake had achieved as an artist as he approached the end of his twenties. In print selling he had failed; as an engraver, he received scraps. It's hard to see how he was surviving.

A painting by Pietro Martini, after Ramber, rather says it all. It depicts the Prince of Wales, escorted by Sir Joshua Reynolds, at the Royal Academy in Somerset House in 1787. The exhibition room is filled with aristocrats and their ladies. A senior clergyman dominates the royal party. The walls from floor to lantern ceiling are packed with substantially sized paintings. Practically every one is a portrait, and where not a portrait, a classical landscape. Blake painted neither. The Prince was knowledgeable about Dutch painting and an enthusiastic collector and supporter of the RA, but he broadly accepted Sir Joshua's rules of taste. William Blake, with his sharp, determined, challenging face, was not someone Sir Joshua would have felt comfortable introducing to His Royal Highness. Blake had challenged Moser and Reynolds himself, yet had produced nothing to astound the Academicians. He had not been to Italy.

Blake could not even lean on Cumberland for moral support. Cumberland had left for Italy on an inheritance in 1785 and would remain on the Continent for five years. In 1787, partly funded by Josiah Wedgwood, Flaxman also departed for Italy. Blake was out on his own, and it is difficult to establish what he was doing in 1786 and 1787 with any precision at all; the dating of drawings and watercolours around this period – such as '*circa* 1785' for the pen, ink and watercolour *Oberon, Titania and Puck with Fairies Dancing* and 'early' sketches of Job, Ezekiel, Joseph, Daniel and other, mainly biblical, subjects – is extremely speculative.[1] Frankly, 1786 is a real mystery. It may be that Blake travelled to a moon of his own.

Blake and the 'English Pagan'

Blake's burlesque or satirical mélange entitled *An Island in the Moon* may have been started in 1786; it may not. He obviously based it on personal experience, not of the moon itself, unlike Swedenborg who had envisioned life on the planets, but rather of people for whom the moon was a source of speculation. Blake might have been thinking of Flaxman's association with Josiah Wedgwood and the 'lunaticks' whose society convened in Birmingham at the full moon, and whose members were close to publisher Joseph Johnson and his radical circle. However, I cannot help thinking Blake had his own lunar speculations around this time.

Alexander Dyce (1798–1869), long-time friend of 'English Pagan' Thomas Taylor, also known as 'Thomas Taylor the Platonist' (1758–1835), reported an anecdote in his *Reminiscences* (*c*.1867–9) concerning Blake and Taylor:

> Taylor, so absurd himself in many aspects, was ready enough to laugh at the strange fancies of others, – for instance, at those of that half-crazed man of genius, Blake the artist. 'Pray, Mr Taylor,' said Blake one day, 'did you ever find yourself, as it were, standing close beside the vast and luminous orb of the moon'? – ['] Not that I remember, Mr. Blake: did you ever?' – 'Yes, frequently; and I have felt an almost irresistible desire to throw myself into it headlong.'– 'I think, Mr. Blake, you had better not; for if you were to do so, you most probably would never come out of it again.'[2]

Poet and Blake expert Kathleen Raine wrote in her classic *Blake and Antiquity* (1979) that while Blake was writing *An Island in the Moon* in 1787, Taylor published his first translation of Plotinus's *Concerning the Beautiful,* followed by his translation of the *Hymns of Orpheus*. It was not only Neo-Platonic philosophy that bound the two men's minds: Taylor was also Assistant Secretary to the Society for the Encouragement of Arts, Manufactures and Commerce (precursor to the Royal Society of Arts), founded by Shipley. Perhaps Blake was trying to obtain support from that body – as a teacher of drawing, for instance – or perhaps recognition for his and Cumberland's etching experiments, which would soon lead Blake to a new method for reproducing illuminated texts.

Technical interests may have dominated their encounters, judging from an entry in the commonplace book of William George Meredith (1804–31), whose uncle, of the same name, was Taylor's patron:

> T. Taylor gave Blake, the artist, some lessons in mathematics & got as far as the 5th . proposit.n. w[hi]ch proves that any two angles at the base of an isoceles [*sic*] triangle must be equal. Taylor was going thro the demonstration, but was interrupted by Blake, exclaiming, 'ah never mind that – what's the use of going to prove it, why I see with my eyes that it is so, & do not require any proof to make it clearer.[3]

This was Blake wagging for effect no doubt, but he had obviously read deeply from Taylor's works. Taylor translated into English many of the Greek-language classics of Neo-Platonism by Iamblichus, Plotinus, Proclus, Porphyry, Olympiodorus and Apuleius of Madaura. Blake found himself very much at home in the Neo-Platonic universe, for Neo-Platonism starts from the point of view that spirit is the primary reality, and it is from a devolution – as well as expression – of spirit that the physical universe is woven. Following Plato, the neo-Platonists maintained the soul's true homeland to be ideal and spiritual. Life is a descent into an inferior reflection of eternal forms in the flux of matter, whose source can be seen by the spirit (mind), but not by matter itself. Nature is blind to its own source and potential; it gropes in metaphorical darkness. The material world exists as the world perceived by the senses, but the senses, while they constitute one avenue of the soul, nonetheless convey a fatally limited or 'constressed' vision of reality.

The philosophy's essence is conveyed in a series of myths, such as the myth of Cupid and Psyche from Apuleius's 2nd-century CE *The Golden Ass* (or *Metamorphoses*). Since this is fundamentally a spiritual philosophy, though not lacking in rationality of expression or logical sequence, *understanding* it actually constitutes spiritual experience, because understanding requires spiritual perception. Spirit sees further than Reason; it knows what reason does not know.

In order to maintain and promote spiritual awareness, Neo-Platonic philosophers favoured sacred rites and purified magic to raise the mind to a level of spiritual receptiveness. Christianity recommends acts of selfless love to the same end, though rituals may assist.

Seen from the highest perspective, natural things may have a sacramental value; that is, particular natural objects can be rendered sacred, when 'linked' and raised in vision to a spiritual level – like the 'bread' and 'wine' of the Christian eucharist. Human love may also be a sacrament so long as it does not fall into 'worship of the body' – that is, mistaking the 'garment' (flesh) for spiritual being.

The problem of life for the soul is that material life induces 'sleep' or unconsciousness, by which means the soul is enticed into the addictive grip of natural forces. Taylor's borrowed ideas would directly influence Blake's *Book of Thel* which, according to Kathleen Raine, he would begin writing in about 1787.

Taylor's spiritual paganism was just one strand of ideas playing in Blake's milieu. In his satire, *An Island in the Moon,* we see an array of babblers competing for vainglorious domination of the mind in a kind of bawdy, drunken haze reminiscent of a Hogarth cartoon.

The characters in Blake's burlesque may be speculatively identified. Thus Taylor has been seen, predictably, as 'Sipsop the Pythagorean'. 'Inflammable Gass' may represent the painter Philip James de Loutherbourg (1740–1812). Loutherbourg was not only famous for dramatic landscapes – his painting of the furnaces of Coalbrookdale (1801) has become the very image of the so-called 'dark Satanic mills' of the Industrial Revolution – he also invented the *Eidophusikon,* a six-foot by eight-foot mechanical 'image of nature' that used coloured glass and projected imagery to fascinate the eye. Employed by David Garrick, Loutherbourg was a highly successful stage designer and was made a member of the Royal Academy in 1781. In 1789 he would embrace alchemy and the magical 'Egyptian Freemasonry' of Cagliostro, fields that would also fascinate George Cumberland.

On the other hand, 'Inflammable Gass' – that which made Lunardi's balloon rise – could be gas-discoverer Joseph Priestley. A transvestite called 'Mr Femality' might be Mademoiselle La Chevalière d'Eon Beaumont, who arrived in London on a mission for Louis XVI in November 1785, causing a stir in the Golden Square area in his/her French feminine finery, worn by order of French King. 'Quid the Cynic' is probably Blake himself. Cynicism, though, does not altogether suit him: he comes over as bitter.

The *Island in the Moon* manuscript opens quite promisingly, in a vein established by Jonathan Swift in *A Tale of a Tub, Gulliver's Travels* and *The Modest Proposal* earlier in the century:

In the Moon, is a certain Island near by a mighty continent, which small island seems to have some affinity to England. & what is more extraordinary the people are so much alike & their language so much the same that you would think you were among your friends.[4]

After that appallingly punctuated, barbed introduction, we head downhill fast, to the point where the thought occurs: 'You want to be a satirist, Mr Blake? Don't give up the day job.' A satirist is generally a creature who excels at satire, and little else. The text evinces a confused mind. Blake even includes in the manuscript, in the mouths of his absurd non-characters, three songs that would only find a decent home in the *Songs of Innocence and Experience*: 'Holy Thursday', 'The Little Boy Lost' and 'Nurses Song' (surely a case of pearls before swine!) as well as a charming, nameless poem WB Yeats christened 'Old English Hospitality' which speaks of the best of English tavern conviviality, and might be a tribute to the King's Arms in Poland Street, or a lament for a tavern visited by Blake in his youth.

Perhaps at the time Blake despaired that his real poetry would ever find any other home. To be kind, one might say that the author's bitterness is really a self-protecting veneer, but one senses that Blake has been disturbed by a world that seems to have no place for him, only for fatuous expressions of half-baked science and insincerity.

Blake was waiting for something to happen; it had something to do with the Moon, but he did not know what it was. In 1793 he would return to the 'Moon' theme in an extraordinary engraving (No. 9) to his *For Children: The Gates of Paradise*. There we see someone about to ascend a ladder from the edge of the earth, surrounded by bright stars in the night, that leads all the way to the moon in her first quarter. The caption says, gnomically: 'I want! I want!' Were we ignorant of the *Desire* theme evident in the emblem books with which Blake was doubtless familiar as a child, we should be at a loss even to begin to understand what Blake thought he was getting at in a text ostensibly dedicated to children. Perhaps the image needs no rationalization, appealing directly to the imagination as it does.

Blake's image and, especially, caption were preceded, as Marsha Keith Schuchard has astutely observed, by statements in Blake's emblem book *There is No Natural Religion* (1788): 'More! More! Is the cry of a mistaken soul, less than All cannot satisfy Man.'[5] Van Bolsvert's image of an angel or 'Soul' chained to the earth, unable to soar to the Desired One, in Herman Hugo's *Pia Desideria* (1634) appears to be echoed in Blake's little emblem in *There is No Natural Religion*. There we see a man chained. Blake's accompanying text reads: 'If any could desire what he is incapable of possessing, despair must be his eternal lot.'

The French mystic Madame Jeanne-Marie Bouvier de la Motte Guyon (1648–1717) was a writer much appreciated by Blake and by Count

Zinzendorf. Madame Guyon's edition of Hugo's emblems, *L'Âme Amante de son Dieu, representée dans les Emblèmes de Hermannus Hugo* (1717; Paris, 1790), was dedicated to the 'interior Christian': 'Lord, all my desire is exposed to your eyes.' Unless worshippers first become like little children before God, their passionate desire for union with Jesus, 'Le Désiré' (the Desired One) would be vain. Blake would refer to Madame Guyon in the poem *Jerusalem* as one of 'the gentle Souls Who guide the great Wine-press of Love.' This was a much healthier direction for Blake to take than the attempted 'clever clever' satire of *An Island in the Moon.* This way, one might actually reach that 'luminous orb'! We see, I think, Blake grappling with his inner survival mechanism, trying to find a way through rejection's despair. That empty zero around the years 1786–7 begins to look pregnant with possibilities.

One event that marked Blake for life was the death of his beloved brother Robert in February 1787. Robert was only 25 when tuberculosis struck him down. Blake stayed up a fortnight nursing the young brother whom he had taught drawing and whose company he loved. According to Mrs Blake, who confirmed the story to John Linnell, when Robert died Blake saw his released spirit rise upwards, clapping his hands for joy. Blake then slept for three days and three nights. He said he remained in spiritual communication with his departed brother, whom he saw in his imagination, and who, notably, inspired him with the secret of illuminated printing that would change Blake's art forever.

The loss of a dear brother was bound to lead Blake's mind towards a powerful desire for union with God, an intense desire for understanding the ways of the spirit and the nature of this life.

It would appear to be around this time that Blake began reading the works of the late Emanuel Swedenborg, whose vision of a world of heaven at last open to human perception meant so much to so many who longed for spiritual clarity and relief from the pit of bereavement.

Swedenborg had himself trod the path of the scientist and had sought life on the moon. A graduate of Uppsala University, Swedenborg came to England in 1710 where he took a particular interest in the works of Royal Society founder, the Rt Rev. John Wilkins (1614–1672).

Uppsala's librarian, Eric Benzelius, had introduced Swedenborg to Hebrew Kabbalah. Swedenborg was delighted to find that polymath Wilkins also favoured Kabbalah, regarding its interpretative tradition as knowledge relating to what 'Adam had in his Innocency' – that is, in Paradise. This Swedenborg found in Wilkins's *Mathematical and Philosophical Works,* published in 1708, a collection that also included Wilkins's *Mathematical Magic* (which showed what wonders could be performed with mathematics and geometry), first published in 1648, and *THE DISCOVERY OF A WORLD IN THE MOON OR, A DISCOURSE Tending to PROVE, that 'tis probable there may be another habitable World in that Planet,*[6] published in 1638.

After a series of shattering visions beginning at Easter weekend 1744, Swedenborg found he could leave his scientific spectacles aside and fly to the moon and beyond in the chariot of his spirit.

I strongly suspect that it was not only Swedenborg who read the thoughts of Wilkins as quoted below. That Blake also read the work seems highly likely both from the title conceit of his private satire on scientific vacuities, and from the fact that Wilkins was also the author of another work, one that Blake would doubtless have loathed even as he would have felt compelled to read it: Wilkins's *Principles and Duties of Natural Religion* (1722, 2 vols, 8th edition).

On page 208 of the first edition of *The Discovery of a world in the Moon*, Wilkins writes:

> Kepler doubts not, but that as soon as the art of flying is found out, some of their Nation will make one of the first colonies that shall inhabit that other world [Blake had recently witnessed the first flight by hot air balloon in England]. But I leave this and the like conjectures to the fancy of the reader; Desiring now to finish this Discourse, wherein I have in some measure proved what at the first I promised, a world in the Moon.

Wilkins added a series of propositions to support his case: 'Prop. 2. That a plurality of worlds do's [*sic*] not contradict any principle of reason or faith ...' 'Prop. 6. That there is a world in the Moon, hath been the direct opinion of many ancient authorities...' 'Prop. 3. That the heavens do not consist of any such pure matter which can privilege them from the like change and corruption, as these inferior bodies are liable unto.' 'Prop. 11. That as their world is our Moon, so our world is their Moon.' 'Prop. 13. That tis probable there may be inhabitants in this other World, but of what kind they are is uncertain.'

Blake's satire tends to resolve the question of Proposition 13. Uncertainty is characteristic of the inhabitants of Blake's *Island in the Moon*. Against this perennial scientific uncertainty, Blake reaches for his 'arrows of desire' and finds he can shoot at the moon directly.

That *Desire leads to fruition,* if the aim be steady and unbroken, is a key principle of Blake's most important philosophical work, *The Marriage of Heaven and Hell,* possibly begun in 1790. *What can be conceived becomes reality.* That is, *Imagination,* not Reason, is the first Practical Cause of man's essential will. The reason knows only *what has been conceived already,* and is always ready to deny what is 'only imagined'. Therefore, Reason inhibits Desire. Desire is not born of Reason but of a pre-existing union that has been obscured or severed. That is why the voice beneath engraving No. 9 in *For Children: The Gates of Paradise* says: 'I want! I want!' and we see a ladder extend to the moon. The Life is in the Thought, not the demonstration. Science was maimed until it was prepared to open its eyes to the inner worlds of thought, of eternity. And this is what Blake knew that Art could do, while Sir Joshua and the smart set wanted portraits of themselves and their tidy gardens to adorn their mathematically constrained houses of death.

The Book of Thel

Scholars are uncertain as to the date of composition of the *Book of Thel.* The fully illuminated text is usually dated between 1789 and 1791 largely on the basis that it appears more sophisticated than Blake's earlier experimentation with a new etching method he began perfecting some time after Robert Blake's death in 1787. Kathleen Raine dated the verse composition of the *Book of Thel* to that year, the year it seems most likely that Blake's thought was charmed, and perhaps challenged, by exposure to Thomas Taylor's translations of Plotinus's *Concerning the Beautiful* and the first *Hymns of Orpheus.*

Shall we find what we're looking for out in planetary space? We shall see.

The *Book of Thel* is a tender, watery, Spenserian fantasy that by means of a beautiful lamentation explores the question: 'Why descend into this earthly experience of misery, longing, sleep, phantom pleasures and decay, when the soul is most at home in the worlds of eternity?'

What is the nature of the desire of the soul?

Thel is about desire and will. The name 'Thel' is the root of the Greek '*Thelema*' which means 'Will', as well as of other words concerning wishing, charms, enchantment. The infinitive 'to Wish' is the noun 'a want' transformed into a verb, that is, into *action*: the energy to act is Desire. But, as Blake's story unfolds, we see a spiritual conflict within the Desire itself: the role of the body will become the great issue of Blake's work and will drive him nearly to insanity.

Strong influences in the poem appear to be Spenser's *Faerie Queen* and Porphyry's account of the *Cave of the Nymphs* which the 3rd-century CE Neo-Platonist found in Homer's account of Odysseus. In Spenser, souls await birth in the Garden of Adonis; in Blake, by the river Adona. Adonis was the beautiful boy of Greek mythology who must be sacrificed. Thel is a beautiful soul; and if she remains in the world below, she must die. Water is everywhere in Blake's poem. That is because in Neo-Platonism, water is the symbol of matter, always in flux, never truly solid. To 'cross the river' is to be held in bondage to the 'sea of time and space', a great desert for the soul, which, paradoxically lacks the 'water of life' that the soul needs to live. The material world is, from the spiritual point of view, tasteless, and is of itself unable to savour the truth.

In Part IV the 'terrific porter' opens the northern bar to Thel, who, entering, sees the 'couches of the dead' of the 'land unknown' – unknown to her, known well enough to us. She is a stranger to the generating world, a stranger to 'a land of sorrows and tears', a 'land of clouds thro' valleys dark'. This gate-man to mortal life seizes the same 'northern gate' that permits the souls into the 'Cave of the Nymphs' in Porphyry's account, the nymphs being the weavers of flesh: the curtain that hides, then suffocates the soul.

In *Thel,* a voice from the pit, or grave, asks: 'Why a tender curb upon the youthful burning boy! Why a little curtain of flesh on the bed of our desire?' The questions seem to be laments for some lost sexual innocence, and that is what they are. But it is the body that has robbed the lovers of their true Desire, separated them from the highest blissful union. It seems to us a hard or impossible doctrine that is being suggested: that the objects of our desire may be deadly, destroying all that they promise.

The material world is one of decay and the dampness hastens the rot that reduces the once blissful body to a sludge in a coffin of lead.

Before Thel is confronted with the grave, she asks questions of living things that seem so beautiful, if humble, in this world. She asks the Lily of the Valley; she asks a cloud; she asks a worm; she asks a humble 'Clod of Clay'. Providence offers the clod of clay and the worm all they need in the grave and they are grateful. They tempt Thel to join them there, but on hearing a terrible lament – the voice of the grave – the Virgin Thel gets up with a start and 'with a shriek' flees back to her home in 'the vales of Har'. Or, as Plotinus would have recommended she do, Thel flees to the 'delightful land' of the Father, whence she came into this world of decay and death and longing and sorrow.

And there we might think Blake might have contemplated suicide. And perhaps he did, but he knew that he had not exhausted his theme, and that the questions posed in *Thel* had not really been answered, being too terrible to contemplate alone.

Furthermore, the poetry of *Thel* was truly beautiful, far better than anything in *Poetical Sketches*, and was there not more to come? Must he surrender before his life had truly begun? And besides, Thel was only contemplating entry into generative life; Blake and his wife were well in the midst of that life. Finding a way *through* it was the problem.

The Little Black Boy

Some time after 1784, Blake wrote the remarkable poem 'The Little Black Boy', to be gathered up to join other *Songs of Innocence* around 1789. Given its daring combination of themes concerning the veil that is flesh, and the slave trade, it would seem to me to be a product of contemplation on historical events of 1787.

> Thus did my mother say and kissed me,
> And thus I say to little English boy.
> When I from black and he from white cloud free,
> And round the tent of God like lambs we joy:
>
> Ill shade him from the heat till he can bear,
> To lean in joy upon our fathers knee.
> And then I'll stand and stroke his silver hair,
> And be like him and he will then love me.

The 'cloud' is a Gnostic image for the body. Was it not a 'cloud' that removed Jesus from the sight of the apostles when assumed to heaven? (Acts 1:9) What is it that inhibits the slave owner from seeing the little black boy as a child of God, like him?

In London in 1787, inspired by Granville Sharp's pioneering anti-slavery campaign, the Rev. Thomas Clarkson formed the Committee for the Abolition of the Slave Trade with William Wilberforce as parliamentary representative. One of the poor blacks who joined themselves to Clarkson's cause was former slave Ottobah Cugoana who, in 1787, published his memoirs. Transported to America as a child, he was freed as a servant in England. Cugoana urged Britain to send a fleet to the Indies to put an end to slavery. In West Africa, meanwhile, Englishman James Weaver, founder of the 'Province of Freedom' on the Sierra Leone Estuary, adopted Granville Sharp's constitution on being elected governor of the freed slave settlers.

If Blake had finished his poem in 1787, he beat brilliant poet William Cowper by a year, for in 1788, Cowper, recovering from mental illness, was commissioned by the Committee for the Abolition of the Slave Trade to write the highly effective 'The Negro's Complaint', which bears comparison with Blake's (then utterly obscure) work:

> Still in thought as free as ever,
> What are England's rights, I ask,
> Me from my delights to sever,
> Me to torture, me to task?
> Fleecy locks and black complexion
> Cannot forfeit nature's claim;
> Skins may differ, but affection
> Dwells in white and black the same.

Blake's poem is more inspirational, and really does get 'under the skin'. It would seem to have been an oversight on Joseph Johnson's part not to have recommended Blake's poetry to the Committee for the Abolition of the Slave Trade. It was, after all, Johnson who had published Cowper's extraordinary six-book blank verse poem *The Task* (1785), followed soon after by a second edition of Cowper's *Poems* in two volumes. Blake would see more of Johnson in 1787, once Flaxman had departed for Italy, for as Blake would write in a poem to Flaxman in September 1800: 'When Flaxman was taken to Italy, Fuseli was given to me for a season'.[7] And Fuseli, as we have noted, was a good friend of Johnson, and a member of the circle that included Priestley, Tom Paine, Godwin, Wollstonecraft and Dr Erasmus Darwin. Being somehow more able to gain Fuseli's attention in and after 1787 would mark a definite shift in Blake's fortunes, together with a mighty energizing of his sense of spiritual and creative freedom. Fuseli saw no reason why an artist should not work entirely from the imagination, painting being a dramatic as well as imitative art.

On the European political front, seeds were planted for what would explode in two years into the French Revolution. On 20 August 1786, comptroller-general Alexandre de Calonne announced that a deficit estimated at £800 million (much of which had gone towards supporting the American War of Independence) would soon plunge France into bankruptcy. De Calonne proposed a universal land tax – rejected by the Estates General on 30 July 1787. A month later, Louis XVI decreed that Parliament retire. Britain, Prussia and the Netherlands allied themselves against France and Austria. Forced to recall Parliament in September, Louis XVI conceded civil status to Protestants. New freedoms were not granted to everyone, though. While the Philadelphia Convention published a Constitution for the United States, Congress planned the colonization of Indian lands. A 'Northwest Ordinance' envisaged up to five new states across the Ohio River.

On the day before Christmas Eve 1787, Commanding Lieutenant William Bligh, aged 33, ordered HMS *Bounty* to weigh anchor for Tahiti. Would they find Paradise there?

TEN

Towards the New Jerusalem

1788

William Blake is sometimes discussed as if his leading ideas were peculiar to himself, an error evident in past treatments of Blake's relationship to Emanuel Swedenborg. To understand that relationship we need to see the bigger picture. What was happening around Blake in 1788–9 as his enthusiasm for Swedenborg reached dizzy heights?

On 6 June 1788, while Blake was in Poland Street absorbing himself in Swedenborg's writings and creating the high-energy illuminated tract *All Religions are One*, the Rev. Ralph Churton received the Bishop of London's nomination to preach a November sermon in His Majesty's Chapel Royal, Whitehall.

A Fellow of Brasenose College, Oxford, Churton had known Dr Richard Chandler since first contributing to his researches in *c.*1774. Chandler was leader of the William Pars and Nicholas Revett 'Dilettanti' Greece-Ionia tour of 1764–6. Churton himself was now a respected member of the British antiquarian establishment. In 1795 he would publish *A Short Defence of the Church of England*,[1] a work that inspired Chandler's friend Richard Gough to write to Churton: 'I look up to you as an able Champion of the Protestant Cause who with Candor and Temper detects every artifice and chicane preached by its Antagonists.'[2] Gough then asked Churton to apply his studies of Prophecy to 'see what can be struck out from present appearances towards discovering future or ensuing events'. All thoughtful men in this period were interested in prophecy. Richard Gough was, of course, the antiquarian responsible for Blake's drawing in Westminster Abbey, a fecund mission for

Gough's still-in-progress masterpiece, *Sepulchral Monuments*.

It was Churton's reputation as a learned defender of the Church of England that elicited the following letter, sent to him on 15 May 1799 by Charles Baldwyn, a Manchester bookseller:

I now write to you, concerning Mr Clowes, Rector of St John's Church, Manchester [...] he has been 29 years Rector of one of our Churches aforesaid a Preacher: a follower of Mr Law's Opinions, as in Agreement with Jacob Behmen [William Law published Jacob Böhme's *Works*, 4 vols, 1764, including Dionysius Freher's engravings, much admired by William Blake]: and since, and to this very time of the Baron Swedenborg: that at this very time he is publishing Swedenborg's Works; and that Mr Bower's[3] 4 Sermons aforesaid (on I Timothy 3:9 [against misleading preaching]) were preached at his Church against him, in his Absence. I am now making Mr Clowes a publick Example – for this reason following.

The Town of Manchester had been pestered with his false Doctrine before the Summer 1783. that somebody, it was thought myself, sent to Beilby Porteus, the Bishop of Chester, a Manuscript Letter, & printed Pamphlets convicting Clowes of the same: in consequence of which, Porteus felt himself forced sore against the grain to summon Clowes to appear before him: he did appear before him: and the Bishop sent him back with a Letter, in which were these, or some such like words: 'Give my Compliments to Baldwyn & tell him that Mr Clowes has behaved before me with such Meekness, Mildness, & Condescension; and has promised that he will not for the future offend anyone.' This letter was read to me 12 November 1783: moreover also, says Bishop Porteus, I'm sure Baldwyn must be the Author of what I've received concerning Clowes. – the Bishop since, set Clowes up for an Example to the rest of our Clergy, 20 in Number. Now, under the Sanction of Bishop Porteus; Clowes has been publishing, and publishing these fifteen years and a half: has been the chief Instrument in setting up a thursday Lecture here, and preached 80 minutes the Introductory one: and printed it: has lately reprinted it or a 2ⁿᵈ Edition: and various other things besides.[4]

Churton's reply has not been preserved. His hands, anyway, were tied, for it was the same Bishop Beilby Porteus who exonerated Clowes that had appointed Churton Whitehall Preacher in 1788! For Churton, the bishop's satisfaction was sufficient unto obedience. Nevertheless, Churton would have sincerely lamented any move that carried members of the Church of England into dissenting bodies; he constantly prayed for those 'misled' into sects to return to what he believed the purest organization of Christ's religion in the world. And in 1788, despite Clowes's urging of Anglicans attending Swedenborgian lectures to remain faithful to the Church of England, moves by Swedenborgians towards a distinct 'New Church' or 'Church of the New Jerusalem' had been in full swing for a year.

This was the confused context in which Anglican William Blake, 'turned on' by Swedenborg's visions, found himself.

At the time that Blake's enthusiasm for the Swedish scientist and visionary reached its height, the Rev. John Clowes (1743–1831) was probably Britain's most significant Swedenborgian, having followed the literary-spiritual path common to a number of intellectual spiritual thinkers who experienced tensions with the established Church. Deeply moved, as John Wesley and Samuel Johnson had been, by William Law's *Christian Perfection* and other English, German and French mystics – including the ubiquitous Böhme – Clowes came to Swedenborg, at the age of 30, through acquaintanceship with the Rev. Thomas Hartley, rector of Winwick, Northamptonshire, Swedenborg's earliest translator into English.

Building on Hartley's groundwork, Clowes translated Swedenborg's *Vera Christiana Religio* ('True Christian Religion', 2 vols, 1781), followed by the *Arcana Coelestia* ('Heavenly Mysteries', 12 vols, 1782–1806), *De Telluribus in Mundo nostro Solari ...* ('Concerning the Earths in our Solar System that are called Planets', 1787), *Amor Conjugialis* ('Conjugial Love', 1792), and *Doctrina Vitae pro Nova Hierosolyma* ('Doctrines of Life for the New Jerusalem').

Blake himself referred to a Clowes translation when, no earlier than 1787, he annotated *A Treatise concerning Heaven and Hell, and of the Wonderful Things therein ...*, a Swedenborg pamphlet translated by Hartley and William Cookworthy, (R Hindmarsh, London, 1784). Blake made the note for himself: 'See N73 Worlds in Universe. for account of Instructing Spirits.' That is, a note to compare the text under consideration with Swedenborg's account of

Spirit-Instructors in the solar system in pamphlet No. 73. Pamphlet No. 73 was Clowes's translation of *Of the Earths in the Universe and of their Inhabitants* (Manchester, 1787), a work clearly showing that Swedenborg had been inspired by Wilkins's *The Discovery of a world in the Moon* (1638; see Chapter Nine, p.114).

Clowes's work also made a great impact on Blake's friend John Flaxman. To mark the fiftieth anniversary of Clowes's induction to St John's, Manchester (1818), a *basso-relievo* tablet was commissioned for the church; Flaxman was the sculptor.

To ask what Blake got out of his immersion into Swedenborg's inner visions and fantastic extra-terrestrial (though equally inner) voyages is a difficult question to answer. Blake, being Blake, would see himself as Swedenborg's spiritual companion, not his student.

First, Blake obtained that pleasant feeling of confirmation of inner convictions that one's ordinary companions rarely supply – a need more likely to be satisfied by the printed page than in the tavern. Blake found a spiritual friend. However, he would have to contend with some discomfort in discovering that he was not alone in his admiration. Inevitably, he would fall out with any system others might build around Swedenborg's thought. Blake was inwardly a loner, and he could be a thoroughgoing cynic too. The same solitariness would inevitably encourage Blake to find differences between his own views and Swedenborg's, as well as grounds for fundamental criticisms of Swedenborg's beliefs. He would, in the future, know times when he held Swedenborg in high esteem and times when he dismissed him as being too bound by conventional Protestant doctrines and the urge to rationalize what reason alone could not grasp or express. But I think Blake knew a fellow traveller when he saw one.

Swedenborg is famous for a doctrine of 'correspondences'. He saw the physical world as the outflow of spiritual causes. Laws of nature reflected spiritual laws. What one sees in the world is an image of a heavenly counterpart or principle. Heaven and earth are intimately linked. Similar correspondences apply to actions. The sexual bliss of a devout couple is registered in heaven. As Blake would put it: 'God is in the lowest effects as well as in the highest causes.'

Blake would often himself see events or images in *at least* two ways: the 'vegetable' image that came *with* the eye, and the spiritual meaning – also expressed as an image – that came *through* the eye. The physical eye delivered an apparent solid, based on sense data conditioned by time and space. The spiritual eye delivered a sign. And a sign forces us to see an object through its significance. The poet's job, as Coleridge would assert, was to 'disembody the soul of fact'. Thus, a thistle on a road obstructing Blake's path could be both a plant and an array of spiritual enemies sent to test him. His imaginative powers being highly cultivated, he could then see his spiritual enemies as figures. The sign, being of spiritual origin, guaranteed the reality of the vision. Conversely, a countryman saying casually 'The gate is open' could enfigure an angel's happy, encouraging announcement that a new stage of life had begun. There is, of course, the famous interchange of Blake with a 'once-born' interlocutor who asked, 'Why, Mr. Blake, when you see the sun rise, do you not see a red disc in the heavens, rather like a golden guinea?' To which Blake replied: 'Oh no, oh no! I see the Lord God Almighty and the whole company of heaven crying out "Holy, holy, holy, Lord God Almighty."'

Furthermore, and this was a doctrine not at all unique to Blake, history and the events of history were open to be interpreted as *signs*. Therefore Blake felt he could write a poetic account of the American or French Revolutions, for example, and call them 'prophecies': forth-tellings of the divine experience of vision. This use of the word 'prophecy' is often misunderstood in Blake. For example, 'America: A Prophecy' does not mean a collection of prophecies on the theme of America, or prophecies concerning America. Those who seek such seek in vain. Blake meant that what he saw happening in America was itself a sign, and to tell it was to prophesy. The state of 'America' itself was a blatant prophecy to those who could see it. What had occurred there was going to occur elsewhere as spiritual principles dictated; America freed was a sign of a New Age, another stone in the building of the heavenly Jerusalem that will transform nature into spirit – unlike materialism, which promises the opposite. As the French Illuminists who gathered about the works of Martinès de Pasqually, Antoine-Joseph Pernety and Louis-Claude de St Martin thought, 'mere' history was a *massa confusa* of external events; *real* history, on the other hand, was the movement of the spirit, expressing itself in time and space. The same can be said of Blake's treatment of the 'French

Revolution'. His version is history *sub specie aeternitatis*. Products of journalism, from this perspective, are practically meaningless.

Now, Swedenborg did not invent the theory of correspondences, and neither did Blake. The idea goes back at least to medieval magical and astrological traditions inspired by the works attributed to Hermes Trismegistus (*Corpus Hermeticum*). Note, for example, the dictum *mundus imago dei*, attributed to the sage Hermes in the Latin *Asclepius*: 'the world is the image of God'. There you have the correspondence. The Hermetic sin *par excellence* is worship of the body (or identification with the enfleshed false self or 'ego'). Worship of the body entailed being misled into corporeal vision, the vegetable eye, or falling in love with the Natural Man, which is but an image of the Real – what Blake calls the 'Poetic Genius' – reflected in the waters of Nature. Blake believed that corporeal vision led to corporeal war. That is why, in the now famous verses, he advocated ceaseless commitment to 'Mental Fight', not corporeal war. Corporeal struggles only change appearances, leaving fundamental and causative spiritual conflicts unresolved.

To ignore the gifts of the spirit is to ignore God's voice; the result is to become a slave to history, a passive performer whose acts are dust: an empty fool who has put his wealth in a house of cards built on sand. Our present culture is precisely in this position. That is why we need to attend to our Blake, and come to understand him well.

Furthermore, the doctrine of correspondence is central to the alchemical philosophy of Paracelsus that was so influential on Jacob Böhme. Knowledge of Paracelsus and Böhme would lead Blake to declare, when he emerged from initial enthusiasm for Swedenborg, that anyone could build up a system like Swedenborg's from knowledge of the latter two sages and the Bible. Well, that is probably, more or less, where Swedenborg was in fact coming from. And so was Blake. He had encountered the giants Paracelsus and Böhme before the American War, or so he implied in a poem to Flaxman in 1800.

There was something of an ego-tickle in Swedenborg as well. He had declared that the opening of the heavenly world to Man, as preface to the spiritualization of the cosmos prophesied in the Book of Revelation, had in fact occurred, in terrestrial terms, in the year 1757: Blake's year of birth, which therefore could be regarded as itself a sign. Blake was, quite literally, a Child of the New Age, and he was conscious, more so, I think, after his thirtieth birthday, that he had a God-ordained role, as artist, poet and seer, in that New Age, such that to mock his mental gift was to mock the Giver of *all* spiritual gifts. Rejection of Blake would then stand as a sign, a judgement, while he himself, in defiance of all appearances, stood with his root and anchor in eternity, unshakeable.

There is another dimension to Swedenborg's visionary dualism that would cause Blake a good deal of inner conflict and marital difficulty.

As in the case of history, so in the case of scripture: according to Swedenborg, behind the literal statements of the Bible lives a spiritual meaning that can come alive in the receptive spirit to serve as interpreter of the 'mere' text. The Bible contains occulted truth: 'that seeing they may see and not perceive; and hearing, they may hear, and not understand' (Mark 4:12). Grace to penetrate the mysteries of the kingdom of heaven was the gift of Him who sent Jesus. This was Swedenborg's approach to the Bible and we may say it was Blake's also, though Blake's inborn and cultivated visionary ability was always likely to see the Bible differently from those of more literal, unimaginative, overly academic and unspiritual minds. Blake was especially at odds with persons who thought the Bible needed to conform to Reason, in order to be believed. This was the supposition that got Thomas Jefferson to cut up the New Testament into self-satisfying morsels and made Joseph Priestley imagine himself a priest of truth.

Blake understood that the Bible is a work that appeals to the imagination first, and is therefore accessible to children and the unlearned in its essential meaning. Unfortunately, as we shall see, those who gathered around the pennant of Swedenborg, born aloft in the London of the late 1780s and 90s, included people of very different perceptual levels, and Blake knew this diversity in capacity was what made sects so sectarian and what would keep him in the broad English Church to the end.

Blake was aware that events unfolding in France in 1788 were signs carrying transcendent messages for the New Age. He followed them as best he could, as we shall. In the meantime, 1788 saw the mute appearance of an extraordinary work printed from a series of exquisite copper plates of only 2 x 2½ inches in size. It was called *ALL RELIGIONS are ONE / THERE is NO NATURAL RELIGION*, and it is positively brilliant.

The text and emblems were produced by etching – that is, the principal design was drawn onto the copper in an acid-resistant substance, after which the plate received a basting in an acidic liquid (*aqua fortis*) that burnt away a layer of copper, leaving the 'etched' letters and designs outstanding, to which ink was then applied and prints taken from the plates.

Incidentally, this process gave Blake his metaphor for the method by which he read the Bible. He said he read it in the 'infernal sense', by which he meant the husk of materialism was burnt away by the fiery 'hell' of the acid, revealing the essential substance. The positive view of 'hell', expressing fatherly wrath, he borrowed from the radical Christian theosophy of Jacob Böhme, which Blake understood and used to great effect, and, not infrequently, consternation. Frederick Tatham was neither first nor last to see the word 'infernal' and think of the 'Devil and all his works' in the conventional or uninitiated sense.

In 24 very short, pithy paragraphs, most no more than a single sentence, William Blake demolished the materialist system of his bugbears, 'Bacon, Newton & Locke' and the 150-year tradition of a 'Natural Religion' conforming to ordinary reason. Blake's positive refutations are dry and dead accurate, but there is great humour behind the lines. Read it too fast and you may miss the brilliance, the subtleties and the devastating meaning. Unfortunately, virtually nobody seems to have read it at the time, and all too few today.

Attributed to 'The Voice of one crying in the Wilderness', the first section is entitled *ALL RELIGIONS are ONE*, an idea that has become a commonplace today, but not so in 1788. Blake begins in agreement with a so-called 'Baconian' scientific principle: 'the true method of knowledge is experiment.' Fine, but he expands on this logically: 'As the true method of knowledge is experiment the true faculty of knowing must be the faculty which experiences. This faculty I treat of.' He then introduces his conception of what it is *in* Man that can experience knowledge. He calls it 'The Poetic Genius' which is the 'true Man'. The outward form or body of Man is derived from the Poetic Genius. He says this idea conforms to classical philosophy wherein all outward forms derive from the 'genius', the parent or transmitting principle (as in 'genes').

The Ancients, he says, called this Genius 'an Angel & Spirit & Demon'. At once we see how Blake combines Art with spiritual philosophy at root. The Genius is 'Poetic' because the Greek '*poiein*' (the origin of 'poetry') means *to make*; creativity is the essential sign of the presence of Genius, and the Genius is the father of Man. This is why Blake would declare: 'Christianity is Art.' The sign of the person in touch with Poetic Genius is creative activity at the highest level; block it and see what happens! True religion is the means of opening up the true inner Man. In the beginning, God creates the heavens and the earth. So the 'Poetic Genius' is God in us, or God-as-us, according to capacity. You have the same idea in modern Magick, which uses the archaic expression 'the Holy Guardian Angel' whose 'knowledge and conversation' is the primary step to realizing the divine Genius, or 'cosmic consciousness'. The 'Holy Guardian Angel' is that Person of the nature of absolute being that has to do with us in this world personally and impersonally: the light beyond reason that is the goal of Kabbalah and authentic Freemasonry, and indeed, as Blake shows, of all mature religion.

Blake then says *everyone* has the Poetic Genius, but as our outward forms are generally the same, but specifically of endless variety, so it is with access to the Poetic Genius. Some 'get it'; some want it, but need it to be brought forth from within; others deny it, obsessed with self, the false self-image standing in their own way, and in the way of others too.

Anyone who speaks and writes from the heart intends to be true, says Blake. Insofar as philosophies seek truth, all are from the Poetic Genius, but 'adapted to the weaknesses of every individual'. One size does not fit all. Blake would have utterly abominated state-controlled curricula, run by state-educated teachers; he saw collective formal education as pernicious. *This man had not been to school*, as Flaxman was only too quick to point out to Hayley!

His 'PRINCIPLE 4' introduces the essence of his challenge to Reason: 'As none by travelling over known lands can find out the unknown. So from already acquired knowledge Man could not acquire more. therefore an universal Poetic Genius exists.' Reason relies on known facts, but the unknown is all around us, and by reason alone we should not realize this. How confident is the one who 'thinks he knows everything'; how close to a fall! Blake then leaps to the principle that the different religions of the nations come from their 'different reception' of the Poetic Genius: everywhere the Poetic Genius is called the 'Spirit of Prophecy'. All religions rely on prophecies; the 'Spirit of Prophecy' *is* the Poetic Genius. Those in touch with the Poetic Genius speak the 'divine word'.

Blake shows understanding of cultural relativity way ahead of his time, but he does not blur the differences. It is the source of prophecy that is 'One'. 'PRINCIPLE 6' brings this point home: 'The Jewish & Christian Testaments are An original derivation from the Poetic Genius.' He adds: 'this is necessary from the confined nature of bodily sensation.' In other words, the biblical text manifests in forms appropriate to the state of ignorance or knowledge and experience of the receiver. The words themselves have been mediated through the limitations of 'the embodied' and are received again according to the limitations of 'the embodied'. The capacity to grasp essence relies on the access of the individual to the same 'Poetic Genius' whence the scripture ultimately derived.

What Blake deals with here is a problem that would dominate 19th-century European theology: what credence could be given the Bible once it was known its constituent works were written by different men at different times of history, when historical and scientific knowledge was relatively confined? Blake dismisses those who deny the value of the Bible on such grounds since – where the text has not been artificially corrupted – the spiritual meaning is absolute and inexhaustible for all time, being derived from the 'Poetic Genius'. The cultivation of the Poetic Genius is as essential to understanding the Bible as it is to scientific progress ('Seek and ye shall find'). Samuel Taylor Coleridge would garner much praise for saying more or less the same thing more than a generation later (*Biographia Literaria*, 1817)! Blake then sums up: 'The true Man is the source he being the Poetic Genius.'

Blake was quick to apply his conception of the 'Poetic Genius' when annotating another Swedenborgian pamphlet, *The Wisdom of Angels, concerning Divine Love and Divine Wisdom*, published in London in 1788. Where Swedenborg (translated by N Tucker) had written in 'point 12', 'The Negation of God constitutes Hell, and in the Christian World the Negation of the Lord's Divinity,' Blake has added: 'the Negation of the Poetic Genius', equating Jesus's 'Divinity' with the Poetic Genius.

The title of the second part of Blake's own tract of 1788 is a straight denial: *THERE is NO NATURAL RELIGION*. But what was Blake denying?

It has been supposed that the Article on Religion in the *Constitutions of the Free-masons* (1723) advocating that Masons adhere to 'that Religion in which all Men agree' refers to what had become known as 'Natural Religion', a religion in tune with nature, not super-nature, and not dependent on historical or scriptural revelation. The principles of Natural Religion were recapitulated as follows in 1730 in Matthew Tindal's *Christianity as Old as the Creation, or the Gospel a Republication of the religion of Nature:*

i)   belief in God
ii) worship of God
iii) doing what is for our own good or happiness
iv) promoting the common happiness

Natural Religion is transparent to human reason; nothing can be a truth of Natural Religion if it is mysterious or not demonstrable. John Toland's *Christianity not Mysterious* (1696) removed anything from Christianity's essence that was mysterious – that is, anything going beyond human reason. God's 'Word' was rational. English philosopher John Locke rejected mystery since it had no 'empirical' basis – that is, no knowledge derived from the five senses. According to Locke's *The Reasonableness of Christianity* (1695), problems deriving from religious diversity could be solved through reliance on reason. Locke adumbrated 'common notions' of religion that may sound familiar to us: belief in a supreme God; the necessity of worshipping him; a reminder of fundamental human duties; the need for repentance; and the doctrine of the afterlife.

Not surprisingly, Blake goes for the jugular, and the jugular is John Locke. He cleverly begins by taking Locke's own view as the preliminary 'Argument' of *THERE is NO NATURAL RELIGION:* 'Man has no notion of moral fitness but from Education. Naturally he is only a natural organ subject to Sense.' This is the fundamental view of many of today's 'behaviourists' and atheist biological theorists. Having had the thought, they have isolated evidence in support of their view; all this passes for 'science' in many quarters of the Western cultural establishment; for many it constitutes a belief system necessitating the labelling and condemnation of opponents as effective 'heretics' from orthodox science.

From Locke's premise, Blake deduces, with sound logic, that Man can only perceive through physical organs. He can, by using reason, only compare and judge what he has already perceived. So, if Man were limited to three senses, he could not deduce a fourth or fifth. If, as Locke maintained, Man possessed only 'organic perceptions', then Man, according to Blake, could only have 'organic thoughts'. Therefore, reason dictates that Man's desires must be naturally limited to his perceptions, because no one, according to Locke's argument, could desire what has not been perceived. Finally, dependent on organs of sense, Man's desires and perceptions must necessarily be limited to sense-objects.

Having stripped bare the argument of the materialist philosopher, Blake poses *his* Argument, based on experiment (experience) and observation.

'Man's perceptions are not bounded by organs of perception.' Man perceives more than sense (however acute) can discover. Reason, which is the 'ratio of all that we have already known', is not 'the same that it shall be when we know more'. Bound by past and current perceptions of knowledge, reason binds, blind to what it does not know.

Blake is now, I think, envisioning diagrams from Newton's *Principia* and the view, widely held by people who do not read very deeply, that Newton had somehow 'explained it all' and shown the universe *in toto* as a rational system reducible to mathematical formulae, agreeable to reason. 'The bounded,' writes Blake, 'is loathed by its possessor.' The same dull round *even of a universe* 'would soon become a mill with complicated wheels'. Blake declares that the Newtonian universe, after the first thrill, is DULL. Intrinsically empty, it grinds; it imprisons. Let's not get carried away with cosmic music and platitudes about the 'final frontier': this universe of science (in its raw state) is aesthetically attractive primarily to people whose income derives, or is hoped to derive, from studying or promoting it. That includes documentary TV producers and presenters – purveyors of the whole panoply whereby music, a dash of rhetoric about personal 'passion', 'wonder' and 'excitement' and dazzling graphics combine with a modicum of mathematical hypothesis to make modern 'science' programmes modes for persuading people that physics is always a 'positive' art that can redeem us gloriously from ignorance.

If Blake was alive today, I suspect he would think that science has had to be 'dressed up' to occupy our curiosity, while the stars shine or stop shining regardless of how we measure their measurable characteristics. Blake was not romantically mesmerized by the prospect of the stars, especially when he saw them in the mind-picture of Newton's universe. There, planetary paths constituted for Blake the 'dark Satanic mills'. Blake's dark Satanic mills were not mill-towns and funnels of black, industrial smoke, full of 'masses' on the verge of socialist salvation. He was thinking of the cycles and ellipses he could see at Joseph Johnson's in books of science: geometrical lines spinning round, reproduced as machines, with clock-like mechanisms that themselves would provide the models for industrial machinery, grinding men and women into their 'infernal machine'. He saw the 'mill-wheels' of the universe translated into the philosophy of mechanism which, combined with the technical practice of mechanics, would dominate 19th-century industrialism, scientific theory and social philosophy. But the mills are in the mind; they bound and bind the universe of reason, with despair the result: the disease of the West we have exported. Think of the mill wheels: great, round heavy stones, pummelling the grain into volatile flour, hour after hour, the cogs creaking slowly as the grain submits to its being crushed to powder. First the thought – then the reality. It is widely held today as a nostrum of learning that without Newton's work, the industrial revolution (wheels again) would not have occurred.

Reason, says Blake, reduces everything, and every one. If Man must live in a world where reason only rules, then to cry 'More! More!' would be the cry of a 'mistaken soul', for 'less than All cannot satisfy Man.' Blake knows that 'desire' far outstrips reason's capacity to satisfy it. Reason, bound by sense-experience, can only say that 'desire' is incapable of possessing what it wants. Reason promises despair: 'If any could desire what he is incapable of possessing, despair must be his eternal lot.' Blake, following Madame Guyon, knows in his heart that the true desire of the heart can be satisfied; he did not learn this through sense-perception, he did not deduce it from Reason; the object of Desire comes from the Poetic Genius which transcends Reason and is not subject to sense-perception; rather, sense-perception reaches its height when in service of Poetic Genius. In prosaic terms, if we apply Blake's thought to our experience of what he considered the world's blindness, the consumer society consumes us, and cannot satisfy true desire, only attempt to smother it. Finite goods will not satisfy the true Man: 'The desire of Man being Infinite the possession is Infinite and himself Infinite.' We are not numbers to be digitized for government convenience.

Blake concludes that the philosophic and experimental enterprises absolutely need the 'Poetic or Prophetic character', or else they 'would soon be at the ratio of all things & stand still, unable to do other than repeat the same dull round over again.'

Having properly laid out his postulates, arguments and conclusion, like a good schoolman, Blake expresses the 'Application', and it ought to astonish: 'He who sees the Infinite in all things sees God. He who sees the Ratio only sees himself only. Therefore God becomes as we are, that we may be as he is'.

Blake was now engaged in 'Mental Fight' with the emerging intellectual culture of materialism, with only the tools of his trade to fight with.

ELEVEN

The Wisdom of Angels

1788–1790

In January 1788, commander Arthur Phillip, having found Australia's Botany Bay uninhabitable, led a British convoy into 'Sydney Cove', carrying more than 700 convicts, 160 of them women. The original roster included 88-year-old rag dealer Dorothy Handland and nine-year-old chimney sweep John Hudson. Phillip reported the future Port Jackson as the finest harbour in the world, but Aborigines failed to see the attraction, or understood it too well, shouting at the disembarking officers, marines and convicts: 'Warra! Warra!', or 'Go Away!' But the British had come to stay.

Meanwhile, reports from Britain's Embassy in Paris warned that a poverty crisis in France made revolt inevitable. Revolt would kindle revolution. In London, Blake, eager for work, continued to 'hang out' with Joseph Johnson's friend, Fuseli. Johnson and Fuseli were happy to provide work when opportunity arose.

Such opportunity came in spring 1788 when Fuseli delivered to Johnson his own translation of a short work by a fellow Swiss, the Rev. Johann Caspar Lavater (1741–1801). Lavater's *Aphorisms on Man* was intended as a 'taster' for his four-volume *Essays on Physiognomy* (first volume 1789), which would become a massive success and establish Lavater's reputation across Europe. Blake executed a fine engraving of Lavater, from Lavater's own drawing, for Johnson, who sold it as a print. For the *Essays on Physiognomy*, Blake engraved a full-page portrait of Democritus, after Rubens – that must have been a task! – and three smaller engravings, after Fuseli.

The Greek rubric of Lavater's *Aphorisms* appealed greatly to Blake: *Gnōthi seauton*: 'Know thyself', an instruction associated with the Oracle of

Delphi and a commonplace of Gnostic-type traditions. In Blake's engraved frontispiece, after Fuseli, the Greek is inscribed on a tablet held up by a cherub. Looking up to the cherub is a seated youth with books and an hourglass. While Blake found Lavater's knowledge of physiognomy instructive (Blake became convinced that the broadness of his forehead above his eyes made him inescapably a 'republican'!), he was more excited by the *Aphorisms*. Copious illuminating annotations added by Blake suggest that it was Lavater's work that inspired him to assemble a phalanx of his own penetrating aphoristic wisdom for his astonishing tract *The Marriage of Heaven and Hell* (1790–93).

When Blake read Lavater's 'The object of your love is your God,' he noted: 'This should be written in gold letters on our temples.' Characteristically, Blake underlined Lavater's encouragement: 'Who in the same given time can produce more than any others, has VIGOUR; who can produce more and better, has TALENTS; *who can produce what none else can, has GENIUS.*'

Blake knew himself.

Blake called the aphorism 'Excellent' that asserted: 'Who, under pressing temptations to lie, adheres to truth, nor to the profane betrays aught of a sacred trust, is near the summit of wisdom and virtue.' Responding to Lavater's conviction that 'Who seeks those that are greater than himself, their greatness enjoys, and forgets his greatest qualities in their greater ones, is already truly great,' Blake added: 'I hope I do not flatter myself that this is pleasant to me.'

Lavater: 'Avoid, like a serpent, him who writes impertinently, yet speaks politely.' Blake: 'a dog get a stick to him.' Lavater: 'He, who is the master of the fittest moment to crush his enemy, and magnanimously neglects it, is born to be a conqueror.' Blake: 'this was old George the second' (showing that Blake had good things to say about kings, as well as bad, as good and bad kings there must be, likewise folk).

Space inhibits inclusion of the many nuggets of wisdom to be found in Blake's silent, but not uncritical, dialogue with Lavater, though exception must be made for some of Blake's one-line comments, since they reveal so much about his philosophy, courage and character: 'I hate scarce smiles I love laughing'; 'damn Sneerers'; 'I hate crawlers'; 'why should honesty fear a knave[?]'; 'I cannot love my enemy for my enemy is not a man but beast & devil if I have any. I can love him as a beast & wish to beat him'; 'no man was ever truly superstitious who was not truly religious as far as he knew [...] True superstition is ignorant honesty & this is beloved of god & man'; 'and consider that *love is life*'; 'pity the jealous'; 'hate the sneerer'; 'True Christian philosophy'; 'Noble But Mark Active Evil is better than Passive Good'; 'O that men would seek immortal moments O that men would converse with God'; 'Great ends never look at means but produce them spontaneously'; 'Superstition has been long a bug bear by reason of its being united with hypocrisy. but let them be fairly separated & then superstition will be honest feeling & God who loves all honest men. will lead the poor enthusiast in the paths of holiness'; 'I seldom carry money in my pockets they are generally full of paper'; 'It is the God of *all* that is our companion & friend, for our God himself says, you are my brother my sister & my mother; and St John. Whoso dwelleth in love dwelleth in God & God in him [I John 4:16]. & such an one cannot judge of any but in love. & his feelings will be attractions or repulses [...] God is in the lowest effects as well as in the highest causes for he is become a worm that he may nourish the weak   For let it be remembered that creation is. God descending according to the weakness of man for our Lord is the word of God & every thing on earth is the word of God & in its essence is God'.

On 12 May, print-seller John Raphael Smith commissioned two plates from Blake: 'The Industrious Cottager' and 'the Idle Laundress', after the very popular, and dissolute, countryman, pig and poultry painter George Morland; they were sold at six shillings a piece.

Three weeks later, provincial parliaments in France revolted against judicial reforms imposed on 1 May by Lord Chancellor Guillaume Chrétien de Lamoignon. Lamoignon's transfer of legislative powers from Parliament to two new bodies incensed a restless bourgeoisie. Street fighting broke out in Grenoble on 7 June as royal troops attempted to disperse a meeting of magistrates opposing the reforms.

Innovative legislation was better received on 21 June when a new US constitution received ratification from nine states. The United States would in due course place executive power in the person of an elected president. Louis XVI would pay dearly for supporting a revolution that had severed a monarch from a rebellious territory. Blake was right: America stood as 'prophecy' for France's destiny.

On 6 July, in Paris's poorest districts, unrest flared up, quelled only when

10,000 troops were deployed. On 19 July, prices plummeted on the Paris Stock Exchange. To allay the crisis, Louis XVI ordered a convening of the Estates General for 1 May 1789 and on 25 August recalled Geneva-born Protestant banker, Jacques Necker, disgraced in 1783, to replace finance minister Loménie de Brienne. Riots followed the announcement, and eight people died. On 23 September, the King abandoned judicial reforms; traditional parliamentary roles were restored. A triumphant parliament reopened for the business of changing the nation the next day.

Across the English Channel, while utilitarian theorist Jeremy Bentham prepared his Priestley-inspired *Introduction to the Principles of Morals and Legislation* for publication in 1789, Catherine Blake's sister Sarah Boutcher moved from Battersea to St Bride's parish, in the City, where the Rev. John Pridden married her to Henry Banes on 16 December. Banes would lease to the Blakes their last home at Fountain Court.

The New Jerusalem Church

On 7 December 1788, 500 letters were circulated from Swedenborgian activists in London, inviting all 'who are desirous of rejecting, and separating themselves from the old Church, or the present established Churches [...] and of fully embracing the Heavenly Doctrines of the New Jerusalem' to attend a conference to be held in Eastcheap on 13–17 April, 1789.[1] Only about 20 Swedenborg readers replied.

While this tumult engaged William and Catherine Blake's serious attention, the government of the country hung in the balance as the King suffered three months of madness for which no doctor, of those consulted, had a cure (it is now generally accepted that he was suffering from cerebral symptoms of porphyria). Legislation for the Prince of Wales's regency was framed as Pitt manoeuvered against the Foxites and *vice versa* and the House of Commons shook with anticipation; the country at large knew for sure only that the King was indisposed. One wonders, however, whether the madness was contagious.

On 13 January 1789, Dr Richard Chandler wrote to the Rev. Ralph Churton from Rolle en Suisse by Lake Geneva, where gathered an enclave of liberal intelligentsia, playing host, at the time, to the Prince of Wales.

The poor King [George III] is, however, sincerely and universally lamented; and the conduct of his Son. *here* by the insensibility it demonstrates to the misfortune of so worthy a father is every where mentioned with indignation. I shall only relate, that while the snow was on the ground, he [the Prince of Wales] went from Geneva to Lausanne & back again in a *traineau* [sleigh], accompanied by a number of English Bucks, in a day, & killed five horses, for a wager of Twenty Pounds. We hope here for a Regency with many limitations. Heaven preserve & bless my Country, I say.[2]

Heaven's guidance was at that moment sought by Blake from a pamphlet by Swedenborg: *Divine Love and Divine Wisdom* (1788). Drawing conclusions from it conforming to his own outlook, Blake realized that Swedenborg's indebtedness to Jacob Böhme matched his own, especially with regard to mystical language using symbolic geometry of the 'centre and circumference' in relation to the heart. In 'point 69', Swedenborg confirmed Blake's belief in the ability of the mind to transcend the sphere of reason.

> But he who knows how to elevate his Mind above the Ideas of Thought which are derived from Space and Time, such a Man passes from Darkness to Light, and becomes wise in Things spiritual and Divine [...] and then by Virtue of that Light he shakes off the Darkness of natural Light, and removes its Fallacies from the Center to the Circumference.

Blake's response to this theme would inform his famous design *The Ancient of Days*, who bounds the universe with the compasses of his hand. Blake was apparently unaware that Swedenborg's categories for expressing Man's relation to spiritual illumination beyond Reason, beyond the comprehension of the 'Natural Man', almost certainly derived from passages in the Third Degree 'Charge' of Freemasonry. Such becomes explicit in Swedenborg's Point 237:

> These three Degrees of Altitude are named Natural, Spiritual and Celestial [...] Man, at his Birth, first comes into the natural Degree ['Entered Apprentice'], and this increases in him by Continuity according to the Sciences, and according to the Understanding acquired

by them ['Fellow Craft' or 2nd Degree], to the Summit of Understanding which is called Rational [Master Mason] ...

Blake fails to see, or chooses to ignore, the Masonic convention implied, and his annotation fulminates with Zinzendorfian fervour against unfeeling reason:

Study Sciences till you are blind
Study intellectuals till you are cold
Yet Science cannot teach intellect
Much less can intellect teach Affection
How foolish then it is to assert that Man is born in only one degree when that one degree is reception of the 3 degrees. two of which he must destroy or close up or they will descend, if he closes up the two superior then he is not truly in the 3rd but descends out of it into meer Nature or Hell

The Masonic Third Degree Charge apparently behind Swedenborg's point reads as follows:

Let me now beg you to observe that the Light of a Master Mason is darkness visible, serving only to express that gloom which rests on the prospect of futurity. It is that mysterious veil which the eye of human reason cannot penetrate, unless assisted by that Light which is from above. Yet, even by this glimmering ray, you may perceive that you stand on the very bottom of the grave into which you have figuratively descended, and which, when this transitory life shall have passed away, will again receive you into its cold bosom.[3]

The parity of ideas here could serve to prove either that Blake was, or was not, a Freemason; certainly as a Swedenborg reader he would have found himself in the company of Masons, and some of a highly 'illuminist' hew. Blake's apparently equating the 'descent' into 'meer Nature or Hell' with the symbolic 'grave' of the Third Degree might suggest either knowledge of Freemasonry or coincidence of idea. (There is a faint echo here of Thel's entering a grave until, realizing her perilous state, she shrieks and flees for the Vale of Har; see p.117.)

Blake's annotations certainly show that Blake was not Swedenborg's uncritical acolyte. Masons learn that 'At the centre of the Circle a Master Mason cannot err.' Where the 'Centre' refers to the Heart, as in Böhme, Blake would doubtless concur with the basic idea, if not entirely with the simplistic, geometrical image. He knew from the William Law edition of Böhme's works that the issue of God's communication with the Heart was more sophisticated than that, as Dionysius Freher's graphic, theosophical illustrations indicated to Blake's delight (*The Works of Jacob Behmen,* 4 vols, 1764–1781).

Blake seizes on Swedenborg's essential points where they agree with his own thoughts. He is particularly fond of the contention that 'the natural Man can elevate his Understanding to superior Light as far as he desires it, but he who is principled in Evils and thence in Things false, does not elevate it higher than to the superior Region of his natural Mind ...' Here we have the doctrine of highest *Desire* combined with a clear distinction between the mind of the natural man and the mind of the spiritual man. This critical distinction is familiar to kabbalists as that between *ruach*, or mind of the ratio of carnal things, and *neschamah*, the mind that receives rays from *above* the contraries inherent to Nature. In short: Blake distinguishes, in line with 'gnostic' traditions, rational mind flooded with its own knowledge, and spiritual mind, watered with Poetic Genius: the Neo-Platonic and Hermetic '*nous*'.

When Swedenborg declares that 'the Whole of Charity and Faith is in Works', Blake leaps to the conclusion: 'The Whole of the New Church is in the Active Life & not in Ceremonies at all.' This conclusion is vital to understanding Blake's relation to the growing clamour for a Swedenborgian Church of the New Jerusalem. He does not want a sect with ceremonies. He wants a dynamic, spiritual body that is realized through the way one lives, bringing the Light forth into the world by creative atonement and attunement to divine levels of consciousness: an idea akin to the Schwenckfeldian Church of the Spirit – not of wood or stone – and to the Rosicrucian 'Invisible Brotherhood' that operates unseen by the world, insofar as its meeting place is 'the House of the Holy Spirit' (that is, the Spirit itself) which the carnal mind of the world cannot see.

As far as outward forms went, Blake was mostly indifferent. Better the Church of England, which at least began, in the primitive sense, with Jesus and was moulded to these shores and their history, than sects full of their differences. Blake would not cease from Mental Fight until Jerusalem was built in England's green and pleasant land. That's what the 'hymn' is actually saying: build a spiritual civilization, a spiritual body, a City 'that is also a Woman', the Bride of Albion, in tune with the Light secreted in the cosmos and open to the Light beyond it, so God would be us, and we would be God, incarnating and discarnating the heart and mind of the Poetic Genius.

And all, one might think, would be well. However, the Blakes became involved with the April 1789 Eastcheap Conference. This can hardly have been their first attendance at a Swedenborgian gathering. The couple would have almost certainly been aware of a Swedenborgian circle centred on the home of Rev. Jacob Duché. Duché had quit America in 1777, having resigned from the chaplaincy to the Continental Congress after suggesting to Washington that 'Independency' had become an idol for which he (Washington) was prepared to kill. The Bishop of London appointed Duché chaplain at the Female Orphan Asylum in Lambeth.

For 14 years, Duché held a Swedenborgian study group at Lambeth on Sunday evenings, encouraging the idea, or experience, of an 'Internal Millennium'[4] visible to the internal eye, illuminated from above. This conception explains Blake's belief that when one abstained from error and chose truth, a 'last judgement' passed upon the penitent: true judgement was forgiveness.

Duché's circle included printer of Swedenborgian pamphlets Robert Hindmarsh, engraver William Sharp, painters Philip de Loutherbourg and Richard Cosway, Dr Benedict Chastanier – formerly of Dom Pernety's Illuminist and High Grade Masonic 'Avignon Society' – and sculptor John Flaxman. Hindmarsh's father, James, was chosen by lots to be the Swedenborgians' first minister. It may have been Blake's fellow engraver Sharp who introduced him to the circle.

From this circle emerged a 'Theosophical Society' in 1783 and, five years later, the first New Church chapel in Great Eastcheap, London, whose first General Conference took place at a public house in April 1789, attended by some 70 persons, including William and Catherine Blake.

What Blake might have known about the Abbé Pernety's 'Illuminists of Avignon' group is unknown to us. There is no doubt, however, that Blake's thought was touched by a millennial, revolutionary spiritual fervour akin in some aspects to that which flourished at Avignon after Pernety had translated Swedenborg's *Heaven and Hell* into French in 1782. While the Avignon Illuminists were regarded as extreme by members of Duché's circle – partly on account of illuminist magical rites and revolutionary potential – Blake's personal position regarding them is unknown. One man who had access to the group – he had supplied biographical details on Swedenborg to Pernety – would have an effect on Blake's eventual attitudes to Swedenborgianism.

Augustus Nordenskjöld (1754–1792), a member of the Swedish Academy of Sciences and a keen reader of fellow mining expert Swedenborg, investigated manuscripts left to the Swedish Academy on Swedenborg's death in 1772, in particular Swedenborg's peculiar *Spiritual Diary*, and his writings on 'Conjugial Love', or sex in marriage. Augustus's brother Carl brought examples of his brother's copies of Swedenborg's manuscripts to Benedict Chastanier in London in 1783. More material arrived in London in 1788 in the hands of Carl Wadström, who that year would be baptised into the New Church.

Wadström and Augustus Nordenskjöld planned a free community at Sierra Leone on Swedenborgian lines, while Wadström co-operated with Thomas Clarkson, William Wilberforce and Granville Sharp in the fight against slavery. A supporter of the Great Eastcheap society, Augustus Nordenskjöld would receive New Church baptism in 1789.

John Augustus Tulk (1756–1845), the Theosophical Society's first chairman, supported the idea of a paper to be signed by all who attended the great Eastcheap Conference as a prerequisite to attending on 13 April 1789. As a result, William and Catherine Blake put their names to this statement:

> We whose names are hereunto subscribed, do each of us approve of the Theological Writings of Emanuel Swedenborg, believing that the Doctrines contained therein are genuine Truths, revealed from Heaven, and that the New Jerusalem Church ought to be established, distinct and separate from the Old Church.[5]

The wording does not necessarily indicate a break with pre-existing Churches, nor does it condemn them, but it might portend such a break. Thirty-two resolutions allegedly passed at the Conference were copied into a 'Minute

Book', preserved at New Church College, Woodford Green, Essex. If the copy is accurate, the resolutions, apparently accepted unanimously, include radical positions.

According to No. 4, 'The Old Church, which means all other churches, is dead.' No. 7: 'While the Old Church lasts, Heaven cannot come to man.' No. 9: 'The idea of a three-person Trinity is dangerous.' No. 12: 'Swedenborgians must separate from the Old Church.' No. 13: 'They should have no connexion with other churches.' No. 26: 'True Christianity exists only in the New Church.' No. 29: 'Swedenborgians must exhibit charity towards the Old Church.' These statements are quite different from the admission manifesto.

We cannot be sure if these, and the rest, were the precise resolutions adopted in April 1789 by everybody; secondly, we do not know if Blake adhered to any of them, even at the time. In fact, the very next month saw a serious split within the new body of Swedenborgians. In May the society withdrew itself from Robert Hindmarsh, Carl Wadström, Augustus Nordenskjöld and three other members. Pages of the Minute Book dealing with events were torn out. Hindmarsh kept silence on the subject in his *Rise and Progress of the New Jerusalem Church in England, America and other parts*, penned in the 1820s.

The trouble appears to have lain principally in Nordenskjöld's wishing to promote and establish Swedenborg's doctrines regarding 'conjugial love' (we would say 'conjugal') and concubinage, found in manuscripts brought from Sweden. What seemed quite acceptable to some forward-looking, Masonic Scandinavians did not register with traditional English Churchmanship – even, or especially, among Methodists. The situation would reach a climax with the publication of controversial passages in 1790, whereafter Blake became hostile towards Swedenborg.

Two days after mutineers took HMS *Bounty* from the command of Captain Bligh on 28 April 1789, George Washington became the United States' first President, having accepted the Constitution the previous September. On 5 May, Louis XVI formally opened the Estates General. On 17 June the French Estates General changed its name to the National Assembly. King Louis closed its Chamber on 20 June but caved in a week later and re-opened it.

On 11 July, newly reinstated finance minister Jacques Necker was dismissed for not attending the King's speech to the Estates General. Necker's dismissal angered Frenchmen everywhere who hoped he would reform the government. Three days later, a Paris mob stormed the Bastille prison, thinking Louis was about to invade Paris with an army. The next day, the electors of Paris established a 'Commune' led by Bailly, the elected mayor of Paris, and the liberal Marquis de Lafayette, the 'Hero of Two Worlds' (the other being America). As head of the National Guard, Lafayette drafted a 'Declaration of the Rights of Man and of the Citizen'.

Necker was recalled by Louis on 16 July but would not co-operate with Lafayette, who tried to maintain order. Slowly Necker lost control of the situation. On 18 July, Camille Desmoulins published the Revolution's first republican manifesto: *La France Libre*.

These events Blake would refer to directly in his poem, 'The French Revolution' (probably written in 1791). In all the excitement, 31-year-old Blake had been busy writing some of his best poetry. His *Songs of Innocence* he would date in printed versions to 1789, even though copies of the illuminated print were not apparently available until 1794.

Blake's manuscript poem 'Tiriel' also appears as a product of 1789. Blake executed a dozen drawings to illustrate the story of a cruel, blind, Urizen-like king who loses his wife and curses his sons (it might even be a covert satire on King George's sickness and his bad relations with his sons). As in Blake's notes for Boyd's *Dante* of 1785, we see that the villain is the most interesting character. Tiriel has a 'silver voice' and is mutable to a degree. The fact that the illustrations and text remained separate suggests Blake might have put the project aside when he developed his new illuminated etching process, to be employed on *Songs of Innocence* and his subsequent poems and prophecies.

It is notable that in his dark wanderings Tiriel is led to the 'vales of Har', whither Thel herself fled after shrieking in the grave of earth (see p.117). The vales of Har seem to be a kind of Eden, a paradise before a Fall. Apparently ageless, Har and Heva are like child versions of Adam and Eve. Their time is absorbed in delightful play, and they find Tiriel frightening.

Like Thel, Tiriel is taken through a series of meetings with various figures whose interchange illuminates aspects of his fatal character. There is something in this of Masonic ritual where Candidates in various degrees are guided to specific points in the Lodge room layout, where questions are put and determinative answers are given – sojourns on a path to self-knowledge.

Blake seems to be engaged in a private war with patriarchal images:

The father forms a whip to rouze the sluggish senses to act
And scourges off all youthful fancies from the newborn man
Then walks the weak infant in sorrow compelld to number footsteps
Upon the sand. &c

The '&c' indicates either the poem was unfinished or the content of this section was slanderous, or both.

In the end, the 'mistaken father of a lawless race' whose 'voice is past' dies 'in awful death' at the feet of Har and Heva. The name Tiriel suggests tyranny and a tyrannical god (Hebrew 'el' = 'god' or 'lord').

In Agrippa's *Three Books of Occult Philosophy*, Tiriel is the name given to the 'intelligence' of Mercury, traditionally associated with cold, slippery, silver things. Blake seems to be anticipating tyranny's end. Its sin: egocentricity and heartlessness. Current events may well have stimulated this expectation. In Gillray's searing, vicious cartoons, French finance minister Necker was identified with freedom; British Prime Minister Pitt with slavery.

On 14 June 1789, set adrift by Fletcher Christian's rebellious mutineers sated with Tahitian paradise and longing to return to free lusts, 'tyrant' Captain Bligh of HMS *Bounty* reached Timor, near Java, after an incredible open-boat voyage of 3,500 miles. God might favour alleged 'tyrants' yet.

On 27 July in New York City, Thomas Jefferson became head of the department of Foreign Affairs, the United States' first executive agency, while a week later, the French Constituent Assembly (another new executive) abolished privileges of nobility. This signal act destroyed at a stroke the social structure of the *Ançien Régime*. On 26 August, inspired by the US Declaration of Independence and Rousseau's works, the Assembly approved the Declaration of the Rights of Man.

The Rights of Man would not be achieved without depriving thousands of their rights. On 10 October, Paris Deputy Joseph Guillotin announced that the most humane mode of execution was a single blow of a blade to decapitate; it was rational, but bloody. On 2 November, all church property was nationalized, or stolen, depending which side of the blade you were on.

In Sierra Leone, the 'Province of Freedom' supported by anti-slavery campaigners in London, and some leading Swedenborgians, was destroyed by local Koya Temne tribal leader 'King Jimmy', unhappy with the agreement struck with the idealistic settlers by his predecessor.

In the flush of revolutionary excitement, fuelled by spiritual millenarianism, William Blake took to wearing the red 'Phrygian' cap of the French revolutionaries in the streets.

His new poems looked like verses for children, but they were rather for a childlike mentality that accepted wholeheartedly the wind of change, the opening of the cage, the free flow of energy near and far, the brotherhood of all beings in God. 'How can the bird that is born for joy sit in a cage and sing?' asked the innocent poet. The Universe unbounded was Blake's Church and there was forgiveness for all.

Thomas Taylor's *Dissertation on the Eleusinian and Bacchic Mysteries* was newly available to Blake in 1790. Kathleen Raine believed he consulted Taylor's account of the Eleusinian Mysteries for two poems written around this period, gathered in 1794 into his *Songs of Experience*: 'The Little Girl Lost' and 'The Little Girl Found'.

According to Greek mythology, the Mysteries of Eleusis derived from Pluto's abduction of Persephone, daughter of Ceres, the corn goddess. The story relates how Persephone was gathering flowers (like 'Har and Heva' in 'Tiriel') when Pluto abducts her to a cavern across a sea, a place of departed spirits. After wandering the world in search of her daughter, Ceres finds her at last at Eleusis. At Eleusis, Ceres teaches the corn mysteries. Taylor wrote in his Dissertation: 'The Lesser Mysteries were designed by the ancient theologists, their founders, to signify occultly the condition of the unpurified soul invested with an earthy body, and enveloped in a material and physical nature.' Pluto is the dark villain. He stands for the world – the world of generation in which Blake's little girl, Lyca, is lost. Entering that world, Ceres carries two torches to light her way: one signifying reason, the other, intuition.

There are several interweaving layers to the poem. On the one hand, there is a prophecy of a world waking up:

In futurity
I prophetic see,
That the earth from sleep,
(Grave the sentence deep)

Shall arise and seek
For her maker meek:
And the desart wild
Become a garden mild.

So opens 'The Little Girl Lost', and we see the pun on sleep, and the 'Grave' that is deep like a prison 'sentence' (cf the grave from which the Mason is raised in the Third Degree). The higher intellect (the mother) must follow the soul in her 'slender dress' (the flesh) in the descent into the world, because mind must experience the tangible world to discover the essential mystery that Hermes revealed as 'That which is above is like that which is below, to work the miracle of the One Thing'. Blake knows from Böhme that Heaven and Hell are born together, of one God.

If you read the poems you soon find elements that don't make sense without the realization that the fatal thing for Lyca to do, in her parents' eyes, is to 'sleep': to become unconscious of her soul and become lost in the reflective body. The lion, who guards the sacred cavern in Mithraic temples, is shown to care for Lyca in her sorrowful sojourn on Earth – the saviour Mithra, incidentally, also wore the Phrygian cap.

When the world wakes up from material sleep, it will see that the empty universe of reason, the 'desart wild', will become 'a garden mild'. Blake looked to a revolutionary change in consciousness, and he must have hoped that the process would be hastened by events on earth that looked wild in the first instance, but would, he believed, reveal the true spiritual freedom of Man, as the fruit of heaven and hell's marriage became manifest. The New Age was unfolding.

Come the crisis, come the man. On 21 February 1790, Dr Guillotin took his ideas of humane killing a step further. His painless-as-possible decapitation machine was laid out in detail. With it, he thought, you could still believe in the brotherhood of Man while killing the ones that got in the way: it was nothing personal. Records survive of more than 13,000 guillotinings during the Revolution, while estimates of the humane device's victims run from 20,000 to 40,000. Of those that escaped its rational horror, about 32,000 *émigres* came to England, and about 130,000 went elsewhere.

After the guillotine: *zyklon B.*

Sex and God

In London, meanwhile, among the Swedenborgians, there was a mighty argument about Sex.

In February 1790, the second issue of *The New Jerusalem Magazine* appeared, funded by John Augustus Tulk. It included a first monthly instalment from Swedenborg's *De Conjugio.* Here are some of the points made by Swedenborg:

> To love the consort is to do good before the Lord, because this is chastity itself; and the Church itself is called virgin and daughter, as the daughter and the virgin of Zion and Jerusalem. Passages [from the Bible] may be quoted.

> Conjugial love has communication with heaven, and the organs of generation have correspondence with the third heaven; especially the womb ...

> Even intercourse from conjugial love communicates.

> That love arises from the Lord's influx alone through the third heaven. The third heaven is the conjugial of heaven; thus marriages are held as most holy in heaven; and adulteries profane.

> Conjugial love increases in potency and effect to eternity, insomuch that it is love as to all power and effect, thence is the life of their souls; but with adulteries love decreases as to power and effect, even so that it becomes impotence and a stock, and scarce of any life.
> It is enough to know that love truly conjugial has immediate communication with the third heaven, and also that love itself with its celestial delight is there preserved in all its variety, and also its acts, such as kisses, embraces, and many other things which delight that heaven,

for that heaven is in the communication of good affections, when the spiritual heaven is in the communication of the thoughts of truth; hence it is evident that filthy affections and thoughts altogether close both heavens.

Protests arose that further publication would open the floodgates of immorality, especially when people realized that when Swedenborg referred to the 'consort', he did not necessarily mean the husband or wife. Following the account of Abraham in the Book of Genesis, and Abraham's taking of Hagar as a concubine when his wife Sarai was barren, Swedenborg stated that a man could, in such instance, take a concubine on condition that he refrained from relations with his wife afterwards (a man was not to have his cake and eat it). The suggestion that women might be held in common for the needs of men violated the sanctity and security of marriage.

But perhaps what was most shocking was simply the idea that heaven kept such a close watch on the sexual life of believers. This would not have surprised Moravians so much, but it certainly upset Anglicans and Methodists, or any traditionally raised Christians. Swedenborg's doctrine of correspondences allowed for the idea that in the context of conjugal love, sexual activity, *as spiritual activity*, could actually be *felt* in heaven. Most Christians had been raised to believe sexuality was a condition of life on earth and its occurrence in marriage was the sole thing that saved sex from taint of sin; and even then, right intention was important. What had heaven to do with such things?

The crisis appears to have put Blake and his wife in a quandary. Catherine was apparently barren. Ten years they had been married, and no children.

There were other implications. Extracts from Swedenborg's 'Spiritual Diary' suggested that the Swedish seer had absorbed ideas from esoteric Jewish circles that states of vision were related to 'virile potency'. That is to say, with the correspondence of sexual organs to the third heaven, there was the implication that sacred conjunctions between devout partners could make spiritual communication with celestial visions possible.

Perhaps 'virile potency' was actually vital to visionary experiences, or an inescapable adjunct. It should be said that while Swedenborg may have seen sexual arousal in relation to visionary powers that could culminate in an ecstatic 'marriage within the mind', for him these things pertained to heavenly

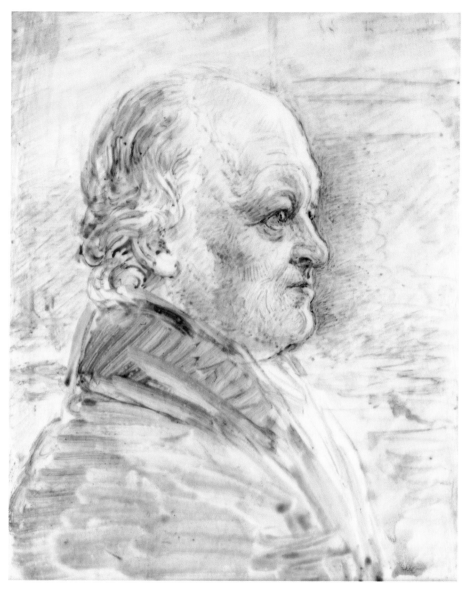

Above: Miniature of William Blake by John Linnell; watercolour on ivory, 1821. (COURTESY OF THE FITZWILLIAM MUSEUM, CAMBRIDGE)

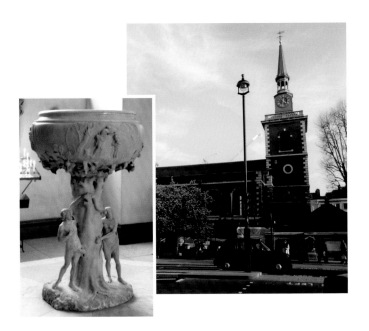

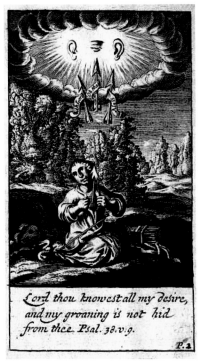

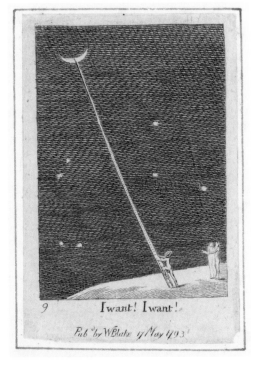

Top: St James's, Piccadilly: here Blake was baptized in 1757. Grinling Gibbons's font depicts the Tree of Knowledge of good and evil. (PHOTOS: PHILIP WILKINSON) **Bottom left:** The *Arrows of Desire*: seen in Herman Hugo's devotional emblem-book, *Pious Desires* (English version, 1690). Arrows from the heart go straight to God. (AUTHOR'S COLLECTION) **Bottom right:** A new emblem for Desire: Blake's 1793 etching 'I want! I want!' from *For Children: The Gates of Paradise*. (COURTESY OF THE FITZWILLIAM MUSEUM, CAMBRIDGE)

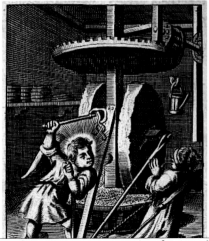

I suppose the World is called a Mill, because it is turn'd about on the Wheels of Time, and grinds and crushes those that most admire it.

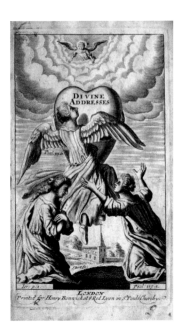

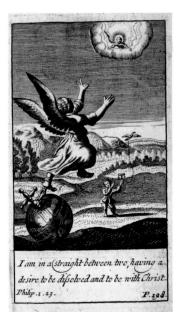

I am in a straight between two, having a desire to be dissolved and to be with Christ.
Philip.1.23. P.198.

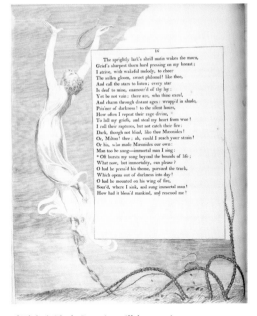

Top left: Here is the origin of Blake's 'dark Satanic mills' – not in industrial landscapes but in Hugo's *Pia Desiderea* ('Pious Desires'), English version 1690: imparted to Blake's mother by Moravian preacher, John Cennick. (AUTHOR'S COLLECTION) **Top right:** *PIA DESIDERIA* or *Divine Addresses*, translated by Edmund Arwaker (1690) with 47 copper plates by Boëce van Bolsvert. (AUTHOR'S COLLECTION)
Bottom left: Engraved emblem from *PIA DESIDERIA* (1690): the Soul chained to earth. (AUTHOR'S COLLECTION) **Bottom right:** Blake's engraving of a yearning, chained Soul: original style, traditional symbolism; from Edward Young's *Night Thoughts* (1797). (BIBLIOTHECA PHILOSOPHICA HERMETICA, WWW.RITMANLIBRARY.NL)

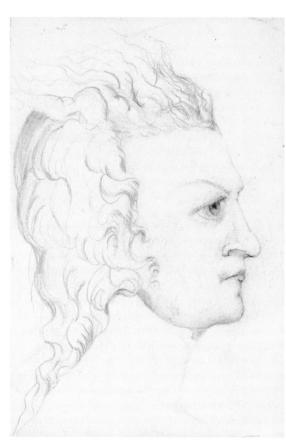

Left: Catherine drew the portrait of her husband as she remembered him at the time they met.
(COURTESY OF THE FITZWILLIAM MUSEUM, CAMBRIDGE)

Bottom left: On 18 August 1782, Blake married Catherine Sophia Boucher at St Mary's, Battersea.
(PHOTO: PHILIP WILKINSON)

Bottom right: *Joseph of Arimathea*, inspired by Michelangelo and the British Druids of Stukeley's *Stonehenge*. Blake's engraving is dated 1773 when he was apprenticed to James Basire.
(COURTESY OF THE FITZWILLIAM MUSEUM, CAMBRIDGE)

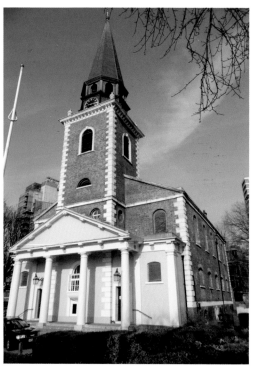

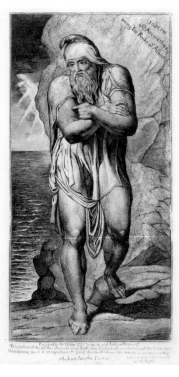

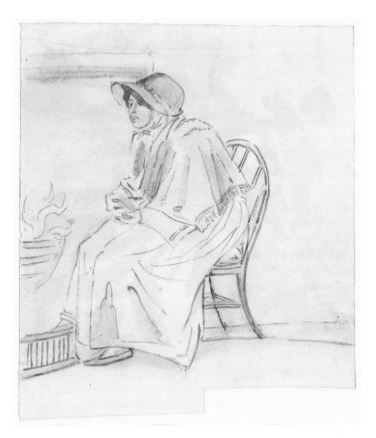

Above: *Catherine Blake,* by George Cumberland; point of the brush, blue wash over black chalk on paper: the only image of Mrs Blake as a young woman. (COURTESY OF THE FITZWILLIAM MUSEUM, CAMBRIDGE) **Bottom left:** 17 South Molton Street, W1, where the Blakes lived on the first floor, 1803–21. **Bottom right:** Plaque commemorating Blake's residence at the address. (PHOTOS: PHILIP WILKINSON)

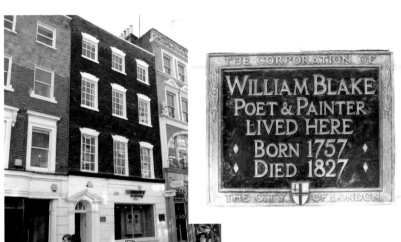

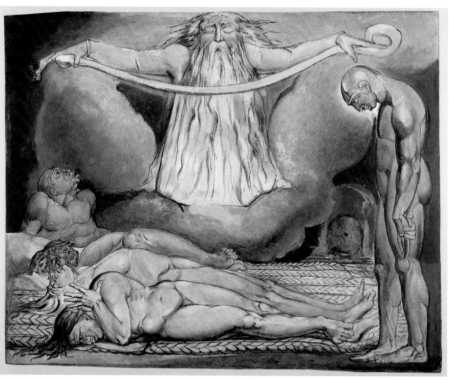

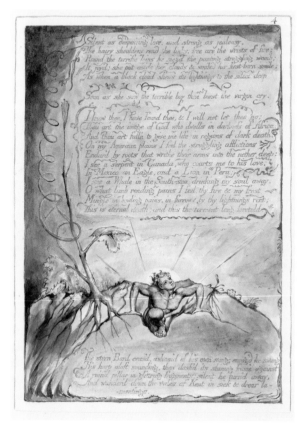

Above: *The Lazar House* print by Blake (Lambeth, 1795): chalk, ink and watercolour. From John Milton's *Paradise Lost* (1667): Adam witnesses the darts of death sent upon the dying. A 'lazar house' was originally a house of lepers, later a hospital for the incurably sick. For Blake, it is an image of the world ruled by the blind pretender-god, *URIZEN*, whom we see with the scroll of Law before him, accusing all. (COURTESY OF THE FITZWILLIAM MUSEUM, CAMBRIDGE)

Left: *Preludium II America: A Prophecy* (plate 4; dated 1793; executed *circa* 1820-25: relief etching print, watercolour). *ORC*, "the terrible boy", nemesis of Urizen, Child of Freedom and Rebellion, emerges from the earth like a revolutionary Superman, his presence felt on the "American plains". (COURTESY OF THE FITZWILLIAM MUSEUM, CAMBRIDGE)

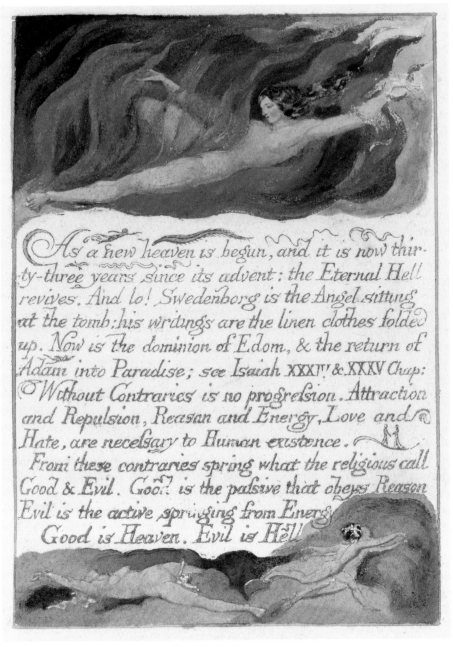

As a new heaven is begun, and it is now thir-
ty-three years since its advent: the Eternal Hell
revives. And lo! Swedenborg is the Angel sitting
at the tomb; his writings are the linen clothes folded
up. Now is the dominion of Edom, & the return of
Adam into Paradise; see Isaiah XXXIV & XXXV Chap:
Without Contraries is no progression. Attraction
and Repulsion, Reason and Energy, Love and
Hate, are necesary to Human existence.
    From these contraries spring what the religious call
Good & Evil. Good is the passive that obeys Reason
Evil is the active springing from Energy
    Good is Heaven. Evil is Hell

Above: From Blake's *The Marriage of Heaven and Hell* (1790); relief
etching, print with watercolour. The New Age will be attended by 'an
improvement in sensual enjoyment': 'Now is the dominion of Edom'.
Serpentine flames rise from the genitalia and the revived body: 'a
portion of Soul discerned by the five Senses, the chief inlets of Soul
in this age.' (COURTESY OF THE FITZWILLIAM MUSEUM, CAMBRIDGE)

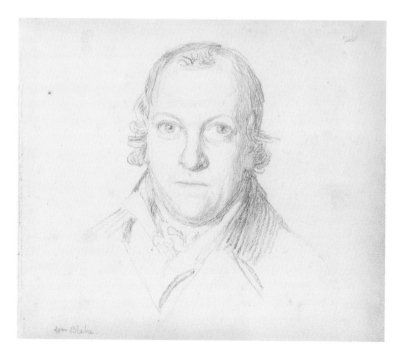

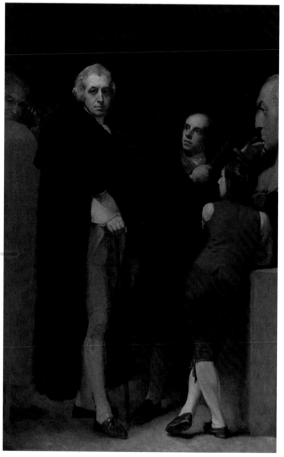

Above: William Blake by John Flaxman; black chalk on paper. Flaxman sketched Blake in 1804, about the time of his trial for sedition at the Guildhall, Chichester. (COURTESY OF THE FITZWILLIAM MUSEUM, CAMBRIDGE)

Left: *John Flaxman Modelling the Bust of William Hayley*, by George Romney (seen to the far left), 1795. Flaxman studies Hayley's profile while Hayley's son, Thomas Alphonso Hayley (Flaxman taught him scuplture), looks on. Hayley's commission for Blake to make an engraving of Thomas Alphonso, who died tragically young on 2 May 1800, would change the direction of Blake's life and bring him into a new, fraught orbit of demanding gentry and watchful aristocracy. (YALE CENTER FOR BRITISH ART)

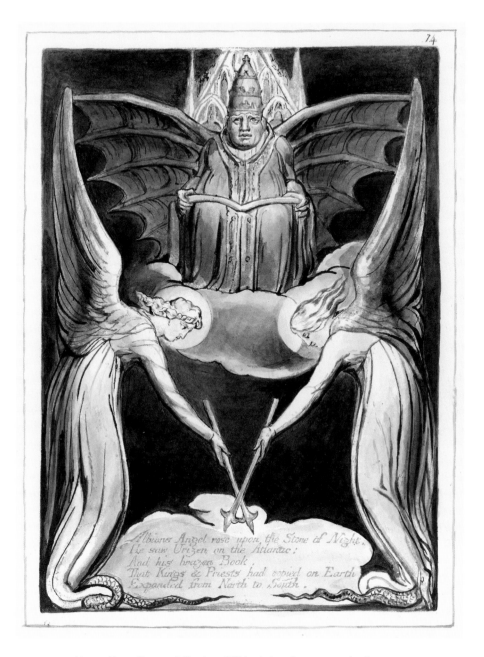

Albions Angel rose upon the Stone of Night.
He saw Urizen on the Atlantic;
And his brazen Book,
That Kings & Priests had copied on Earth
Expanded from North to South.

Above: From *Europe: A Prophecy:* 'Albion's Angel rose upon the Stone of Night'; watercolour and red ink (dated 1794 but executed not before *circa* 1820-21). Blake presents King George III in a papal crown with Satan's wings. Was this sedition or satire? (COURTESY OF THE FITZWILLIAM MUSEUM, CAMBRIDGE)

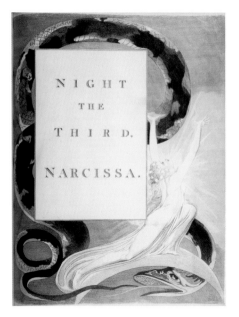
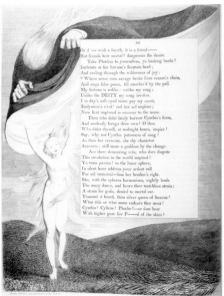
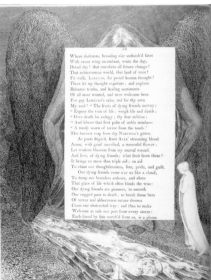
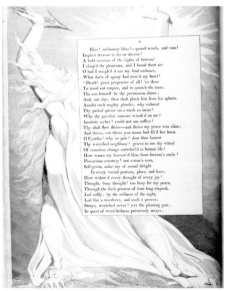

Above and following page: Striking examples from Blake's 43 engravings for Edward Young's *Night Thoughts* (1797), commissioned by publisher Richard Edwards in late 1794 or early 1795. Blake executed over 500 watercolours in preparation for the deluxe edition. Blake received little reward for his extraordinary efforts. (BIBLIOTHECA PHILOSOPHICA HERMETICA, WWW.RITMANLIBRARY.NL)

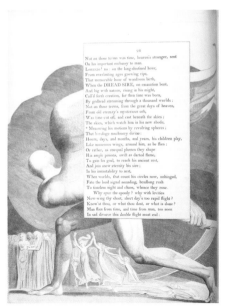

Not on those terms was time, heaven's stranger, sent
On his important embassy to man.
Lorenzo! no: on the long-destined hour,
From everlasting ages growing ripe,
That memorable hour of wondrous birth,
When the DREAD SIRE, on emanation bent,
And big with nature, rising in his might,
Call'd forth creation, for then time was born,
By godhead streaming through a thousand worlds;
Not on those terms, from the great days of heaven,
From old eternity's mysterious orb,
Was time cut off, and cast beneath the skies;
The skies, which watch him in his new abode,
Measuring his motions by revolving spheres;
That horologe machinery divine.
Hours, days, and months, and years, his children play,
Like numerous wings, around him, as he flies;
Or rather, as unequal plumes they shape
His ample pinions, swift as darted flame,
To gain his goal, to reach his ancient rest,
And join anew eternity to rest,
In his immutability to rest,
When worlds, that count his circles now, unhinged,
Fate the loud signal sounding, headlong rush
To timeless night and chaos, whence they rose.
Why spur the speedy? why with levities
New-wing thy short, short day's too rapid flight?
Know'st thou, or what thou dost, or what is done?
Man flies from time, and time from man, too soon
In sad divorce this double flight must end;

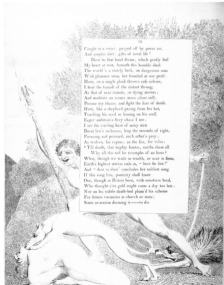

Caught at a court; purged off by purer air,
And ampler diet; gifts of rural life?
    Blest be that hand divine, which gently laid
My heart at rest, beneath this humble shed.
The world's a stately bark, on dangerous seas,
With pleasure seen, but boarded at our peril;
Here, on a single plank thrown safe ashore,
I hear the tumult of the distant throng,
As that of seas remote, or dying storms;
And meditate on scenes, more silent still,
Pursue my theme, and fight the fear of death.
Here, like a shepherd gazing from his hut,
Touching his reed, or leaning on his staff,
Eager ambition's fiery chase I see;
I see the circling hunt of noisy men
Burst law's enclosure, leap the mounds of right,
Pursuing and pursued, each other's prey;
As wolves, for rapine; as the fox, for wiles;
Till death, that mighty hunter, earths them all.
Why all this toil for triumphs of an hour?
What, though we wade in wealth, or soar in fame,
Earth's highest station ends in "here he lies!"
And "dust to dust" concludes her noblest song.
If this song live, posterity shall know
One, though in Britain born, with courtiers bred,
Who thought e'en gold might come a day too late;
Nor on his subtle death-bed plann'd his scheme
For future vacancies in church or state;
Some avaricious deeming it——to die.

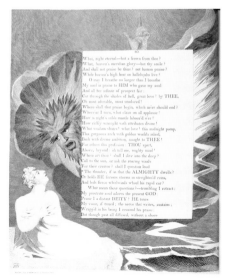

What, night eternal?—but a frown from thee?
What, heaven's sweetest glory?—but thy smile?
And shall not pause be thine? nor human praise?
While heaven's high hour so hallelujahs love?
O may I breathe no longer than I breathe
My soul in praise to HIM who gave my soul
And all her infinite of prospect far;
Cut through the shades of hell, great love! by THEE,
Oh most adorable, most unadored!
Where shall that praise begin, which ne'er should end?
Where'er I turn, what claim on all applause?
Here is night's sable mantle labour'd o'er?
How richly wrought with attributes divine!
What wisdom shines! what love! this midnight pomp,
This gorgeous arch with golden worlds inlaid,
Built with divine ambition, nought to THEE?
For others the profusion? THOU apart,
Above, beyond! oh tell me, mighty mind!
Where art thou? shall I dive into the deep?
Call to the sun, or ask the roaring winds
For their creator? shall I question loud
The thunder, if in that the ALMIGHTY dwells?
Or holds HE furious storms in straighten'd reins,
And bids fierce whirlwinds wheel his rapid car?
    What mean these questions?—trembling I retract;
My prostrate soul adores the present GOD,
Praise I a distant DEITY? HE tunes
My voice, if tuned; the nerve that writes, sustains;
Wrapt in his being I resound his praise;
But though past all diffused, without a shore

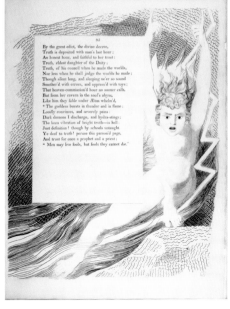

By the great edict, the divine decree,
Truth is deposited with man's last hour;
An honest hour, and faithful to her trust;
Truth, eldest daughter of the Deity;
Truth, of his council when he made the worlds,
Nor less when he shall judge the worlds he made;
Though silent long, and sleeping ne'er so sound,
Smother'd with errors, and oppress'd with toys;
That heaven-commission'd hour no sooner calls,
But from her cavern in the soul's abyss,
Like him they fable under Ætna whelm'd,
The goddess bursts in thunder and in flame;
Loudly convinces, and severely pains;
Dark demons I discharge, and hydra-stings;
The keen vibration of bright truth—is hell;
Just definition! though by schools untaught.
Ye deaf to truth! peruse this parson'd page,
And trust for once a prophet and a priest;
"Men may live fools, but fools they cannot die."

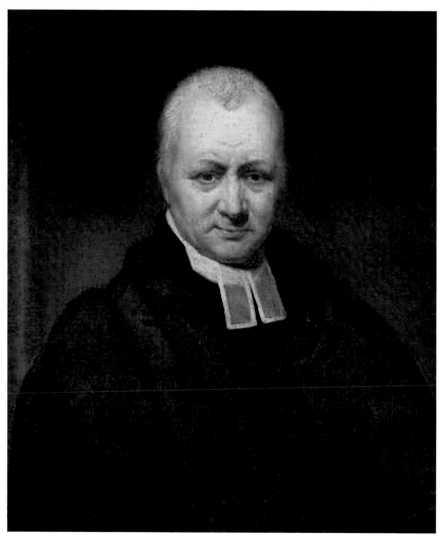

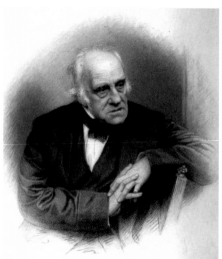

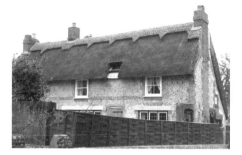

Top: Portrait of Archdeacon Ralph Churton (1754–1831) by Thomas Kirby. (PHOTO: PATRICIA CHURTON) Bottom left: Henry Crabb Robinson, aged 86, engraved by William Holl the Younger. (AUTHOR'S COLLECTION) Robinson interviewed Blake at Fountain Court in and after December 1825. Bottom right: Blake's cottage at Felpham.

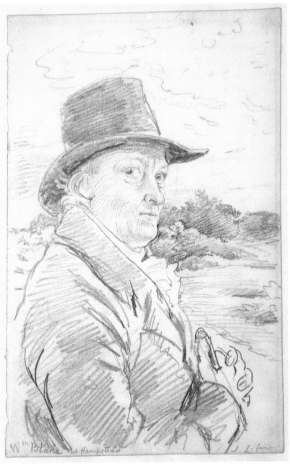

Left: Blake on Hampstead Heath *circa* 1825, by John Linnell; graphite on paper. (COURTESY OF THE FITZWILLIAM MUSEUM, CAMBRIDGE)

Below: 'Savoy Buildings': the site of the old entrance to Fountain Court in the Strand. Here the Blakes lived and worked 1821–27. (PHOTOS: PHILIP WILKINSON)

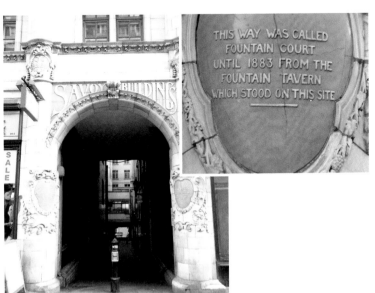

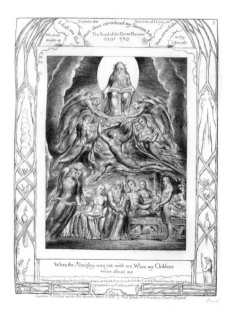

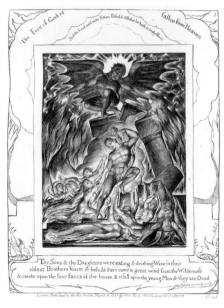

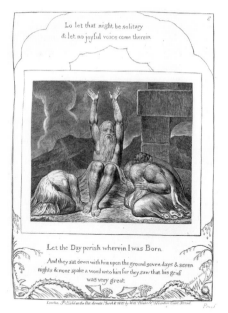

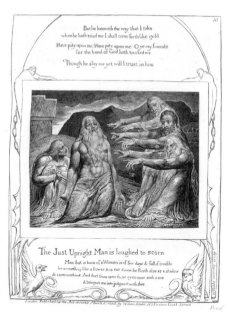

Above and following page: Eight of the twenty engravings completed by
Blake after 25 March 1823, when, aged 65, he was commissioned by John
Linnell to make a series from the Book of Job. Blake's *Job* is justly regarded
as the work of a master artist and engraver, endowed with genius, at the
height of his powers. (BIBLIOTHECA PHILOSOPHICA HERMETICA,
WWW.RITMANLIBRARY.NL)

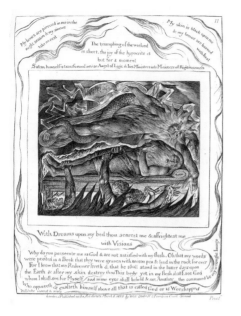

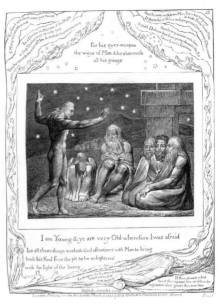

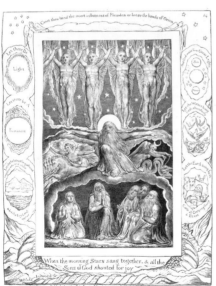

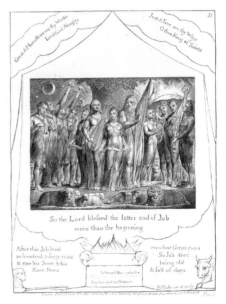

Above: The story of Job and his trials spiritualized by the creative mind of William Blake, and published in 1826. At last, great men were willing to admit there was a genius of the highest order living at Fountain Court. (BIBLIOTHECA PHILOSOPHICA HERMETICA, WWW.RITMANLIBRARY.NL)

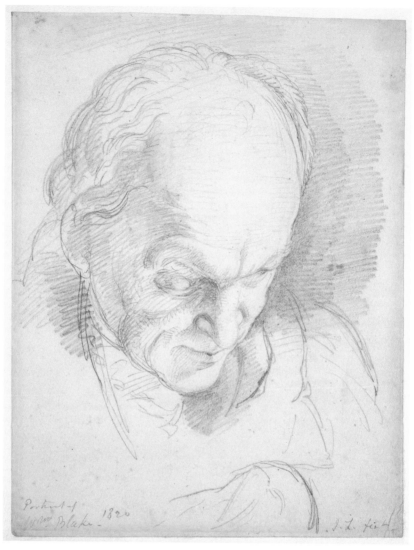

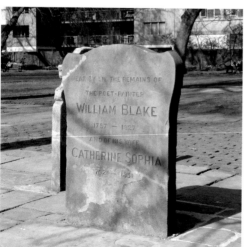

Above: Drawing of William Blake by
John Linnell (1820). (COURTESY OF THE
FITZWILLIAM MUSEUM, CAMBRIDGE)
Left: Stone erected to mark the burial
of William and Catherine Blake at
Bunhill Fields, 38 City Road, London
EC1. In fact, Blake's burial place is
unmarked, situated on the edge of an
amenity lawn in the distance. (PHOTO:
PHILIP WILKINSON)

states and were heavenly blisses strictly, not earthly ones. Nevertheless, it is hard to imagine that such an idea would not have seized Blake's innocent imagination, at least for a while, and possibly confused him too. Indeed, his next major work, *The Marriage of Heaven and Hell,* which he began to write in 1790, reads in parts like the testament of a person who has just discovered sex after a lifetime spent, or misspent, in a straitjacket and padlocked codpiece. Did Blake begin to think that a practice of 'cosmic sex' would help free his mind from time and space? And did he doubt whether his wife was 'up for it'? Such was the idea pursued by Marsha Keith Schuchard in a book originally entitled *Why Mrs Blake Cried.*[6]

Schuchard's basic hypothesis with regard to Blake's alleged 'sexual path to spiritual vision' is that Blake absorbed from contemporary counter-cultural influences a theory that sexual energy could be employed for spiritual means, to access high visionary states where the heavens opened to the conscious mind and communication with 'spirits' could take place, giving the seer powers of prophecy and trans-temporal vision. Boosting the theory was the supposed 'permission' offered by Swedenborg to engage in such activities lawfully from the Christian point of view.

Other contemporary encouragements were already available, such as Rev. Martin Madan's eccentric work *Thelyphthora: Or a Treatise on Female Ruin*[7] (1780), which advised polygamy as a palliative against venereal disease and prostitution, rather like Dr James Graham's argument for his celestial bed. Madan justified his ideas by an appeal to the Old Testament: concubinage was lawful among the patriarchs if the wife was barren. William Cowper – Madan's first cousin incidentally – had already written a poem, *Anti-Thelyphthora,* that parodied Madan as a creature gone mad and bad. We have no evidence that Blake favoured Madan or Cowper.

The problem with the theory appears straightaway. We have two separate issues that have been artificially joined. First, Catherine's apparent barrenness; second, visionary experimentation, if such did indeed take place. Visionary experimentation is not a cure for barrenness, nor, I suggest, is it a substitute for the absence of progeny, nor for the sating of a frustrated sexual appetite. However, let us examine the principal 'evidence' offered in the theory's support.

The theory's lynchpin is a report of Gilchrist. After relating JT Smith's anecdotes about the perfection of Mr and Mrs Blake's relationship, of how

Kate was 'rigid, punctual, firm, precise', of how 'She shared his destiny and softened it, ministering to his daily wants,' Gilchrist offers a snippet of discord, from what source we know not:

> Such harmony there really was; but, as we saw, it had not always been unruffled. There *had* been stormy times in years long past, when both were young; discord by no means trifling while it lasted. But with the cause (jealousy on her side, not wholly unprovoked), the strife had ceased also. In age and affliction, each grasped the reward of so wise a reconciliation, in an even, calm state of companionship and mutual helpfulness.[8]

And Gilchrist would add another anecdote in a similar vein:

> 'Do you think,' he [Blake] once said in familiar conversation, and in the spirit of controversy, 'if I came home and discovered my wife to be unfaithful, I should be so foolish as to take it ill?' Mrs Blake was a most exemplary wife, yet was so much in the habit of echoing and thinking right whatever he said that, had she been present, adds my informant, he is sure she would have innocently responded: '*Of course not!*' 'But,' continues Blake's friend, 'I am inclined to think (despite the philosophic boast) it would have gone ill with the offenders.'[9]

However true the anecdote may, or may not be, it does not refer either to sexual mysticism or to a response to barrenness. The quote could just as easily be used to prove that Blake and his wife had fully absorbed Mary Wollstonecraft's ideas about women's equality and the right to choose lovers according to mutual consent.

The crucial step necessary to the hypothetical 'Why Mrs Blake cried' scenario came within a decade of Gilchrist's first edition of his Blake biography. Poet Algernon Charles Swinburne accused Gilchrist of passing over too lightly some details of Blake's life. Swinburne, on no direct authority, asked readers of his insightful essay on Blake to believe that the artist had once tried to add a concubine to the household, but at Mrs Blake's tearful remonstrance had abandoned the idea for her sake.[10] This story was repeated by WB Yeats and Edwin John Ellis in their collection of Blake's work published in 1893.[11]

Ellis went on in his own biographical treatment of Blake to suggest it was all part of Blake's attempt to 'educate' his wife, an idea that Schuchard's hypothesis runs with.

Again, we have hearsay and speculation, with no reference to sexual mysticism, only to sexual appetite. It is most likely that Swinburne simply added Gilchrist's jealousy story to some teasing, *risqué* comments that Blake is known to have made to the critic Henry Crabb Robinson in 1826. Gilchrist had access to, and used, the manuscript of Robinson's *Reminiscences* (published in 1869), but chose not to include the following reference, doubtless observing Robinson's warning that repetition would harm Blake's reputation.[12] These comments are worth showing in full; Robinson himself was aware of their shock value (which is why he put them in German):

13 June 1826
Called early on Blake. He was as wild as ever with no great novelty except that he confessed a *practical* notion which would do him more injury than any other I have heard from him. He says that from the Bible he has learned that *Eine Gemeinschaft der Frauen statt finden sollte* [there ought to be a confraternity, or community, of wives; that is, wives should be in common]. When I objected that *Ehestand* [matrimony] seems to be a divine institution he referred to the Bible – 'that from the beginning it was not so.'[13]

Again, Blake's approach seems to be one that invoked a kind of sexual innocence. Blake elsewhere declared to Robinson that there could be suffering in heaven, as there could be pleasure too. Sexual pleasure Blake held to be something heavenly. He told Robinson that the poet John Milton had appeared to him to ask him to correct a notion from his *Paradise Lost* that the pleasure of sexual intercourse arose from the Fall; how could something good derive from something bad? Blake asked.

Blake also spoke to Robinson of androgyny being the heavenly state of man and the idea that division of the sexes was the result of the Fall of Man; so it is difficult to get any precise idea of what Blake thought might 'go on' in heaven. However, his point that the pleasure of sex is itself innocent and that it is human self-wilfulness that perverts its joys is consistent throughout his work. It would be fair to say that Blake believed that lovemaking was an essentially spiritual experience, and the more so, for spiritually conscious people. But this is quite a difference from making Blake into a kind of would-be sexual magician, manipulating sexual energies for specific willed ends, such as encountering spirits. He encountered 'spirits' anyway, as personified aspects of *mind*, or the Poetic Genius.

Furthermore, Blake's comments to Robinson on Swedenborg are revealing of the depth of consideration, and perhaps anguish, exercised by Blake in response to problems within Swedenborg's sexually oriented material, and indeed, of much else Swedenborg had to say:

> 10 December 1825
>
> Yet he [Blake] also said that *Swedenborg* was wrong in endeavouring to explain to the *rational* faculty what the reason cannot comprehend. He [Swedenborg] should have left that.[14]

Specifically, and remarkably, Blake singled out what he called Swedenborg's 'sexual religion' for censure. Crabb Robinson noted from comments made by Blake on 10 December 1825 at the Aders's house: '*Swedenborg*. Parts of his [Swedenborg's] scheme are dangerous. His sexual religion is dangerous.'[15] Sadly perhaps, there is no elucidation of this point, but the word 'dangerous' is strong and suggests a prohibition.

All this sets Blake's reaction to the events of May 1790 – when the Swedenborg society split over the 'conjugial love' issue – into a more complex, troubling pattern. Schuchard's hypothesis regards Blake's Moravian-influenced upbringing as one conducive to linking spirituality and sexuality ('sexualized spirituality'), Christ and flesh. Blake was 'cool', we might say, about visions and about a divinely ordained sexual nature, within marriage anyway. His wife, however, is considered to have had a traditional upbringing that might have made her listen to the protestors against 'conjugial love' and feel guilty at participating in anything like 'free love' within marriage, or anything that made her feel uncomfortably unrighteous. She is supposed to have revolted at the least thought – let alone practice – of becoming a kind of Tantric sex partner for the visionary benefit of her husband, even as he allegedly embraced an apotheosis of Priapism in the Richard Payne Knight mode.

It is worth looking closely at George Cumberland's brush drawing of Catherine Blake, seated before a fireplace, executed in about 1785.[16] She sits primly, leaning slightly forward on her Windsor chair, buttoned up to the neck in a shawl, her striking face with strongly defined, aquiline nose framed by a bonnet pulled round and bowed under her well-defined jaw. Her hands are clasped together on her lap. Her lips are full, sensuous, but the face is taut. Her dark eyes stare fixedly, seriously, intensely, not at the fire before her, but into her own concerns, dreams perhaps. This is a woman focused, intense, energetic and devoted. *Intense* is the word. She is disciplined, and she is inwardly tough, physically strong. This is not a woman to be trifled with; she knows her own mind and is self-contained. Nothing flighty about this lady, nothing you would care to take advantage of. One imagines she was the kind of person who could take a lot, and take a lot in without saying too much, but also one who, pushed that bit too far, would explode in a way no decent man would ever forget, or wish to provoke again.

In Schuchard's scenario, much of Blake's personal anguish running through the 1790s and into the first decade of the 19th century was caused by a profound spiritual and sexual frustration as his wife resisted his desire to use sex to break through the barriers of time and space and voyage into 'paradise', returning with a visionary and revolutionary store for the enlightenment of humanity. This anguish is held to be evident in a handful of unpublished poems that can be interpreted as evincing tensions in the marriage, and, specifically, in the manuscript giant of a poem, *Vala*, whose phallic and vaginal imagery has been obscured, and, where not 'rubbed out', sanitized.

According to this scenario, some time after the 1790s Catherine finally settled down into a complementary sexual-spiritual role and gave her husband what he wanted, resulting in spiritual harmony and much visionary verse. This does sound somewhat like a tale from sexually oriented marriage guidance counselling with quite a lot of post-1960s Californian domestic Tantrism mixed into the recipe. That is, the scenario bears an anachronistic ring, not because I think the 18th century was prudish and hid its real self, but because the imposed narrative obscures categories and distinctions that meant so much to Blake himself. More to the point, had we not heard the hypothesis, would the 'evidence' have naturally suggested it? The 'evidence' put forwards bears many other possible interpretations, and the distinctions at the time were much finer than the kind of broad 'sexual revolution' versus 'Victorian religious prudes' conflict that informs the hypothesis in question.

First, we have no compelling evidence whatsoever that 'Mrs Blake cried', or that concubinage was an issue for the Blakes specifically, only that it was an issue for Swedenborgians. Gilchrist's original anecdote simply says that there had once been an issue of jealousy, and when Blake removed the cause, harmony reigned. I dare say this is true of many marriages. There is no evidence at all that Blake was ever sexually involved with another woman after his marriage, or that he particularly wanted to be, though it would be extraordinary had his eye never strayed nor his fancy speculated on the eternal 'what if?' He had, after all, met Catherine Boutcher 'on the rebound' and it may have taken many years for him to see her as the sole object of romantic worship in his inner life; indeed, it is quite possible that he was never spiritually monogamous or even 'in love' with his wife in the sentimental sense, though he certainly loved and respected her: they were loyal partners in all. If Blake truly 'boasted' he would not be devastated to find his wife had been unfaithful, it suggests they had a relationship with imaginary gates left open, and loved each other in such a way, or perhaps were so fundamentally insecure, or wise, as to one another, as never to have passed through them, though the idea might occasionally have appealed. Blake hated repression.

> Thou hast a lap full of seed
> And this is a fine country
> Why dost thou not cast thy seed
> And live in it merrily

> Shall I cast it on the sand
> And turn it into fruitful land
> For on no other ground
> Can I sow my seed
> Without tearing up
> Some stinking weed

Eternity

He who binds to himself a joy
Does the winged life destroy
But he who kisses the joy as it flies
Lives in eternity's sun rise[17]

Soft Snow

I walked abroad in a snowy day
I asked the soft snow with me to play
She playd & she melted in all her prime
And the winter calld it a dreadful crime
[*deleted line*: 'Ah that sweet love should be thought a crime'][18]

One or two poems might suggest Blake's sex life was not all he wanted it to be, but there are other, equally valid, interpretations of the poems' meanings. His poems frequently comment on dark consequences issuing from *others'* enforced chastity, though not his own – even unto being the causes of war.

Blake's and Catherine's marriage might have gone through the usual ups and downs; it might not. Given the paucity of hard evidence I am not sure we are at much liberty to speculate. That Blake held revolutionary views about sexual freedom and energy cannot be doubted, but that is quite different from the view that Blake's *Marriage of Heaven and Hell* was composed primarily as a 'blistering satire' on New Church prudes who could not cope with Swedenborg's conceptions of 'conjugial love'.

It is just as likely that Blake himself found the 'new' Swedenborg material disturbing at a deep personal level. Was it perhaps uncomfortably invasive – as Moravian advice concerning remarriage had been to his mother? And if he himself did not find it so, then his wife would almost certainly have done. She had the most to lose from accepting *as a divinely ordained instruction* that a barren wife could be put aside because the couple had no children. Blake may have toyed with the notion, or even, *in extremis*, have teased his wife with it, but he had bigger fish to fry, as *The Marriage of Heaven and Hell* makes abundantly clear.

The fact is we know nothing of Blake's sex life other than that it did not issue in any children. Everything else suggests they were happy together, living in great intimacy for very many years without, as far as we know, separation. Blake's annotations on Swedenborg gain in venom from 1790. Here are just a few of his comments (and they are typical) of his annotations to the pamphlet of Swedenborg's *The Wisdom of Angels concerning the Divine Providence* (London, 1790): 'Lies and Priestcraft'; 'Cursed Folly!'; 'Predestination after this Life is more Abominable than Calvins & Swedenborg is Such a Spiritual Predestinarian – witness this [Note] number and many others'; 'Read N[ote] 185 & There See how Swedenborg contradicts himself & N[ote] 69.'

Blake concludes that Swedenborg is fundamentally a Calvinist with as repressive an underlying belief in predestined damnation as any other illiberal Protestant. I think it is obvious that Blake needed to find himself a way out of Swedenborg and his brood: he had become fed up with the whole thing. Indeed, it is likely that it was *precisely* the events at Eastcheap of April and May 1790 that sealed it for Blake. He did not join the New Church and never, as far as we know, attended New Church services. He was not interested in a Swedenborgian Church, and, when it came to it, he was in no need of Swedenborg as a personal prophet or seer: he had *himself,* as is quite plain from his soon to be produced *Marriage of Heaven and Hell,* which is a rebuttal not simply of prudishness among New Church readers or any other repressors of 'Eternal Energy', but of Swedenborg's general approach, as Blake saw it at the time. That is to say, having found some of his own ideas confirmed by Swedenborg, Blake exploded Swedenborgianism into something else entirely. He began to develop his own system, using a mythology of his own spiritual experience. Swedenborg would be Blake's John the Baptist, but having served as herald, Swedenborg's job was done. Indeed, already Blake saw the seeds of failure in the Swedenborgians' attempt to turn the revelation into an organization. This, he was sure, had never been Swedenborg's intention, any more than Wesley wanted to institute a Methodist Church, separate from the Church of England. It is followers who make sects, not true masters.

TWELVE

The Lust of the Goat is the Bounty of God

1790

According to Samuel Johnson's dictionary, the word 'bounty' comes from the French *bonté* and means generosity, munificence or liberality; not charity. A Royal 'bounty' is a free gift coming from a character of liberality.

Shortly before the great Eastcheap Conference, Captain Bligh reported the events of the *Bounty* mutiny to the Admiralty: HMS *Bounty* had been stolen by Master's Mate Fletcher Christian and redirected to an island, 'Otaheite' (now Tahiti), where something like sexual innocence reigned. The incident was reported in detail in the *Oxford Journal* of 20 March 1790. Was this a sign of the times?

On 31 March, Maximilien de Robespierre was voted president of the radical Jacobin Club in Paris. On 15 June, Protestant militia massacred some 300 Catholic aristocrats in Nîmes. Four days later, hereditary nobility was abolished in France. The question in England was: *are you for or against the revolution in France?*

Foxite Whigs still looked favourably upon the tide of events across the Channel, but in October Irish statesman and conservative Whig Edmund Burke (1729–1797), a supporter of the American rebellion, published his *Reflections on the Revolution in France*, asserting, contrary to Rousseau, that man had no natural rights in a state of nature. Civil rights applied only in civil societies under law. The State was not a partnership agreement ('social contract') to be dissolved by parties as it suited them. Human society evolves by slow process, and the social order is not to be suddenly overturned, nor fundamentally assaulted in heat of passion or political enthusiasm.

Prophetically, Burke foresaw bloodshed inevitably succeeded by 'some popular general' who would 'establish a military dictatorship in place of anarchy'. He was right, of course. Burke also looked to his own countrymen and attacked revolutionary sympathizers who did not truly grasp the stakes, misreading the signs of the times.

A year later, revolution-supporter Tom Paine, friend of Joseph Johnson, wrote the second part of his incendiary *Rights of Man*. Dedicating it to George Washington, Paine attacked Burke's *Reflections*. For Paine, the revolution was simply 'justice' answering centuries of injustice. Man's 'rights' gave 'the people' the right to judge what was good for them. Times had changed and there was no going back. Blake now expressed what he believed was the essence of the transformation:

> As a new heaven is begun, and it is now thirty-three years since its advent: the Eternal Hell revives. And lo! Swedenborg is the Angel sitting at the tomb; his writings are the linen clothes folded up. Now is the dominion of Edom, & the return of Adam into Paradise; see Isaiah XXXIV & XXXV Chap:
> Without Contraries is no progression. Attraction and Repulsion. Reason and Energy, Love and Hate, are necessary to Human existence. From these contraries spring what the religious call Good & Evil. Good is the passive that obeys Reason[.] Evil is the active springing from Energy.
> Good is Heaven. Evil is Hell.

And with that, Blake announced his solution to the times: a paradox that is *The Marriage of Heaven and Hell*. Energy is what matters: 'Energy is Eternal Delight.' Enthusiasm, passion, these are forms of dynamic energy without which nothing can change: the lust of the goat is the bounty of God. *The Marriage of Heaven and Hell* is a fiery fanfare to energy, showing that the spiritual and physical worlds are really one world of dynamic, energetic movement. You can read it as a comment on the French Revolution, or as a comment on Swedenborgianism. Or you can take it as a universal philosophy of life: many have.

The 'Marrriage' arrived in the form of an etching, some copies of which were coloured, others not. Illustrations abound; figures fly about the words and monumental, incisively drawn men and women spread themselves across its pages, betokening extreme mental and physical states. One of *Marriage's* 'Proverbs of Hell' famously announces: 'The road of Excess leads to the palace of Wisdom.' It all reads like a basic tract of spiritual revolution. What here is Art, and what philosophy? In fact, *The Marriage of Heaven and Hell* appropriately combines the two, as the narrative combines the contraries of divine creation. It is a prophecy, theosophical prophecy, if one must call it something. It is a product of what Blake called the Divine Genius: set free! Had there ever been anything like it? Yes, there had. It bears striking resemblances to books of the Bible.

Let us first look at that mighty broadside with which we began. It follows a poetic 'Argument', a kind of comment on the times: 'Rintrah roars & shakes his fires in the burdend air; Hungry clouds swag on the deep.' There are fires in heaven and tumult below: do not trust appearances. The villain may look like a sweet, reasonable fellow:

> Now the sneaking serpent walks
> In mild humility.
> And the just man rages in the wilds
> Where lions roam.

These lions can tear flesh, and Blake's 'Rintrah' stands for wrathful energy, the just wrath of the prophet; Rintrah is on the rebel's side insofar as the rebellion expresses spiritual liberty freeing itself from repression.

It is hard to know what *The Times*, now nearly three years old, would make of Blake's work viewed as a kind of prophecy regarding current world events. These were not signs *The Times* could readily decipher. Blake's references may be to historical events and people, but nearly all his indices are esoteric.

It is 33 years since the 'advent' of the 'new heaven', declares Blake: 1757, Blake's birth year, was the date Swedenborg gave to the establishment of the new heaven. It was widely believed Jesus was crucified aged 33. Therefore, we have an opening scene set in a new cave-tomb of resurrection (Luke 24:1–12;

John 20:1–12), and we may presume Blake is now himself 33 and a participant in the new resurrection. Swedenborg is the Angel sitting at the tomb. Who is the other? we may ask, for the Gospels have two angels at the tomb. One of them poses the question: 'Why seek ye the living among the dead?' Is Blake saying: 'Don't expect too much from Swedenborg'?

Using Jacob Böhme's terminology, the 'Eternal Hell' (Nature) revives. 'Angel' Swedenborg can only announce that he whom the women at the tomb seek is elsewhere, and Swedenborg's writings are the linen clothes of Jesus, folded up in the tomb. The linen had wrapped the corpse of the crucified – it bore the blood; the writings are done with: the saviour has departed the tomb. 'Now', Blake tells us, 'is the dominion of Edom', when Adam returns into Paradise. We are instructed to look at Isaiah chapters 34 and 35, which we better had: 'For it is the day of the Lord's vengeance, and the year of recompenses for the controversy of Zion [Jerusalem],' announces Isaiah 34:8.

And look! The abolition of nobility, *predicted*: 'They shall call the nobles thereof to the kingdom, but none shall be there, and all her princes shall be nothing' (Isaiah 34:12). And with the fall of nobility and monarchy, Britain ('the island') will be the place where the 'wild beasts' meet: 'And thorns shall come up in her [France's?] palaces, nettles and brambles in the fortresses thereof: and it shall be an habitation of dragons, and a court for owls. The wild beasts of the desert shall also meet with the wild beasts of the island, and the satyr shall cry to his fellow; the screech owl also shall rest there, and find for herself a place of rest' (Isaiah 34:13–14). Island Britain is where the new Jerusalem will be built: 'And the ransomed of the LORD shall return, and come to Zion with songs and everlasting joy upon their heads: they shall obtain joy and gladness, and sorrow and sighing shall flee away' (Isaiah 35:10).

We are getting a powerful idea, but the intended meaning of Blake's 'Now is the dominion of Edom' seems hard to pinpoint precisely.

Isaiah 34 announces a judgement of slaughter that is to fall on Idumea, another name for the Biblical 'Edom' (meaning 'Red'), named after Isaac's son Esau, who, born red all over, surrendered his inheritance for a mess of 'red pottage' and went to live in Edom (where King Herod came from): 'For my sword shall be bathed in heaven: behold, it shall come down upon Idumea, and upon the people of my curse, to judgement' (Isaiah 34:5).

The negative view of Jewish scripture with regard to 'Edom' led Jewish commentators to identify Edom with Babylon (which held Jews captive), with Rome (which imposed Idumean monarchy over Israel), and, subsequently, with Christianity, which, after Constantine, was imposed on Palestine. At first sight, this rather confuses a neat interpretation of Blake's prophetic announcement, an announcement made more resonant by the realization that the name 'Adam' (who is going to enter Paradise) is derived both from the Hebrew *'adamah'* ('earth') and from *'adam'* meaning 'to be red'. Adam was made of the 'red earth'. In the preceding 'Argument' Blake refers to 'Red clay brought forth' 'on the bleached bones', a clear reference to the resurrection of men envisioned by the prophet Ezekiel (Ezekiel 37:1–14).

So 'Edom' is the Gentile world; 'Edom' is an 'Adam' who is returning to Paradise; and 'Edom' is a place where first, bloody judgement will be enacted, and afterwards will be transformed from a desert into a place where 'waters break out'. Where once were dragons, Edom will be 'grass with reeds and rushes'.

A green and pleasant land …

There is more to the 'dominion of Edom'. Consider Jacob Frank (1726– 1791), self-proclaimed successor to Jewish pseudo-messiah Sabbatai Zvi (1626–c.1676). Frank astonished Polish Catholic leaders in the 1750s and subsequently with his declaration that he acknowledged the kabbalistic text, the *Zohar* (or 'Book of Splendour'), which in Frank's view allowed for a Trinity, over the Talmud, while seeking a complete *rapprochement* of his many Jewish followers with the Church.

In the critical year of 1757, the bishop of Kamenetz-Podolsk presided over a debate between Talmudists and anti-Talmudists or 'Zoharists'. The bishop decided the anti-Talmudists winners of the debate, at which point Jacob Frank appeared in Iwana claiming, as Zvi's successor, to be a man in receipt of messages from heaven. Negotiations took place to reconcile Frank and his followers to Catholicism. Protestant Churches also competed for these Jewish converts; some of Frank's followers joined the Moravian Church. London Moravian circles became aware of the curious events in far-off Poland.

By 1790, some 26,000 Jews had been baptised in Poland. Furthermore, Frank, amid all his mystical messages, asked his followers to adopt what he called the 'religion of Edom' (Christianity), as a step towards a future religion he called '*das*', meaning 'knowledge' – that is to say, *gnosis*. Frank's followers saw themselves as people who had been set free from the law of Rabbinic Judaism to embrace the journey on the 'highway' established in the redeemed Edom of Isaiah chapter 35: 'the way of holiness' (Isaiah 35:8–9). This 'way' would be characterized by love, song, 'joy and gladness', and a non-repressive attitude to the human body, when directed to a heavenly ascent.

It is the transformed 'Edom' bathed pure by the sword of heaven ('nor shall my sword sleep in my hand') that Blake celebrates in *The Marriage of Heaven and Hell*, a marriage made possible by uniting the contraries, something made possible only by divine means, for God's ultimate being is limitless:

The ancient tradition that the world will be consumed in fire at the end of six thousand years is true, as I have heard from Hell.

For the cherub with his flaming sword is hereby commanded to leave his guard at [the] tree of life, and when he does, the whole creation will be consumed and appear infinite and holy, whereas it now appears finite and corrupt.

This will come to pass by an improvement of sensual enjoyment.

But first the notion that man has a body distinct from his soul is to be expunged; this I shall do by printing in the infernal method by corrosives, which in Hell are salutary and medicinal, melting apparent surfaces away, and displaying the infinite which was hid.

If the doors of perception were cleansed everything would appear to man as it is, infinite.

For man has closed himself up, till he sees all things through narrow chinks of his cavern.

A good book could be written on these radiant passages alone. We may ask: whence came Blake's hyper-vision? The Poetic Genius?

Blake will not pussyfoot around the issue of sex: this new heaven and new earth will be the result of an improvement of sensual enjoyment. There was certainly need for improvement. The whole subject was mired in myth and mystery. Blake seems to have made a breakthrough, possibly as a result of his conflict with Swedenborg's thinking.

The full recovery of Man requires the relationship between body and soul to be purified and understood: 'Man has no Body distinct from his Soul for that calld Body is a portion of Soul discernd by the five Senses. the chief inlets of Soul in this age'. What an amazing idea! What we call body is a portion of the soul discerned by the five senses. Are the senses physical or psychological?

It is the mind that creates the sensation of material existence. Sensual existence can be heightened until the senses are themselves transcended, when 'we shall see things as they are: infinite.'

Incredible. Inspiring. But what does it mean?

Readers and would-be readers of Blake are often confused by his ideas about 'contraries' uniting, while elsewhere remaining distinct. That may be because the distinct ideas were not his to begin with. Blake's contrast of 'Hell' and 'Heaven', along with idiosyncratic use of the words 'Evil', 'Devils', 'Angels' and 'Fire' together with expressions like 'Eternal Nature', 'Eternal Hell' and 'Eternal Delight' can be attributed to Blake's sometimes ironic and sometimes direct employment of theosophical categories derived from his spiritual master and, in his maturity, spiritual brother, Jacob Böhme (1575-1624).

Who was this man and what did Blake get from him?

Blake and Böhme

Jacob Böhme had two things in common with Blake: he was a craftsman (a shoemaker), and he was a visionary. Of prosperous farming stock, Böhme spent most of his life in Görlitz, east of Dresden in Lusatian Saxony, close to the Polish border.

Aged 25, Böhme underwent a major spiritual experience. He later wrote of how he felt penetrated by 'the Light of God', and 'saw and knew' more in a quarter of an hour than if he had been 'many years in a university [...] I saw and knew the Being of Beings, the Byss and the Abyss, the eternal generation of the Trinity, the origin and descent of the world, and of all creatures through divine wisdom'.[1]

Abraham von Frankenberg (1593–1652), one of his followers, believed that Böhme's key spiritual experience occurred in 1610, when, gazing at the reflection of the sun in a pewter dish, the 35-year-old Böhme realized that the brightness was only visible on account of the darkness of the surface from which it was reflected. He grasped visually the paradoxical character of light and darkness: the contraries. Von Frankenberg wrote how the experience introduced Böhme 'into the innermost ground or centre of the [...] hidden nature.'[2]

Böhme expanded on his experience in his manuscript *Aurora or Morning Redness*, the circulation of which was halted by Görlitz pastor Gregory Richter. Despising the idea of a tradesman with pretensions to theological learning, Richter had the magistrates expel Böhme, but they allowed him back in 1613, so long as he published nothing more for the rest of his life.

Böhme spent the rest of the decade in publishing silence, but clarity had infused his mind: a metaphysical structure had appeared that accommodated both Renaissance schemes of planetary interaction and opposition, and the alchemical theme of the transformation of base matter. The alchemical 'marriage of the contraries' symbolized in the *rebis*, the androgynous figure symbolizing sulphur and mercury embodying a mutual polar opposition, chimed with Böhme's insights into the *necessity* of internal opposition in the projection of the divine being. One immediately thinks of Blake's *Marriage of Heaven and Hell*: 'Without Contraries is no progression.'

The influence of Swiss physician and freelance theologian Paracelsus (1493–1541) looms large in Böhme, as it does in Blake. The title of Böhme's *Mysterium Magnum* (1623), for example, is the Paracelsian term for the great matrix of nature – the Mystery, the *prima materia* of all things, whose masculine opposite is the 'Archeus' or 'Separator'.

The *Archeus* is the differentiating aspect of divine mind within the undifferentiated *massa confusa* that extends endlessly throughout creation like the entwined roots and branches of an infinite, even sinister forest.

Paracelsus' triadic system of salt (matter), sulphur (soul) and mercury (spirit) is deeply ingrained in Böhme's system: a triad interpreted by Böhme as a dynamic spiritual process of purgation, illumination and transformation (or union). Indeed, Böhme sees the cosmos as a continuous dynamic expression of these principles. Blake saw the whole process in one word: *forgiveness.*

Kabbalistic influence is also present in two of Böhme's basic symbols transmitted into Blake's thought: the 'ungrund' or primal abyss, and the archetypal Man or original Adam. They resemble the *En Sof* – unknowable limitless light – of the Kabbalah's ultimate Deity and that tradition's image of

'Adam Kadmon' whose body contains the universe. We shall see him in Blake's figure 'Albion', the Ancient Man.

One can see in all this the Paracelsian conception that the universe is a divine riddle, encoded with deep secrets awaiting the inspired and pure decryptor. It is little wonder that Böhme himself would come to be so closely associated with the fictional brotherhood of the Rose Cross, even to the point of being seen as a kind of honorary member. For Böhme's most devoted followers, Böhme had apparently cracked it.

Böhme's works promised a veritable 'science of God', and in doing so made some of his followers feel the world could no longer be denied the fruit of Böhme's inspiration. On New Year's Day 1624 they published several of his tracts under the title *Der Weg zur Christo* ('Way of Christ'). This event precipitated ecclesiastical harrassments that would trouble the mystic's life until his departure from this world.

On the day of his death, Böhme was heard to remark that he could hear the strains of sweet music – as William Blake was also reported to have heard on *his* deathbed 200 years later. Böhme blessed his family and murmured quietly, 'Now I go hence to Paradise.'[3]

What Böhme left behind would shape Blake's thought fundamentally. The following passage comes from Böhme's *Of Heaven and Hell* (which ought to sound familiar). In it we glimpse Böhme's great theme of the opposite worlds of 'Wrath' and 'Fire' in dynamic relation to 'Love' and 'Light'. Note also the phrase 'Eternal Delight' which sounds so Blakean, but is Böhme's; Blake tells us that 'Energy is Eternal Delight' in his *Marriage* of the lower order with the higher.

And as the Light hath quite another Property than the Fire hath, for It giveth and yieldeth Itself forth; whereas the Fire draweth in and consumeth itself; so the holy Life of Meekness springeth forth through the Death of SELF-Will, and then God's Will of Love only ruleth, and doth ALL in ALL. For thus the Eternal ONE hath attained Feeling and Separability, and brought Itself forth again with the Feeling, through Death in great Joyfulness; that there might be an Eternal Delight in the Infinite Unity, and an Eternal Cause of Joy; and therefore that which was before Painfulness, must now be the Ground and cause of this Motion or stirring to the Manifestation of all Things. And herein lieth the Mystery of the hidden Wisdom of God.[4]

The two contrary worlds of Böhme's theosophy arise from what Désirée Hirst considered 'the most startling doctrine Böhme developed'[5], that of the 'Eternal Nature'. 'Evil' does not enter the world through Adam's sin, but was there from the beginning *in potentia*. Eternal Nature exists *before* creation; it arises from the 'Abyss', the 'Ungrund', the Unknowable God, by God's mysterious will to know Himself.

The *Eternal Nature* is expressed in three principles. The first two are defined thus: '…with the stern Fire-world, according to the Father's Property, and according to the Light and Love world is the Sonnes Property; and yet it is, but One only substance undivided, but One God; as Fire and Light is One.'[6] What Böhme is saying is that for the 'Ungrund' or 'Abyss' (that is, *infinite depth*) to know itself required a reflexive manifestation of opposites: Father/Fire and Son/Light. By analogy, I cannot 'know myself' without creating, in thought, an 'I' to know and a 'myself' to be known: two phases of being even though I and myself are one.

Once Böhme's two opposite principles are manifest, their *contrarium* produces a reaction, a 'flash' like a spark from force of friction, from which a third principle is produced: the 'Outbirth', with a momentum of its own. From that 'outbirth' our universe is derived.

Note, however, that 'Light and Darkness are in One another'.[7] In their manifestation God 'sees' what we cannot, for we are creatures of the duality, or at least it is from this that we derive our senses.

Böhme chose to illustrate this pattern in the imagery of dynamic globes and circles. He drew a dark circle touching a light one, with a third circle underneath both. A 'lightning flash' or creative spark marks the contact between the light and dark principles. This ignited flame of vitality is akin to the belief in an alchemical fire hidden but present in all things, latent from creation's first birth. The universe derives from a metaphysical combustion. Blake's *Marriage of Heaven and Hell* is full of creatures surrounded by flames: eternal energy, eternal delight. Plate Three announcing the 'Dominion of Edom', for example, shows a woman from whose genitals emanate streams of fire: like a salamander, she seems to live in fire. Fire burns but fire is life; love is in fire. The same fire is in the lust of the goat and in man and woman. The sexual energy is fundamentally creative, not shameful: *love is on fire!*

As Böhme maintained, the first two 'worlds' are in reality one, as 'fire' and 'light' are one. So God exists as 'Father' insofar as Will is Lord of Fire and Power; God is 'Son' insofar as Will is the bearer of the light-principle.

> The being of all being is but a single being, yet in giving birth to itself, it divides itself into two principles, into light and darkness, into joy and pain, into evil and good, into love and wrath, into fire and light, and out of these two eternal beginnings into a third beginning, into the Creation itself as his own love-play between the qualities of both eternal desires.[8]

The image of a 'Big-Bang', currently favoured by many cosmologists as a working-theory for the universe's origin, is not entirely alien to this visualization – the archetypal spark of ignition is there. The essence of the idea is ancient. As Abraham von Frankenberg observed, Böhme's system was very close in principle to that of the Valentinian Gnostics as expressed by their opponent Irenaeus in his *Adversus Haereses* (*c*.180 CE).

Where does Man fit into all of this? For in Blake's scheme, Man-rebuilt must be the hero of any marriage of heaven and hell. According to Böhme, Man was originally a spiritual, androgynous being in whom the two sexes were one.

This being fell into matter, a catastrophe involving division into separate sexes followed by the sin and disobedience mythologized in the Eden story. Put another way, Adam gave way to Nature. Before that: 'Adam was a Man, and also a woman, and yet none of them (distinct), but a Virgin full of [...] modesty, and Purity, viz. The Image of God: He had both the Tinctures of fire, and light, in him; and in the Conjunction of which, the own Love, viz. The Virgineall Centre, stood, being the faire Paradisicall Rose-Garden of delight, wherein he loved himselfe; as we also in the Resurrection of the Dead...'[9]

Adam was a Man, and also a woman. Blake will describe Albion's lost consort 'Jerusalem' as 'a city, yet a woman', giving us the clue that the rebuilding of 'Jerusalem' is the reconstitution, redemption and revival of *Man*: this is what Blake understood by the Christian idea that 'by one Spirit are we all baptised into one body' (1 Corinthians 12:13).

Another Behmenist 'contrary' pertinent to the fate of Man is that of Will and Desire. (In England, Böhme was known as 'Jacob Behman'.) Neither are, in themselves, evil. In the *Marriage* Blake writes: 'Those who restrain desire, do so because theirs is weak enough to be restrained; and the restrainer or reason usurps its place & governs the unwilling. And being restrained it by degrees becomes passive till it is only the shadow of desire.' Put another way, the virile are loathed by the impotent. The 'heart's desire' was at the essence of Blake's religious upbringing and nothing but the highest could satisfy it.

Where desire does partake of evil is when its focus is so limited on self that it severs itself from Father and Son. Man must die to self to be reborn in God; God must be reborn in man.

The divine will advances in self-knowledge as it manifests itself as human self-consciousness. Ultimately, the human will, itself a manifestation of the Divine Will, is transformed into the Divine Will through an ongoing dialectical process. God becomes humanity as humanity becomes God: 'The Son of God, the Eternal Word in the Father, who is the glance, or brightness, and the power of the light eternity, must become man and be born in you, if you will know God: otherwise you are in the dark stable and go about groping.'[10]

For this magical process to be enacted, men must rise from self-centredness, cease babbling and permit God to be heard in the heart.

Redemption comes through the New Man, the appearance of the original type. The New Man is Christ, in whom there is no confusion of human and divine Will. Through Him man is brought back – redeemed – to the original bliss. At the Last Day, Man will rise as Adam was first created.

When Blake wrote *The Marriage,* he seems to have thought such a dénouement was imminent.

Adam's essential error was to give way to that part of himself which was reflected in Nature: '... for the properties of the Creation, which all lay in Adam [...]awakened and rose up in its own self, and drew the free-will into it, and would needs be manifested.'[11]

Having 'fallen' once from heaven, and for the second time from Eden, Man's 'Double Fall' involved him in a sleep, unconsciousness, and amnesia.

As long as Man 'stood in heaven his essences were in Paradise; his body was indestructible ... the elements stood in awe of him.' Unfortunately, 'tired of unity, Adam slept and his imagination turned away from God. ... He brought will and desire from God into selfhood and vanity; and he broke himself off from God, from his divine harmony ... Sleep was succumbing to the world's powers, and Adam became a slave to just those powers which previously had served him. Now the elements ruled him.'[12]

In Adam, Blake envisioned a process of painful awakening, of becoming free from the lower elements that had held Man captive since time immemorial, elements manifested in tyrannical rule and distortion of religion.

Böhme armed Blake with his critique of the commonly understood sense of the Bible, as well as the blade to dissect the errors of Milton, as Blake saw them. So Blake could write in *The Marriage of Heaven and Hell,* under the rubric 'The voice of the Devil', of the Bible's Jehovah as 'No other than he who dwells in flaming fire':

The history of this is written in Paradise Lost, and the Governor or Reason is called Messiah.

And the original Archangel or possessor of the command of the heavenly host is called the Devil, or Satan, and his children are called Sin and Death.

But in the book of Job, Milton's Messiah is called Satan.

For this history has been adopted by both parties.

It indeed appeared to Reason as if desire was cast out, but the Devil's account is, that the Messiah fell. & formed a heaven of what he stole from the Abyss [Böhme again].

This is shewn in the Gospel, where he prays to the Father to send the comforter or Desire that Reason may have ideas to build on, the Jehovah of the Bible being no other than he, who dwells in flaming fire. Know that after Christ's death he became Jehovah.

But in Milton, the Father is Destiny, the Son a Ratio of the five senses. & the Holy Ghost, Vacuum!

Note. The reason Milton wrote in fetters when he wrote of Angels & God, and at liberty when of Devils & Hell, is because he was a true Poet, and of the Devil's party without knowing it[.]

The flaming fire is Böhme's first principle of divine essence expressed. As Blake put it, it is 'Energy, call'd evil'. In these fires dwell devils as 'living spirits in the Essences of the Eternal Original'. Angels live in the principle of light, and each spirit must be confined to its principle. Blake always had some sympathy for the devils.

One can feel Blake enjoying a joke at Böhme's expense in his first 'Memorable Fancy' (of three) in *The Marriage of Heaven and Hell:* 'I [Blake] was walking among the fires of hell [he was walking in the country, the natural world in one aspect], delighted with the enjoyments of Genius, which to Angels look like torment and insanity.' The angels can only see their side of the *contrarium*; Blake feels free to 'walk' in the energy of desire: the fire principle. And to Blake, of course, 'Energy is Eternal Delight'.

Most readers of Blake will be familiar with how the poem 'The Tyger' (from *Songs of Experience,* 1794) vividly describes the creation of the tiger's 'fearful symmetry'. The unresolved question haunts the believer: 'Did he who made the lamb make thee?'

In his *Aurora* (1612), Böhme wrote that evil beasts were never intended in the divine plan, originating in Lucifer and his fallen angels' corruption of the world. Without the deviant angels' Fall, there would have been no snakes, toads or venomous insects. But Lucifer focused his admiration on his selfhood, exalting himself, so poisoning the fountains of creation. The life principle took on evil forms, 'as a fiery serpent, or Dragon, and imaged and framed all manner of fiery and poisonous forms and Images, like to wild, cruel and evil Beasts'. According to Böhme, Lucifer 'half killed, spoiled and destroyed the source of life'; so the beast which had most of the fire, or the bitter, or the astringent quality became also a hot, bitter and fierce beast. 'Tyger, Tyger burning bright,/ In the forests of the night;/ What immortal hand or eye,/ Could frame thy fearful symmetry?' And what are these 'forests of the night'?

Adam, who might have lived on the 'fruits of life' (a Böhme phrase used by Blake), chose the earthy nature of the tree. In 'The Poison Tree' (*Songs of Experience,* 1794), we find the words 'wrath', 'poison' and 'anger', highly reminiscent of Böhme in his treatments of the 'Double Fall'. Böhme asks, 'Why did God suffer this Tree to grow [in Eden], seeing Man should eat it? Did he not bring it forth for the fall of Man? And must it not be the Cause of Man's destruction?'

Kathleen Raine observed: 'From this "deadly root" of poison and wrath the Mystery [Nature] branches and extends endlessly.'[13] These extended branches with their infinitely twisting roots are the dark forests of fallen Nature all about us (Blake's Eternal Hell).

In Blake's second story in *The Marriage* under the title 'A Memorable Fancy', he describes a scary journey in which an Angel takes him through a church and down into a vault, then through a mill at the vault's end, then to a winding cavern until they come to a void, boundless beneath them. They grasp the roots of trees above them and, suspended, hang above the void. Blake says he wants to fall into the void and find out if providence exists there. The Angel warns him of presumption and says he will see his 'lot which will soon appear when the darkness passes away':

> So I remained with him sitting in the twisted root of an oak. he was suspended in a fungus which hung with the head downward into the deep:
>
> By degrees we beheld the infinite Abyss, fiery as the smoke of a burning city; beneath us at an immense distance was the sun, black but shining[;] round it were fiery tracks on which revolv'd vast spiders, crawling after their prey; which flew or rather swum in the infinite deep, in the most terrific shapes of animals sprung from corruption.

How Blake's compelling story resolves I shall have to leave for the reader to discover, though we have seen enough to perceive how Blake has taken Böhme's ideas about the corruption of Nature and used them creatively. As to Blake's emblematic 'Tyger', 'Yea!' Blake seems to say, 'the Tyger is awe-inspiring, fearful, magnificent – and doesn't he make you think?'

Kathleen Raine relates the 'Tyger' to Böhme's 'wrath fires' of the Father in one of Blake's many dizzyingly brilliant 'Proverbs of Hell' in *The Marriage*: 'The tygers of wrath are wiser than the horses of instruction.' I believe this aphorism appeared on the walls of the Sorbonne as student graffiti during the rebellious events of 'Mai '68' in Paris. Blake might have wished it had appeared on the same walls in Paris in 1790, for that year he saw its sense everywhere.

Blake turned Böhme's theosophy into ammunition for Mental War against abstracted Reason and sexual repression, military and corporate stateism and industrialization. But his greatest fight was with materialism, the worship of mere Nature in its outer aspect, the quantifiable and measurable universe, the external world as seen by the cold eye of abstracted science: what he called 'Newton's sleep'. And as his war was against external vision, Blake knew that the struggle that mattered was not primarily through external politics and laws but *via* spiritual transformation and freed energy.

Blake famously saw the hidden energy, the vast eternities in the apparently microscopic: 'To see a heaven in a grain of sand/ and a heaven in a wild flower/ hold infinity in the palm of your hand/ and Eternity in an Hour' (from Blake's *Notebook*, undated). Now hear Böhme, though not as succinct: 'If thou conceivest a small minute circle, as small as a grain of mustard seed, yet the Heart of God is wholly and perfectly therein: and if thou art born in God, then there is in thyself (in the circle of thy life) the whole Heart of God undivided.'[14]

Blake seems to have derived almost his whole notion of movement, velocity, force, change and momentum from Böhme's dynamic theosophy. Everything is forced into a change and transformation. Morality and physics jump and dive and dig and cut together.

In the poem 'The Poison Tree', the Poison Tree grows from 'wrath' and the 'apple bright' from anger. For Böhme this tree is also Nature: 'it grew out of the Earth and has wholly the Nature of the Earth in it'. Earth is corruptible, so shall Nature 'pass away in the End, when all goes into its Ether'. Commenting on this parallel, Kathleen Raine exclaimed how 'He [Böhme] might be paraphrasing Paracelsus.' Of the two trees in the legend – the Tree of Life and the Tree of Good and Evil – Böhme holds that they are one tree, but manifested in two different principles: the light of heaven (Son) and the fires of Hell ('the wrath of the anger of God', the Father).

The ambivalence of the divine 'wrath' preoccupied Blake. The issue surrounding this fiery and decidedly unliberal issue reaches its apex in the famous question provoked by contemplation of the 'Tyger': 'Did he who made the Lamb make thee?' Kathleen Raine wondered if we should consider an answer through the prism of Böhme's words: 'The God of the holy World, and the God of the dark World, are not two Gods; there is but one only God. He Himself is all Being. He is Evil and Good; Heaven and Hell; Light and Darkness; Eternity and Time. Where his Love is hid in anything, there His Anger is manifest.'

Raine came to the conclusion: 'This is the god of the Alchemists, beyond the contraries.' 'Too great,' Blake would add, 'for the eye of man.'

The roaring of lions, the howling of wolves, the raging of the stormy sea, and the destructive sword, are portions of eternity too great for the eye of man.[15]

The Marriage of Heaven and Hell, whence this aphorism derives, is such a trove of wisdom, containing so many of Blake's most memorable insights, that it simply must be read in its entirety. From the biographical perspective, it reveals Blake's ongoing unspoken dialogue with Swedenborg. Under the title 'Opposition is true Friendship', he makes further, no-holds-barred digs at Swedenborg:

I have always found that Angels have the vanity to speak of themselves as the only wise; this they do with a confident insolence sprouting from systematic reasoning. Thus Swedenborg boasts that what he writes is new; tho' it is only the Contents or Index of already publish'd books. A man carried a monkey about for a shew, & because he was a little wiser than the monkey, grew vain, and conciev'd himself as much wiser than seven men. It is so with Swedenborg: he shews the folly of churches & exposes hypocrites, till he imagines that all are religious, & himself the single one on earth that ever broke a net. Now hear a plain fact: Swedenborg has not written one new truth. Now hear another: he has written all the old falshoods [sic]. And now hear the reason. He conversed with Angels who are all religious, & conversed not with Devils who all hate religion, for he was incapable thro' his conceited notions. Thus Swedenborgs writings are a recapitulation of all superficial opinions, and an analysis of the more sublime, but no further. Have now another plain fact. Any man of mechanical talents may, from the writings of Paracelsus or Jacob Behmen [Böhme], produce ten thousand volumes of equal value with Swedenborg's, and from those of Dante or Shakespear an infinite number. But when he has done this, let him not say that he knows better than his master, for he only holds a candle in sunshine.

That would have brought no delight to Flaxman, but he was far away in Rome.

Blake closed his extraordinary tract with 'A Song of Liberty' that looks ahead to his poems 'The French Revolution' and 'America: A Prophecy'. The liberty song starts with what may be the text for the illustration of the woman akimbo, flames pouring from her genitals, a text based on St Paul's writing of the 'whole creation groaning in travail until now for the revealing of the sons of God' (Romans 8:18–23):

1. The Eternal Female groan'd! it was heard over all the Earth:
2. Albion's coast is sick silent; the American meadows faint!
3. Shadows of Prophecy shiver along by the lakes and the rivers and mutter across the ocean: France, rend down thy dungeon;
4. Golden Spain, burst the barriers of old Rome;
5. Cast thy keys, O Rome, into the deep down falling, even to eternity down falling
6. And weep!
7. In her trembling hands she took the new born terror howling;
8. On those infinite mountains of light, now barr'd out by the atlantic sea, the new born fire stood before the starry king!

The identity of the 'new born terror' or 'new born fire' who will challenge 'Starry Jealousy' or the lord of the bounded universe is kept for another writing. The little terror will emerge as 'Orc', child of freedom and rebellion who becomes manifest when spiritual feeling is repressed: a wild child for sure. And should he not be finally identified with the figure depicted in the famous watercolour known as *Glad Day* discussed in Chapter Seven (see p.88). For there he stands on the infinite mountains of light, free at last!

The verses end with a cry that will return word for word in 'America': 'Empire is no more! And now the lion & wolf shall cease.'

And if that were not enough, there is a final chorus, one that appears to attack both the black-gowned Churchmanship that condemns Man's sexual nature as shameful, as well as, in veiled words, a Freemasonry ('accepted brethren' called 'free': a long-unnoticed, highly potent reference to London's 'Grand Lodge') that is putting a roof on the formerly infinite Lodge in touch with the heavens by venerating the Great Geometer that is Reason the Restrainer.[16]

Let the Priests of the Raven of dawn, no longer in deadly black, with hoarse note curse the sons of joy. Nor his accepted brethren, whom, tyrant, he calls free: lay the bound or build the roof. Nor pale religious letchery call that virginity, that wishes but acts not!

For every thing that lives is Holy.

Every thing that lives is holy! Had Great Britain entertained an Inquisition, Blake and his 'sons of joy' would have been roasted.

There was providence in the void.

All this visionary apotheosis of 'Man' may lead us to forget who, in particular, had to benefit from Blake's marriage of heaven and hell. Much on Blake's mind in this period were the little men and women to be seen everywhere on London's 'charter'd streets'. 'What about the children?' asked Mrs Banks, the banker's wife, in *Mary Poppins* before the dance of the chimney sweeps showed the Bankses something they were missing of life. Was there an apocalyptic hope for the children? In Blake's heart, there was, for it was in this period that he wrote 'The Chimney Sweeper', included, not without dark irony, in the *Songs of Innocence.*

Conditions among the little boy sweeps were appalling. Many died before maturity from respiratory conditions; many were killed in pursuance of tireless, unremitting work, forced up crumbling chimneys too narrow even for their cold, hungry bodies. In the harrowing story of Blake's 'Chimney Sweeper' we hear of a little boy whose mother died when he was in infancy, who was then sold by his father into the trade: 'in soot I sleep.' He describes little Tom Dacre who wept when his curly hair was shaved for the job, and how he made a joke of it: at least the soot wouldn't spoil it.

> And so he was quiet, & that very night,
> As Tom was sleeping he had such a sight,
> That thousands of sweepers Dick, Joe, Ned & Jack
> Were all of them lock'd up in coffins of black,
>
> And by came an Angel who had a bright key,
> And he open'd the coffins and set them all free.

Then down a green plain leaping laughing they run
And wash in a river and shine in the Sun

This was indeed a vision. On 21 December 1790, the first cotton mill to use new technology was opened on Rhode Island in the United States. Its owner, Sam Slater, had been apprenticed to the water frame's English inventor, Richard Arkwright. Slater used water and children to operate his mill.

In England, reaction to new technology was often violent. Robert Peel (1750–1830), the son of a Lancashire mill owner, used James Hargreaves' innovative 'spinning Jenny'. It was broken by handweavers who saw their livelihoods disappearing. Peel moved to Burton upon Trent, Staffordshire, where he built three mills and a canal (4,000 miles of waterways had been constructed since 1760). Peel hit on the idea of recruiting stray children off the streets of London and putting them to work as 'apprentices' in the mills. Thus made rich, Peel decided on a political career and bought nearby Tamworth's pocket borough. His son Robert would become Prime Minister in 1834.

THIRTEEN

What is now proved was once, only imagin'd

1791

No bird soars too high. if he soars with his own wings.
[...] What is now proved was once, only imagin'd

(The Marriage of Heaven and Hell, 1790–93)

Mr and Mrs Blake began the year 1791 on something of a high. They had a new house, having moved south the previous autumn from Poland Street across Westminster Bridge to 13 Hercules Buildings, Lambeth. Catherine Blake's mother and aunts came from Lambeth, so she might have found family and friends there.

There wasn't much to Lambeth in those days. Apart from the Archbishop of Canterbury's palace, there were, amid lanes, fields and marshes, a few rows of fairly new houses, built 20 years earlier, of which Blake's was one. Timber yards occupied the Thames bank. Across the road stood the Royal Asylum for Female Orphans, the workhouse where Swedenborgian Jacob Duché had served as chaplain until 1789. In 1774, Duché's extemporaneous prayers at the American rebels' first Continental Congress had profoundly touched John Adams and the historic assembly. Duché's wife Elizabeth's brother, Francis Hopkinson, was in fact a signatory to the Declaration of Independence. Blake almost certainly knew Duché, for Duché maintained his discussion groups with moderate and radical Swedenborgians until he returned to the United States in 1793.

Number 13 Hercules Buildings had three floors and a basement, and each floor had two well-proportioned rooms, with three feet of panelling, handsome cupboards and marble mantlepieces. Blake could look down on his narrow garden from his workroom; the whole place, judging from his prolific output there, suited him.

According to Flaxman's sister-in-law, Maria Denman, Blake planted a fig tree and a vine arbour, but refused to prune the vine out of a belief pruning was wrong. The Blakes sat there in the summer with Flaxman, surrounded by cascading fruit, luxuriating in a south London bacchanal, singing songs. Not surprisingly, perhaps, a story circulated among students at the Academy in later years that the Blakes had on occasion sat there naked. Surprised by a visitor, Will and Kate allegedly celebrated their innocence by declaring they were Adam and Eve! Samuel Palmer vehemently repudiated this story, declaring it both apocryphal and completely out of character, but one can't help wondering nonetheless. Perhaps it was simply the idea of the dreamer Blake amid the grape that conjured the image from wishful thinking.

At the garden's end grew a peach tree, by which stood a summerhouse, with a privy beneath poplar trees. Two other significant buildings stood in the vicinity: the Bethlehem Hospital for Lunatics (its presence adding to the myth of Blake's madness that would develop in the 1790s) and, three streets away, Astley's Amphitheatre, owned by John Conway Philip Astley, who lived in a house in the garden of 15 Hercules Buildings.

Astley was quite a character. In 1799 he would co-found the Masonic Benefit Society (now the RMBI), patronized by Grand Master George, Prince of Wales, and busied himself raising extra income amid the uncertainties of war. The Society enjoyed the support of both rival 'Grand Lodges': the Grand Lodge of England (est. 1716–23), and the 'Antient' Grand Lodge (est. 1751). An Antient Freemason (as Blake's father might have been), Astley was in 1787 a member of the Lodge of Temperance No. 22 (now 169). Astley founded another lodge, Royal Grove Lodge No. 240, becoming its Master in 1788 (it lasted till 1836).

Astley owned Astley's Royal Grove Circus in Dublin and Astley's Amphitheatre in Lambeth. The Circus specialized in equestrian acts and comedy, and had a band. A horse-rider called Samson played the flute while riding two horses at once without reins. There was Billy the miniature Learned

Horse who counted numbers, ungirthed his own saddle, took kettles of boiling water off a fire and could act as a waiter at tea parties. It says something of the times that Billy would be brought up on a charge of witchcraft; accusations were dismissed: Reason reigned, after all! Perhaps the strangest attraction was the Scientific Pig who could read minds (he read ladies' minds only by permission). The pig could also spell, read handwriting and tell the time from a person's watch in the audience – he was, in short, better equipped than many children leaving school today. The pig's death so disturbed his owner that the poor man was consigned to Edinburgh's Asylum.[1]

Tatham's manuscript 'Life' of Blake (1832) relates how the artist, standing one day at one of his windows 'which looked into Astley's premises', was struck by the sight of a boy, hobbling along with a log attached to his leg, of the kind used to keep horses from straying. Asking his wife why such a thing should be, he was told it must have been punishment for some 'inadvertence', whereupon Blake's blood boiled with indignation that such a thing should ever be done to an Englishman, an act inexcusable in the treatment of a slave. He stormed down to demand the boy's release. Astley, with like vehemence, approached Blake's door demanding why his judgement with regard to the boy should have been crossed. The argument, according to Tatham, nearly came to blows, such was Blake's fury and Astley's matching indignation. However, when Blake explained the matter, Astley cottoned on: the punishment was too degrading. The two men parted with mutual forgiveness and respect; Astley apparently admired Blake's humane sensibility.

The confrontation is a pure illustration of Blake's own verse of wisdom: 'I was angry with my friend. I told my wrath; my wrath did end.'

Comfortably ensconced in Lambeth, it seems Blake's new etching technique was perfected some time in 1791. He attributed his invention to the spirit of his departed brother, Robert. It was based on a technique called relief etching, described in an anonymous work: *Valuable Secrets concerning Arts and Trades* (reprinted many times after 1758). The aim was to engrave with *aquafortis* to make a work resemble *basso relievo*. Blake added his own innovation: a liquid that was impervious to acid, used to write on copper. John Jackson (1801–1848) made a study of Blake's method.[2]

The subject is drawn onto the copper plate in Burgundy pitch (spruce resin), or any appropriate substance that resists *aquafortis* (nitric acid). When the substance in which the drawing has been made has become hard, the plate is surrounded by a 'wall', and *aquafortis* is poured onto the plate. The unprotected parts are corroded, leaving the drawing in relief. The chief advantage of this method for Blake's intentions was to enable him to write copious amounts of illuminated poetry on the plate, whereas to incise the words into copper would have been interminable labour. Even so, the writing had to be done in reverse, using a mirror, so that it would be legible when the copper received the paper impress. Blake's patience with the process was admirable.

There were other problems. Blake used a rolling or copperplate press for his metallic relief engravings, the impression being obtained from the lines, as in a woodcut. It was difficult to corrode the white parts to sufficient depth to avoid their being touched by a dauber or ball in the process of inking. To avoid soiling, Blake and his wife had to wipe out surplus ink from the hollows. This took longer than inking the plate, so printing was slow.

Complete illuminations required painting by hand. Blake and his wife ground the watercolours themselves on a piece of statuary marble, using common carpenter's glue as a binder. The early Italian painters used it; Blake attributed the 'secret' to the revelation of the holy carpenter St Joseph.

Colours used were indigo, cobalt, gamboge, vermilion, Frankfort-black and, occasionally, ultramarine, applied with a camel's hair brush. Each illuminated book made thus became a unique artwork, something that appealed in itself. Likewise, when he made prints, he delighted in the accidental transformations that could be wrought on a basic design by varying the blend of watercolours.

As far as we can tell, Blake would not advertise the existence of his illuminated work until October 1793, when six works 'in Illuminated Printing' were made available to the public.

Blake obviously still hoped in 1791 to get his poetry published in the conventional manner. A set of proofs survives, dated 1791: *THE FRENCH REVOLUTION. A POEM, IN SEVEN BOOKS. BOOK THE FIRST. LONDON: Printed for J. Johnson, No 72, St Paul's Church-yard. MDCCXCI. (Price One Shilling)*. The 'Advertisement' at the head of the proofs claims that the remaining books of the poem were finished and would be published in order. If they were ever written, they have not survived.

'The French Revolution' was by no means Blake's finest work. The mode is rather like the voice of 'Chorus' introducing and commenting on a Shakespearean play. Unfortunately, the play in question was real enough, proceeding with mounting violence across the Channel – in a country the author had never visited, and never would visit. Imagination without direct experience has its limitations when dealing with historical subjects. There is therefore an anaemic quality to the work. It is not worth speculating too much on why Johnson did not publish it. Perhaps politically it was too dangerous: William Pitt's spies were on the lookout for anyone who considered Great Britain ripe for revolution.

Perhaps Johnson just couldn't see a market for it – it's hard to say, and impossible to know. Publication would not have done Blake any good; and, proud as he was, he needed all the help he could get.

Perhaps in his way Blake was trying to be popular, to come up with a more immediately accessible work. Genius and the meat-market seldom mix. Blake seems to have confused Louis XVI with his own poetic tyrant, Tiriel, with a touch of Shakespeare's crook-backed Richard III for good measure. The work tries too hard, I think, to show physical manifestations as the expression of brooding, overbearing spiritual movements: the resulting verbal canvas exhibits such a rough-brush manner as to render the Hermetic axiom 'As above; so below' a satiric commonplace. You would never think Jacques Necker was a finance minister to read Blake's less than prophetic effusion.

> Troubled, leaning on Necker, descends the King, to his chamber of
> council; shady mountains
> In fear utter voices of thunder; the woods of France embosom the
> sound;
> Clouds of wisdom prophetic reply, and roll over the palace roof heavy.

If one may quote from *The Marriage of Heaven and Hell:* 'Enough! Or Too much.'

In the France of flesh and blood, 16 January 1791 saw the formation of a new national police force, the *gendarmerie.* Meanwhile, secret police thrust their tentacles into hitherto private realms. Revolutionary states never trust anyone.

As the Jacobins saw it, the Roman Catholic Church still exerted counter-revolutionary influence, holding France captive to its past. On 20 January, Talleyrand had to resign the bishopric of Autun for having sworn allegiance to the new civil constitution imposed on the Church by the state. The Papacy could do very little but attack its own representatives. Tom Paine was delighted: 'There is a dawn of reason rising on the world,' wrote Paine in the second part of his *Rights of Man*. On 13 April, Pope Pius VI offered priests who had sworn allegiance to the civil constitution 40 days to recant. Failure to revoke state obligations would be punished by excommunication.

Five days later, the National Guard prevented Louis XVI and his family from leaving Paris. Another brave attempt to escape the capital was foiled on 25 June at Varennes. Louis' powers were temporarily suspended, as if he were a naughty boy. The 23-year-old Louis-Antoine de St Juste exalted in the wonder of it all in his overblown book, *The Spirit of the Revolution*. 'Bliss it was in that dawn to be alive/ But to be young was very heaven,' as Wordsworth would write in *The Prelude* concerning *his* French sojourn in 1791. Young or not, revolutionary enthusiast St Juste would be guillotined three years later.

In London, radicals' publisher Joseph Johnson had not forgotten Blake's engraving skills. Johnson was publishing a major work by Freemason Dr Erasmus Darwin, who in 1781 had moved from Lichfield, Staffordshire, to Derby. *The Botanic Garden* (first part) would duly earn the praise of Samuel Taylor Coleridge for its combination of science and poetry – something we don't see much of these days. It transpired that Blake had a connection with the subject Johnson wanted him to engrave.

It was Sir William Hamilton who had first brought the Roman 'Barberini Vase' to England after purchasing it in 1778. Margaret, Dowager Duchess of Portland bought it in 1784, whence it passed to her son, the Duke of Portland. Flaxman was invited to see the 'Portland Vase' and was impressed by a wonder of classical cameo-glassmaking that seemed to depict spiritual rebirth after discarding the garment of the body. Kathleen Raine thought the images from antiquity might have inspired Blake's poem 'The Little Girl Lost'.[3] Flaxman, who designed for Josiah Wedgwood, wrote to his employer, extolling the vase as the apex of the perfection Wedgwood sought; Flaxman suggested Etruria produce a replica. In April–May 1790, the vase replica in jasperware was exhibited in Greek Street. Blake probably went to see it. Copies later went on sale in London showrooms. It was an instant hit. The publicity did Flaxman no harm at all.

Erasmus Darwin (grandfather of Charles) wanted to include an engraving of the original vase in *The Botanic Garden*. On 9 July 1791, Darwin wrote to Josiah Wedgwood: 'Mr Johnson's engraver now wishes much to see Bartolozzi's plates of the vase, & will engrave them again if necessary [...] the name of the engraver I don't know [Blake], but Johnson said he is capable of doing anything well ...'[4] On 27 July, Johnson wrote to Darwin referring to Blake: 'Bartolozzi's plates cannot be copied without Hamilton's consent.'[5] Johnson said it would be best if Blake had access to the vase. Whatever access he may have had, Blake's transcription of the vase was perfect, and put him in the mainstream of high-quality publishing. *The Botanic Garden's* second part, *The Loves of the Plants*, has been called 'the sex life of plants', and the poetry was appropriately romantic with some erotic elements: the whole divided according to what Darwin called the 'four elements of the Rosicrucians'. The book evinced an antislavery stance – Wedgwood himself wrote against slavery for the book – support for the French Revolution, and some speculations regarding evolution that would be taken up in time by Erasmus's grandson, Charles.

Blake also executed another remarkable engraving for *The Botanic Garden*. His 'Fertilization of Egypt', after Fuseli, was signed *Blake sc.* (from *sculpere*, to carve, engrave) to the right of Fuseli's design credit. It depicts the jackal-headed god Anubis, bestriding the Nile like the Colossus of Rhodes. Beyond the pyramids, a divinity with thunderbolts in his hands casts rain over the soil-rich country. Engraved with a striking sense of perspective and drama, the bearded god strongly resembles Blake's later images for his figure Urizen, hardly distinguishable from the 'God of this world' he called 'Old Nobodaddy'.

While Darwin busied himself with publication of his latest book in Derby, to the south, in Birmingham, a 14 July banquet to mark the Storming of the Bastille caused a riot when a mob incited by an Anglican clergyman attacked the house of the host, Joseph Priestley. Priestley quit for London, then the United States.

On 12 August, having been given the vote in Paris and having been denied it by planters, black slaves in Santo Domingo (now capital of the Dominican

Republic) rose in revolt. This event, and others like it, may have inspired the stirring stanzas that would appear in 1793 in Blake's *America: A Prophecy*:

> Let the slave grinding at the mill, run out into the field:
> Let him look up into the heavens & laugh in the bright air;
> Let the inchained soul shut up in darkness and in sighing,
> Whose face has never seen a smile in thirty weary years;
> Rise and look out, his chains are loose, his dungeon doors are open.
> And let his wife and children return from the oppressors scourge;
> They look behind at every step & believe it is a dream.
> Singing. The Sun has left his blackness, & has found a fresher morning
> And the fair Moon rejoices in the clear & cloudless night;
> For Empire is no more, and now the Lion & Wolf shall cease.

Apart from the repeat of the last line that would grace *The Marriage of Heaven and Hell*, self-published in 1793, we should observe that the lines probably do not refer to British mill workers, as is readily supposed, especially by those under the 'dark satanic mills' misapprehension, but to the real slaves working in the Indies and French Louisana at sugar mills, where sugar canes were ground in wooden or metal rollers with cogs and wheels, and the detritus burnt in furnaces.

Mary Wollstonecraft

Mary Wollstonecraft (1759–1797), writer, philosopher and feminist, had been involved with Joseph Johnson's circle since 1787 when Johnson published her *Thoughts on the Education of Daughters*. She became Johnson's translator, reader and editorial assistant. In 1788, Johnson published her children's book, *Original Stories from Real Life*, as well as her translation of Jacques Necker's *Of the Importance of Religious Opinions*. Through Johnson she met several leading political radicals, including John Horne Took and Blake's friend, painter Henry Fuseli, with whom Miss Wollstonecraft would embark on an adulterous affair in 1789. That year, Blake was called upon to provide unsigned engravings for her translation of Christian Gotthilf Salzmann's *Elements of Morality, for the Use of Children* – Blake would in due course self-publish an 'alternative' children's book, *For Children: The Gates of Paradise* in 1793.

Two editions of Mary Wollstonecraft's *Vindication of the Rights of Men* appeared in 1790, published by Johnson, with her name on the title page. Wollstonecraft began writing the feminist classic *A Vindication of the Rights of Woman* in September 1791, the same month in which appeared the second edition of her children's book *Original Stories from Real Life: with Conversations, Calculated to Regulate the Affections and Form the Mind to Truth and Goodness*, this time with six engravings by Blake. Ten pen and wash sketches, from which five of the engravings were taken, are now in the Library of Congress, Washington, DC; they were formerly owned by the Gilchrist family.[6]

For those who find Blake's mythical painting daunting, these sketches might provide a way in to appreciating his all-round skills. One imagines their usefulness to costume designers for lavish BBC productions, so charming are Blake's depictions of teacher Mrs Mason and her two girl pupils, very gracefully attired in 'empire lines'. Mrs Mason wears a dark Tudor bonnet-like hat with a high, very broad crown and brim; the girls with curling locks sport oval straw summer hats. Not all is nursery freshness, however. A number of the sketches offer Blake an opportunity to express his humane cynicism. The title 'Oeconomy and Self-Denial are Necessary' is illustrated by Mrs Mason and her charges entering the sparse interior of a cottage where a desperate, hungry family gathers round an empty grate, weeping for want of food and warmth. The face of 'A Starving Woman with Two Children' is reminiscent of a horrified visage from some tormented spirit figure in Blake's designs for *Young's Night Thoughts* (1797). The figure of 'Mrs Mason' probably reflects Wollstonecraft's approving women's participation in 'adopted' lodges of Freemasonry in France, dedicated to social, philanthropic and philosophical work. The Revolution was pushing Masonic lodges, including 'adopted' women Masons, into dormancy.

While in England the imaginary 'Mrs Mason' brought a concept of social responsibility to her young charges, in Paris 43-year-old playwright and gender equality activist Olympe de Gouges, an associate of the *Loge des Neuf Soeurs* (Nine Sisters Lodge), pipped Mary Wollstonecraft to the post by five months by publishing her *Declaration of the Rights of Woman and the Female Citizen* in September 1791. The brave Olympe would be guillotined in the Place de la Révolution on 3 November 1793. Her crime: alliance to a different revolutionary faction (the Girondins) to the prevailing one (the Jacobins). The guillotine exercised no gender preference.

In November 1791, Mary Wollstonecraft met William Godwin for the first time at one of Johnson's literary dinners. She did not like him; in fact, Wollstonecraft became more obsessed with Fuseli than ever, an ungovernable passion that in the autumn of 1792 boiled over when she called at Fuseli's house with a proposition to him and his wife Sophia: that since their love was innocent, they should all live together as *a ménage à trois*. One can only guess at Blake's reaction to the scandal involving his friend and occasional benefactor. Could Wollstonecraft's willingness to play concubine have lain behind Blake's remark years later to Crabb Robinson that Swedenborg's 'sexual religion was dangerous'? Mary Wollstonecraft would marry the journalist, philosopher and novelist Godwin in 1797. Their daughter, the future Mary Shelley, was the author of *Frankenstein* (1818): a warning, and a plea for the necessity of a stable, loving family to prevent the monster-*Man* becoming a living nightmare.

These were crazy times and we today can hardly imagine the excitement, the sense of social and atmospheric tremor, the creaking and cracking of an old world crumbling and peeling away to reveal startling, invigorating, frightening, earth-quaking visions of untrammelled, apocalyptic liberty, which stirred the heads and hearts of the *avant garde*. In the dizzying heat of it all, it comes almost as cooling relief to find that the first known letter of William Blake to anyone, anywhere, concerned an engraving commission for a work of crisp antiquarian scholarship, albeit one of the greatest such works of the century.

On 18 October 1791, a month before his thirty-fourth birthday, Blake received the compliments of editor Willey Reveley with an enquiry asking whether Mr Blake wished 'to engrave any of Mr Pars' drawings for the Antiquities of Athens'. If Blake could 'do them' by the end of January 1792, Mr Reveley would be glad to send 'some to him'.[7]

Blake had reason to be chuffed. It was his master James Basire who had executed most of the engravings for the first volume of *The Antiquities of Athens,* back in 1762. William Pars was, of course, the younger brother of Henry Pars, young Blake's drawing master. In 1764, Pars had been with Dr Richard Chandler and Nicholas Revett to Asia. Reveley was now editing Volume 3 of James Stuart and Nicholas Revett's series. William Pars would contribute some of the engraving.

Blake replied to Reveley that, 'tho full of work', he was 'glad to embrace the offer of engraving such beautiful things' and would do what he could to meet the deadline. In fact, his engravings were not ready until the beginning of April. Blake had very little sense of, or interest in, time. That very November, Nancy Flaxman wrote from Rome to her sister-in-law, Maria Denman, to 'pray call on Mr Blake & beg of him to answer your Brother's Letter directly.' Bentley doubts if Blake even responded to this.[8]

John Gabriel Stedman was a Scottish-Dutch retired soldier of fortune, poet and painter. On 1 December 1791, he confided to his journal that he had received through the offices of publisher Joseph Johnson about 40 engravings for his projected *Narrative, of a five years' expedition, against the Revolted Negroes of Surinam, in Guiana, on the Wild Coast of South America*. Stedman, while putting down slave revolts, had acquired a great respect for 'my brother the negro' and wanted the world to know about the hideous abuse of slaves by jealous old white women whose husbands and relatives exhausted themselves with uninhibited black women. Stedman's account of the many tortures unjustly inflicted on slaves gave ammunition to the anti-slavery movement, though Stedman did not write against the slavery system itself. He was content to target what he saw as its inhuman abuses. Stedman was outspoken, maintaining that control of slave islands was only achieved through the admirable fighting skills of 'slaves in red coats' – that is, negroes recruited for security services.

Despite Stedman's writing to Blake to congratulate him on his – now famous – contributions to the book, Stedman would not meet Blake for some years. His chaotic *Journal* is nevertheless punctuated with multiple references to the artist.[9]

That month of December, flames of revolution blew closer to home when in Dublin the Protestant lawyer Wolfe Tone founded the Dublin Society of United Irishmen, calling for full independence from the Union while seeking military support from Paris.

On 5 December, in Vienna, Wolfgang Amadeus Mozart died of fever at the age of 35: one less genius, and the world carried on regardless.

FOURTEEN

'Works of Extraordinary Genius and Imagination'

1792–1793

It has often been reported that Blake, with no lack of courage, wore the woollen *bonnet rouge* of the revolutionaries in the streets, and was a 'liberty boy' and a lifelong republican. But what kind of 'radical' was Blake really? Was he a romantic radical, like Wordsworth in his hot youth, caring little for ideological detail but swept into a euphoria of 'equality, fraternity, liberty' for all? – or did he rather pick and choose: more of the liberty, less of the equality? Not Deist, but spiritual. Did he want to 'man the barricades,' or was Blake fundamentally a millenarian, seeing the revolution as a sign of a spiritual epiphany unfolding, its material manifestations incidental?

What does this word 'radical' mean?

Learned Divine Dr Thomas Townson, Archdeacon of Richmond, friend and benefactor of Rev. Ralph Churton, died, aged 77, on 15 April 1792. According to Churton's manuscript *Reminiscences:*

> A man who called on him (Dr Townson) soliciting subscriptions to some projected publication, being invited to drink, said, 'Give me a toast!' 'I'll give you Church & King,' said Dr Townson. 'A very good toast,' he said, and drank it in all appearance heartily; and then said, 'Now Sir, I will give you a toast, Alderman Trecothick's toast; "Here is, Old England freed from the tyranny of priests & Kings!!"'[1]

Barlow Trecothick (?1718–1775) was a wealthy merchant, educated in Boston, Massachusetts. He served as a London alderman (1764–74), then as Lord Mayor in 1770, afterwards as MP for the City of London. Trecothick assisted the repeal of the hated Stamp Acts, liaised with City and merchant interests, and cautioned successive governments through the 1760s that a policy of conciliation, not hard pressure, would ease tensions with American merchants. After the 'Boston Massacre', Trecothick spoke up in the Commons, accusing Britain's representatives of behaving 'like bullies', standing on 'phantom honour' rather than reason. Surely, Trecothick reasoned, the state should forego taxes for the greater benefits of a trade monopoly.

Trecothick's alleged 'toast' looks back to 'Old England' freed from arbitrary rule. And that is pretty much the general stance 'radicals' had in common. They tended to be critical, at least, of the dominance of the Church, and intolerant of monarchical prerogatives. More radical positions included extension of the franchise (the poor had no voice to ameliorate their wretchedness) and improvement of workers' conditions. A minority dreamt of an overthrow of the state by the 'popular will'. Some were rationalists, some were idealists: some both. But radicals disagreed with one another as much as with their 'enemies', real or imagined. Trecothick, for example, was on hostile terms with 'fellow radicals' John Wilkes and John Horne Tooke, a friend of Blake's friend George Cumberland. Tooke and Wilkes fell out as well. The question of radicalism boiled down to how far the individual was prepared to go in challenging the law, and how far the state was prepared to go in suppressing dissenting views. Most radicals favoured rhetoric and writing, but as the revolution in France became bloodier such methods came under closer government scrutiny, and intolerance of political dissent grew.

On 25 January 1792, the London Corresponding Society was established, modelled on the Jacobin Club in Paris. Blake, aged 34 at this time, did not join; Johnson and Cumberland did. In Paris, the revolution had split wide open. On 29 June, Lafayette tried, but failed, to get the National Guard to break up the Jacobin Club. Relative moderates lost control. On 10 August a mob of 'sans-culottes' seized the Tuileries palace; the King was imprisoned. The next day, a revolutionary commune was formed. The first journalist to be guillotined was Du Rozoy, director of the *Gazette du Paris*, on 24 August. His crime? Raising money for *émigrés*. On the shores of Sussex, the Prince of Wales wept at the sight of French gentility, clergy and aristocracy pouring off boats, fleeing the galloping Terror. Some of them he recognized as former guests at races and dances and dinners, and not a 'Scarlet Pimpernel' in sight.

A few weeks later, in London, flush from a fiery public meeting and delighted by news that the department of Calais had elected 'Citizen' Paine to the National Convention, Tom Paine gave Johnson's regular literary dinner a last taste of his rhetorical force. According to Gilchrist, Blake offered Paine timely advice to get out quick following his speech. But it was Tatham, many years later, who provided Blake's lines to Paine: 'If you are not now sought, I am sure you will be.' (A drawing in Blake's *Notebook*, arguably of Paine, is the only evidence he and Blake ever communicated.) In fact, it was well known that the government's suit of a seditious libel against Paine for his latest *Rights of Man* required Paine's presence in court in September. When the order arrived, conveniently late, to detain Paine at Customs, he had already – after a hostile reception – passed through and boarded his ship for France. Most likely, the government wanted Paine out, rather than handing him an opportunity to whip up support as a martyr in court. Paine never returned.

Communal madness broke out in France on 4 September. Paranoid that a Prussian army was marching on Paris (a threat of the Duke of Brunswick in the event of the King being harmed), revolutionary partisans dragged prisoners from their cells and hacked them to death while an almshouse full of prostitutes and young orphaned girls was violated and its inhabitants grotesquely slaughtered. Across the country, life became cheaper than bread.

Three days later, Blake's mother, Catherine, died, three weeks short of her sixty-ninth birthday. Catherine Blake, the girl from Nottinghamshire, was not interred in the Moravian cemetery in Chelsea, but lay by her husband in Bunhill Fields. We have no record of Blake's reaction to the loss.

On 19 September, Paris welcomed Tom Paine as a renegade from 'tyranny'. He dined the next night on news that Kellerman's revolutionary army had trounced Brunswick's men at Valmy. The next day, monarchy was abolished in France.

Positioned militarily on France's northern border against an Austrian-Prussian coalition, Lafayette, defender of the King and Queen against extremists Danton and Robespierre, watched his back. Fast losing his troops' confidence, certain he was next for the guillotine, Lafayette tried to escape through Austria to a Dutch port as an American citizen (which he was). Counted by Austria's Emperor as a dangerous anti-monarchist, he was gaoled by the Austrians at Wezel. These events stimulated largely incoherent verses from Blake, confided in his *Notebook*. They reveal that Blake, at least at the time, could happily have drunk Trecothick's toast:

> Let the Brothels of Paris be opened
> With many an alluring dance
> To awake the Physicians thro the city
> Said the beautiful Queen of France
>
> Then old Nobodaddy aloft
> Farted and belchd and coughd
> And said I love hanging & drawing & quartering
> Every bit as well as war and slaughtering
>
> Then he swore a great & solemn Oath
> To kill the people I am loth
> But if they rebel they must go to hell
> They shall have a Priest & a passing bell
>
> The King awoke on his couch of gold
> As soon as he heard these tidings told
> Arise & come both fife and drum
> And the ['Famine' crossed out] shall eat both crust and crumb
>
> The Queen of France just touchd this Globe
> And the Pestilence darted from her robe
> But our good Queen quite grows to the ground
> And a great many suckers grow all around

Additional lines suggest Blake thought Lafayette had misspent his tears on the King and Queen: instruments of a tyrannical conception of God.

Fayette Fayette thourt [thou art] bought & sold
And sold is thy happy morrow
Thou gavest the tears of Pity away
In exchange for the tears of sorrow

A 'song of innocence'? In 1798, *ESSAYS MORAL, ECONOMICAL AND POLITICAL by FRANCIS BACON, BARON OF VERULAM AND VISCOUNT ST. ALBANS* was published in London.[2] Blake annotated his copy with fury, pointing out Bacon's innumerable self-contradictions and what Blake regarded as Bacon's lily-livered, foolish sophistries in argument and exposition. Anyone who rates Bacon highly should read Blake's unsettling criticism.

Pages 38 and 39 of the original book deal with critical issues of sedition. Bacon's view of sedition was that it came under the category of *envy*: 'This envy, being in the Latin word 'invidia', goeth in the modern languages by the name of discontentment; of which we shall speak in handling sedition. It is a disease in a state like to infection ...' Bacon goes on to say that 'public envy' is chiefly aimed at 'principal officers or ministers, rather than upon kings and estates themselves'. Blake's annotation to this is direct: 'A Lie Every Body hates a King Bacon was afraid to say that the Envy was upon a King but is This Envy or Indignation[?]'.

Blake meant that what Bacon associated with sedition was probably simple indignation, aimed directly at kings because the King bore ultimate responsibility for government. Now, Blake knew that everybody did not 'hate a King'. When the king was associated with things people liked, he was cheered; if not, he was jeered. Often, the king took steps to avoid public contact to dodge affronts to dignity. 'Every Body hates a King' has been taken as evidence that Blake hated kings, forgetting that Blake loved painting the deeds of past kings in history, even though he was alive to the terrible things that kings had done in the past and bad things done by the King or in the King's name that he abhorred in his own time.

It is probably true that everybody at some time hates a king. I suspect King George III had hard feelings, to say the least, against Louis XVI when the latter gave support to rebellion in America; George IV couldn't stand Czar Alexander I. Blake hated tyranny of all kinds, whether exercised by a king, or by the boss of Astley's circus over a naughty boy. He also knew there were clergymen who did their calling great credit with their saintliness, though it never looked 'Christian-like' to see a representative of the Church-by-law-established praying for a felon on a Tyburn gibbet.

By and large, Blake was sympathetic to radical causes, but only to a point. He would have said that kings reap what they sow; if models of Christian service, they did themselves credit; if they put themselves before what was right, then they were tyrants and should be dipped in the water. He read his Bible. The two Books of Kings showed that God Himself favoured the king that did His will; the others came to sticky ends. Blake was not idealistic about every single man and woman on the planet; he knew that there were those whose tendencies would be the ruin of any system of liberty: 'You cannot have liberty in this world without what you call moral virtue, and you cannot have moral virtue without the slavery of that half of the human race who hate what you call moral virtue.'[3]

Blake was an enthusiast for several radical causes, but he was not at all convinced that radicals had all the solutions. The faults were many; the cure was rare. Those who would lump Blake in with the automatic rebel who hates authority because it is there should take into account that he rather shocked Samuel Palmer, admittedly in old age, by saying there was probably more practical liberty in a Papal state than there was in a secular state, for the principal virtue of Catholicism he understood to be *forgiveness*: for Blake, *the* cardinal Christian virtue, from which subtended an understanding of the realities of human nature and the predicament of the tempted. By contrast, the secular law is indifferent, or oblivious, to the spiritual state of the offender. Blake was for an Englishman's freedom, the right of the individual to be individual, but he recognized that you could seldom expect an outright majority to support the best path: 'One law for the lion and the ox is repression.'

By November 1792, the London Corresponding Society, led by shoemaker Thomas Hardy, had grown from nine to six hundred and fifty. Members produced pamphlets on extending male suffrage (then restricted to property-owners of a certain value), justice in land and law, regular parliaments, and state-supported provision for the poor and old. The French National Convention had that year extended the vote to all males over 25; Hardy's society sent a delegation to the Paris Convention in November, a move that alerted the government to dangers of revolution at home, and, after the September Massacres across France, convinced it of the menace of contagion.

On 13 December, the British Parliament voted support for Pitt's war preparations as France's revolutionary army took more French cities amid great bloodshed, perpetrated with especial violence against the Church. Two days later, Louis XVI appeared before the National Convention to hear charges against him. Nothing could be plainer to Tories in Britain: removal of the King's authority meant anarchy, savagery and general misery.

On a cold, overcast day, 21 January 1793, Louis XVI was guillotined in the Place de la Révolution. To deflect reactionary shock, France declared war on England and the Netherlands on 1 February. Now it was anarchy, savagery, misery. Even for many radicals, the penny began to drop: the dream was over.

A day later, an advertisement appeared in London for 'A Splendid Edition of Barlow's Aesop's Fables' to be printed by John Stockdale, Piccadilly; engravers were named, but a third of them, including Blake, did not sign their work. For the rest of the decade, Blake declined to put his name to journeyman jobs, investing his identity in a burgeoning portfolio of elaborate solo projects.

Possibly the first of the 1793 projects, *The Gates of Paradise* opens with an extraordinary, slightly disturbing emblem. A caterpillar on a leaf appears to keep watch over a human face, sleeping, wrapped in a chrysalis. The caption, 'What is Man!' is dated 17 May 1793. Turn a leaf and the etched title page appears: *For Children The Gates of Paradise Published by W. Blake 13 Hercules Buildings Lambeth and J. Johnson St. Paul's Church Yard.* The design is elegant, determinedly homemade, adorned only by a free-flying figure, released from gravity. There is much gravity in the contents, though.

'Children', for whom the work is ostensibly intended, are presented with 17 etched designs of a most peculiar character. Allowed to enter directly into the imagination, they are unforgettable. Attempt too quickly a rational explanation, and they repel all boarders. Perhaps turning his mind away from the tide of terrible events, Blake enters a personal dreamworld. As in many dreams, the elements are crisply delineated, packed with elusive meaning. Were it not for some additional titles in Blake's manuscript *Notebook,* we would probably be at a loss to see what Blake was driving at.

Continuing the strange binding of human figures to the lower elements of the natural order, the second etching depicts a woman gathering a child out of the ground by the head, as one might a mandrake. The caption 'I found him beneath a Tree' sounds like a confession. Blake's manuscript *Notebook* offers a little more: 'I found him beneath a tree in the garden.'[4] One thinks of Eden, of guilt, rebuke and salvation. Is this the tree of good and evil – that is, the world of the Contraries: Nature, a poisoned tree?

We then have an etching each for Nature's four Elements: four striking designs of great originality and linear flair depicting a distressed male figure deluged by water; caverned by dark earth; detached on a cloud in the air beneath the fate of stars; and, finally, looking slightly more alert, risen up in fire with shield and spear, the spear pointing downwards (arrows of desire go upwards). Page 91 of the *Notebook* shows that the reference is to Milton's *Paradise Lost* (Book One): 'he rears from off the pool/ his mighty stature': a premonition of Blake's fiery warrior and all-round troublemaker, 'Orc'.

The seventh image has that bluish, dreamy quality of those late 18th-century inn signs of the 'Eagle & Child' type, though it is monochrome. We see a winged child breaking free from a shell: 'At length for hatching ripe, he breaks from the shell' (the words from Dryden's *Palamon and Arcite*). We may also think of Blake's spiritual brother, German mystic and poet Angelus Silesius (1624–1677): 'My body is a shell in which a chick lies closed about;/ Brooded by the spirit of eternity, it waits its hatching out' (from *The Cherubinic Wanderer*).

There follow a series of emblematic designs, all of them powerful and, one would think, fairly unsuitable for children. But the children addressed are the children of nature, those subject to a patriarch, whose presence haunts the potent, mysterious images. The implication is that of Jesus's key to his teaching: 'Unless ye be as these little children, ye cannot enter.'

The principal key to the 'gates of paradise' is provided by the first and last images. The image 'titles' are taken from the book of *Job*, in which Job pits Man against the existential facts of corruption, loss, disease and death – indeed, all the experiences that make men curse God or deny His existence. Job exerted great fascination on Blake, inspiring a series of paintings of the afflicted man, and, of course, the matchless engravings that brought appreciation and some profit to his final years. The first caption, then, 'What is Man!' (question or assertion?), is taken from Job 7:17: 'What is Man that thou shouldst magnify him and that thou shouldst set thine heart upon him?'

Why should the baleful, damned 'worm of sixty winters' (Blake's phrase for Man assessed by Reason) engage the attention of Almighty Anything? Blake seems to have an answer. According to Erasmus Darwin's understanding of the Eleusinian Mysteries in *The Botanic Garden*, of which the Portland Vase was considered an allegorical illustration, the *butterfly* is an emblem of the soul. Realizing this, we may now look again at the first image, captioned 'What is Man!' The human face in the chrysalis, enclosed, asleep, is the hidden God.

The final image bears the rubric: 'I have said to corruption, thou art my father, to the worm thou art my mother and my sister' (Job 17:14). The design is startling. In the shadow of tree roots (the fire-world of Böhme's Nature-Hell), a figure is seated on the ground. She wears a hood, like a maiden or priestess. The face is one of hapless innocence, neither distressed nor passionate. She holds a plain upright staff: the 'golden rule' perhaps. Wrapped about her feet a worm is coiled that may even be attached to the androgynous figure like a tail: then she would be the 'worm' who is mother and sister to Man. To enter the gates of Paradise, one must first enter the world of Nature, understand its source, and learn at last, through 'Death's Door' (the penultimate image), that the light is secreted in the 'fire'. Blake has married his heaven and hell.

Visions of the Daughters of Albion

And then there was colour. As if to announce his breakthrough in illuminated design, Blake splashes a rainbow across the title page of his next work of 1793, *Visions of the Daughters of Albion*. In spite of the colour blaze, the dichotomy underlying the poem is starkly displayed. There is Blake's 'Father of Jealousy', Urizen, glum in bright red fires, looking down on a wary free spirit dancing towards us from out of the page, watching his vulnerable back as the commander of law hovers above him like a hostile space ship.

The whole production is washed in seaside colours of aquamarine and rocky browns and seaweed greens, as pink and purple passions streak across the skies. But this seaside is not the place of holiday outings. This seaside is the perilous sea of time and space in which the figures find they are trapped.

The villain, though not the only one, is 'Urizen', whose name combines 'Reason' or 'Your reason' and the Greek *'ourizein'*, which means 'to set limits', 'to bound' or 'encompass'. The universe of the imagination is unlimited and boundless, but Urizen bounds it and makes a finite hell from infinite heaven.

The theme of *Visions* is the binding of the genitals, the suppression of love and the rape of integrity. Urizen is Blake's idea of Böhme's God who dwells in flaming fire: the wrath of the Father.

The Daughters of Albion are not only Albion's daughters within the mythological psyche-scape, of whom 'Oothoon' (raped by the patriarchal 'Bromion') is the principal, but are also the girls and women of Britain whose rights, though invisible to Church and State, have recently been declared by Mary Wollstonecraft. The social battles of Blake's modern England are prefigured in *Visions*. What do the events on earth signify?

Visions opens with a confession: 'I loved Theotormon/ And I was not ashamed.' But the daughters of Albion are 'enslav'd'. To begin with, 'Theotormon', the object of desire, appears to be 'the soft soul of America', for which the daughters pine. The daughters want fraternity and sorority with a new spirit of a new America, even as another power 'Bromion' seems to dominate the 'soft American plains': 'The voice of slaves beneath the sun, and children bought with money./ That shiver in religious caves beneath the burning fires/ Of lust.' Hypocrisy is everywhere, even in newly 'liberated' America: 'They are obedient, they resist not, they obey the scourge: Their daughters worship terrors and obey the violent.' The Britain and America love-theme quickly disappears as the poem extends into a multi-level, wide-ranging symbolic tale of love thwarted:

> They told me that the night & day were all that I could see;
> They told me that I had five senses to inclose me up.
> And they inclos'd my infinite brain into a narrow circle.
> And sunk my heart into the Abyss, a red round globe hot burning ...

The lamentations are many-faceted, running the gamut from nostalgia for the 'joys of old' to tirades against blind capitalists, 'fat cats', a heartless system that lives on the sweat of the poor to 'build him castles and high spires. where kings & priests may dwell./ Till she who burns with youth. and knows no fixed lot; is bound/ In spells of law to one she loaths'. The horrors of a forced marriage that obscures 'the clear heaven of her eternal spring' are painfully depicted, along with the bitter fruits of unwanted children 'that live a pestilence and die a meteor & are no more'.

The poem is highly erotic in parts, the illustrations likewise. The lines, 'Oothoon weeps not: she cannot weep! Her tears are locked up;/ But she can howl incessant writhing her soft snowy limbs./ And calling Theotormons Eagles to prey upon her flesh,' are graphically depicted as Oothoon is spread-eagled over a cloud, her legs akimbo, pecked at by a great eagle whose bites are like kisses – for eagles signify spiritual aspiration.

Visions' most striking image perhaps depicts naked lovers chained back to back in a cave by the sea, unable to conjoin and bound in sexless disunion by hypocritical jealousy.

So increased is the erotic charge towards the poem's climax, we may suspect its being the product of some enormous sexual frustration on the part of the poet. He laments the presence of a 'creeping skeleton/ With lamplike eyes watching around the frozen marriage bed'. Is the frozen marriage bed Blake's? Perhaps. The lines follow a hymn to the secret joys of masturbation in men and women:

> The moment of desire! the moment of desire! The virgin
> That pines for man; shall awaken her womb to enormous joys
> In the secret shadows of her chamber; the youth shut up from
> The lustful joy, shall forget to generate. & create an amorous image
> In the shadows of his curtains and in the folds of his silent pillow.
> Are not these the places of religion? the rewards of continence?
> The self enjoyings of self denial? Why dost thou seek religion?

However, while one might speculate that Blake has taken feelings from his own marriage and universalized their significance to humanity in general, the overall feeling suggests his poem is the product of wide observation of the world and its secrets, not merely an expiation of a private hell in which Catherine does not give the poet all that he knows he wants, and what he knows that she wants. That is not to say, however, that Blake was not also attempting to educate his wife into a higher, spiritual conception of the 'marriage bed'.

Blake revisits the worm of the 'gates of paradise':

Does not the eagle scorn the earth & despise the treasures beneath?
But the mole knoweth what is there, & the worm shall tell it thee.
Does not the worm erect a pillar in the mouldering church yard?
And a palace of eternity in the jaws of the hungry grave
Over his porch these words are written. Take thy bliss O Man!
And sweet shall be thy taste & sweet thy infant joys renew!

The cry of Nature everywhere speaks a wisdom that Man will not see:

And trees. & birds. & beasts. & men. behold their eternal joy.
Arise you little glancing wings, and sing your infant joy!
Arise and drink your bliss, for every thing that lives is holy!

And Blake cries: 'Love! Love! Love! Happy happy Love! free as the mountain wind!' And that's what the Daughters of Albion want to hear. Theotormon doesn't 'get it', so Theotormon doesn't get It.

As if that salty blast were not sufficient for the year, Blake in a frenzy of inspiration produced *AMERICA/ a/ PROPHECY/ LAMBETH/ Printed by William Blake in the year 1793.*

In spite of the promising title, the text of *America: A Prophecy* seldom offers the kinds of riches we might expect now that we are so used to movies where the word 'America' echoes in *basso profundo con mucho machismo* through sweeping aerial images from Manhattan to the Grand Canyon and on to the Golden Gate Bridge! We are still at the 13 States stage, and the West had not been 'won'.

The real joy of *America* lies not in the language, which is patchy in inspiration, but in the incredible power of the images, arresting even in the uncoloured early versions of the work. The painted version in the Fitzwilliam Museum, Cambridge (dated 1821), is a wonder to behold. It must have shocked sensibilities by its sheer Olympian originality, revolutionary sense of space and movement, and daring subject matter. Blake found his style, created a genre, and let rip in *America*.

The frontispiece depicts a huge winged angel, chained to a pedestal amid ancient monuments. Dwarfed by comparison, a mother and child lament the muscular figure whose head is bowed in despair: titanic energy constrained brings lamentation.

The text's main purpose seems to be to introduce in stark terms the fiery boy, Orc – the 'red Orc' of Blake's prophecy. Orc is Mars made flesh, and in plate 3 we discover him chained to the earth beneath an overhanging tree. Orc's howling is channelled through the roots of Nature and echoes in the dungeon hells below. *America* is really the 'Adventures of Orc in America'. Very rarely seen, plate 4 shows Orc climbing free from a divot in the earth like a god new-born. It is hard to resist comparing this crystalline, hypnotic image to the emergence of Nietzsche's 'Superman' in *Also spracht Zarathustra*. Poised like a sprinter in the Olympics, Orc looks to the heavens for the starting signal.

The signal is, of course, the conflict between the colonists and the 'wicked patriarch', King George III – 'wicked' because the king does not see that Orc is really behind this rebellion and what it therefore represents. 'When thought is closed in chains then love shall show its roots in deepest hell'.[5] Blake paints the War of Independence in the broadest possible colours, with plenty of famous name-drops (including Tom Paine, Franklin and Washington and his fellow commanders) but with precious little interest in history as we know it. He presents the conflict in symbolic, allegorical and semi-apocalyptic terms. Thus, the 13 states have 13 angels, and they gather decisively on the imaginary island of Atlantis between the shores of London and Boston. The angels direct the drama: history is the outflow beneath of spiritual powers above that reside in the human breast. History records the show. Blake's point is to show the prophetic meaning. And for him, that is simple enough. What happened in America is now happening across the world. America itself is the prophecy.

On 29 August 1793, slavery was abolished in French-held Santo Domingo. This is the kind of event that generates the poem's best verses, notably those quoted earlier, beginning: 'Let the slave grinding at the mill, run out into the field ...' Washington, of course, kept slaves, so 'America' is a prophecy for the *future* of America too: 'Free, Free at last!' The slaves will be set free and 'the Lion & Wolf' of Empire shall cease. That's your prophecy. For Blake, the movement is one of resurrection, and not for the first time he uses the image of Ezekiel's valley of dry bones combined with the Gospels' account of Christ's revival:

The morning comes, the night decays, the watchmen leave their stations;
The grave is burst, the spices shed, the linen wrapped up;
The bones of death, the cov'ring clay, the sinews shrunk & dry'd.
Reviving shake, inspiring move, breathing! Awakening!
Spring like redeemed captives when their bonds and bars are burst ...

As Orc has now been let loose upon the imprisoned world, the text and imagery are full of red fire. 'Urthona', the Earth in the poem, will not know peace until Orc's work is done and the spiritual energies that keep him enflamed have done their will upon the world. That work was still being celebrated in 1968 when the US poetic rock band The Doors sang of the 'Wild Child, full of grace: saviour of the human race'. Listeners have long been bemused by Jim Morrison's throwaway line at the end of the song: 'Remember when we were in Africa?' The reference is almost certainly to Blake's 'Preludium' to *America*. The 'terrible boy', 'the hairy boy' Orc, aged 14, has been distracted from his pains by a naked daughter of Urthona (Earth) – naked, that is, but for clouds around her loins. Excited by the virgin, Orc rends the chains, whereupon:

Round the terrific loins he seiz'd the panting struggling womb;
It joy'd: she put aside her clouds & smiled her first-born smile;
As when a black cloud shews its light'nings to the silent deep.

Soon as she saw the terrible boy then burst the virgin cry.

I know thee, I have found thee, & I will not let thee go;
Thou art the image of God who dwells in darkness of Africa;
And thou art fall'n to give me life in regions of dark death.

For Blake, Orc is the first, ancient image of God perceived in Africa by men driven by long suffering to fight. 'Remember when we were in Africa?' That's what the late, lamented Jim was getting at.

The benefits of the American revolt were felt not only among the 'fierce Americans'. In Britain, 'priests in rustling scales' rush to the 'reptile coverts, hiding from the fires of Orc,/ That play around the golden roofs in wreaths of fierce desire,/ Leaving the females naked and glowing with the lusts of youth

[...] They feel the nerves of youth renew, and desires of ancient times,/ Over their pale limbs as a vine when the tender grape appears'.

Composition of such lines may have sent Will and Kate into amorous excess among the grapes and vines of 13 Hercules Buildings, Lambeth, in 1793. Perhaps the neighbours got used to it.

Proud of his year's works, the 35-year-old Blake issued a prospectus on 10 October from an engraved plate, printed in blue on a leaf of some 11 x 7½ inches.

To the Public.
The Labours of the Artist, the Poet, the Musician, have been proverbially attended by poverty and obscurity; this was never the fault of the Public, but was owing to a neglect of means to propagate such works as have wholly absorbed the Man of Genius. Even Milton and Shakespeare could not publish their own works.

This difficulty has been obviated by the Author of the following productions now presented to the Public; who has invented a method of Printing both Letter-press and Engraving in a style more ornamental, uniform, and grand, than any before discovered, while it produces works at less than one-fourth of the expense.

If a method of Printing which combines the Painter and the Poet is a phenomenon worthy of public attention, provided that it exceeds in elegance all former methods, the Author is sure of his reward.

Mr. Blake's powers of invention very early engaged the attention of many persons of eminence and fortune; by whose means he has been regularly enabled to bring before the Public works (he is not afraid to say) of equal magnitude and consequence with the productions of any age or country: among which are two large highly finished engravings (and two more are nearly ready) which will commence a Series of subjects from the Bible, and another from the History of England. The following are the Subjects of the several Works now published and on Sale at Mr. Blake's, No. 13, Hercules Buildings, Lambeth.

1. Job, a Historical Engraving. Size 1 ft. 7½ in. by 1 ft. 2 in.: price 12s[hillings].

2. Edward and Elinor, a Historical Engraving. Size 1 ft. 6½ in. by 1 ft.: price 10s. 6d [sixpence].

3. America, a Prophecy, in Illuminated Printing. Folio, with 18 designs, price l0s. 6d.

4. Visions of the Daughters of Albion, in Illuminated Printing. Folio, with 8 designs, price 7s. 6d.

5. The Book of Thel, a Poem in Illuminated Printing. Quarto, with 6 designs, price 3s.

6. The Marriage of Heaven and Hell, in Illuminated Printing. Quarto, with fourteen designs, price 7s. 6d.

7. Songs of Innocence, in Illuminated Printing. Octavo, with 25 designs, price 5s.

8. Songs of Experience, in Illuminated Printing. Octavo, with 25 designs, price 5s.

9. The History of England, a small book of Engravings. Price 3s.

10. The Gates of Paradise, a small book of Engravings. Price 3s.

The Illuminated Books are Printed in Colours, and on the most beautiful wove paper that could be procured.

No Subscriptions for the numerous great works now in hand are asked, for none are wanted; but the Author will produce his works, and offer them to sale at a fair price.

The fact that Blake put Joseph Johnson's bookshop address as a publisher's address on *The Gates of Paradise* suggests that that is where the prospectus was principally available. There may have been inspection copies of some of the works at Johnson's, but those wishing to order further copies were expected to make their way to Lambeth. As this was a 'prospectus', some of the works may have been unfinished. 'Songs of Experience', for example, may not have been available until 1794.

Six days after the prospectus was officially issued, Marie Antoinette was guillotined in Paris. An 'anti-suspect law' having been passed by the Convention on 17 September whereby all 'enemies of the revolution' could be held until the end of the war enabled Robespierre to imprison senior military 'suspects' as well as moderate Girondins. Twenty-one Girondins followed Marie Antoinette to the guillotine on 31 October.

Eight days later, Girondin poet Mme Roland, standing heroically by the red scaffold that would in a matter of moments take her life, beheld the statue of 'Liberty' that overlooked it, and declared: 'Oh Liberty! What crimes are committed in thy name!'

On 20 November, Nancy Flaxman wrote from Italy to her sister-in-law Maria in London: 'know you anything of Stothard or Blake?' Blake had not been keeping contact with his old, dear friends. He was, in fact, busy on the last 10 plates for Stedman's *Narrative* of the Suriname slave revolt.

For the following two years, Blake would become Stedman's most trusted London-based friend.

Living in Tiverton, Devon, Stedman first met Blake in person on 21 June 1794. Contacts were maintained through 1795, when Stedman visited Blake several times, as Johnson encountered a string of technical difficulties in printing Stedman's work. Thanks to Stedman we know that in 1795 Blake was 'mobbed and robb'd', but we don't know why. Was it for radical associations? The reference to a mob suggests so.

Two notable events occurred in France around Christmas 1793. On 19 December a certain Napoleon Bonaparte, having been forced to quit his native Corsica by freedom-fighter Pascale Paoli, distinguished himself as captain of artillery in the retaking of Toulon from British and French royalists. Then, on Christmas Day, Robespierre declared his support for the policy of Terror, thus unleashing the full force of extreme scorched-earth tactics that ever since have characterized the heartless depths of revolutionary fanaticism.

Orc knew no bounds …

FIFTEEN

Singular Shapes and Odd Combinations

1794

'Frenchmen were always brutal, when unrestrained. With their own domestick misery and wickedness they never were satisfied. In these latter days, they have been *neighing* after the constitutions of their neighbours in the lawless lustihood.'[1] So wrote scholar and satirist Thomas James Mathias (*c.*1754–1835), whose *The Pursuits of Literature, A Satirical Poem* was first published in 1794. While Mathias has been dubbed a reactionary critic of radical English literature, French revolutionary behaviour in the period 1794–98 earned his literary castigation in the eyes of most of his countrymen.

A revolt in the Vendée in January 1794 provoked the Terror's wrath: mass murder of men, women and children, mostly peasants, was joined to wholesale demolition and a scorched-earth policy. The Robespierre-led Committee of Public Safety with its Revolutionary Tribunal stood in effective control.

On 4 February, the Convention abolished slavery in all colonies. Leading revolutionary Georges Danton, who strove to moderate the Terror, believed abolition of slavery would stimulate uprisings against the British. 'Today,' declared Danton, 'Pitt died.' Danton was guillotined on 5 April; Pitt lived. Eight days later, Danton was followed to the scaffold by fervent anti-Christian and scourge of the Girondists, Pierre Gaspard Chaumette (1763–94). It was Chaumette who had organized the 'Festival of Reason' (10 November 1793) whose gaudy accoutrements featured an actress dolled up as the Goddess Reason on a platform in Nôtre Dame. Robespierre opposed Chaumette's Cult of Reason with his Deist Cult of the Supreme Being.

Pertinent to our story was Chaumette's crossing intellectual swords with Louis-Claude de St Martin in 1790. The logical child of Rousseau and Voltaire – two of Blake's principal bugbears – Chaumette regarded Christians as 'enemies of reason' and Christian ideas as 'ridiculous', taking people out of the 'real world'. Chaumette believed education would make people what you wanted them to be: reason ruled.

So akin are Blake's ideas to those of Louis Claude de St Martin (1743–1803) that one might consider Blake St Martin's English representative! However, it seems they had common sources, in Böhme and Paracelsus – sources that led kindred spirits to like conclusions. St Martin's philosophical presentation of ideas shared with Blake help us to understand Blake better.

St Martin came out of the French 'Illuminist' stable fathered by Martinès de Pasqually (*c*.1709–1744), founder of the 'ultra' Masonic Order, The Order of Knight Masons, Elect Priests of the Universe (1766). St Martin joined in 1768. The Order practised theurgic rituals in an attempt to recover the pristine faculties of Adam before the Fall.[2] Directly opposed to Chaumette's rationalist reductionism, St Martin launched a wide-ranging critique of Reason (*L'HOMME DE DESIR*, Lyon, 1790; *Ecce Homo,* Paris, 1792).

According to St Martin, true enlightenment conforms neither to the senses nor to calculations of the brain: it is a supernatural gift. The True Cause is not subject to the brain; it is an Active Intelligent Being, capable of things unimaginable and incalculable to unaided reason. St Martin believed the Fall could be overcome, even though its effect had been to shatter and scatter the primal faculties of Man. Like a mirror, the parts could not reflect light until reunified and regenerated. 'Rectification' was possible through the sacrificial act of the 'Réparateur' who could restore the 'man-God' (the *Réparateur*, or 'repairer', is basically Böhme's idea of Christ). This conception makes sense of Blake's enormous, unfinished poem of psychic disintegration and reintegration, *Vala* or *The Four Zoas*, which he would begin in 1797.

Having discovered Böhme in 1790, St Martin dropped Freemasonry. It is the divine 'Sophia' – Wisdom as a feminine figure – that enables return to true being. Sophia is analogous to Blake's female 'Jerusalem'.

St Martin developed the man-God idea further: he is co-operator and minister of the divine will with a mission of salvation – a role Blake himself would take on explicitly, if privately, in the early 1800s (if he had not done so before and kept it wisely to himself).

Introduced to the works of Mme Guyon, St Martin perhaps borrowed her ideas about 'desire' to write in praise of what he called the 'hommes de désir', the 'Men of Desire' – Blake, remember, had his *arrows of desire*. Ordinary men become *Men of Desire* when they actively desire to rescue the divine life from the bondage of the fallen human condition. Such people imitate Christ. They incarnate consciousness of the divine word and wisdom; they expiate the world through their sacrificial suffering, denying 'selfhood' – reflexive egotism. St Martin called for the people of desire to participate in the Great Work of Reintegration. When the call was heeded, humanity would be showered with divine mysteries that the rationalist, so-called 'enlightenment' rejected outright.

St Martin also foresaw the reintegration of 'Eternal Nature'. He believed the Imagination was the spiritual part of humanity: imagination possesses the vision of all things. Through imagination we grasp the spiritual unity of the universe. The 'kingdom of heaven' is a simile and metaphor for a spiritual reality; our eyes do not reveal the whole truth. St Martin advocated a new tongue, a new spiritual language and tool for interpreting history (did Blake's 'prophetic books' contribute to this?). History's value lay in signs encoded within it; historical events were symbolic of, not instruments of, the reintegration of humanity.

How much, or how little, of St Martin had been brought to Blake's attention through Swedenborgians who knew the French Illuminists personally we do not know. But the channels were there. Jacob Duché's son, for example, had visited the Avignon base of *illuminatus* Dom Antoine-Joseph Pernety, inspired by Swedenborg in 1782 to write *The Marvels of Heaven and Hell and the Planetary and Astral Territories*. Like Blake, Illuminists responded to the Enlightenment's elevation of Reason by recognizing that while reason constituted the inner eye of the mind, its function needed to be clarified, or illuminated, by the light beyond time and space, beyond the external senses.

Such thoughts seem to have inspired Blake's own illuminated work of 1794, *EUROPE a PROPHECY*, self-published shortly before Blake's biggest and most blatant attack on Reason: *THE BOOK of URIZEN*.

We could describe *EUROPE a PROPHECY* [3] as 17 plates of unadulterated genius without having read a word of it. The range and explosiveness of the imagery alone convince us that we are in the presence of a master visionary, a great artist. Most people will be familiar with the unforgettable first plate, sometimes called *The Ancient of Days*, a timeless figure of which Blake was very proud, and one that he made every endeavour to improve right up to the week of his death.

An apparent gift of eidetic memory, the grand figure of the bearded god combines Blake's respect for the grandeur and terror of the Creator with his spiritual critique of the image of the 'bounder' who limits and encloses infinite spirit.

And that is only page one!

Europe opens with a poem about the five senses: 'Five windows light the cavern'd Man,' writes Blake: 'thro' one can look./ and see small portions of the eternal world that ever groweth.'

We are swiftly led into the world of what I have called the *patriarchetypes*. Blake's mythic beings present us with an idea of unconscious archetypes operating 'behind' human history. History *as lived* is a manifestation of spiritual dynamics, its real life operating 'from above', that is, *within* the psychology of each person. Simultaneously, these beings are also 'patriarchs' and 'matriarchs', the primal fathers and mothers of our mental being, the origins of our gods and goddesses: the faculties; and how like a warring family they interact! This is the story of transcendent, psychological life flowing into historical processes, then across and beyond time into meta-historical symbols. Such an artistic combination was, to say the least, daring and original; it still is, and many have chosen to skip over Blake's 'prophecies' as being too demanding. Skippers skip over a great deal.

So, *Europe* begins around the time of the birth of Christ (on earth), which Blake appears to have known was about 6 or 7 BCE: 1,800 terrestrial years before Blake was writing. A 'shameless shadowy female' with 'snaky hair' arises from the breast of Orc. She wails to their mother, Enitharmon, who is a kind of Queen of Heaven, or like her consort Los a link between the human mind and the world of spirit: inspiration, or the goddess of the 'Poetic Genius'.

Already, though rooted in the heavens, the shadowy female's fruits are surging and foaming and raging into life on earth. It is as though a matrix of energy has entered being to withdraw again, as in the obscure comings and goings of sub-atomic particles. Something has been born on earth: 'The deep of winter came;/ What time the secret child,/ Descended thro' the orient gates of the eternal day:/ War ceas'd, & all the troops like shadows fled to their abodes.' It was perhaps wise of Blake to use the subtlest allegory here (as well as an allusion to Milton's poem *On the Morning of Christ's Nativity*) and elsewhere, for what Blake was saying was that Orc, whose head Enitharmon will crown 'with garlands of the ruddy vine', was born in the world as Jesus.

What was that? Yes, Orc was born in the world as Jesus.

Enitharmon seizes the moment as the time to exert a 'Female will'. She sends into the world her children Rintrah and Palamabron (Prophecy and Science) so that 'Woman, lovely Woman' may 'have dominion':

> Go! Tell the human race that Womans love is Sin!
> That an Eternal life awaits the worms of sixty winters
> In an allegorical abode where existence hath never come:
> Forbid all Joy, & from her childhood shall the little female
> Spread nets in every secret path.

Blake was no feminist in the contemporary sense: the female has no monopoly of virtue in power relations. Blake could be wary of feminine powers in general. The use of sexual power or mystery for entrapment, for example, was a horror to Blake.

Failing to grasp the daemonic message of Orc-Jesus, the world is caught up in the net of a religion in which heaven is remote and where the sexual sense, too frightening to confront fully, is suppressed by hypocritical chastity. Urizen rules through the orthodox reading of the Bible that keeps Jesus bound to the Ten Commandments amid the thunders and slaughters of Sinai.

Eighteen hundred years pass under the thrall of the great anti-sexual, anti-spiritual message of the Church whereby 'Man was a Dream! [...] Eighteen hundred years, a female dream!'

The curtain re-opens on an England smarting in the wake of American defeat. Albion's Angels have been hit hard by the loss and England painfully rises again in 'troubles mists o'erclouded by the terrors of struggling times'. The problem, as Blake sees it, is that the 'fiery King' and his ministers just can't see that they are opposing Orc, their own salvation, and are exhausting themselves in the process, instead of taking a leading role in the transformation of earth according to heaven.

Insofar as the country opposes its own True Will, problems mount up, and Blake envisions the growth of what he calls the 'ancient temple serpent-form'd/ That stretches out its shady length along the Island white'. This serpent temple image he will develop further as the religion of the Druids, who took the religion of the patriarchs who dwelt in Albion and reduced it to human sacrifice. Blake sees this human sacrifice in the sending of young men to war against their own best interests, which are true religion and science: the Science of Man.

Blake employs a clever pun where the serpent is concerned. The alchemical image of infinity has long been a snake swallowing its own tail. Blake implies that in the new mills of Satan the circle is closed completely, made finite, bounded in circumference and radius:

> Then was the serpent temple form'd, image of infinite
> Shut up in finite revolutions, and man became an Angel;
> Heaven a mighty circle turning; God a tyrant crown'd.

Blake refers allegorically to attacks on radical writers. These attacks have denied to youth in England materials necessary to feed the quest for understanding. Youth is taught to look to an end of the world for hope, not to the eternal world within and, unseen, about them:

> For Urizen unclasped his Book: feeding his soul with pity
> The youth of England hid in gloom curse the paind heavens; compell'd
> Into the deadly night ...

Blake's vision is considerably darker than Wordsworth's relatively tame 'Shades of the prison house' that close upon the 'growing boy' in his famous poem, 'Intimations of Immortality' (published in 1807).

In May 1793, 6,000 members of the general public signed a petition saying they supported the London Corresponding Society, led by Thomas Hardy, John Thelwall and John Horne Tooke. It is clear that Blake supported it too.

Enitharmon awakes from her 1,800-year dream to find Orc freshly engaged: 'Arise O Orc and give our mountains joy of thy red light.' Here surely is the 'missing caption' to Blake's watercolour known, for no good reason, as *Glad Day*, or *Albion Rose*. We should rather see the image as an epiphany of young Orc, who is something, I believe, of Blake's idealized self – the child born not of James and Catherine Blake, but of poetry and inspiration: Los and Enitharmon. Had the 18th century possessed the technology and visual culture we have today, this image would have made an effective trans-continental tee-shirt: a 'whose side are you on?' public challenge.

> But terrible Orc, when he beheld the morning in the east,
> Shot from the heights of Enitharmon;
> And in the vineyards of red France appear'd the light of his fury.
>
> The sun glow'd fiery red!
> The furious terrors flew around!
> On golden chariots raging, with red wheels dropping with blood;
> The Lions lash their wrathful tails!
> The Tigers couch upon the prey & suck the ruddy tide:
> And Enitharmon groans and cries in anguish and dismay.
>
> Then Los arose his head he reard in snaky thunders clad:
> And with a cry that shook all nature to the utmost pole,
> Call'd all his sons to the strife of blood.

St Martin also looked at the 'strife of blood', realizing that while the ultimate aim of the 'Reintegration' was otherworldly, the process transformed the world of sense through a *parergon* or by-product of the spiritual process (*ergon*). World events had real meaning. Thus, for St Martin, the French Revolution was a terrestrial hieroglyph of humankind's quest for right order, according to the inner desire for reconciliation and reintegration with God's will; its violence, a sign of punishment for past indifference to the True Cause. Although this was a profound and painful lesson, a sacrifice, it foreshadowed a far greater liberation of humanity still to come.

Blake was there already, and he could write and paint and carve, as well as sing and think, and he was bright on the barricades of desire.

Blake's next missile was devoted to the villain of the piece. *The First Book of Urizen* turned out to be the *only* Book of Urizen, but one would think that sufficient, unless the second Book was written in the blood of history. Startling as the imagery undoubtedly is (28 dynamic plates in the version held by the Yale Centre for British Art), it makes stimulating, if grim, reading. Here is the creation of the inner and outer universes without the fancy space-music or the optimistic, awe-struck voice of the modern commentator on the 'wonders of the cosmos', as if a trip to the limits of cosmological knowledge was a pleasant afternoon's run past pretty planets and glittering stars.

I hope readers will take a trip instead to the 'blakearchive.org' website and see the words in their proper visual context, and compare different versions. You will not be disappointed by what you find.

The Book opens with the phenomenon (unnamed) of Newton's universe, what Blake calls the 'soul-shuddering vacuum' of Newtonian space. Diagrammatically, the cycles and ellipses of the planets look quite graceful, clockwork-like, even cool and value-free, but Blake takes you beyond the clean geometry of the page and plunges you head-first into a universe that is more like a charnel house and butcher's yard combined, with only the fires that eat into the cosmic hulk like all-devouring plankton to see by.

The Book opens with the question, 'who made this "abominable void"?', to which some answer: 'It is Urizen.'

But no one knew for sure.

Urizen remained 'unknown, abstracted/ Brooding secret, the dark power hid'. Blake exposes him. And what do we see? This Urizen, this blind power, has many forms, is guilty of many sins, and he looks like the common idea of God Almighty, the Great Architect, maker of heaven and earth. But Urizen did not make it all; he only *thinks* he did, because he has bound it according to his nature. And that nature is the faculty of Reason, worshipped by Chaumette, adored by the radicals, turned into God by theologians, and called 'Life' by biologists. He is the maker of Law, and the Accuser, and he knows no power above him – which claim identifies him very closely with the 'Demiurge' of the Gnostics, the conglomerated, strutting ego of the material universe, killer of the prophets and the attempted murderer of Jesus.

When Blake saw the tablets of the Ten Commandments hanging above the altars of English churches, he saw Urizen. One only had to look from the Law to the condemned, crucified below, to get the Idea – well, *he* did.

The imagery of the Book is truly terrifying. Blake seems to have gone fathoms deep into himself, perhaps far too deep, and extracted from the miseries of his vision of the formation of suns and planets, and organic matter, and gases, and voids, a new psychological landscape. Internal mental processes are wrenched into three dimensions and given phantom life, and the horror of the tiny scream shorn of relative scale and made cosmic is practically unbearable: it is meant to be. Blake's inner universe is stripped to the bone, then ground to the marrow and mashed into a sea of molten brass in which parts of life bob up and drown in terror and 'dismal woe'.

What is wrong with Urizen? He is abstracted. He is isolated. He is cold. He has no heart. No heart.

No heart!

The Book, of course, is intended for the lighthearted, for only the light-hearted will get the marvellous joke that runs right through the searing drama. Only those who have borne the heaviest thoughts know the virtue of the light heart, and only such light-hearted will be able to bear it.

Never before had there been anything like Blake's painted images of Urizen extracted from the screaming form of Los, the Time-Spirit, the Great Prophet: he who pounds out in hammered rhythm the links of chains of time, and day, and week, and age to come and past. Urizen's wound after being separated by lymph and limb from Los will not heal. We see blood and fibre pouring from Urizen's brain into a conglobed mass of messy bloody and fleshy, fibrous horror, as his form changes uncontrollably. In one image, Urizen appears next to frightened Los as a skeleton poking through some form like the flash of an X-ray:

> From the caverns of his jointed Spine,
> Down sunk with fright a red
> Round globe hot burning deep
> Deep down into the Abyss:
> Panting, Conglobing, Trembling
> Shooting out ten thousand branches
> Around his solid bones.

It would make a spectacular horror film. But it could equally be a science documentary, for Blake shows us the 'Big Bang', the diminution of the 'Eternals' into chaotic forms, whirling round like wheels : 'As glasses [telescopes] discover Worlds/ In the endless Abyss of space,/ So the expanding eyes of Immortals/ Beheld the dark visions of Los,/ And the globe of life blood trembling.'

We see the first female appear. And Los is attracted. Blake has probably seen Erasmus Darwin's latest book *Zoonomia* (1794), in which Darwin writes that animal forms are not fixed but adapt and evolve – anticipating his grandson's evolutionary theories of adaption by half a century. For the first 'Infant form' does not appear until what begins as a worm in Enitharmon's womb manifests as a serpent. The serpent, in its turn, transforms into 'many forms of fish, bird & beast', before Enitharmon – the first female, called 'Pity' – produces 'a man Child to the light'. In fierce flames the Eternals witness the 'birth of the Human shadow'. Los seizes the child, bathes him 'in springs of sorrow' and they name him ... ORC. 'Beneath Urizens shadow' they take Orc to the top of a mountain, like Abraham with Isaac, and they chain 'his young limbs to the rock/ With the Chain of Jealousy' (for Urizen is a 'jealous God'). Then Urizen forms a plummet and line to divide the Abyss.

Blake's – or rather Böhme's – 'Abyss' corresponds to the the ancient Gnostics' *Bythos* (that is, 'Depth'): the unfathomable ocean of God, from which God's 'First Thought' emanates in the Gnostic Valentinian creation system. Blake appears to take another idea from this 2nd-century CE theosophic scheme.

As Piloo Nanavutti observed in 1976, the Valentinian story of the fall and redemption of 'Sophia' (Lady Wisdom) 'elucidates many passages of Blake's prophetic books.'[4] In the Valentinian drama, Sophia, independent of her partner-in-*syzygy*, 'Theletos' (God's *Will* respecting Sophia),[5] cannot accomplish perfect creation, as her 'Unknowable Father' can. From her ungovernable yearning to 'know the Father', all the abstracted Sophia can produce, is an 'Ectroma' or abortion – a fatal, unbalanced, incomplete universe whose spiritual origins have degenerated into mortal, changing, deficient matter. Isolated from the divine *Pleroma*, or 'Fullness', Sophia's divine *pneuma* or spirit is distressfully trapped in the deficiency her ignorance has engendered. This horror story has undoubtedly informed the *First Book of Urizen*, though Blake does not simply reproduce it: he moulds it to his purpose.

Thus, when the isolate Urizen, separated from *his* emanation, or partner,

Ahania, goes into the Abyss to fathom and divide its mysteries, he too attempts, by his own powers alone, an act of creation. The result is a disturbing world, teeming only with:

> Portions of life, similitudes
> Of a foot or a hand or a head
> Or a heart or an eye.

In the still unpublished 'Askew Codex', recovered from Egypt and brought to the British Museum in 1785, *Pistis Sophia* – 'Faith Wisdom' lost in the world – accomplishes from her creative exertions only 'formless fruit'. In *Urizen*, the Eternals are shocked at the work of Urizen's perverted science. They move to confine it: 'For Eternity stood wide apart,/ As the stars are apart from the earth.'

The Valentinian myth is perfectly adapted to Blake's own purposes, for we see in it a dramatic mode for expressing that 'Reason' cannot comprehend that which is above itself. Reason's attempts to usurp the powers of supra-rational Genius, the holy spiritual light above – powers on which Reason, in fact, depends for life and function – only produce Frankensteinian horrors. Mary Shelley's monster, you may recall, is created from bits of condemned humans 'galvanized' by the ambitious rationalist Frankenstein, high on his own portion of scientific knowledge.

In the end it was the cold application of reason by logic-chopping, razor-dangerous politicos with egalitarian know-all systems that generated the prospects of inhuman horror, nature-destruction, warped technology and pseudo-science that made the superstitious efforts of even the worst 'medieval' or 'unenlightened' oppressors look positively amateurish by comparison. And it started with the great divider: the guillotine that Chaumette himself advocated with such passion for Louis XVI.

We live in the shadow of Urizen's awful, life-denying, radioactive creations. And still the point has not been registered, as our teachers persist in subjecting infinite spiritual knowledge to limited rational categories – where, that is, there is any interest in spiritual knowledge at all. Blake saw it all unfold as he looked *through*, not *with*, his eyes, and told us a myth so that we could better grasp the 'parable'.

Separated from higher influence, 'self-conglobing' and armed with dividing rule, massy weights and a brazen quadrant, pure ego Urizen forms golden compasses to limit the infinite. He plants 'a garden of fruits'. This is Eden's Tree of Knowledge of Good and Evil, whose fruit, when eaten, will condemn Man.

Urizen next creates the 'Net of Religion' and all the systems that would tie down the 'Giants' of old and make them forget 'their eternal life': 'No more could they rise at will/ In the infinite void, but bound down/ To earth by their narrowing perception.' The reference is to the 'Nephilim' of Genesis 6; and through them to the stark human predicament, reflection on which has given us religious legalism, existentialism and nihilism:

> They lived a period of years
> Then left a noisome body
> To the jaws of devouring darkness
>
> And their children wept, & built
> Tombs in the desolate places,
> And form'd laws of prudence, and call'd them
> The eternal laws of God

Here endeth the *First Book of Urizen*, an instalment from Blake's on-going 'Bible of Hell'.

SIXTEEN

The Song of Los and Sedition

1794–1795

Blake's trouble was that he was too radical for the conservatives and too spiritual for the radicals: he was concerned with truth. His spirit was innocent, turned part-cynic by experience, but open to higher spiritual influence. Little wonder he would one day rail against his fate: 'O why was I born with a different face?/ Why was I not born like the rest of my race?'[1] In 1794–5 he put these feelings into a series of drawings and watercolours on the theme of 'Job's Complaint': 'What is Man that thou shouldst Try his Every Moment?' (Job 7:17–18). The trials in question may not have been merely personal: late 1794 would bring the most significant state-sponsored trials of radicals in the decade.

Seriously alarmed by the turn of events in Paris and what conservatives took to be their reflection in English radical circles, the government acted. Leading Whigs sensed the wind, trimmed their sails, and jettisoned residual revolutionary enthusiasms. Enjoying sufficient consensus in the Commons, and the backing of the King, the government could get moving; the situation could not be permitted to get out of control, as it had in France.

On 7 May, Robespierre insisted the National Convention decree 'the existence of a Supreme Being and the immortality of the soul'. If it were not so tragic, this would have been comic: the absolute decreed into existence by a transient body of voters! Indeed, such was Robespierre's sudden concern for natural philosophy that the next day Lavoisier, who had discovered the chemical composition of water, was executed. A month later, the Celebration of the Supreme Being was held in the Champs de Mars. Mars was a good choice for such vanities, for two days later there appeared a new law: revolutionary tribunals would no longer tolerate preliminary questioning, nor a defence: they simply chose between acquittal and death.

On 27 July, the Convention, suspecting Robespierre had identified himself with the Supreme Being, ordered his arrest. He was guillotined the next day with 21 companions.

In the circumstances, the publication in London of *The Pursuits of Literature, A Satirical Poem* seems somewhat suspect: perhaps it was government-sponsored propaganda. Running through seven editions by 1798, this clever work by Royal Society Fellow Thomas James Mathias (*c.*1754–1835) attacked contemporary authors whose works for one reason or another upset conservative, genteel opinion; which is to say, works Tories in particular disliked. Blake knew several of the chief targets, either personally or by association.

Mathias's first poem sets French revolutionary inspirers in its sights: Voltaire, d'Alembert and Condorcet are singled out for their impious and subversive thought. On page 22,[2] the blast of disapproval comes closer to home: the 'vulgar illiterate blasphemy of Thomas Paine, and the contemptible nonsense of William Godwin. I feel for mankind when they are insulted by such writers.'

On page 29 it is radical John Horne Tooke's turn: 'Mr Horne Tooke, for instance, is out of the reach of art' (but not of the government, it transpired). Tooke, a former lawyer and priest, lived in Wimbledon, where a local bookseller sold his works. Mathias recommends establishing a 'bidental' at the bookseller's door to give the French a target 'on their first invasion'. In ancient Rome, a 'bidental' was a place struck by lightning and thus singled out for a *templum* where special priests (*bidentales*) sacrificed two-year-old sheep (*bidens* means 'having teeth on each side'). Walls or palisades separated *bidentals*; it was not permitted to walk over them. Mathias's implication was that Tooke was both traitor and priestly obfuscator.

Next in the firing line (page 50) is Joseph Priestley: 'If I may write, let Proteus Priestley tell, he writes on all things, but on nothing well.' Interestingly, Mathias next casts a swipe at William Hayley, the poet Cowper's liberal friend. Mathias dismisses Hayley's poetry as 'too feeble, tedious, and insufferably prolix' (page 56). Blake would reach the same conclusion when Hayley became Blake's 'patron' six years later. On page 57, Erasmus Darwin is lined up – radical associations again: 'Dr Darwin is certainly a man of great fancy ... good writing and good poetry require something more.' Mathias advises Darwin to look through Nature to Nature's God: a view Blake would surely have risen to challenge.

On page 68, Mathias's ire is reserved for the unnamed author of *The Worship of Priapus,* printed for the Society of Dilettanti in 1786. The author is unnamed because Mathias declines to add currency to a book 'with numerous and most disgusting plates'. The book, of course, spoke of sexual energy and the powers of divine creation as having been, in classical times, viewed as one and the same: to worship a phallic image, the book suggested, was to worship a divine symbol. That went down like a lead balloon with defenders of true religion in England. It should be recalled that Richard Payne Knight's Priapist enthusiasm was shared by Blake's friend, artist and radical George Cumberland (friend of Tooke), and by classical art collector Charles Townley. Mathias does not refer to Townley by name. Townley was a Fellow of the Royal Society, as was he. However, Mathias ridicules the Society of Dilettanti itself, presenting it as a source of risible classical enthusiasms (such as republicanism), and a thing of absurdity, for its members conducted mysterious, private rituals dressed in *togas*! Mathias believed there existed a healthy classicism (his) and an unhealthy one (that of radicals and 'Priapic antiquarians', to borrow Schuchard's phrase). Denouncing Knight's poetry as hopeless, the 1796 edition would attack *The Worship of Priapus's* author by name ('RP Knight') since Knight had himself revealed in print he was the Priapus book's author.

While these are the kinds of men Mathias suspects for crimes against art, greater crimes are imputed to Tooke and Paine. Their views are nothing less than a downright betrayal of their country to vicious Frenchmen. They cannot go unmarked; the government, it is implied, should look to the nation's security. It seems clear Mathias had not made his way to Lambeth to dip into the works of William Blake. Perhaps Blake's work had not circulated sufficiently to attract Mathias's brand of public opposition. It would be easy, should it ever do so, to dismiss it as eccentric, at best. Rumours of Blake's 'madness' begin at this time.

Regarding Blake's circulation, and the rumour of madness, Joan K Stemmler discovered at the Bodleian Library, Oxford, fascinating correspondence between antiquary Richard Twiss and bibliophile Francis Douce, Fellow of the Society of Antiquaries, concerning recently seen illustrated books. On 13 September 1794, Twiss informed Douce how 'a Lady' had shown him 'two curious works of Blake N° 13 Hercules Build⁵ Lambeth. One was "the gates of Paradise" with 16 etchings the other "Songs of Innocence" printed in colours. I suppose the man to be mad; but he draws very well. have you anything by him? [*sic*]'³

This is the first reference, outside of Blake's 1793 *Prospectus*, to either work. Twiss presumed Douce was already familiar with Blake's name. Douce would later acquire Copy I of the *Book of Thel* (1789) and, in 1821, *The Marriage of Heaven and Hell*. Writing to Douce again on 25 September 1794, Twiss informed him that 'Blake's Paradise' could be viewed the following Saturday (27 September); he, Twiss, would have books ready for him at the Black Bull, Holborn, adding: 'You will see several more of Blakes books at Johnsons in St Pˢ Ch.yᵈ [St Paul's Churchyard].' So we know you could see at least some of Blake's productions in the City. The 'Lady' may have been Mrs Bliss, an appropriate name for the possessor of one of the five copies of *For Children: The Gates of Paradise* and copy 'P' of the *Songs of Innocence and Experience* (Twiss's not mentioning 'Experience' as well as 'Innocence' would be a common oversight).

It is just possible that that curious whiff of 'madness' might have protected Blake from suspicion in relation to trials that took place immediately following Twiss's and Douce's correspondence. However, an exchange of letters between George Cumberland and fellow radical John Horne Tooke indicate that Tooke probably did not know Blake's name until February 1798, though one letter makes it clear Cumberland was well aware of Blake's radical inclinations. Blake, after all, had included seditious thoughts in the *First Book of Urizen* with this barbed couplet, arguably attributed to the 'villain':

> One curse, one weight, one measure
> One King, one God, one Law.

Cumberland wrote to John Horne Tooke on 19 February 1798 about alleged obscurity in William Sharp's newly engraved frontispiece to Tooke's *Diversions of Purley*. Cumberland sent Tooke an alternative drawing and motto:

> If you approve them, both the Motto and the drawing will be honoured
> by appearing, as you propose, with your second volume – in which case
> I shall take the liberty to recommend that neglected man of genius,
> and true son of Freedom Mʳ William Blake, as your engraver, both on

account of the pleasure I know he will have in executing a work with your portrait in it, and the general moderation of his charges[.][4]

'Son of Freedom' or no, Tooke disregarded Cumberland's suggestion.

The French National Convention's offering of fraternity to foreign revolutionaries forced the British government into the *Suspension of Habeas Corpus Act* of 7 May 1794. *Habeas Corpus* was duly suspended on 16 May, a measure intended to last eight months permitting the arrest without charge of any conspiring against His Majesty's person or government. Arrests of leading radicals followed: government spies had well penetrated the London Correspondence Society.

On 2 October, a bill of indictment was found in the grand jury, at the Sessions-House, Clerkenwell, against Thomas Hardy, leader of the London Correspondence Society, and against John Horne Tooke, JA Bonney, Stewart Kydd, Jeremiah Joice, Thomas Wardell, Thomas Holcroft, John Richter, Matthew Moore, R Hodson, John Baxter, John Martin and leading radical orator John Thelwall.

While Parliament debated the suspension of *Habeas Corpus* and the apprehending of members of alleged seditious societies, the arrested men were kept close prisoners in the Tower until brought to solemn trial before a special commission at the Old Bailey on 25 October.

On 6 November, Thomas Hardy and the other alleged agitators charged with treason and conspiracy in London were acquitted. Scottish radicals were not so fortunate. Savage sentences were passed on political suspects by the Scottish judge Lord Braxfield. With fears of revolution spreading, anyone proposing change of the 'perfect' constitution was regarded as an enemy of the state. Leading Unitarian Thomas Palmer was sentenced to seven years' transportation; he had written a pamphlet condemning war. Lawyer Thomas Muir, founder of the Scottish Friends of the People and forger of links with Irish Republicans in Paris, was sentenced to 14 years' transportation for sedition, while a secret convention in Edinburgh concluded its verdicts with punitive transportation and a death sentence.

The government's calculated intimidation policy worked. There would be discontent, occasional outbursts of hostility towards the King and his government, but there would be no revolution in Great Britain. Government was preparing for one of the greatest trials of the nation's history: the Napoleonic Wars. The revolutionary party was definitely over.

The Song of Los

The year 1795 opened with a Song, a strange sad song: 'I will sing you a song of Los, the Eternal Prophet,' it began. Why is Los the 'Eternal Prophet' in Blake's prophetic poems? He is so because he is the Time principle: he past, present and future sees. Los is often depicted as a mighty smith with a great hammer, not un-phallic by any means, beating rhythm; for time is the essence of poetry, of meter and measure and song. But also, as Thomas Taylor showed Blake from Plato: 'Time is the moving image of eternity.' Infinity is a sequence in time; eternity is unconditioned by time and space. What eternity is to spirit, time is to the world. For this reason, Los, the 'moving image', kept his link to the Eternals, and *through* 'Los'– that is, through the spirit of Poetry (the 'Poetic Genius') that transcends time even as it is constructed within time – Man may converse with paradise still. In a sense, Los is the custodian of divine imagination.

When things got difficult, Blake would go with Los to his paradise.

The *Song of Los* begins with a conundrum: how could poetic language be used by Urizen to bind people through 'his Laws to the Nations'? Blake creates a funny picture: 'Adam shuddered! Noah faded! black grew the sunny African/ When Rintrah gave Abstract Philosophy to Brama in the East.' The problem was not language as such, but abstraction. Rintrah represents prophecy. Blake seems to be saying that, in Asia, philosophy was put forward in the guise of prophecy, in holy books. He mentions the Hindu source of creation, 'Brama'. In 1785, Charles Wilkins completed the first English translation of the *Bhagavad-Gita*. Blake painted a picture of Wilkins with his text, sadly now lost, and took an interest in Hindu philosophy and religion. Blake's problem was how to understand the 'Gita' (meaning 'Song'). Was it philosophy or religion? Was it abstract ideas made into allegorical stories and dialogues, or pure imaginative access to the spirit? The Sanskrit *Brahman*, or underlying reality to everything in and out of this world, has been called, despite Brahman's being technically undefinable, 'being, consciousness, bliss'. The 'Parabrahman' of the Vedantins (philosopher-interpreters of the *Bhagavad-*

Gita, the Upanishads and the *Brahman Sutras*) has also been identified with the *Mysterium Magnum* or 'Great Mystery' of Paracelsus, the source of forms, out of whose essence everything is derived. Paracelsus's *Mysterium* was much on Blake's mind; it would emerge prominently in Blake's next prophetic poem, *The Book of Ahania*.

Under *The Song of Los's* sub-heading 'Africa', Blake considers the role of abstraction in the development of religion. He takes Africa as the place where religion first appeared, believing the whole continent was once called 'Egypt'. His poetic treatment of the theme is, however, suddenly interrupted by present political realities:

> (Night spoke to the Cloud!
> Lo these Human form'd spirits in smiling hypocrisy. War
> Against one another; so let them War on; slaves to the eternal Elements)

Blake turns from the contemporary clamour, back to the main current of his *Song*; the outside world is but a drop in an ocean. Are we seeing the beginning of Blake's long withdrawal into 'paradise' and the 'realms of Day'? 'Night' is ignorance and the 'cloud' is the body: Politics is ignorance addressed to the 'garment', not the True Man, which is the Poetic Genius.

Blake embarks on a theme that will gain greater force in works to come. He is against abstract philosophy. He even objects to aspects of religiously oriented philosophy such as the *Hermetica*, attributed to ancient sage Hermes Trismegistus: 'To Trismegistus. Palamabron gave an abstract Law:/ To Pythagoras Socrates & Plato.' Blake's objection is not against thinking as a road to truth itself, but the principle that spiritual realities can be understood by unaided reason, and where not understood, passed over. God does not 'explain' himself in modes cut and dried for rational understanding. Believing the Hebrews superior by far to the Greeks, Blake is suspicious of an England passing its Bible by, venerating the classical sophists and the clever men; perhaps he would have found some common ground with Mathias here, for it is a conservative and a spiritual vision.

In the *Song of Los*, Orc is chained to Mount Atlas, and howls. Jesus hears the voice of Oothoon, separated from 'wretched Theotormon' (since *Visions of the Daughters of Albion*). Jesus thus receives 'a Gospel' from him, and it makes him 'a man of sorrows'.

Following the suppression of Jesus's true voice, the 'human race began to wither'. Blake refers to the monastic movement, self-condemned by its shunning sexual knowledge: 'for the healthy built/ Secluded places, fearing the joys of Love/ And the diseas'd only propagated.' Blake suggests that the giving of 'a loose Bible' 'to Mahomet' by 'Antamon' (prince of the 'pearly dew' or male seed) and 'Leutha' (sex under Reason's domination) was an effort to restore some sexual maturity to a sex-denying religion.

Another reaction to Christianity's emasculation is envisioned when the northern god Odin receives a 'Code of War': a means to 'reclaim his joy' after having apparently suppressed 'Diralada', another name for 'Thiralatha', Blake's female figure from *America*. She is associated with erotic dreaming. Love inhibited, the Vikings make war.

Blake then re-presents his beloved Gothic era in negative terms, the architectural structures mentioned possibly derived from the history of Masonry in the *Constitutions of the Free-Masons* (1723; 1738). Again, the theme is emasculation, the stifling of the instinctive knowledge of humanity as a whole. It all matches the climate of political crackdown:

> These were the Churches: Hospitals: Castles: Palaces
> Like nets & gins & traps to catch the joys of Eternity
> > And all the rest a desart:
> Till like a dream Eternity was obliterated & erased

Blake is saying: 'You think you know your history, and the bounds of religion? You know nothing. You know not what you've lost!' This is Blake's personal song of Loss.

> Thus the terrible race of Los & Enitharmon gave
> Laws & Religions to the sons of Har binding them more
> And more to Earth: closing and restraining:
> Till a Philosophy of Five Senses was complete
> Urizen wept & gave it into the hands of Newton & Locke

Having completed a first section under the title 'AFRICA', Blake comes to 'ASIA'. Asia is at first awoken from its 'web' by the 'thick-flaming, thought-creating fires of Orc' in Europe, but soon looks back to a world where Sultans and Pashas could do as they pleased, where arbitrary power meant strength: where cruelty was 'manly'. Hope is in Europe, so long as the howls of Orc can be heard.

Blake's designs and, we may suppose, Catherine Blake's painting of the etchings, are again sources of joy and surprise. The lost children of innocence, Har and Heva, are shown in moving distress, orphans of the storm, the elements against them: 'Since that dread day when Har and Heva fled,/ because their brothers and sisters lived in War & Lust.'

There is only one complete copy of the six plates of the *Book of Ahania* of 1795; it is in the Library of Congress. It could be called the 'Further Adventures of Urizen', and though it takes its title from Urizen's separated emanation or consort, Ahania, Urizen's son Fuzon takes most of the action – in revolt against his father. The full-page design that opens the short work shows a beautiful woman looking for some distant hope while Urizen behind her hides his giant face behind his petrified hair. Perhaps Ahania was partly modelled on an idealized Catherine: there is something very warm and sympathetic about the naked figure, kneeling close to a being whose fists are clenched, unable to express any affection. The delicate title page design in a lustrous blue anticipates the delicacies of Chagall's fantasy by more than a century. But for a truncated, obese Urizen, literally cut off by the words at the end of the 'book', that is the sole imagery expended on this work. Was Blake exhausted?

Fed up with his dad, an exasperated Fuzon asks:

> Shall we worship this Demon of smoke,
> Said Fuzon, this abstract non-entity
> This cloudy God seated on waters
> Now seen, now obscur'd; King of sorrow?

Urizen fashions a 'Globe of wrath' and hurls it across the immensities towards his son, indifferent to the division in his 'cold loins' and the needs of 'his parted soul' named Ahania, whom Urizen calls 'Sin'.

Fuzon is hit by a poisoned rock fired from his father Urizen's 'Bow black' (black from the 'clouds of secresy'). Fuzon's 'light' literally goes out; the rock falls to earth, to Sinai, and is, of course, the Decalogue or Mosaic Law.

Beneath Urizen, because he had 'shrunk away from Eternals', his pained root has spread beneath the petrified seat he sat upon, and created a 'thick tree', the 'Mystery'. This is an image from Paracelsus, transmitted through Paracelsus to Böhme. It is the 'Eternal Nature' expressed in the wrath-world of the Father, the world of fire, but separated from the world of the 'Son', the world of love and light.

Urizen's role in the creation of the 'Mystery' directly parallels Paracelsus's conception of the 'Yliaster' or primordial matter out of which the universe was formed at time's beginning. The Yliaster is the world's eternal constructor, the universe's carpenter and sculptor of forms. Franz Hartmann described the role of the Yliaster in creation thus: 'When creation took place the Yliaster divided itself; it, so to say, melted and dissolved, and developed out of itself the Ideos or Chaos (*Mysterium magnum, Iliados, Limbus major*, or Primordial Matter.)'[5] Blake gives this philosophical account a sinister twist to implicate Urizen, divided, in the evil of the cosmos. Those who would try to put the world to rights must engage in a spiritual struggle.

> For in Urizen's slumbers of abstraction
> In the infinite ages of Eternity:
> When his Nerves of Joy melted & flow'd
> A white Lake on the dark blue air
> In perturb'd pain and dismal torment
> Now stretching out, now swift conglobing.

Urizen hangs his son Fuzon on a Tree: 'The corse [corpse] of his first begotten/ On the accursed Tree of MYSTERY:/ On the topmost stem of this tree/ Urizen nail'd Fuzons corse.' The reference is clearly to the poetic writings of the Norse *Edda*, to Odin, god of war and wisdom and poetry, who for nine days hung himself on a tree as a sacrifice to himself, pierced with a spear. Odin's tree is usually identified with the 'world Ash', Yggdrasil, whose roots plunge to the depths and whose branches extend into the heavens. Blake's Fuzon-bearing tree, however, is shown in Böhme's terms of Hell's ever-extending roots of nature: 'The Tree still grows over the Void/ Enrooting itself all around/ An endless labyrinth of woe!' The fruit of this tree is pestilence.

From this primordial drama, Asia, with its seed of abstract philosophy, emerges from 'the pendulous deep'. As Fuzon groans on the Tree, Urizen's latest misshapen, diseased children 'reptilize upon the Earth,' a reference apparently to discoveries of dinosaur bones, associated with Urizen's warped offspring: the 'bones' of his 'army of horrors'.[6]

This *Ring*-like conflict continues with the 'lamenting voice of Ahania'. Reading her lament makes one think immediately of Wagner, and ask why no composer has yet fully embraced the operatic libretto-potential of Blake's epics.

> Where is my golden palace
> Where my ivory bed
> Where the joy of my morning hour
> Where the sons of eternity, singing [...]

> Then thou with thy lap full of seed
> With thy hand full of generous fire
> Walked forth from the clouds of morning
> On the virgins of springing joy,
> On the human soul to cast
> The seed of eternal science.

Blake's Africans

According to John Gabriel Stedman's chaotic journal for 1795, his *Narrative* concerning the slave revolt at Suriname (published in 1796) caused much aggravation between him and Joseph Johnson. Stedman had to make numerous trips to London from his Tiverton home to try to sort out plates and printing. He dined at Blake's house several times, and, on one of these occasions, bought Mrs Blake a blue sugar cup. On 24 June, Stedman received proofs of volume 1, but the text was marred. When the Blakes entertained Stedman for three days in August, Blake offered to mediate between Johnson and Stedman when the latter returned to Devon. The following month, Stedman's diary recorded Blake's being 'mobb'd and robb'd', the story behind which calamity Samuel Palmer intended to tell Blake aficionado JC Strange in the 1850s, but never did.

Unimpressed by some of Bartolozzi's plates, Stedman had nothing but praise for Blake's brilliance. Anyone who sees Blake's splendid *A Coromantyn Free Negro, or Ranger, armed*, for example, will understand Stedman's delight: Blake's engravings retain a living force, definition and presence that show he inwardly understood something of the impact of the Suriname experiences on Stedman's psyche. In every engraving of Africans, slave or free, Blake brings out their dignity and beauty, as well as the sorrow and suffering inflicted upon them. One of the most striking of the 16 signed plates is an allegory of 'Europe supported by Africa and America'. Europe is presented as a naked white woman, Africa and America by naked black women. They embrace each other in sorority, with a hint of eroticism that is both sensual and sisterly, betokening oneness under the skin. While the slaves bear the rings of bondage, it is clear that 'Europe' needs them, and not only economically.

The Prints of 1795

While Blake's poetic fire might have been caught in the political crossfire of the times, he had energy to spare for a potent series of colour prints. Today, the 1795 prints constitute his best-known, most widely appreciated artworks, the more famous of them being permanently exhibited at Tate Britain. Most of the titles are familiar to aficionados: *Elohim creating Adam*; *Satan exulting over Eve*; *God judging [or speaking to] Adam*; *Lamech and his Two Wives*; *Naomi entreating Ruth and Orpah to return to the land of Moab*; *Nebuchadnezzar*, *Newton*; *Pity*; *Hecate*; *The House of Death*; *The Good and Evil Angels struggling for possession of a Child [or Good and Evil Angel]*; and *Christ appearing to the Apostles after the Resurrection*.

The disappearance of one subject from the 1795 print series is a great loss: *Wren*, a representation of Sir Christopher Wren and St Paul's Cathedral, has been untraced since 1880. DG Rosetti's *Academy* review (1863) maintained that *Wren* shared its 'general arrangement' with Blake's famous *Newton* print. Wren's 'hands trail along the ground'. On the *verso*, according to Rossetti, 'the hands are up to the chin, expressing great tension of mind in a forcible manner'.

Just as *Newton* expressed Blake's stinging critique of Newton's legacy, an analogous critique was intended for the honorary Grand Master of Freemasons, Christopher Wren, whose classical St Paul's had replaced the

Gothic structure destroyed in the Great Fire. In Blake's view, classical formalism was too abstract to 'house the Lord'; the God of Jesus did not, Blake believed, belong in philosophic temples – altogether too cold and insufficiently alive.

What do we mean by a 'print'? Tatham, as usual, got it wrong when he informed Rossetti how Blake made his prints, claiming that an outline was drawn strong and thick in ink or colour on common thick millboard before blotting on oils in profusion to merge for accidental effects; a 'loose press' being then employed to take the print. Blake did not use oils, but tempera, which he insisted on calling 'fresco'. His version of what he believed authentic fresco consisted of a ground of whiting and carpenter's glue, passed over several times in thin coats. Grinding his own colours, he mixed them with a small amount of the same glue. It was Blake's use of the glue, rather than the egg yoke of true tempera, that probably initiated the accidental darkening, with time, of some of his paintings, though he also confessed to darkening some paintings deliberately to suit the taste of others or because, his mood having changed, he doubted his original feel for brightness. Also, contrary to Tatham, Blake did not repaint the millboard 'plate' for further impressions. As a result, subsequent 'prints' lost intensity, requiring greater attention for finishing in watercolour and pen and ink. In some cases, Blake would take the print of the outline before overprinting it with the 'fresco' treatment; in others, there was only colour printing. Blake's priority appears, therefore, to have been the *textural quality* of the print, rather than the limited reproduction potential of the method. He did not take many such prints of his works.

Prints much commented upon need little to add from this author. However, a few details as to encoded meanings that might otherwise be missed, or avoided, need mentioning. The *Elohim creating Adam*, for example: while debate never ends on whether the use of the Hebrew plural noun-ending (*-im*) for 'God' ('Elohim': literally 'gods') in Genesis 1 means, or once meant, 'gods', or was always, or became, an acceptable Hebrew word for the singular God introduced to Moses as Jahveh, we know that Blake entertained the Gnostic supposition of a confusion of sources in the creation of Man from the earth ('And God said, Let *us* make man in *our* own image, after *our* likeness'; Genesis 1:26, my italics). Man's manifestation in matter was not, for Blake, unambiguous, nor was it innocent.[7]

The Gnostic conception was that the creator of material being was a subordinate angel to the Father. The angel, sometimes called 'Saklas' or 'Fool', was blind to his origin, and did not accept anything above him, and was therefore 'jealous'. The winged figure fashioning Adam's woeful face with one hand while embracing a subterranean or sub-aqueous solid substance in the other might, if one were kind, be seen as an 'aspect' of God, but the isolate look and unmistakable visage of the blind Urizen mark the figure out as a usurping divine power: he who applies chains of 'jealousy' and poisons the sexes; he who sets thought against thought. Adam's body has the serpent coiled about it already – the serpent supplying the plural of the Elohim's Satanic, or stolen, powers – and we may look in Blake's *First Book of Urizen* for elucidation on *that*.

Similarly, the Eve over whom Satan exults is wrapped in the serpent whose coils extend throughout Nature. Satan's spear points towards earth, the dust *qua* dust that is Satan's empty dominion, for in Blake's thought, Satan's kingdom of Nature is illusory; in reality of essence, nothing of it is real – all is appearance mediated through the five senses. Urizen is also visible in his flames as 'God' judges Adam in the print of that title, though 'condemns' – in the sense of 'The Accuser condemns Man' – would be more appropriate than 'judges', for God's left hand rests on a tablet of law that he himself has framed from his condition.

Note also the sheet that is mysteriously cast over what might be earth in *Lamech and his Two Wives*. The sheet emanates like a wave from the two women. This is probably the same symbolic sheet we see bizarrely extending from *Newton's* head to the floor of his geometrical diagram: he emanates materialism like a spiritist's ectoplasm. This is the 'garment, not the man', the 'cloud' or body that occults or secretes the divine genius, during man's sojourn in time and space, according to Blake. There is certainly more meaning to be located in *Lamech and his Two Wives*. The story of the first polygamist, Lamech, is in Genesis 4:18–24. In the story, Lamech kills a young man who has wounded him. His dismay reflects that of Cain, whom Blake also painted as Abel's murderer in the striking work to which the Lamech print is linked, for Lamech was the sixth-generation descendant of Cain. Blake chose his subjects carefully.

The almost three-dimensional Good Angel saving the vulnerable child from the blind, chained Evil Angel bears comparison with the print called *Pity*.

A couple flying past on a spiritual horse take pity on a mother who has apparently died in childbirth. The mounted woman takes the infant newborn that is rising towards her. She is doubtless Blake's 'first female form, now separate' whom the Eternals called 'Pity' before fleeing from her. And the child, if we look at his face, is no other than the man William Blake! To paraphrase the Gospel: 'Unless ye be as the little children, ye cannot enter the kingdom of heaven.'

Then, by contrast, we must look at poor, mad, beast-like *Nebuchadnezzar*, coupled visually, and not without reason, with *Newton*. They seem to inhabit similar space. But what kind of space is it? Look carefully at the growths upon the rock in which Newton has embedded himself and made into a kind of throne. The 'earth' is the mushiness of the seabed; the life is that of molluscs and sea anemones and things which cling to rock and suck on it. Yes, this abstracted Newton's habitat is nowhere else but the Sea of Time and Space, and he is beneath its waves, he breathes in the fluxious realm of matter. From Newton's 'garment' that pours from his head emanates a scroll, on which Newton places his great dividers. The compasses are Urizen's tools, and we see in their application the binding of the universe into abstraction, measure, height, weight, number, fraction, depth; and 'modern science' is content with, nay, rejoices in these sense-categories, which in Blake's vision obliterate the infinities and close the doors of perception. There is a Satanic gleam in Newton's eye as he points to his diagram of a triangle and an ellipse as if it were God's message for mankind: 'divide, and rule.'

Blake's 1795 prints reverse the premises of materialist civilization. He declares, contrary to the direction of thought in his time, that Man is a spiritual being in a living and spiritual universe, that Man contains infinite worlds within him. While the Church *preaches* a kingdom of heaven within, it yet denies us access with the thud of Law. The Church has closed off, at worst, or made remote, at best, the heavenly kingdom, by its capitulation to rationalism, classical abstraction and sex-phobia. As for mere government, it is murderous and exists for power alone.

Blake's prints restate the message of his prophetic poems.

It may even be the case that Blake chose his 'print' method specifically, and literally, to 'give the impression' by practical analogy (mixing paint powder and glue and water) of his dramas taking place in the 'sea of time and space':

that image so familiar to Blake and Thomas Taylor, taken from Neo-Platonist philosopher Porphyry's *De Antro Nympharum* ('the Cave of the Nymphs'), which Taylor translated in the hope of awakening youth to what he considered pure Platonic spirituality, but whose essence, Blake believed, ante-dated Plato. Blake blamed Plato for trying to rationalize spiritual essence with anti-sexual overtones, but he would execute a remarkable painting of Porphyry's myth, full of Neo-Platonist symbolism, in 1821. Discovered on a shelf amid broken glass and scraps at Arlington Court, Devon, in 1947, Blake's tempera is now known as 'The Sea of Time and Space'.

It seems highly likely that the print series of 1795 is a true series whose common theme and production method are intrinsically related to the principal subject encoded in the apparently disparate image sequence. As with Blake's 'infernal' printing method, one must burn away the superfice to reveal the Poetic Genius. Denial of Blake's esotericism will lead you nowhere. These are are not 'prints' for quantity, but for quality, and should be considered as supremely experimental.

A final note on Blake's prints: look carefully, if you can, at *Christ appearing to the Apostles after the Resurrection*. Christ, golden, his spiritual body redeemed from the power of death and the vision of the world, stands. All the disciples, save only Magdalene, have fallen to their knees, and cannot look at him; prostrate, their eyes are directed to the earth, to matter, the disciple at the front even tugging at Christ's *garment* as it scrapes the earth, kissing it (like Nebuchadnezzar eating earth), pre-echoing precisely Blake's jibe aimed at 'The Accuser who is The God of This World': 'Truly My Satan thou art but a Dunce/ And dost not know the garment from the Man/ Every Harlot was a Virgin once.'[8] The symbolism could not be more obvious. There are marks, or signs, of past suffering in Christ's visible body, but no blood (as Zinzendorf would have liked): all is healed. As Swedenborg maintained, the spiritual being in heaven can suffer pain as well as feel joy. But the disciples do not *see*: they are still worshipping the image, the flesh, and are still in the 'tomb' – unlike the Woman – and therefore, paradoxically, will shape a gospel *from fear of the body*. The 'harlot', who is Wisdom, sees the true Man, the Poetic Genius.

Lenore

Some time in 1795 William Miller of Old Bond Street employed Blake to execute three designs for Gottfried Augustus Bürger's horror poem *Lenore*, translated by the handsome Whig MP and Fellow of the Royal Society and Society of Antiquaries, John Thomas Stanley (1760–1850). Printed by S Gosnall, *Lenore* was published in February 1796. Designed by D Chodowiecki, *Lenore's* frontispiece was engraved by Harding. The choice of Blake for further illustrations may have been a suggestion of Fuseli's, as the poem dealt with dreamscapes, as one can glean from the first few lines of Stanley's translation:

> Now in the moonshine, round and round,
> Link'd in hand the spirits fly;
> And as they dance, in howling sound,
> Have patience! Patience! Loud they cry.

Artist and Swedenborgian Richard Cosway may also have suggested Blake, since Cosway, like Stanley, was a Fellow of the Society of Antiquaries. Perhaps Stanley himself enjoyed some link to Blake, through Johnson perhaps.

Engraved by 'Perry', Blake's designs are remarkable, looking forward again to illustration styles we normally associate with the followers of Chagall, visible in children's books published in the 1960s and 70s. On page 103 we see a fantastically elongated horse, vividly stylized and sharp as a pin. It heads star-wards like a rocket, breathing flame, spurning the earth with flashes of fireworks. The horse bears William, clutched around the waist by a terrified Lenore. William waves to an airy crew of terrible and wildly joyful creatures, some just bones like denizens of the grave set temporarily free. Across the face of the full moon, a naked bevy of three men and two women dance above human figures, stuck firm in the earth. Blake clearly loved the commission and let his childhood imagination loose before subjecting the design to great formal, linear discipline.

The second engraving shows Lenore and her mother observing soldiers returning from war while three youths form a band with fife and drum. A husband and wife embrace, while the child clings to its father's leg: another powerful, thoughtful design.

Blake's last design is based on Stanley's new ending for *Lenore*, from a passage in 'Night V' of *Young's Complaint, or Night Thoughts* beginning: 'He most affects the forms least like himself.' We see Lenore start from her couch, as though awaking from a dream, as William rushes towards her, followed by her mother. What is interesting here is that Blake would in 1796 receive a commission from bookseller Richard Edwards of New Bond Street for a new edition of *Young's Night Thoughts*, while Edwards' brother James, bookseller of Pall Mall, also in 1796, produced another translation of *Lenore* (called 'Leonora'), this time by WR Spencer, with designs by Lady Diana Beauclerc (*née* Lady Diana Spencer, known as 'Lady Di'). Perhaps Blake's commission stemmed from his work on Miller's competing publication.

All this suggests how poor our knowledge is of the details of Blake's life at this time. While he may have spent much of his time 'in paradise', there was probably time left for making business connections and socializing – more than we might imagine, anyway.

Blake produced one more illuminated work in 1795, his last self-published illuminated poem for over a decade. The only surviving copy of *The Book of Los* consists of five plates, with only two full-page illustrations: the frontispiece and title page. The title-page is bluntly arresting: a vast brownish rock, like the earth's crust or a vast mountain, exhibits a tiny cleft in which is stuffed, rammed or imprisoned an indefinite form, or deformation: an inhuman being mangled, from human form distorted, bloated, bruised, alone and utterly constrained, suffocating – if indeed breath were possible to it – and crammed into ever-imprisoning rock. The image is viscerally horrific, uncompromising and utterly anti-romantic.

The frontispiece is a sad, forlorn, baleful depiction of 'Eno, aged Mother' sitting beneath 'the eternal Oak' bewailing the 'Times remote' when 'Love and Joy were adoration:/ And none impure were deem'd': a time of abundance before covetousness 'broke his locks and bars', before Los was bound in a chain 'Compell'd to watch Urizens shadow'. Blake is, I think, fulminating on the crackdown of society, the withdrawal from the promise of change and revelation, of freedom and brotherhood, of revolutionary new things, energies, wonders unexpected.

But melancholy Los will fight back. He forms his anvil and builds his furnaces and beats his phallic hammer and heats 'those infinite fires/ The light that flow'd down on the winds', condensing the 'subtil particles in an orb'. He forms a great orb of power, of fire, a glowing mass like a great whirling, magic discus which he casts down, zooming into the deeps. It finds its quarry: the 'vast spine of Urizen'. Urizen struggles in 'dark vacuity' and 'fierce torments'. The title page depicts the grisly retributive climax of the poem, as Urizen:

> ...his Brain in a rock, & his Heart
> In a fleshy slough formed four rivers
> Obscuring the immense Orb of fire
> Flowing down into night: till a Form
> Was completed, a Human Illusion
> In darkness and deep clouds involvd.

And there, with perhaps much wishful thinking, the remains of Urizen are left for another day, another night.

SEVENTEEN

The Edge of Dawn

1795–1796

Rev. Ralph Churton's diary, 19 November 1795:
'At Northampton at the meeting to address His Majesty on his Providential
Escape. Five or at most I believe six held up their hands against it. An old
Dissenting Teacher was one of the five.' Ralph was rector of Middleton
Cheney, a Brasenose College living in Northamptonshire. The entry shows
the provincial reflection of an event that took place in London on 29 October.
Note how dissenters were unwilling to thank God publicly for the King's
deliverance, and Churton's implication, based on experience, that religious
dissent made for suspicion of disloyalty to the Crown.

Two years into the war with France, despite some trades benefiting from
government purchases, the loss of Continental markets fuelled discontent.
Another harvest was bad, near-famine conditions existed in parts of the
country; prices were rising and wages had not kept pace. Ordinary people's
living standards deteriorated.

On his way to open Parliament on 29 October, King George's coach was
surrounded by cries of 'Bread! Bread! Peace! Peace! No King!' A gunshot
was fired into the coach as it passed into Old Palace Yard.

A providential escape, but the return journey was worse. Hails of stones
smashed the coach windows, then poured inside. The King was hit. Taking
a stone from his cuff, the King gave it to Lord Onslow, saying: 'I make you a
present of this, as a mark of the civilities we have met with on our journey
today.' So hostile was the reception, the coach had to be rescued by the Horse
Guards. Louis XVI's decapitation had lessened the aura of sanctity about the
King's person.

Within weeks, Parliament passed the Seditious Meetings and Treason Acts. Public meetings were restricted to a maximum of 50 persons. Such meetings would now require a magistrate's license. Rooms hosting critical discussions regarding laws or administration were branded as houses of disorder; they would be closed. Blake's optimistic interpretation of the situation seems to have been that while 'Urizen' had got himself into a jam of self-destroying measures, 'Los' was actually calling the tune, spiritually speaking. If this is so, Blake was optimistic, and optimism is merely a state of mind.

On 6 December, Blake wrote to George Cumberland to congratulate him on designs he had commissioned Blake to engrave for his forthcoming *Thoughts on Outline* (1796). Blake emphasized that it was right and proper for designers to execute their own work (even *Locke* thought so!), and better it would be if it were always so. He then instructed Cumberland how to 'lay the Wax' on a copper plate to be etched. Blake didn't mind Cumberland doing his own engraving, but while Cumberland saved money by taking tips from the master, he wanted Blake's hand in his work. Blake provided eight plates.

Blake added a pointed jibe at the antiquarians to whom Cumberland was aiming his work (Townley, Richard Payne Knight, Cosway), while at the same time suggesting that he, Blake, badly needed more income, and perhaps Cumberland might encourage the antiquarians to come to him:

Now you will, I hope, shew all the family of *Antique Borers* [my italics] that Peace & Plenty & Domestic Happiness is the Source of Sublime Art, & prove to the Abstract Philosophers that Enjoyment & not Abstinence is the food of Intellect.[1]

Cumberland did his best.

Among Cumberland's plates, several illustrated the myth of Cupid and Psyche. Thomas Taylor had published his interpretation of Apuleius's story in *The Golden Ass* earlier that year (1795). Blake wrote how Ovid's *Metamorphoses* and Apuleius's *Golden Ass* 'contain Vision in a sublime degree, being derived from real Vision in More ancient Writings.'[2] Cupid (erotic desire) was a character in Ovid's work. Blake would incorporate the myth into his next prophetic poem, though *Vala* would go unpublished for a century or more.

According to Erasmus Darwin's *Botanic Garden*, the fable of Cupid and Psyche formed part of the Eleusinian mysteries, arguably depicted on the Portland Vase – the soul being represented as a butterfly, a significant image to Blake. Taylor wrote of Psyche as follows:

> Psyche, then, or soul, is described as transcendently beautiful, and this is indeed true of every human soul, before it profoundly merges itself in the defiling folds of dark matter. In the next place, when Psyche is represented as descending from the summit of a lofty mountain, into a beautiful valley, this signifies the descent of the soul from the intelligible world into a mundane condition of being, but yet without abandoning its establishment in the heavens. Hence, the palace which Psyche beholds in the valley, is, with great propriety, said to be 'a royal house, which was not raised by human, but by divine hands and art.'[3]

Back in the mundane, Stedman's troubles continued. On 18 December, he sent Christmas geese to Blake and to Johnson; Johnson sent Stedman a blurred index. On 27 December, portraitist Richard Cosway thanked Cumberland for his design representing Leonardo, suggesting Blake ought to engrave it, as few of Leonardo's works had been engraved, and a print of such work should pay Blake 'very well'. Cumberland had taken the hint and asked Cosway's assistance in keeping the wolf from Blake's door. A Swedenborgian who knew himself to be God's intimate, Cosway believed he could raise the dead, and that the Virgin Mary had sat for him. Cosway and Blake together would have made stimulating company.

Two months later, Cosway made another verbal contribution to Blake's welfare. According to the diary of landscape artist Joseph Farington (1747–1821), Farington was present at a meeting on 19 February 1796 of fellow Royal Academicians Benjamin West, Richard Cosway and Ozias Humphry: 'West, Cosway and Humphry spoke warmly of the designs of Blake the Engraver, as works of extraordinary genius and imagination.' Farington deferred from the general admiration.[4]

On 16 March 1796, Nancy Flaxman wrote that 'a friend of ours' was most beautifully designing Young's *Night Thoughts* in watercolours, a friend 'whose genius soars above all rule'.[5] It was Richard Edwards of New Bond Street who saw Blake's potential for the elaborate *Night Thoughts* publishing project. Blake would make 537 designs for Edwards, doubtless hoping this would be the 'one' to lift his and Catherine's fortunes. Men of influence were speaking up on Blake's behalf. In the event, only 43 of Blake's designs made it to the final (unfinished) publication in 1797.

Men of influence were indeed curious to know what Blake was about. The Liberal poet William Hayley's young son, Thomas Alfonso, apprenticed to Flaxman, was advised by his father to journey to Lambeth to see the engraver whose name, if not fame, was beginning to circulate. On 18 June Thomas Hayley wrote to his father: 'I have not been able to call on Blake as I intended but I will lay hold on the first opportunity. You know it is a great distance from us.'[6]

On St John the Baptist's Day (24 June), while Freemasons busied themselves in Great Queen Street with their annual feast, Joseph Farington received an evening visit from Henry Fuseli. Fuseli stayed till midnight. Perhaps wine oiled his tongue. According to Farington's diary, conversation turned to Blake. Fuseli spilled the beans regarding 'Blake the Engraver, whose genius and invention have been much spoken of'. Farington noted that Fuseli had known him 'several years, and thinks he has a great deal of invention, but that "fancy is the end and not a means in his designs."' Fuseli appears to have furnished Farington with the view that 'the whole of his [Blake's] aim is to produce singular shapes & odd combinations.'

Such a view is a calumny. On another occasion, Fuseli maintained Blake was 'good to steal from' – thieves often denigrate their targets. Farington learned of Blake's executing designs 'to encircle' the framed text of Young's *Night Thoughts*. According to the diary, 'Blake asked 100 guineas for the whole.' While bookseller Richard Edwards set aside 900 sheets for the task, Edwards said he could only afford 20 guineas for the entire commission: a sum JT Smith would dismiss as 'despicably low'. Nevertheless, 'Blake agreed.' Farington added: 'Fuseli understands that Edwards proposes to select about 200 from the whole and to have that number engraved as decorations for a new edition.'

Farington then reported how Fuseli confided to him something Fuseli might better have kept to himself: 'Fuseli says, Blake has something of madness about him. He acknowledges the superiority of Fuseli: but thinks himself more able than Stothard.'

Farington's tongue reached far. If Fuseli, being Blake's old friend, said such a thing, who might not believe it? Fuseli even informed Farington that the now '38 or 40 years of age' Blake had 'married a maid servant, who has imbibed something of his singularity. They live together with a servant at a very small expence [*sic*].'[7]

Unlike Farington, Cumberland had confidence in Blake and was happy to spread the word. When he registered his *Thoughts on Outline* at Stationer's Hall on 22 November, Cumberland's book not only contained Blake's eight plates but also acknowledged what Cumberland felt he owed to Blake's 'extraordinary genius and abilities'.

Thoughts on Outline's engravings revelled in 'the human form divine' as seen by classical Greeks and Romans. Cumberland's explicit design for 'The Conjugal Union of Cupid' would have given Mathias the vapours; Cumberland, however, was *au fait* with Richard Payne Knight's priapic perspectives. Blake finally got round to thanking Cumberland for his copy on 23 December: 'thou real Alchymist!' exclaimed Blake, who knew how to express enthusiasm when he wanted to. Blake may also have been expressing a cool jibe at Richard Cosway and Swedenborgian John Augustus Tulk who, inspired by French Illuminists and Masonic Magus Cagliostro, were experimenting with alchemy on the quiet. For Blake, the 'quintessence' of mature alchemy was the highest state of mind that generated the purest Art. Blake had imbibed alchemical symbolism through Böhme, through the Pietist tradition, and through Paracelsus and British Rosicrucianist Thomas Vaughan. Man was a microcosm containing in himself the Light and the Fire worlds, and was therefore a micro-*theos,* a sleeping god.[8]

Such was not the voice of established propriety. In September, the conservative *British Critic* (which would be purchased by Anglicans Joshua Watson and Henry Handley Norris in 1811), concerned that it had strayed from soundness, ran a critique of *Lenore*'s illustrations for daring to portray 'imaginary beings, which neither can nor ought to exist'. Joseph Johnson's November *Analytical Review* also knocked the book's 'perfectly ludicrous, instead of terrific' designs.

On 22 December, bookseller and now publisher, Richard Edwards penned a lukewarm advertisement for *Night Thoughts*: 'the bold and masterly execution of this artist cannot be unnoticed or unadmired,' he gushed, or rather, failed dismally to gush. He lacked confidence in what he had let loose on the world; perhaps Edwards had been 'got at' by the insidious smirk of hostile criticism. Strange thoughts flew about Blake's mind in 1796. At some point, judging from the paper watermark indicating that year, he sketched some obscure, erotically charged, drawings. The subjects appear derived from the Ethiopic *Book of Enoch* that James Bruce had brought back with him from Egypt. No complete English translation existed, as far as we know, until 1821, so if Blake did take from the newly discovered work the subject of 'Nephilim' overwhelming human women with lust and science (and massive penises), introducing sinfulness into humanity on the grand scale, it is something of a mystery how he managed it, though translation work was probably going on somewhere. However, verbal debate on the subject of the 'evil Watchers' who seduced the beautiful women of earth and begat a race of giants could have been gleaned in outline from Genesis chapter six. Blake was fascinated by the story, since the myth of the wicked 'Nephilim', or fallen angels (the 'Watchers'), was one of the root myths central to the Gnostic religion's development – something Blake intuitively understood and was perfectly at home with.

Thinking about the sexual desires of angels doubtless took Blake's mind back to his engagement with Swedenborg's sexual doctrines. This material continued to haunt him.

EIGHTEEN

The Four Zoas

1797–1800

Wright's coffee house, 12 January 1797: five Royal Academicians meet to discuss the recent discovery of the secret of Titian's colouring.

According to Joseph Farington's diary, the subject turns to Blake: ironic since Blake loathed Venetian colour techniques, a prejudice the gathering would have found perplexing.

Supping at Wright's with Farington were portraitist John Hoppner, famous for brilliant colouring, painter John Opie, Blake's friend Thomas Stothard, and historical painter John Francis Rigaud:

> Blake's eccentric designs were mentioned. Stothard supported his claims
> to genius, but allowed He had been misled to extravagance in his art,
> & He knew by whom. [Fuseli, presumably] – Hoppner ridiculed the
> absurdity of his designs, and said that nothing could be more easy than
> to produce such. – They were like the conceits of a drunken fellow or
> a madman. 'Represent a man sitting on the moon, and pissing the Sun
> out – that would be a whim of as much merit.' – Stothard was angry
> mistaking the laughter caused by Hoppners description.[1]

Hoppner also attacked Flaxman's drawing, but Farington reckoned Hoppner's 'description of Flaxmans figures was equally ridiculous as that of Blakes fancies'.

Blake was about to commit another 'fancy'. Possibly inspired by *Night Thoughts*' division into individual 'Nights', beginning with 'Night the First', Blake began his manuscript *VALA OR The Death and Judgement of the* [Eternal]

<Ancient> Man/ a DREAM of Nine Nights by William Blake 1797.[2] Blake replaced the adjective 'Eternal' with 'Ancient' in the title page draft, though the idea of an archetypal god-man is the same. Blake would return to the manuscript throughout the next decade, completing its 133 pages *circa* 1807. In an early erased stratum of page 3, the title was 'the Book of Vala', but confusion is endemic to the manuscript, the pages having lost their original order before WB Yeats and EJ Ellis approached them in the 1890s.[3] Yeats and Ellis claimed to have seen another title on the *verso* of a drawing: 'The Bible of Hell, in Nocturnal Visions collected. Vol. 1. Lambeth'.

If the book be considered autobiographical, then *Vala* seems riven with persistent depressive, frustrated states, reflected in *Vala*'s epic account of the psychic disintegration of 'Albion the Ancient Man'. This is hardly surprising, for Blake took as his rubric *Ephesians* chapter 6, verse 12: 'For we wrestle not against flesh and blood, but against ... spiritual wickedness in high places.'

Blake announces he has martialled his verses 'for the day of Intellectual Battle'. He was taking on the spiritual intrigue behind the *status quo*, giving its protagonists infinite space in his infinite imagination. It is fortunate that he did not have infinite supplies of paper, for, at first sight, the work seems unbearably long. *Vala*, however, cannot be ignored, if only for the insight it affords into Blake's psycho-spiritual system of the *Four Zoas*. Anticipating by a century Jung's structure for the 'unconscious' psyche, Blake's Psyche – or Mind of the Eternal Man – is certainly conscious of herself as she experiences crack-up, with Blake as recording angel.

Blake's 'Four Zoas' correspond in a general way to Jung's balanced 'quaternity': his four psyche-functions of Reason, Intuition, Feeling and Sensation. These Zoas (or 'life-minds') are four personified aspects of a living spiritual being; they have vivid adventures. In their un-fallen state, Urthona, Urizen, Luvah and Tharmas are living essences in the eternal world. They are the founts of the psyche, the ancient, archetypal lineaments of Mind. If there be strife on earth, it is the reflection of strife in the psyche of 'Albion'.

The figures relate also to the body: Urthona to the loins; Urizen to the head; Luvah to the heart; and Tharmas to the body-senses in general.

Analogous to the emanated 'Aeons' or divine 'thought-forms' of Gnostic systems, each Zoa projects 'emanations' (or emanates projections). Urthona's emanation is Enitharmon: that which cannot be attained from Nature alone – *inspiration*. Her consort is Los, their child is Orc; we have met them before. The entire Zoa corresponds to Blake's 'Holy Ghost': the divine Imagination, or 'Poetic Genius', involved in a subtle way with the fifth sense, touch, sexual pleasure, when touch is seen in its original state, as a gateway to heaven.

Urizen's emanation is Ahania, or Wisdom, also subtly associated with pleasure. The Zoa Urizen corresponds to the Christian 'Satan', or reason derived from Nature alone. Luvah's emanation is Vala, or Nature, derived at one level from the heart's yearning for knowledge of pristine, spiritual and ideal forms. As the Zoa of the heart, Luvah also corresponds to the Son of God, and to Love.

The emanation of Tharmas is Enion, a kind of earth-mother, derived from division of an ancient unity: mistress of the sensual world. The five senses *perceive* Nature into form: the manifest world, according to Blake, is that part of the soul perceived by the five senses.

Armed with this knowledge, we can grasp what Blake meant by his ideal of 'fourfold vision', the harmonious state of vision extolled in this famous verse sent to his friend Thomas Butts on 22 November 1802:

> Now I a fourfold vision see,
> And a fourfold is given to me;
> 'Tis fourfold in my supreme delight
> And threefold in soft Beulah's night
> And twofold Always. May God us keep
> From Single vision & Newton's sleep!

Fourfold vision is the dynamic *union of the Zoas*; when united, their individualities are transcended in divine ecstasy. 'Single vision', on the other hand, is any one of the Zoas isolated, associated with either gross sense perception (seeing *with*, not *through* the eye) or a state of abstract rationalism, though intuition shows us the relation of these two states – abstract reason is slave to sense perception – both opposed to love and inspiration, bound to time and space. 'Beulah' is the married state: the promise of perfect union.

A century before Freud and Jung, Blake has shown us a dynamic psyche working on principles of which most are unconscious, while maintaining the spiritual character of human mind abandoned by strict Freudians and our 'behaviourists'. Had Blake been born in Germany, he would have been considered a great philosopher.

Kathleen Raine has observed that Vala 'makes the descent Thel refused; and her figure is enriched by attributes of Psyche [from Apuleius's *Cupid and Psyche*]. She too comes to the Northern Gate, and the porter admits her; but she does not enter the world alone: she is accompanied by a divine lover who has prepared a garden for her. Blake's Luvah ... tells of his love for Vala, "the sinless soul": "I loved her, I gave her all my soul & my delight ..."'[4]

That the epic *Vala* is concerned with sexual pleasure's denigration is evinced in the numerous explicit images Blake sketched around his manuscript. They lament the degradation of sexual delight into misdirected erotomania or enforced chastity: parodies of sexuality's true role in divine vision. Some images have been rubbed out, or sanitized, by either Linnell or Tatham or both, including one showing collective worship of an enormous phallus, rather like a cargo cult where ignorant persons worship things whose true origin has been lost: a nagging hint of intuition that maybe there was a time when the genitals were not objects of shame, sin or abstracted sensual titillation, but glorious and blessed organs of divine, spiritual life.

Another remarkable image shows the body of a woman, whose womb opens out like Gothic altar gates into a chapel and shrine. Blake was as concerned with the 'Female Will' that used this power to manipulate men, as he was by men's and women's collective ignorance of the God-given glories denied us by our misperception of the true value of our sexual natures: our link to heaven. An undated poem from Blake's *Notebook* may serve as the text for the drawing:

> I saw a chapel all of gold
> That none did dare to enter in,
> And many weeping stood without,
> Weeping, mourning, worshipping.

Bad sex denigrates a sacrament, and bad sex is single-vision sex. Blake points us in the direction of a sacramental ecstasy in 'fourfold vision' hardly glimpsed by our pornographic culture, still worshipping the 'garment', not the Man.

Vala was, I think, Blake's attempt to write a new 'Genesis' and 'Revelation' for the unbounded, spiritual Church of the New Jerusalem. And it is a Bible of Hell, because it has been written from the fires of eternal energy and delight. What could be more biblical – or more moving – than Enion's lamentation from 'Night the Second'?[5]

What is the price of Experience do men buy it for a song
Or wisdom for a dance in the street? No it is bought with the price
Of all that a man hath his house his wife his children
Wisdom is sold in the desolate market where none come to buy
And in the witherd field where the farmer plows for bread in vain

It is an easy thing to triumph in the summers sun
And in the vintage & to sing on the waggon loaded with corn
It is an easy thing to talk of patience to the afflicted
To speak the laws of prudence to the houseless wanderer
To listen to the hungry ravens cry in wintry season
When the red blood is filld with wine & with the marrow of lambs

It is an easy thing to laugh at wrathful elements
To hear the dog howl at the wintry door, the ox in the slaughter house
   moan
To see a god on every wind & a blessing on every blast
To hear sounds of love in the thunder storm that destroys our enemies
   house
To rejoice in the blight that covers his field, & the sickness that cuts off
   his children
While our olive & vine sing & laugh round our door & our children
   bring fruits & flowers
Then the groan & the dolor are quite forgotten & the slave grinding
   at the mill
And the captive in chains & the poor in the prison, & the soldier in
   the field
When the shatterd bone hath laid him groaning among the happier
   dead

It is an easy thing to rejoice in the tents of prosperity
Thus could I sing & thus rejoice, but it is not so with me!

Blake has looked aside for a moment from the inner struggle and turned its collective gaze upon the world of human society. The vision immediately reveals what mere journalism never could: the outer world manifests the internal, 'invisible' story. 'Night the Seventh' erupts into a lucid vision of the industrial revolution and its attendant 'alienation' going on all about Blake and the public realms of war:

And all the arts of life they changd into the arts of death
The hour glass contemnd because its simple workmanship
Was as the workmanship of the plowman & the water wheel
That raises water into Cisterns broken & burnd in fire
Because its workmanship was like the workmanship of the Shepherd
And in their stead intricate wheels invented Wheel without wheel
To perplex youth in their outgoings & to bind to labours
Of day & night the myriads of Eternity. that they might file
And polish brass & iron hour after hour laborious workmanship
Kept ignorant of the use that they might spend the days of wisdom
In sorrowful drudgery to obtain a scanty pittance of bread
In ignorance to view a small portion & think that All
And call it Demonstration blind to all the simple rules of life

If you can find the time, go to the end of *Vala*. You will be able to say: 'I have been somewhere, and I have seen something beyond ...' Blake brings the battered ship home: 'How is it that we have walkd thro fires & yet are not consumed/ How is it that all things are changd even as in ancient times [...] The war of swords separated now/ The dark Religions are departed & sweet Science reigns/ End of the Dream.'

That 'sweet science', incidentally, is not the stuff we learn at school: Blake means 'innate science' or spiritual knowledge, without which quantitative science is rudderless.

In 1797, Blake's fortieth year, the 'war of swords' still raged. Churton's diary for February and March records discussions with Edward Farington (the diarist's brother) of Brasenose College, Oxford, about the Cavalry Act, passed to license volunteer cavalry regiments to counter a united threat from Spain, France and Holland; students would be tempted to sign up.

On 4 March, Churton was in Banbury: 'And there heard that Admiral Jervis with 15 ships has beaten the Spaniards with 26, much larger, taken 2 [ships] of 112 and 2 of 84 guns. D.G. [*Deo Gratias* = Thanks be to God]'⁶ The Battle of Cape St Vincent of 14 February brought temporary relief to the country, but war depressed the art market.

Published in November 1797 with 43 outsize marginal illustrations by Blake, *Young's Night Thoughts* was a casualty, though its merits did not go entirely unnoticed. Nancy Flaxman wrote to a friend whose 'favourite Bard' was the author Edward Young (1681–1765): 'Blake is the artist's name, "Native Poet he["]&c one who has sung his wood notes wild – of a Strong and Singular Imagination – he has treated his Poet most Poetically – Flaxman has employ'd him to Illuminate the works of Grey for my library.'⁷

By the year's end, Blake was out of pocket. The war depressed not only the art market: it stifled artistic expression as well. In 1798, George Cumberland planned to publish his utopian novel *The Captive of the Castle of Senaar: An African Tale; in Two Parts,* in which the narrator learned from 'his master a Jew' about the island of Sophis, run 'according to nature'. *Sophia*, Wisdom, is implied in the island's name. The society, somewhere in Africa, has liberated women, no slaves, and no war. No King or Prime Minister Pitt either. It has free love: 'Oh Holy Energy ... Thou art Love!' No shame is attached to organs of the body.

Cumberland confided a copy to a friend who urged him that 'it would be dangerous, under Mr Pitts, [*sic*] maladministration, to publish it'.⁸ The edition was cancelled. Unlike Platonist purist Thomas Taylor, who scorned 'the mere union of bodies', Blake was delighted with his copy: 'Your vision of the Happy Sophis I have devoured. O most delicious book,'⁹ he enthused.

Thomas Butts

Blake's financial problems moved him towards the position of his Illuminist contemporary, Antoine Fabre d'Olivet (1767–1825). Following a spiritual crisis (1800–1805), Frenchman d'Olivet would write of the very rare 'Providential

Men' who understand what d'Olivet calls the 'Tradition': primordial knowledge of how to bind Will to Providence – God's will, foresight and provision.[10] Providential Men know the way back to the unity behind all phenomena. Providential Men do not confuse mere 'rationality' with 'reason'; the latter, according to d'Olivet, being a spiritual power knowing what ordinary reason does not. Spiritual truths transcend rationality: contrary to Kant's philosophy, they can *be known*. It was 3rd-century CE neo-Platonist philosopher Plotinus who referred to the Greek *nous*, or the 'higher reason' ('mind' or 'spirit'), as 'king'.

On 26 August 1799, Blake wrote to Cumberland: 'I live by Miracle.' Since *Night Thoughts,* he confessed, 'Even Johnson & Fuseli have discarded my Graver.' Yet Blake laughed at Fortune and would 'Go on & on'. He trusted in Providence: 'I think I foresee better Things than I have ever seen. My Work pleases my employer, & I have an order for Fifty small Pictures at One Guinea each.'

The 'employer' was Thomas Butts (1757–1845), clerk in the office of Commissary General of Musters, and Butts's own employment was ironic, for it involved provisioning the army; as it turned out, Butts provisioned the 'Intellectual Battle' as well. Perhaps Blake knew Butts from his Poland Street days (Blake moved out in 1790): the Butts family occupied a fine house that also housed Mrs Butts's boarding school for girls, just around Poland Street's corner at 9 Great Marlborough Street.

As well as buying new works, Butts would, over the years, commission from Blake 135 illustrations to the Bible, in both tempera and watercolour. A tempera work of 1799, 'Christ blessing the Little Children', can be seen at Tate Britain. It is only 27cm x 39cm, but it packs power of reverence and perception. Jesus suffers the little children to come to him, and one can see why they would do so. Jesus's seated form seems to grow from the tree behind him. He holds two children to his heart. One boy, his back to us, seems focused wholly on Jesus's pelvic region. Behind the oak tree, a classical scene reminiscent of Poussin's and da Vinci's rural backdrops reunites England with a pristine, bucolic holy land.

In May 1799, 41-year-old Blake exhibited Butts's commission in tempera, 'The Last Supper: "Verily I say unto you, that one of you shall betray me"' (Matthew 26:21) at the Royal Academy. Butlin observed how the figures recline at table in the Roman style, as in Poussin's Eucharist paintings from his two series on the Seven Sacraments, both of which passed through London in the 1780s and 1790s.[11]

Interestingly, Judas is shown counting his money at the table, before Jesus's arrest. Blake's message was probably that the worldly obtain their illusory treasure early: true rewards come in heaven. And it should delight those who believe that Da Vinci's *Last Supper* depicts an androgynous Magdalene close to Jesus, that Blake, without a trace of ambiguity, depicts the feminine Magdalene seated intimately on Jesus's left, their shoulders rubbing – she gazes lovingly at him – while the other disciples sit at a distance from the couple. Blake appears familiar with the Gnostic identification of the Magdalene with *Sophia*, Wisdom.

> But I thy Magdalen behold thy Spiritual Risen Body
> Shall Albion arise? I know he shall arise at the Last Day

> (*Jerusalem*; Chapter 3, plate 62)

Perhaps Blake's exhibiting at the Academy in May encouraged Charles Townley to persuade Henry Blundell to consider Blake as engraver of artefacts from Blundell's classical collection at Ince Hall, Cheshire (now demolished), for on the 23rd Townley's diary reveals his taking Blundell to meet Blake: 'I took him to See the progress of the plates now in hand – called on Mr Blake engraver N^r 13 Hercules Buildings, Lambeth[.]'[12] If only Blake had left a record of the occasion, would he have considered urbane, Catholic Townley as one of the 'Antique Borers' he'd referred to in 1795 to Cumberland?

Bentley speculates an additional purpose, derived from poet William Hayley's having called on Townley on 1st May. Hayley's new book *An Essay on Sculpture* required an engraving of Townley's bust of Pericles, for which Flaxman provided the drawing, and Blake, subsequently, the engraving. In the process, Blake probably visited Townley's famous collection in Park Street, near Grosvenor Square.[13] The link between Townley, Flaxman and Hayley would shortly change Mr and Mrs Blake's lives.

A New Century, a New Move

The year 1800 began very well, for John Flaxman. He was elected a full member of the Royal Academy on 10 February. Perhaps Hoppner had got over his criticisms of Flaxman's drawing; perhaps Townley had put in a good word. Anyway, Flaxman's opinion now carried more weight; and he extended his largesse towards his old friend, recommending Blake for Hayley's engraving needs.

Author of the successful *The Triumphs of Temper, The Life of Milton* and lately *An Essay on Sculpture – in a Series of Epistles to John Flaxman Esq. R.A.* (T Cadell Jr and W Davies, in the Strand, 1800), Hayley was a genial, liberal character, a good classical scholar and a real lover of art. His poetry was easy to digest, exhibited learning, and was anaemically uninspired. The copy of *An Essay on Sculpture* that I inspected had had its two Blake engravings removed, leaving the reader bereft in a sea of more than 250 pages of verse unadorned by interruption of genius. It was tasteful for its time. And yet, Hayley was a friend of one of the era's greatest poets, William Cowper, whose *The Task* Joseph Johnson had published. And here lay Blake's greatest misfortune. For, as he drew closer to Hayley's patronizing orbit, pushed by Flaxman for Blake's 'own good', Blake would find himself 'gatecrashing' a very personal 'love-in' that had united Hayley, portrait painter George Romney, Lady Hesketh, her second cousin William Cowper, and Cowper's friend John 'Johnny' Johnson, rector of Dereham, Norfolk: all denizens of a blissful idyll at Eartham Hall, West Sussex. From Lady Hesketh's point of view, the poor Londoner Blake always appeared an interloper. Everything about the timing was wrong, but the 42-year-old Blake took little convincing that Providence had taken a hand, and if not Providence, then Fortune.

Flaxman taught sculpture to Hayley's illegitimate teenage son Thomas Alphonso Hayley, but the youth suffered from a spinal disease. Hayley was desirous to show his love for the boy by a gift of an engraving. Blake's initial effort failed to match Hayley's expectation, as did his second. Time was running out; an operation failed to arrest the disease. Then, on 25 April, William Cowper died at Dereham, a grief compounded a week later by the death of Hayley's son (2 May).

On 6 May, Blake extended his condolences with an account of how he was still in daily conversation 'in the Spirit' with his late brother Robert. 'Every Mortal loss is an Immortal Gain,' Blake reassured Hayley: 'The Ruins of Time builds Mansions in Eternity.'[14]

Blake enclosed a proof of Townley's 'Pericles' for Hayley's sculpture book frontispiece. Hayley's tender feelings must have warmed to Blake's 'brother's Sympathy' and he began nursing ideas of how 'gentle visionary Blake, sublimely fanciful & kindly mild',[15] might be induced to come and shed some of his warmth of heart upon the south coast. Hayley, after all, now had two very large gaps in his life. He decided to fill them with work, and what could be more appropriate than a *Life* of the departed Cowper, employing the humble engraver at Hayley's personal direction?

In June, Blake visited Hayley at Felpham, close to Bognor Regis, where Hayley, who called himself 'Hermit', had built a 'Turret' with a library he planned moving into, renting out Eartham Hall for income. Blake brought with him a roll of prints sent by Townley *via* Flaxman for Hayley, possibly in return for a copy of the *Essay on Sculpture* that featured one of Townley's prized Grecian possessions.

On 2 July, Blake wrote to Cumberland, bearing his soul. He had, he confessed, begun 'to Emerge from a Deep pit of Melancholy, Melancholy without any real reason for it, a Disease which God keep you from & all good men'.[16] Blake had noticed that things were getting better for artists in London, as if guilty at thoughts of leaving: 'We remember when a Print shop was a rare bird in London & I myself remember when I thought my pursuits of Art a kind of criminal dissipation & neglect of the main chance, which I hid my face for not being able to abandon as a Passion which is forbidden by Law & Religion, but now it appears to be Law & Gospel too, at least I hear so from the few friends I have dared to visit in my stupid Melancholy.'[17]

Unbeknownst to Blake, Hayley had been fencing with Lady Hesketh over who should write Cowper's *Life*. On 22 July, he suggested she do it as a series of letters to Earl Cowper, also informing her that 'a most worthy, enthusiastic Engraver' had so attached himself to him that 'He has taken a cottage in this little marine village to pursue his art in its various Branches under my auspices, & as He has infinite Genius with a most engaging simplicity of character I hope he will execute many admirable things'. This missive cut little ice with Lady Hesketh.

Lady Hesketh

Born Harriet Cowper, Lady Hesketh (d.15 January 1807) was wife to Sir Thomas Hesketh, and sister of Cowper's early love, Theodora. She was personally involved in Cowper's life and legacy. Her own health and nerves had been shattered attending the mentally ill Cowper at Weston, near East Dereham: Cowper had recurrent bouts of mania, believing he was eternally damned. Any hint of madness repelled her.

On 22 October 1801, she would write to relative the Rev. 'Johnny' Johnson, after complaining of Hayley's asking questions about their cousin Cowper's life she couldn't answer, that Cowper's 'excellent friend in Staffordshire' had said that 'he always feared that Cowper would suffer from the Methodists'.[18] Cowper, she asserted, was a lifelong Anglican with no truck for 'Enthusiasts' or sectarians. The reference was plainly to Blake, whom she was ever unwilling to name. Hayley's calling Blake 'enthusiastic' was ruinous to Lady Hesketh's idea of him, a view emphasized in another letter to 'Johnny' of 18 February 1802. Lady Hesketh reckoned Hayley's desire for a 'superb and pompous' monument to Cowper in East Dereham church was due to Hayley's desire to elevate Flaxman, someone she clearly thought little of:

> You know dear Johnny Mr Hayley's Enthusiasm for *Artists* of all Descriptions and his particular regard for Flaxman and for the Art of Sculpture tho' I rather wonder that his ardor on this subject is not a little cool'd as the Son he so much regrets fell a Sacrifice to it, but it certainly is not, and he is wild upon the Subject.[19]

Such was the character of the invisible turmoil Blake entered in September 1800 when he rented a thatched Felpham cottage from the Fox Inn's landlord, a field away from the sea, at £20 per annum. He was paying for a spiritual prison cell, but was slow to catch on. He might have realized sooner had he seen the pretentious and, frankly, treacherous letter Flaxman wrote to Hayley on 19 August:

> I hope that Blake's residence at Felpham will be a Mutual Comfort to you & him, & I see no reason why he should not make as good a livelihood there as in London, if he engraves & teaches drawing,

by which he may gain considerably as also by making neat drawings of different kinds but if he places any dependence on painting large pictures, for which he is not qualified, either by habit or study, he will be miserably deceived – [20]

Hayley put Blake to work on plates for a charity project. 'Hermit' had written a ballad on 'Little Tom the Sailor' for a bereaved widow's fund.

Nevertheless, on first moving out of London to the cottage, Blake experienced a spiritual liberation. He found he could more distinctly see and hear the voices of 'celestial inhabitants'[21]. Perhaps he was experiencing improvement in his 'sensual enjoyment' with Kate. Presumably he was progressing with *Vala*, and it looked like sufficient work was coming his way to keep the visionary flight aloft. On 1 September, he wrote to Cumberland at Bishopsgate, Windsor Great Park, that he had fallen in love with the cottage and had 'better prospects than ever', telling Cumberland he had already obtained 12 months' work with more in the offing: 'I call myself now Independent. I can be Poet Painter & Musician as the Inspiration comes.'[22]

It seems Blake was trying to convince friends that the curious move was all for the best. The latter comments, however, are ironic, as independence was something he had surrendered, and Hayley had no use for him as a poet, painter or musician, except, in due course, as a painter of *miniatures*, a skill Hayley claimed to have taught Blake in letters to friends! Hayley treated Blake and his wife rather like exotic pets, to be humoured and walked about as display pieces. The situation was awful and got worse.

On 12 September, Blake wrote to Flaxman as 'Dear Sculptor of Eternity' and 'a Sublime Archangel'.[23] Blake's naïvety, asserting to Swedenborgian Flaxman that 'the time is now arriv'd when Men shall again converse in Heaven & walk with Angels', is distressing to read, even after over 200 years.

He wrote to Thomas Butts on 23 September as 'Dear Friend of My Angels', with an account of Mr and Mrs Blake's long but cheerful journey by seven different *chaises* from Lambeth to Felpham. Butts's reply is fascinating.

Butts doubted the 'Title' was dignified since he was unsure whether Blake's angels were black, grey or white! He rather suspected Blake was under the protection of the 'blackguard'. He thanked Blake nonetheless, for if he was denied access to 'other Mansions' he might yet find welcome in 'his Highness's Court'. Butts suspected Blake was more of the Devil's party!

> Whether you will be a better Painter or a better Poet from your change of ways & means I know not; but this I predict, that you will be a better Man – excuse me, as you have been accustomed from friendship to do, but certain opinions imbibed from reading, nourish'd by indulgence, and riveted by a confined Conversation, and which have been equally prejudicial to your Interest & Happiness, will now, I trust, disperse as a Day-break Vapour, and you will henceforth become a member of that Community of which you are at present, in the opinion of the Archbishop of Canterbury, but a sign to mark the residence of dim incredulity, haggard suspicion, & bloated philosophy ...[24]

Blake's reply of 2 October addressed Butts as 'Friend of Religion and Order': not a 'Title' Blake would have liked used of himself. There is a sense in which clever Blake was sporting with Butts. Blake then added apparently spontaneous verses about his visionary states. He said he saw the 'Light of the Morning' as 'particles bright', and as he gazed into each particle, he saw it was 'a Man'. Curiously, one of the titles the ancient Gnostics gave to their figure of the 'primal Man', or *Anthrōpos*, was *Phōs*, that is: 'Light'. Blake's imagination then led him to a vision wherein every particle of sand was also a Man. He was trying to convey a vision of the 'humanation' of the universe. When all the particles were combined, they became 'as One Man', a Messiah, a 'Ram horn'd with gold'. Blake then remained 'as a Child' seeing Mr and Mrs Butts by the 'fountains of Life'. His eyes, his inner eyes, kept expanding. It was as though Los had leapt from the page and repainted the Sussex coast and gleaned it over with Blake's liquid soul, a glue mixed with light as particles and waves until the artist, lost in ecstasy, returned to himself, and spoke of Chichester, and the 'Genuine Saxons' who dwelt in the villages, 'handsomer than the people about London'.[25]

Readers of Blake's letters of sudden, explosive contentment at Felpham have been blinded to the actual conditions of England at the time, blending Blake's brief joys with ideas of romantic rural life in poetic cottages with roses around the door, surrounded by genial country folk.

In the late autumn of 1800, the Rev. Ralph Churton wrote from Middleton Cheney to Henry Addington (1757–1844), formerly of Brasenose College, now Speaker of the House of Commons. Churton was genuinely concerned about the artificial maintenance of the English grain price and a pressing need for cheap imports to save rural people from starvation. Replying from his family estate at Woodley, Berkshire, on 6 November, Addington maintained that while Churton was 'a Person, whose understanding, & Principles I truly respect', the grain price could not 'be brought lower in the immediate'.[26]

Winter 1800–01 was pocked with riots. Volunteer army units tried to quell them, but volunteers proved unreliable. In Wolverhampton a unit refused to act against food rioters, while several volunteers in Devon actually led riots against farmers and millers who to them appeared as co-conspirators against the poor.

In March 1801, Henry Addington succeeded William Pitt the Younger as Prime Minister.

NINETEEN

Enthusiast in the Establishment

1801–1803

Hayley was keen for Lady Hesketh to appreciate Blake. He wrote to her in February 1801, promising her delight when she at last beheld a miniature of her late cousin William Cowper by the hand of the 'excellent enthusiastic Creature, a Friend of Flaxman'.[1] Receiving Blake's miniature, Lady Hesketh wrote at once: 'the Sight of it has in *real truth* inspired me with a degree of horror, which I shall not recover from in haste! [...] I think it *dreadful! Shocking!*'[2]

Getting Lady Hesketh's support was important to Hayley's schemes: he bided his time. Meanwhile, when not at the cottage engraving 'Michelangelo' for Fuseli's *Lectures on Painting* (Joseph Johnson, 1801), Blake painted portraits for the panels of Hayley's new library in his Felpham Turret: Cowper, Spenser, Chaucer, Cicero, Voltaire, Shakespeare, Dryden, Milton, Tasso, Camoens, Ercilla, Pope, Otway, Dante, Demosthenes, Homer, Klopstock and Thomas Alphonso Hayley all received the gift of Blake's vision and sympathy.

Lady Hesketh, meanwhile, took her objections to Johnny Johnson who had visited Hayley in early March, and had met, and evidently liked, Blake and his wife; but Lady Hesketh had an *idée fixe* that Cowper (even in death) would suffer from 'Methodists'. She associated Hayley's 'engraver' with Methodists because the word had come to mean 'enthusiasts' of religion, dissenters from the establishment.

Four years after John Wesley's death in 1791, Methodism had broken with the Church of England, creating rival sacraments in individual parishes, threatening a religious and civil establishment already disturbed by political moves for 'Catholic Emancipation'. Though Catholic Emancipation had support from Pitt, the King vowed never to permit any measure that violated his coronation oath to defend the established Church.

Ralph Churton's diary gives us an exact idea of how defenders of the Church saw religious dissent:

> An old Anabaptist, (as he proved to be) a dissenter from the Church, on my inquiring whether he came to church, ran on strangely with words without meaning, 'The soul is all' – 'new birth' – 'verily verily' 'Christ died for sin' – 'dominion of Satan.' The inward test seemed all in his account; nor could I learn, though I tried a good deal, whether he thought it necessary to abstain from sin and subdue lusts. I hope he does. O Lord pity our ignorance, forgive our errors; & of thine infinite mercy bring back those that have gone astray, that they may be one fold under one Shepherd, Jesus Christ.[3]

Lady Hesketh may not have been disposed to pray for those she perceived as obstructive, but despite her hostility, as spring turned to summer, the 44-year-old Blake received plentiful requests from local families for flattering miniatures. So long as he served, all was well; his sweet singing, amiable humour and gentle voice charmed Hayley's cultured visitors.

At July's end, Flaxman mediated between Blake and collector Rev. Joseph Thomas of Epsom. Thomas commissioned a series of watercolours: scenes from Milton's *Comus* and from Shakespeare.

Hayley, meanwhile, was pressing on with his *Life and Posthumous Writings of William Cowper Esquire*, to be published by Joseph Johnson (1803–4). Beginning in September 1801, Blake would engrave six plates for the three-volume work, the most troublesome being the print from Romney's portrait of Cowper.

Between September and November, Hayley penned a curious poem to his deceased son, calling on his spiritual guidance for Blake: 'My Angel Artist in the Skies/ Thou mayst inspirit and control/ a Foiling [failing?] Brother's Hand & Eyes/ or temper his eccentric Soul.'[4] Hayley, of course, never realized that where his relations with Blake were concerned, he was dealing with 'Orc' repressed. Flaxman required no intercessions. In October, Hayley commissioned him to fashion a marble monument for his late wife, Elizabeth, daughter of the Dean of Chichester, who had died in 1797. Chichester Cathedral would serve again as a gallery for Flaxman's skills when Hayley arranged for Flaxman to sculpt Alderman Francis Dear's funerary monument.

On 3 October, Ralph Churton, in Northamptonshire, expressed the national relief when he recorded that a peace settlement had at last been made with the French:

> Now that PEACE is concluded. Blessed be His name who is the God
> of Peace – But, O Lord grant us peace and unity among ourselves in
> Thy Truth, that so public peace may be a real and desirable blessing.[5]

In Sussex, Blake was characteristically less guarded, pouring forth enthusiastically to Flaxman on 19 October: 'The Kingdoms of this World are now become the Kingdom of God & his Christ, & we shall reign with him for ever and ever. The reign of Literature and Art commences. [...] I hope that France & England will henceforth be as One Country and their Arts One, & that you will Ere long be erecting Monuments In Paris – Emblems of Peace.'

The Treaty of Amiens in May 1802 concluded negotiations with Napoleon. During that time Blake and Hayley appeared to be cosying up to one another; unspoken tensions, however, persisted. Hayley's diary for 26–27 April records his reading the German poet Klopstock to Blake in his library. Some such session led Blake to later recount his frustration listening to Hayley with his tongue rooted in his mouth. A few years earlier, Blake had responded in his *Notebook* to Klopstock's denigration of English verse (heroic hexameters were apparently un-English) with some satiric lines of his own:

> When Klopstock England defied
> Uprose terrible Blake in his pride
> For old Nobododaddy aloft
> Farted and belched and coughd
> Then swore a great oath that made heavn quake
> And calld aloud to English Blake

'English Blake' (a telling soubriquet) was 'giving his body ease/ At Lambeth beneath the Poplar trees' but started from his (lavatory) seat and cast a churning spell that disturbed Klopstock's bowels to the point of such agony that Old Nobodaddy begged Blake to cease, which he did from pity: 'If Blake could do this when he rose up from shite/ What might he not do if he sat down to write'.[6] One wonders how Hayley would have received Blake's vulgarities, for Hayley worshipped Friedrich Gottlieb Klopstock (1724–1803).

Keen to help his friend, Hayley coined the idea of giving Blake the benefit of his name and reputation in a publishing project. Hayley would write a series of poems devoted to animals; Blake would engrave the animals. Thus was launched Hayley's *Ballads Founded on Anecdotes relating to Animals with Prints* [14 of them], *designed and engraved by William Blake.*

The work tends to get caught in the crossfire of Blake's problems with Hayley and today suffers from the mildness of Hayley's verses, but the engravings are very fine, full of tenderness, freedom, comedy and grace.

Blake suffered to produce them. In May, he and Catherine went down with draught-induced rheumatism and severe colds, but still Blake got up to work on the frontispiece: 'Adam surrounded by animals.' Perhaps Hayley thought a general sympathy for animal subjects among the English, and the innocence of the engravings, would lull Lady Hesketh into helpful embrace of the scheme. She received specimens of the engravings to show to society to promote distribution. Predictably, Lady Hesketh claimed herself ignorant of matters of art but said that she would, for Hayley's sake, submit the works to those whose taste commanded respect – Lady Hesketh was on speaking terms with the King's daughters.

In June, Flaxman was happy to subscribe to the *Ballads*, and to provide copies for friends. Things were looking up. Then, in July, Lady Hesketh took Blake's Elephants to Bath. Bath, she informed Hayley, was too dull that time of year to advance the *Ballads'* cause, or that of their engraver. When comment came, however, she encountered a reaction. The engravings lacked taste and were poorly proportioned. The 82-year-old Bishop of Worcester, Richard Hurd (1720–1808), was particularly scathing; old he was, but the bishop had *taste.*

But Johnny Johnson loved the Elephants, and the Eagles. Hayley sent Lady Hesketh Blake's 'Eagle' engravings too, but she didn't like them, nor did people of 'taste'. Such people, Lady Hesketh insisted, found them confusing.

Blake's views on 'taste' may be found in his annotations to *The Works of Sir Joshua Reynolds* (ed. Edward Malone, London, 1798): 'The Enquiry in England is not whether a Man has talents & Genius. But whether he is Passive & Polite & a Virtuous Ass: & obedient to Noblemens Opinions in Art & Science. If he is; he is a Good Man: If not he must be Starved.'[7]

The trouble was that the word 'genius' meant different things to different people. In the religious establishment of the time we find the following:

> The Bishop of Bristol is a genius, that is a clever but rather an odd eccentric man; and his daughters, by William's account, seem to be geniuses also.[8]

On 15 July, Hayley wrote a careful reply to Lady Hesketh, unwisely taking the tack of trying to get her ladyship to see similarities between Blake and Cowper, specifically his tenderness of heart, his devotion to the Bible, his 'perilous' powers of imagination, even 'little Touches of *nervous Infirmity*, when his mind is darkened by any unpleasant apprehension.'[9] If Hayley believed he could secure Blake in Lady Hesketh's regard by setting him up in any manner as a replacement for the deceased Cowper, his sympathies had overtaken his reason. As for his praises of the Blakes' near-perfect marriage – Hayley described their life as a perpetual 'honeymoon', which may suggest the Blakes enjoyed a bed of spiritualized sexuality – nothing could have annoyed Lady Hesketh more. The idea of a sentimental *ménage* influencing her friend's judgement over her own was unconscionable.

On 19 August, she wrote to Johnny Johnson. Hayley would not take her hints that people of taste had no regard for Hayley's engraver's work. The unnamed 'engraver' was simply unworthy to undertake Hayley's *Life* of Cowper. It seemed Lady Hesketh might have commerce on her side, for that month the *European Magazine* gave the *Ballads* a lukewarm reception: copies were returned unsold. Blake, it seemed, could not 'cross over' to the mainstream.

Resistance to a character like Blake's was a priority of establishment politics at the time. The grounds of resistance were laid out in 1802 with forensic, penetrating erudition at the Oxford University Bampton Lectures, that year given by past Bampton Lecturer Ralph Churton's colleague, Oriel College

Fellow, George Frederick Nott (1767–1841), in eight published sermons entitled *Religious Enthusiasm considered*.

> The first conduit of divine illumination in the mind of the Enthusiast is owing to the inordinate action of his imagination, which when vehemently excited, is known to represent ideal objects so vividly to the apprehension, that they are mistaken for material ones. His subsequent belief in the reality of this illumination arises from the natural defect, or from the willful perversion, of his reason; in consequence of which he is either unable or unwilling to detect the fallacy of those pretensions by which he is deluded. [...] it is observable that the Enthusiast is uniformly occupied in procuring his own exaltation, often by asserting his individual excellence, and always by contriving some system of which he is to be honoured as the father, and feared as the governor; we cannot but argue, that the love of distinction, and the hope of preeminence, were the causes which first called forth the powers of his imagination. To the unworthy but powerful passions therefore of pride, of vanity, and of ambition, all Enthusiasm perhaps should be, in strict propriety, referred. [...] But it is the peculiar character of pride that it knoweth no bounds.[10]

Devastating. Anyone at the time reading a letter from Blake to Thomas Butts of 22 November 1802 might think Nott was contending with Blake personally. According to Blake's brother James, Blake had somehow offended Butts. Blake began by asserting his skills as a painter.

> There is nothing in the Art which our Painters do that I can confess myself ignorant of. I also Know and Understand & can assuredly affirm, that the works I have done for You are Equal to Carrache or Rafael, or Else I am Blind, Stupid, Ignorant and Incapable in two years' Study to understand those things which a Boarding School Miss can comprehend in a fortnight. [...] My Pictures are unlike any of these Painters [Carrache, Rafael, Corregio], and I would have them to be so. I think the manner I adopt More Perfect than any other; no doubt They thought the same of theirs.[11]

Blake apologized for not accomplishing a promised miniature of Mrs Butts, but when confronted by Nature he could not do historical painting. That is, portraiture was not consistent with imaginative art. He then confessed he had been very unhappy, but was so no longer. He had battled 'in the Abysses of the Accuser' and emerged into the light of day: 'My Enthusiasm is still what it was, only Enlarged and confirm'd.' He wrote another letter the same day promising Butts more pictures 'with all possible Expedition'. He then added a long poem, indicating the sense of opposition he felt from his friends – from his wife's sister (who was living with them), from Butts himself, from Flaxman, from Fuseli: 'Because I give Hayley his due respect'. 'Must Flaxman look upon me as wild[?],' he asked, before concluding with his verse on Fourfold Vision, begging not to be judged by 'Single vision & Newton's sleep'.

On 29 December, Lady Hesketh wrote to Hayley that she had received his biography of Cowper. In a startling *volte face* she added: 'I must tell you that I admire Romney's head of all things! Now it is *Softened*[;] of the engraving [by Blake] I pretend not to judge, but I like it.' Why she had hated the miniature now became clear. Cowper in miniature had a 'distracted and distracting look'. In other words, Blake had picked up Romney's suggestion of Cowper's insanity, something hugely unnerving to Lady Hesketh. With that hint removed, the image of her beloved cousin was whole again.

It would have been interesting to hear old James Basire's view on his long-parted apprentice's new work; alas, Blake's old master had died in the autumn, and poor Blake had found no like respect in the established mainstream. Was his genius, and his own knowledge of it, his greatest enemy?

Spiritual Enemies of such Formidable Magnitude

Blake wrote a confessional letter to Butts from Felpham, dated 10 January 1803. Mr and Mrs Blake had been ill, Mrs Blake 'so very ill', with ague and rheumatism, that apologies were necessary for tardiness in declining Butts's offers of help. 'Incessant labour' would keep them afloat. Despite Hayley's new commission for six engravings at 10 guineas each for the twelfth edition of his poem *The Triumphs of Temper*[12], Blake felt deeply frustrated. Some reasons are obvious. If we look at the title page of Hayley's published poem, we read (after the title): 'With New Original Designs by Maria Flaxman'. No mention of Blake, despite his technically exquisite work. Experimenting with darker shading than usual, he approached Miss Flaxman's gloomy interiors with style; the two dream images are beautifully refined and dramatically effective. But the designs were Miss Flaxman's.

Blake felt assailed by spiritual enemies and natural obstacles, while 'on all hands' he found 'great objections to my doing any thing but the meer drudgery of business and intimations that if I do not confine myself to this I shall not live. [...] This from Johnson & Fuseli brought me down here & this from Mr H[ayley] will bring me back again, for that I cannot live without doing my duty to lay up treasures in heaven is Certain and Determined.'[13] This would be his last winter at Felpham.

Spiritual values kept him going. He was 'under the direction of Messengers from Heaven, Daily and Nightly', and would rather his works 'should be preserv'd in your [Butts's] Green House [...] than in the cold gallery of fashion. – The Sun may yet shine, & then they will be brought into open air.'[14]

Blake's next significant statement to Butts is one that would elicit from a critic the question: '*Who does this man think he is?*' Was he artist, preacher or messiah? Blake declared: 'The thing I have most at Heart – more than life, or all that seems to make life comfortable without – Is the Interest of True Religion & Science, & wherever any thing appears to affect that Interest (Especially if I myself omit any duty to my ['self' deleted] Station as a Soldier of Christ), It gives me the greatest of torments.'

Much of Blake's philosophy is contained in those words 'True Religion & Science'. For Blake, true religion meant the fullest exercise of God-given talent, with no burying of that talent 'in earth' (Matthew 25:14–30). The art of life was the life of art. By 'Science' Blake indicated the root-essence of what he elsewhere called 'innate science' and we – in a restricted moral sense – call 'conscience'. 'Science', for Blake, was *spiritual knowledge*. I think it would be fair, in our terms, to say that Blake worked for Art and *gnosis*: eternal values.

On 30 January, Blake informed his brother James by post of his intention to return to London. Hayley, he asserted, was secretly nervous his reputation would suffer scrutiny should London society suspect him of mistreating the artist. Blake imagined himself on top of things; Hayley felt compelled to appear more solicitous for him; he was making Hayley treat him with more respect. His time had not been wasted (note the family guilt). Blake claimed he'd learned the secrets of publishing from Hayley: 'The Profits arising from

Publications are immense,'[15] he said, truly. But if Blake thought such profits were going his way, he was fooling himself and his brother.

Without notice, Blake raised his prices to secure Hayley's respect. He told Butts he'd suffered enough of Hayley's 'genteel Ignorance and polite Disapprobation'.[16] Emotionally, raising his price was a bid to regain independence, but while Hayley felt pushed into doing more for Blake, he was hurt by the price increase and began, under Lady Hesketh's influence, to lose faith in Blake's motives. In a letter, Hayley enquired of Joseph Johnson regarding Blake's new prices. Johnson replied on 4 January that Blake should be paid liberally, but his prices were greater than 'good artists here'. Hayley wondered if Blake wasn't getting above himself.

Johnson took the opportunity to complain at Hayley's insistence on having Cowper's life printed by Joseph Seagrave in Chichester rather than by a London printer (Mrs Blake came in to assist the actual printing). Seagrave's delays meant that Cowper had missed the valuable 1802 autumn season when town was full with little competition for new reading.

Hayley was feeling the pressure. A letter of 3 March from the poet Anna Seward, the 'Swan of Lichfield', busy on her *Memoir* of Erasmus Darwin, further stoked up Hayley's doubts. In receipt of three of the *Ballads,* Seward said bluntly: 'you write them for the multitude.' She made no comment on the engravings.[17]

And the world turned again. On 11 March 1803, Ralph Churton noted in his diary:

> Intelligence of a message from the King to Parliament that the French are arming &c. Press warrants issued in consequence. O Lord, be Thou our Defence & Shield; & let not those who would overturn the world prosper; Pardon, unite, and save us for Thy dear Son's sake.[18]

'Press warrants' permitted the army and navy to 'press' men into service. The south coast was anxious about 'press gangs' grabbing men off the streets and piling them into His Majesty's ships. Blake probably fumed as Prime Minister Henry Addington ordered the construction on the coast of defensive Martello Towers and the raising of some 600,000 men-at-arms – not that such feelings found their way into pious letters to Thomas Butts, for whom Blake was painting Bible pictures, such as the 'Riposo' depicting the Holy Family reposing on their sojourn to Egypt.

Blake informed Butts in July that his Sussex sojourn was coming to an end, with Hayley's blessing. Hayley had new work for him: an edition of Cowper's translations of Milton's Latin and Italian poems with engravings taken from designs by Blake, Romney and Flaxman. Profits raised from the subscription were intended for a monument of Cowper at St Paul's or Westminster Abbey. Blake assured Butts of the War Commissariat that 'Mr Addington & Mr Pitt are both among the Subscribers.'[19]

Blake hoped his 'three years trouble' would end in 'Good Luck at last', its 'Memento', as he described it, being a 'Sublime Allegory' completed into a 'Grand Poem'. This may have been what would become the illuminated poem *Milton* (dated 1804), though he might have been thinking of *Vala*, or even *Jerusalem* (also dated 1804). The synchronicity of Hayley's 'Milton' project with the title of Blake's eventual publication seems more than coincidental. Anyhow, Blake considered his new work 'the Grandest Poem that this World Contains', whose 'Authors are in Eternity'.[20] Hayley had looked at it, and Blake could see by Hayley's look of contempt that it must be good. Hayley, Blake exclaimed, was as averse to his poetry as he was to 'a Chapter in the Bible'. This was surely to curry favour with Butts: if Blake had been so put off by Hayley's liberalist indifference to the Bible, why had he stayed so long in Felpham?

Blake no longer pulled his punches over Hayley: 'I know myself both Poet & Painter, & it is not his affected Contempt that can move me to any thing but a more assiduous pursuit of both Arts.'

A week after Blake posted his letter to Butts, Ralph Churton's diary recorded a 'Circular letter from Lord Lieutenant [of the County of Northamptonshire] about, Defence of the Nation, a superintendent for each Parish. – answer it.'[21] While there had been parliamentary debate about how, or whether, to respond to French rearmament, the surrender of the King's forces to General Mortier in Hanover on 3 June ended all dispute: England faced a French invasion. Patriotism centred on the King, but there was concern about collaborators.

If Blake's letters suggest obliviousness to the invasion threat, so do Hayley's;

Hayley had a new project. Artist George Romney had died the previous November; Hayley planned to write his *Life*, writing to Flaxman in August for reminiscences, while explaining some of the difficulties Blake had encountered 'with the Ladies' – Lady Hesketh and her sister Theodora – over previous engravings, including those for the new edition of *The Triumphs of Temper* (Lady Hesketh had indicated disapproval to Hayley on 1 July). Hayley hoped fortune would favour Blake more with his work for the *Life* of Romney. He then confided to Flaxman that:

> Blake surprised me a little in saying (after we had settled the price of 30 guineas for the first, the price which He had for the Cowper) that Romney's head would require much Labor & he must have 40 for it – startled as I was I replied I will not stint you in behalf of Romney – you shall have 40 – but soon after while we were looking at the smaller & slighter drawing of the Medallion [of Romney, complete] He astonished me by saying I must have 30G[uineas] for this – I then replied – of this point I must consider because you will observe Romney's Life can hardly circulate like Cowper's & I shall perhaps print it entirely at my own risk – So the matter rests between us at present – yet I certainly wish to have both the portraits engraved.[22]

Fortune now gave Blake the hardest kick of his life. Five days after Hayley penned his grievances to Flaxman, Blake emerged from his cottage to find a soldier, billeted at the Fox Inn down the lane, hanging about his garden. Unbeknownst to Blake, the soldier had been co-opted by the gardener to assist. When Blake insisted the soldier cease trespassing and get out, the man became abusive, whereupon Blake, in his accustomed state of righteous indignation, seized the soldier's arms and, with the power of pent-up zeal, pushed him all the way to the pub, where the soldier threatened Blake in a manner so loud that some locals could not but overhear the rumpus. It was Friday 12 August 1803, and the matter would not rest there.

On 15 August, after consultation with his comrade Private Cock of His Majesty's First Regiment of Dragoons, John Scolfield made his complaint official with the local Justice of the Peace. Scolfield accused Blake of a storm of seditious outbursts: that England was like a parcel of children who would play with fire until they got burnt; that when Napoleon came he would be ruler of Europe in an hour, and that when he set foot in England, all men would have the choice of having their throats cut or joining the French; and the strongest man would conquer. He said Blake damned the King, the country and its subjects; that soldiers were all bound slaves, as were all poor people, whereupon Blake's wife came up and said that so long as she had blood, she would fight with Napoleon. Scolfield's complaint hammered on: Blake said he had told more important men than Scolfield his views and accused Scolfield of having been sent by his Captain or by Esquire Hayley to hear what he had to say. In Scolfield's words, 'his [Blake's] Wife then told her said Husband to turn this Informant [Scolfield] out of the Garden'. Scolfield then claimed he had turned to leave 'peaceably' when Blake pushed him out and down the road, twice taking 'the Informant' by the collar without the Informant resisting, while Blake at the same time 'damned the King, and said the Soldiers were all Slaves'.[23]

That was more than enough to get 'Miniature Painter' Blake – as Scolfield described him in the *Complaint* – transported to Australia for life, or even, given the highly charged nature of the times, hanged, lest 'leniency' encourage dissent or treason.

A warrant was issued against Blake by Chichester magistrate John Quantock on 16 August. To avoid arrest, William Hayley paid Blake's initial bail of £100. This kindness would utterly change relations between Blake and the man he only days before had regarded as an enemy to his true will.

Fortunately, Blake had witnesses to support his defence. Mrs Haynes, Mr Hosier, Mr Cosens and Mr and Mrs Grinder could all testify that Blake had not made the seditious comments at the inn or on the road and that Scolfield had been observed swearing and threatening to knock Mr and Mrs Blake's and William the gardener's eyes out; Mr Hosier had heard the soldier say he would be revenged and would have Blake hanged if he could. According to the witnesses, Blake said he ordered the soldier out for saying something he considered insulting. They were not in the garden together long enough for all the things to have been said that were alleged. Mrs Grinder heard the soldier say he could have Blake's house searched as he had misunderstood Blake's profession and thought him a 'Military' rather than 'Miniature' Painter (that is,

Scolfield suspected Blake was a spy, recording British military positions), and therefore may have come to the garden with ill intent in the first place.

On 24 August Flaxman wrote to Hayley: 'I am heartily grieved for Blake's irritability, & your consequent trouble.' Blake's mind was thrown into profound turmoil, though he was confident the soldier had foolishly perjured himself. However, Blake was going to have to face the justice of THE LAW. And when Blake thought of Law, he thought of *The Accuser;* he thought of Urizen; and he thought of chains. He must have been terrified to the core.

On 7 September, Ralph Churton was at 'Brackley at a meeting of Deputy Lieutenants, Inspectors & Superintendents of Parishes for Volunteers – £748.10 [10 shillings] subscribed.'[24] There would be a Review of the Brackley & Chipping Warding Yeomanry near Marston on 4 November.

As gathering gloom thickened into darkening tension, the Michaelmas Quarter Sessions were held at Petworth, Sussex. On Tuesday 4 October, charges against Blake of sedition and assault were heard before Charles Duke of Richmond, John Sargent and George O'Brien Wyndham, Third Earl of Egremont. Blake was ordered to appear at the next sessions. Bail was again set at £100, of which Chichester publisher Joseph Seagrave paid £50, with £50 from Blake; Hayley probably lent him the money.

It must have eased Blake's shadowed mind somewhat when he and Kate returned to London in the autumn, to upstairs rooms at 17 South Molton Street, north of Oxford Street in the parish of St George. Charles Townley had a townhouse there, as did artist Richard Cosway.

Blake wrote to Hayley on 7 October as his 'devoted rebel', lamenting that: 'Art in London flourishes. Engravers in particular are wanted. [...] Yet no one brings work to me.' He signed it: 'To Eternity yours, Willm. Blake.'[25]

He was back in London just in time for King George's review of more than 12,000 men of the City of London Volunteer Corps on 26 October. Attended by exiled Bourbon princes and his seven sons, the King alighted from his coach at the entrance to Hyde Park and mounted a charger. An estimated crowd of 200,000 cheered wildly and Lord Eldon declared it the finest sight he had ever witnessed. Was Blake tempted to join the throng, to demonstrate loyalty to the cause? Around 46,000 men from the London area joined the Volunteers.

In fact, on that day, Blake wrote to William Hayley. The *Ballads* project was failing: 'I called on Mr Evans [a bookseller], who gives small hopes of our ballads; he says he has sold but fifteen numbers at most, and that going on would almost certainly be a loss of expenses.'[26]

On 27 November, Lady Hesketh decided the time had come to express her views on Blake directly to Hayley: 'but if I may give credit to some reports which reached me at that time, Mr. B: was more *Seriously* to blame [for the Scolfield incident] than you were at all aware of I believe – but I will only add on this Subject – that – *if he was*, I sincerely hope that you are no Stranger to it!'[27]

Had this potentially incriminating letter got into the prosecution's hands, it could have been ruinous. Hayley wrote back repeating that the allegations against Blake were untrue: vengeful lies from a soldier reduced to the ranks for ill conduct. We can but wonder as to the source of Lady Hesketh's intelligence about Blake.[28] Blake himself suspected after the events that he had been targeted or set up from on high on account of his beliefs and the extremity of the times. His poem *Jerusalem* repeatedly demonstrates what might be called an obsession with the characters and names of persons connected with his trial, still vivid years afterwards. How could Blake regard the events as accidental, when he believed that every physical event had a spiritual cause?

Flaxman tried to obtain work for him. On Christmas Day, he wrote to Prince Hoare, Secretary of Foreign Correspondence of the Royal Academy, to secure a commission for engraving, from Flaxman's sketch, a newly found bust of Ceres. Blake accepted the commission, but as Christmas faded, how could he be sure he would live to accomplish the work?

TWENTY

Lady Hesketh's hair stands on end

1804–1805

In 1633, the Rev. Peter Studley, vicar of St Chad's, Shrewsbury, published *The Looking-Glass of Schism*. It included an account of churchwarden Thomas Hickes, who took it upon himself to smash a churchyard cross in Tewkesbury. Hickes's family immediately suffered a series of monstrous births. Failing to recognize divine retribution, Hickes took the stones secreted by parishioners beneath the church and made of them a pig-trough; the pigs died. Studley concluded that their deaths, and Hickes's subsequent, abominable suicide, derived from the original blasphemy; Hickes, Studley believed, was a fanatical vandal of sacred monuments.

When John Brickdale Blakeway (1765–1826), the historian of Shrewsbury, brought the account to Rev. Ralph Churton's attention in March 1804, Churton replied:

> The mirror of Schism 1633, must, I dare say, be a curious book. The increase in Methodists & Sectaries in Shrewsbury is a circumstance to be lamented, but not alas! peculiar to that town, but common I fear to the whole nation. I think it was Bishop Butler's notion, that nations are like individuals, have fits of insanity, & I fear we are not perfectly sane at present, & when we may be so, God alone knows, & may He heal us! We have the worst sort of sickness, are sick of being well, & loath our manna, the best liturgy & best Church on earth since the days of the Apostles.[1]

Churton perceived the extremes of 17th-century Protestant iconoclasm as 'curious'; but extremism persisted in other forms of dissent and religious 'enthusiasm'. Indeed, extremes of enthusiasm might conceivably swell into tempting imaginings so seductive that the religious enthusiast might even envision Napoleon Bonaparte as God's instrument for delivering the country from an alleged 'tyranny' of Church and King. Here lies the essential conflict at the root of Blake's trial: dissent *versus* order. The suspicion that Blake was of the former tendency explains both his personal terror – Kate nearly perished of fright – and Lady Hesketh's increasing attacks on Blake's character and motives. If Art was on the side of 'Enthusiasm', then it was as likely a cousin of dissent, and dissent could make traitors, as had notoriously occurred in the case of the Gunpowder Plot. Blake was in serious trouble.

New Year's Day, 1804. Hayley wrote to ebullient 'Johnny' that he hoped he would get to the 'Turret' on the 10th to see Hayley's lawyer, Samuel Rose (1767–1804), 'eloquently & successfully defend our interesting Artist'.

Auguries were not promising. The trial, due for Chichester Guildhall's Quarter Sessions, was delayed by a day due to pressure of work. Then, a few days before the trial, key character witness William Hayley was thrown from his horse. Dr Guy attended Hayley's bad head injury: would he be well enough to attend?[2] More disturbing was the fact that the senior of the seven magistrates was Charles, Duke of Lennox (1735–1806), 3rd Duke of Richmond, Lord Lieutenant of Sussex; it was Richmond's responsibility to raise militia for the country's defence, to which defence Sussex was key. His Grace was also a Field Marshal, having served as Colonel commanding the 72nd Regiment of Foot and the Royal Horse Guards. His father fought with Cumberland at the crushing of the Jacobites at Culloden. A former Whig and proponent of parliamentary reform, Richmond had joined Pitt's government in 1784 and changed into an anti-reformist Tory. He liked Neo-classical portraiture and had patronized Sir Joshua Reynolds. His nephew Charles Lennox sat for the artist John Hoppner, Blake's dismissive critic.[3] Blake was probably unaware that the Duchess, Lady Mary's portrait had been engraved by William Ryland, he whom a teenage Blake believed would be hanged (and was); see p.59.

Stimulated by the national crisis, Richmond was in no mood to tolerate abuse of regular or volunteer soldiers – seldom welcome in civilian streets at the best of times – or to treat seditious men lightly. According to Hayley's *Memoir*, the old Duke 'was bitterly prejudiced against Blake', making 'unwarrantable suggestions in the course of the trial, that might have excited prejudice in the Jury'.[4]

Richmond wanted an example.

Beginning well, Blake's counsel Samuel Rose declared that whereas he would never defend anyone he believed had uttered seditious words, the defendant Blake was 'as loyal a subject as any man in this court: – that he feels as much indignation at the idea of exposing to contempt or injury the sacred person of his sovereign as any man: – that his indignation is equal to that, which I doubt not every one of you felt, when the charge was first stated to you.'[5]

It is just as well Rose had not seen plate 12 of *Europe: A Prophecy*, where above the words, 'He saw Urizen on the Atlantic:/ And his brazen Book/ That Kings & Priests had copied on Earth', appears a seated figure in the robes of a priest, with the wings of a demon and the face, it appears, of King George III, topped by a papal crown!

Having demonstrated that witness testimony did not match Scolfield and Cock's account, poor Rose suddenly, and dramatically, collapsed. Unable to continue, he would eventually succumb to a 'rheumatic fever in the head'. But Rose had sufficiently established the case to convince the jury that to accept the soldiers' testimony would be to impugn the honesty of the witnesses.

The Duke of Richmond was displeased. When Hayley congratulated him on 'seeing an honest man honorably delivered from an infamous persecution,' Richmond replied bluntly: 'I know nothing of Him,' to which Hayley, on the verge of euphoria, replied: 'True, my Lord, your Grace can Know nothing of Him; & I have therefore given you this Information: I wish your Grace a good Night.'[6] This exchange and the account of the duke's prejudice were excised from the printed version of Hayley's *Memoirs*.[7]

Blake's acquittal exploded into widespread jubilation testifying to the excellent relations Blake enjoyed with Felpham and Chichester's inhabitants since his first visit in 1800; it was not he but the soldiers who were outsiders.

That the incident leading to trial was unlikely to have been staged as a strategem of secret government may be argued by the fact that, however hostile Richmond was to Blake, either personally or impersonally, the best case to question Blake's loyalty could have been drawn from his own works; no such attempt was made. Their circulation and contents were too obscure to provoke government intervention. Nevertheless, Hayley's imputation of prejudice leaves open the question of how far influence from other parties may have coloured Richmond's judgement.

The larger part of the literary and artistic establishment would, in times to come, insulate itself from poor engraver William Blake, conveniently dismissable by his enemies as mad or eccentric: imbalance of mind being the source of a 'genius' vulnerable to exploitation.

Blake returned to South Molton Street, where his release summoned Kate back from death's door. For the next two years, Blake became Hayley's humble London agent, prosecuting his interests in the Cowper and Romney *Life* projects. Some of his letters to Hayley, shorn of Blakean flourishes, could have been written by, well, anyone. By paying his bail and lending Blake his lawyer and reputation, Hayley had saved the artist's bacon, and Blake knew it. Who now was the angel? What price salvation?

Blake needed support. Fleeting triumph had hardly subsided when, on 1 February 1804, a review in the *Literary Journal* of Prince Hoare's *Academic Correspondence* attacked Blake's goddess Ceres plate, from Flaxman's sketch: 'Surely [...] the Royal Academy of England might have offered an engraving worthy of the subject and of the country.'[8] The review did not prevent one more commission, in 1806, from the Academy's Secretary of Foreign Correspondence.

On the same day the bad review appeared, Lady Hesketh offered belated congratulations to Hayley and the 'kindness and Eloquence of our good Rose' on the 'acquittal of your friend'. She then added, pointedly: 'You are so Staunch and Jealous in your friendships once made that you cannot be too careful in your choice.'[9] Translation: Blake was *his* friend, not hers, and he had better choose better ones.

In March, Hayley started pushing Blake to come up with two outstanding plates for the third volume of his *Life* of Cowper. Friends were anxious to obtain the final instalment. Blake parried attempts to get him to work to order by delaying replies and making excuses; the work was finally delivered at the end of April. Hayley's friend Samuel Greatheed wrote to praise Blake's frontispiece engraving of Cowper's tomb at East Dereham: it was so good it obviated the duty of visiting the original.

By May's end, Blake was writing to Hayley in a composed, literary style, thanking Hayley for lending him volume 2 of John Marshall's *Life of George Washington* (Philadelphia, 1804–07):

> I suppose an American would tell me that Washington did all that was done before he was born, as the French now adore Buonaparte and the English our poor George; so the Americans will consider Washington as their god. This is only Grecian, or rather Trojan, worship, and perhaps will be revised in an age or two.[10]

By June, Hayley was determined to engage Caroline Watson as engraver for the Romney *Life*, not Blake. Lady Hesketh had adamantly promoted Watson's cause. Flaxman, who was employing Blake for three engravings for his *Odyssey of Homer* (1805), suggested that while this was a matter between Hayley and the engraver, he found Watson unimpressive; choosing her would 'be unsatisfactory to all persons concerned'.[11]

Hayley also fancied employing a friend of Flaxman's Hayley called 'Cromak', to engrave Romney's *The Shipwreck*. Flaxman replied in August that 'Cromek' (Robert Hartley Cromek, 1770–1812) was fully engaged and suggested that since Romney's original *Shipwreck* was then with Blake, it would be problematic to withdraw it from him. Flaxman began to wonder if Blake hadn't been all too prophetic when he had written to him earlier in the year that, as far as the trades went, London was a 'City of Assassinations'.

On 7 August, aware that Hayley was considering other artists to contribute to the Romney book, Blake wrote to him plaintively: 'Profit never ventures upon my Threshold, tho' every other man's doorstone is worn down into the very Earth by the footsteps of the fiends of commerce.'[12]

Hayley knew very well of Blake's impecuniousness. At the end of September, he received Blake's letter asking for 'the favour of £10 more' for *The Shipwreck* while also fishing for employment on a worthy engraving of Romney's 'Tobias and Tobit', hanging at Eartham. Blake signed the letter: 'Your sincere and obliged humble servant.'

While Hayley to'd and fro'd, effectively betraying the man who was serving him while carrying Flaxman and his sister along, Blake had a kind of artistic religious experience at an exhibition on the New Road, in sight of the countryside, opposite Portland Place.

Joseph, Count Truchsess had brought to England a collection of German, Flemish and Dutch Masters to sell to a company for the public benefit. Notwithstanding leading portraitist Thomas Lawrence's low opinion of the exhibition, which opened in August 1803, Blake informed Hayley it had had such an effect on him that 'I was again enlightened with the light I enjoyed in my youth, and which has for exactly twenty years been closed from me as by a door and by window-shutters. Consequently I can, with confidence, promise you ocular demonstration of my altered state on the plates I am now engraving after Romney.'[13]

The reference to '20 years' is something of a mystery. Ironically, 1784 was the year Flaxman wrote to his (then) new friend William Hayley of Blake's 'Poetical Sketches': 'his education will plead sufficient excuse to your Liberal mind for the defects of his work.' Full-circle indeed!

It is as though Blake were denying his mature career. Did he want to begin again, with the savour of mind that once sprung fresh from youth? He was now 47. Middle age has its drawbacks, though none were evident in his magnificent engraving of *The Shipwreck*, a work anticipating Géricault's *Raft of the Medusa* by some 15 years, its epic dynamism sufficient to induce seasickness, or relief to be on land.

Lady Hesketh wrote to Hayley on 14 November, insisting ardently 'that no inferior or middling artists, may ever more be suffered to lay their insufficient Hands on any future work of yours!' She had, she said, already written to Caroline Watson to tell her the commission was hers.[14]

Watson would engrave *Romney* after designs by Maria Flaxman.

Did *nobody* want Blake to succeed on his own terms? His personal revelation at the Truchsessian Gallery found no public outlet: a breakthrough with no breakthrough, Blake's silent triumph soon dissolved.

On 18 December, he wrote to Hayley: 'I am again in want of £10' – for *The Shipwreck*: how apt. Wishing Hayley a 'merry Christmas', Blake informed the landed gent that Mrs Blake's recovery from miserable rheumatic swelling of legs and joints had been greatly assisted by *Birch's Electrical Magic* 'which she has discontinued these last three months'– presumably for want of funds.[15] Joseph Johnson had reprinted John Birch's *Essay on the Medical Application of Electricity* in 1802; so impressed was Blake by Birch's use of electricity to restore health to Kate's body that he translated the idea into his unfinished poem

Milton, where Albion's sleeping body is regenerated by Milton's sudden arrival – 'Feeling the electric flame of Milton's awful precipitate descent'. The Blakes needed a shock of cash.

Ten days later, Blake's trial advocate, Samuel Rose, died.

He will poison him in his Turret

Seven months on, Lady Hesketh still insisted it was only 'the pains' 'our poor Rose took in that affair'[16] that had saved Blake. Hayley's charity, she maintained, blinded him to the truth:

> Surely my dear Sir you are gifted with *more* true Charity, than falls to the lot of most mortals, (or that perhaps one wou'd wish there *should*) if you can not only forgive but continue to protect, and cherish, one, (whom for your sake, I ever *tremble* to think of, and whom certainly I will not name) ...[17]

She named him on 31 July 1805 in a letter to Johnny Johnson:

> My hair stands on end to think that Hayley & Blake are as dear friends as ever! He talks of him as if he was an Angel! How can you Johnny suffer our poor friend to be thus impos'd upon? – I don't doubt he will poison him in his Turret or set fire to all his papers, & poor Hayley will consume in his own Fires.[18]

On 1 August, Hayley replied. He 'smiled' at Lady Hesketh's notion of his having '*super-abundance of Christian charity*'. He would simply be a 'despicable mortal' not to have protected a well-meaning and '*very industrious*, tho not very *successful* artist' from the quarrelsome brutality of 'a degraded sargent' (Scolfield). Hayley believed Lady Hesketh's 'striking Intimation' derived from malevolent reporting. For himself, he would be:

> ever glad to do Him [Blake] all the little good in my power, & for extraordinary reasons, (*that may make you smile*) *because* He is *very apt to fail in his art*: – a species of failing peculiarly entitled to pity *in Him*, since it arises from nervous Irritation, & a *too vehement desire to excell*. – I have

also every wish to befriend Him from a motive, that, I know, our dear angelic Cowper *would approve*, because this poor man with an admirable quickness of apprehension & with uncommon powers of mind, *has often appeared to me on the verge of Insanity* [...][19]

The verge of Insanity ...

TWENTY-ONE

The Mocker of Art is
the Mocker of Jesus

1805–1807

On 22 March 1805, Henry Fuseli became Master of the Royal Academy. It may have been this potentially advantageous event, coupled with Flaxman's determination to see Blake employed, which encouraged the opportunistic engraver-turned-publishing entrepreneur Robert Cromek to employ 47-year-old William Blake as both designer and engraver on a new project. The project was billed in Cromek's first *Prospectus* as: 'A New and Elegant Edition of BLAIR'S GRAVE, Illustrated with FIFTEEN PRINTS From Designs Invented and to be Engraved by *WILLIAM BLAKE* with a Preface containing an Explanation of the Artist's View in the Designs, and A Critique of the Poem.'

The Grave, a poem by Scotsman Robert Blair (1699–1746), had long been popular, despite its apparently dire subject: the Grave and Last Judgement. Fortunately, Blair's work had humour as well as spiritual meaning.

Twelve Royal Academy members provided the bulk of advance subscribers. They included the President, Benjamin West, Richard Cosway, Henry Fuseli, John Flaxman, Thomas Lawrence, Joseph Nollekens, John Opie and Thomas Stothard. The absence of John Hoppner's name is noticeable.[1]

On 18 October, Flaxman informed Hayley that several Academicians had seen specimens of Blake's drawings for *Blair's Grave* and had been favourably impressed. Flaxman himself was particularly struck by a composition called *The Gambols of Ghosts according with their affections previous to the final Judgement*. This was one of a series of 20 drawings with watercolour wash that Blake sold to Cromek – considered lost until rediscovery (with one missing) at a Glasgow bookshop in 2001! Separated from its context, the immensely charming *Gambols of Ghosts* was sold at Sotheby's Old Master Drawings sale on 30 January 2013 for $722,500.

Flaxman also admired *Wicked Strong man dying:* sold at Sotheby's in 2006 for $1.5m. In 1805, Blake struggled to pay his rent and Cromek was no philanthropic patron of the arts.

Meanwhile, off the southwest coast of Spain (as Ralph Churton noted in his diary):

> 21st October. Monday. On this day (as we learnt afterwards Nov.7th) 19 French warships & Spanish ships were taken by our fleet off Cape Trafalgar – but alas! the ever to be lamented death of Lord Nelson was the price of the victory.[2]

Sacrificing greatness was apparently in the air: Flaxman's information was that 'Mr Cromak' had commissioned 40 drawings, 20 of which would be engraved by the designer (Blake), but when Cromek's first *Prospectus* appeared around the end of November, Blake's 20 engravings had been reduced to 15. Then it appears something about Blake's specimen white-line etching of *Death's Door* shocked Cromek. Comparing it with the drawing today, one can perhaps see why. The drawing is full of light; the etching looks like the lights have gone out, doubtless consistent with the solemnity of the subject. In the process, the refinement of the drawn lines was exchanged for emotional force. Perhaps Cromek had heard Hayley's doubts about Blake's levels of consistency and, with so much at stake, panicked. Such is likely, for another *Prospectus* was hastily issued, also dated November 1805. It made devastating reading for Blake. *Blair's Grave* was now 'Illustrated with TWELVE VERY SPIRITED ENGRAVINGS by *LOUIS SCHIAVONETTI* From Designs Invented by *WILLIAM BLAKE.*'

Third Billing to Blair! Schiavonetti! Where were the 'Fifteen Prints' by William Blake? What about the money? What was going on?

Flaxman wrote to Hayley about Blake on 1 December 1805:

Blake is going on gallantly with his drawings from the Grave, which are patronised by a formidable list of R.A's and other distinguished persons – I mentioned before that he has good employment besides, but still I very much fear his abstracted habits are so much at variance with the usual modes of human life, that he will not derive all the advantage to be wished from the present favourable circumstances.[3]

Not exactly supportive. Judging by Blake's resigned letter to Hayley of 11 December 1805, Blake fully twigged that his earthly fortunes were to plummet again.

In a passionate sermon that must have embarrassed the hell out of 'nominal Christian' (*if that!*) Hayley, Blake gave his answer to anyone who considered spiritual 'Enthusiasm' was to be avoided by Christian people, who believed that rational order should preside over spiritual experience and who believed that the forces of the state, however subtly, should be employed to suppress the living spirit of Man:

Receiving a Prophet As a Prophet is a Duty which If omitted is more Severely Avenged than Every Sin & Wickedness beside. It is the Greatest of Crimes to Depress True Art & Science. [...] I know that such Mockers are Most Severely Punish'd in Eternity. I know it, for I see it & dare not help. The Mocker of Art is the Mocker of Jesus. Let us go on, Dear Sir, following his Cross: let us take it up daily, Persisting in Spiritual Labours & the Use of that Talent which it is Death to Bury, & of that Spirit to which we are called.[4]

Hayley did not feel 'called': had he not informed Lady Hesketh that any good he did was simply a gentleman's response to the challenge of injustice? Hayley humoured Blake's spirituality; he did not share it. Blake's letter probably did more to turn Hayley definitively away than any other single stimulus. Hayley was never going to recognize the artist as 'Prophet' or accept that criticism of art could be blasphemous; Hayley and Blake were worlds apart, and always had been.

Statuary Flaxman takes a break

In his own mind, Flaxman was probably tired of, even frustrated with, as he saw it, finding a profitable niche for Blake. Perhaps he found other business more pressing; certainly he found it more attractive.

In December 1805, Sir Roger Newdigate (1719–1806), former MP for Oxford, antiquary, collector and public benefactor, gave the university £2,000 for the purpose of moving the Arundel or 'Pomfret' Marbles out of a dingy space near the Bodleian Library into the Radcliffe Library, or 'Camera' as it is now known, a circular Neo-classical, domed construction opposite Brasenose College, dedicated to scientific study.

Assembled by the great art collector Thomas Howard, 21st Earl of Arundel (1585–1646), the Marbles had been bequeathed to Oxford in two parts, latterly by the mother of the 2nd Earl of Pomfret in 1755, a transaction overseen by Sir Roger when sitting for Oxford.

Sir Roger requested his good friend Ralph Churton, recently collated to the archdeaconry of St David's, to undertake delicate negotiations with the university and to arrange appropriate appointments. That is how the name of Flaxman entered Churton's diary, for John Flaxman was chosen to arrange the proposed exhibition, to mend broken statues and to record the transfer to the highest standards.

On 2 January 1806, Churton was in London. There he met up with his daughter's godfather Richard Gough (of *Sepulchral Monuments* fame), and with 'Statuary' Flaxman, as Churton referred to the sculptor in his diary.

While a certain poor engraver in South Molton Street fumed over his abandonment, Flaxman went on 21 January to Banbury, close to Churton's living at Middleton, whither he and the Archdeacon journeyed together by coach to Sir Roger Newdigate's seat at Arbury Hall, Warwickshire. Conversation probably encompassed the business in hand and, doubtless, the classical world, a world Churton was as familiar with, as a scholar, as Flaxman was as a sculptor. The name of Charles Townley would probably have cropped up, as Townley had assisted Churton's antiquarian research through the auspices of mutual friend TD Whitaker before Townley's death, less than a year before; Farington and Nollekens would have been other names of mutual interest. Had the subject of Flaxman's Swedenborgianism come up, one can only guess at what might have passed between the two men! Churton's sense of humour was better developed than Flaxman's. Did thoughts of poor Blake flash through Flaxman's mind as the coach entered the gorgeous gardens of the Gothic Revival Arbury Hall, where, welcomed inside, the men soon gazed up at Romney's fine portrait of Sir Roger Newdigate?

As matters transpired, their business dragged on to the end of the next year, until stubborn resistance from Radcliffe's Librarian Thomas Hornby finally put the project on ice.[5] Hornby insisted the arts and sciences remain distinct. Blake might have contributed to the discussion, but his was a voice few wished to hear.

Reaction and Persecution

Dependent now on Thomas Butts's appetite for Blake's paintings (Butts had engaged Blake as son Tommy Butts's drawing master), the artist vented his spleen in a letter defending Fuseli's controversial painting of Count Ugolini from a malevolent write-up in *Bell's Weekly Messenger*. In July, Richard Phillips's *Monthly Magazine* published Blake's attack on mindless connoisseurs who judge everything from acquired canons of taste. He was, of course, defending himself, while perhaps expressing gratitude to Fuseli, whose portrayal of Count Ugolini had captured something of Blake's own condition: Ugolini's sons 'suffer him to indulge his passionate and innocent grief, his innocent and venerable madness and insanity and fury'. As well as pointing towards his own 'agony', Blake's letter pleaded for the common man's right to judge pictures from the heart: 'But O Englishmen! I know that every man ought to be a judge of pictures, and every man is so who has not been connoisseured out of his senses.'[6]

Blake's democratic critique of academic authority may not have passed unnoticed. That same month, the *Literary Journal* reviewed *Memoirs of his Child* by Benjamin Heath Malkin MA, FSA. Hired by Cromek to write the Preface to *Blair's Grave*, Malkin had commissioned Blake to engrave a portrait of his deceased child for the reviewed book's frontispiece. Confronted by Malkin's praise of Blake in the introduction to his *Memoirs of his Child*, the *Literary Journal* was scathing: 'we cannot extend our approbation to the irrelevant panegyric upon Mr. William Blake, painter and engraver. Of that gentleman, here forced upon our notice as a poet, we shall have occasion to speak [...] at the conclusion of this critique'.[7] Blake's poetry was ridiculed for having 'heightened' the 'modern nonsense'; 'Laughing Song' from *Songs of Innocence* was pilloried. The *British Critic* of September 1806 added its influence, dismissing Malkin's encomium as 'one of the most idle and superfluous works that we have ever seen'. The *Monthly Review* weighed in with its views in October, dismissing Blake's 'inferior' versifications.

Such a unanimous venting of venom cannot have been accidental. A general campaign in the conservative press against 'Methodism' may have inspired the attacks, which would intensify. From the government point of view, the issue was one of national unity in the face of common danger. Unity implied uniformity.

The Canterbury Pilgrims

We may imagine something like paranoia enveloping Blake's sensitive soul, for events would soon convince him that Cromek had stolen one of his best ideas. That Cromek had already taken bread from Blake's mouth and passed it to Schiavonetti provided justification in Blake's mind for seeing Cromek as a crook. Blake would claim he had made preliminary sketches for a treatment of Chaucer's Canterbury Pilgrims before anybody else had considered the idea.

Blake's procession of distinct characters – publically exhibited in a tempera treatment in 1809 – is surely Blake's statement about 'uniformity'. In Chaucer's pilgrims, Blake saw an image of the onward march of the 'great army of God' to 'Jerusalem', of an England where every human characteristic had its place in the whole movement. The *Canterbury Pilgrims* is a political statement against repressive uniformity, for every pilgrim, good, bad or indifferent, has his and her place in the tapestry of life, while all journey in quest of the miraculous and all may be forgiven. 'Gothic' was not simply for Blake an attractive style, it was a spiritual approach to life.

That Blake had the idea is not in question. What is in question is whether or not Cromek, having seen sketches, took the idea to Blake's friend Thomas Stothard and commissioned a commercialized version of it. Cromek claimed the original idea was *his*. Cromek's son TH Cromek reckoned his father was inspired around October 1806 after reading Chaucer's work. Stothard's daughter-in-law recalled the painter George Stubbs wanting to see Stothard's *Canterbury Pilgrims* in 1806. Since Stubbs died in July, that would make an early date for the commission.[8] But Stothard painted equine pictures and it's possible there was confusion and that Stubbs, an animal painter, had come to see these. Nevertheless, the story as related by Stothard's biographer Anna Eliza Bray specifically mentions that Stubbs was fascinated to see how Stothard dealt with so many horses in one design.

What is difficult to understand is why Blake was still prepared to have any business at all with Cromek in 1807 if he was sure he had been subject to theft of idea in 1806. Blake submitted a bill to Cromek in May 1807, and there, while he criticized Stothard's Pilgrims as 'low and contemptibly treated'[9], no accusation of skullduggery on Cromek's part is made. But Blake was on tender ground, for *The Grave* had not yet been published, and as conceived by Cromek its frontispiece sported an engraved portrait of Blake after Thomas Phillips. It was essential to Blake's career he benefit from the fraught publication: Cromek had him over a barrel.

The problem for Blake in later life was that he accused *Stothard*, his longtime friend, of profiting from stolen goods, causing a rift that was never healed. There is no compelling reason to believe that Stothard knew about Blake's idea before his commission from Cromek; he always protested innocence and felt aggrieved at the accusation. The issue then is whether Cromek stole the idea and presented it as his own.

Judging from a curious letter Cromek wrote to the poet James Montgomery on 17 April 1807, seeking praise for the brilliance of his ideas, and particularly the *Pilgrims*, Cromek had the make-up of a professional magpie. After ridiculing and belittling Blake for living in 'Fairy Land', he proceeded to echo Blake's own phraseology and concepts as a means of elevating himself before Montgomery. In a clumsy, perhaps unconscious, parody of Blake's style, Cromek laments to Montogomery that the 'Man of Genius', the butt of the 'Mock & scorn of Men', is:

A Pilgrim & stranger upon Earth travelling into a far-distant Land, led by Hope & sometimes by Despair, but − surrounded by Angels & protected by ye immediate Divine presence he is the light of the World. Therefore Reverence thyself, O Man of Genius![10]

A man who could thieve the thoughts and language of another in this manner, passing them off as his own, was certainly a man who could convince himself he was innocent of theft. I suspect Cromek accounted his personal creativity – even genius - lay in an ability *to recognize a good idea,* while simultaneously grasping *how to exploit it.* In his own estimation, this knack made him an individual of stupendous originality. From such a conceit, it was short work to imagine the original idea was his also; after all, *what is an idea without exploitation?* The exploitation of potential was truly his creation! How many art dealers have harboured resentment of an artist's alleged 'genius', while inwardly elevating their more practical gift for transforming paint into hard cash? Besides, did not Chaucer belong to the world? Only a 'genius' like Cromek could see what poor men like Blake could not: that there was cash in art if one were smart.

Cromek's clever presentation of Stothard's *Canterbury Pilgrims,* and Schiavonetti's and Heath's lucrative engraving after it, amounted to a masterpiece of marketing. The painting went on tour; thousands saw it, many bought the print. It was a 'win-win' situation. In March 1807, Hoppner showed Stothard's painting to the Prince of Wales. 'Prinny' permitted Cromek to dedicate a print to him. No wonder Blake thought Stothard had stolen from him. What Stothard's work had taken away, albeit inadvertently, was the chance for Blake to show the wide world his most accessible wares. Stothard had effectively taken away Blake's *fame,* his future, leaving him and everyone else at the mercy of crooks like Cromek. And, what is more, Stothard's painting, superb as an illustration, conveys not a jot of Blake's essential political and philosophical idea. It illustrates, but it does not penetrate. In fact, the work itself was part of a unified canon of good taste, chocolate-boxy, and very acceptable to the *status quo*: one of the most successful prints of the century. It could even be conceived as patriotic: *this* was what we were fighting for! Good Old England! Michael Powell and Emeric Pressburger seized this propagandist idea brilliantly in their movie *A Canterbury Tale* (1943): first Chaucer, then the Spitfire!

Spiritual work always throws up the ironies implicit in reality.

On 17 April 1807, Cromek informed Montgomery that Blake's drawings for *The Grave* had been presented to the 'Queen and Princess at Windsor'. Her Majesty wished the work dedicated to her. So delighted was Blake that he produced a design for the dedication with a poetic address 'marked', according to Cromek, 'with his [Blake's] usual Charcteristics – Sublimity, Simplicity, Elegance and Pathos, his wildness *of course*.'[11] Blake signed his poem: 'Your Majesty's devoted Subject & Servant William Blake.' The poem is undoubtedly sincere: 'O Shepherdess of England's Fold/ Behold this Gate of Pearl and Gold.' In May, Cromek returned Blake's sketched '*vignette*' dedicated to the Queen, along with Blake's 'demand' for four guineas for it. Cromek insisted Blake was ridiculous to expect him to pay for an honour visited upon Blake personally; besides, the sketch wasn't worth the money. But, said Cromek, rather than deny Blake any advance to his reputation deriving from it, he had been prepared to pay Schiavonetti 10 guineas for etching a plate from the drawing!

Cromek launched into a pointed, spiteful and vicious rant against Blake: 'When I first called on you, I found you without reputation [...] What public reputation you have, the reputation of eccentricity excepted, I have acquired for you. [...] Why did you so *furiously* rage at the success of the little picture of 'The Pilgrimage'? [Stothard's *Canterbury Pilgrims*] Three thousand people have now *seen it and have approved of it*. Believe me, yours is "*the voice of one crying in the wilderness!*"'[12]

Let us give to Anna Eliza Bray's *Life of Stothard, R.A.* the last word on Cromek's amazing self-vaunted generosity. According to a letter of Stothard's reproduced by his biographer, the entrepreneur who raked handsome profits from Stothard's work only ever paid him £60 of an agreed completion fee of £100.[13]

But *The Grave* turned out to be Cromek's own: his career entered a swift decline after its publication in 1808; he died in 1812, aged 42. He will be remembered always for calumniating Blake.

In Blake's mind, he had now lost two of his oldest friends. His *Notebook* contains lines headed 'On F— & S—' – clearly meaning Flaxman and Stothard:

> I found them blind I taught them how to see
> And now they know neither themselves nor me[14]

Blake would turn to spiritual friends.

Milton

Cumberland probably visited Blake in London in summer 1807. In notes made after 6 June, Cumberland observed: 'Blake has eng.[d] [engraved] 60 Plates of a new Prophecy!'[15]

Bentley thinks these 60 plates must have been for *Jerusalem* (which eventually ran to 100 plates), but they are as likely to have been for *Milton*. The Library of Congress's 'Copy D' of *Milton* (1818), with the poem divided into two 'Books', consists of 50 plates. A partly masked white line on the title page (visible most clearly on copies 'B' and 'C') suggests the poem was originally intended to be presented as *12* 'Books', rather than two, so we may have lost a number of plates, or perhaps they were turned to other uses. We know of 51 plates Blake made for *Milton* altogether, but no copy has them all; there might once have been a 60-plate version.

Milton lifts material straight out of *Vala*, so Blake may have made some, now lost, plates from the *Vala* manuscript (we have no engraved version of the *Vala* text) before turning to *Milton*; Tatham destroyed many of Blake's copper plates. It is also possible Cumberland remembered '60', having heard '50' or a variant. Either way, *Milton*, like *Jerusalem*, is dated '1804'; it was produced sometime between 1804 and 1811, and the tumultuous 'Preface' at least, as well as numerous passages on the mocking of Art, fit Blake's anguish of 1806–07 well:

> Rouze up O Young Men of the New Age! Set your foreheads against the ignorant Hirelings! For we have Hirelings in the Camp, the Court, & the University: who would if they could for ever depress Mental & prolong Corporeal War. Painters! on you I call! Sculptors! Architects! Suffer not the fashionable Fools to depress your powers by the prices they pretend to give for contemptible works or the expensive advertizing boasts that they make of such works; believe Christ & his Apostles that there is a Class of Men whose whole delight is in Destroying. We do not want either Greek or Roman Models if we are but just & true to our own Imaginations, those Worlds of Eternity in which we shall live for ever, in Jesus Our Lord.

This is the golden moment when Blake gives us the lyric of what we know better as the 'hymn' 'Jerusalem':

And did those feet in ancient time
Walk upon Englands mountains green,
And was the holy Lamb of God
On Englands pleasant pastures seen!

And did the Countenance Divine
Shine forth upon our clouded hills?
And was Jerusalem builded here
Among these dark Satanic Mills?

Bring me my Bow of burning gold:
Bring me my Arrows of desire:
Bring me my Spear: O clouds unfold!
Bring me my Chariot of fire!

I will not cease from Mental Fight,
Nor shall my Sword sleep in my hand:
Till we have built Jerusalem,
In Englands green & pleasant Land.

This beauty is followed by a quotation from the first part of Numbers 11:29: 'Would to God that all the Lord's people were Prophets, and that the LORD would put his spirit upon them!' The setting of the quote from Moses is the holy camp in which the young men of Israel prepare for Canaan's conquest. This makes plain *Milton's* opening. Blake sees the young men of England as potentially holy warriors of a Mental Fight to regain the lost ground fit for Jesus's feet to walk on.

In effect, Blake is saying : 'Don't be afraid to take on the Classics, and the men who worship Greece and Rome!' This was the high watermark of the classical revival; politicians could be seen at home or at clubs wearing togas. *Milton's* opening tirade accuses Homer, Ovid, Plato and Cicero of stealing and perverting into artifice the true inspiration of the 'Sublime' Bible. Shakespeare and Milton, he declares 'were both curbd by the general malady & infection from the silly Greek & Latin slaves of the Sword'. He might have been talking about Flaxman, whose *Iliad* he had recently worked on.

In *Milton*, John Milton himself comes to earth to confess his errors.

The title page says that *Milton* is 'To Justify the Ways of God to Men': Blake's intention is theological. He speaks as a prophet. 'Book the First' makes it clear that, though sublime, the Bible has been misconstrued by the enemies of Jesus: 'till Jesus, the image of the Invisible God/ Became its prey; a curse, an offering, and an atonement,/ For Death Eternal in the heavens of Albion.' If St Paul believed that crucifixion was necessary for atonement, then he was a crucifier. Blake calls the people of England to a vision of Albion that can save them from the pit of Urizen and pacified minds, unknowing, oppressed, with nothing but death at the end.

> Then Los and Enitharmon knew that Satan is Urizen
> Drawn down by Orc & the Shadowy Female into Generation

It is Satan who divides the nations, who has made of Albion 'Canaan', 'closing Los from Eternity in Albions Cliffs/ A mighty Fiend against the Divine Humanity mustring to War'. Blake is talking about the war with Napoleon and its price:

> Satan! Ah me! Is gone to his own place, said Los! Their God
> I will not worship in their Churches, nor King in their Theatres

Blake sees the Druidic sacrifices 'among the rocks of Albions Temples' revived, offering human victims throughout the Earth. Blake was not romantic about Stonehenge; such was the home of 'Satans Druid sons' made alive again through loss of spiritual light, now battling it out for an empire built on oppression. The powers of darkness desire to 'devour' Albion and 'Jerusalem the Emanation of Albion'.

In a magnificent plate, Blake reveals the great Milton in his heavenly majesty before descending to Earth, the realm of Death:

> With thunders loud and terrible: so Miltons shadow fell
> Precipitant loud thundering into the Sea of Time & Space.

Then first I saw him in the Zenith as a falling star,
Descending perpendicular, swift as the swallow or swift;
And on my left foot falling on the tarsus, entered there;
But from my left foot a black cloud redounding spread over Europe

Blake's etched and painted image showing the moment when 'Milton' actually enters Blake's foot is astonishing. As the naked, 'electrified' poet leans backwards, his arms outstretched in an erotic posture of total acceptance, a starry comet blazes down and cracks like a firework into his left heel and toes. The figure has a healthy erection, obscured in some copies of the plate by underwear (plate 32 of the Library of Congress copy, for example), applied for reasons of 'taste' by either Tatham or Linnell. The application is in the worst possible taste.

The erection is important.

Blake is familiar with the esoteric significance of the big toe of the left foot. According to Swedenborg's *Spiritual Diary* (1758), the state of the feet is directly related to the spiritual state of the person. In sections 5105–07, for example, Swedenborg sees Luther condemned in heaven for vexatious quarrelling, being ignorant of the higher light, angry with all who disagreed with him. When Luther is cast into a hell for 'vastation' (that is, purification), 'It was perceived that he is now vastated under the soles of both feet; for, when he was cast down into that hell, cold, such [as occurs] when spirits are fully vastated, took possession of the soles of the foot for two hours.' Milton's being cast down to Earth in Blake's work exactly mirrors Luther's purgation. Blake, experiencing Milton's spirit, feels Milton's spiritual, and physical, symptoms.

Swedenborg specifically relates the big toe of the left foot to the genitals (a Tantric doctrine also), and its stimulation by the spiritual condition of the person brings to the left foot a 'fiery' sensation linked to the fire in the genitals:

Pain was felt in the great toe of the left foot [by Luther]. The reason is, because the great toe of the left foot corresponds to those who speak from faith derived from the Word and continually quarrel about doctrinals. They induce pain in that great toe. Therefore, also, that great toe communicates with the genitals; for the genitals correspond to the Word, as has been largely and very frequently shown. It has been often granted to sensibly perceive that communication.[16]

Blake not only experiences *gnosis* from Milton, who has realized he mistook the natures of Satan and of sexuality in *Paradise Lost,* but gets mightily turned on sensually at the same time: for Blake, spiritual ecstasies are reflected in the senses, even when the ecstasy is that of realizing an error. Truth is spiritual orgasm, for truth is energy, and 'Energy is Eternal delight'. Blake would tell Crabb Robinson in December 1825 that Milton himself had explained how in heaven he had realized his mistake in thinking sensual pleasure a result of the Fall – that is, related to sin and evil. How could something good come from something evil? Blake asked. A beautiful etched plate (no. 38 in British Museum Copy 'A') showing a naked man languidly embracing his wife on a rock by a choppy sea while a dark eagle hovers above, could be 'Milton within his sleeping Humanity' or Albion, or it might be an idealized Blake and wife Kate by Felpham's shore, though the rocks look too menacing for that: 'The Spectre of Satan stood upon the roaring sea & beheld/ Milton within his sleeping Humanity' (from plate no. 39 in Copy 'A'). Whoever is intended, the figure is depicted plainly with a smooth, stylish erection, though it has been deliberately obscured – that is, censored – on other copies for 'reasons of taste' that would make Urizen proud.

As for the 'black cloud redounding over Europe' from Blake's left foot, Blake saw the war as a product of not realizing the secrets of the sexual nature of man, of perverting spiritual life with corporeal, not mental war: a staggering insight for Blake's, and for our, time. Urizen knows not himself; his emanation Ahania knows. In the pages of Blake's manuscript *Vala* we find a curious drawing of Ahania gazing intently at Urizen's Big Toe, for Urizen is self-cast from the Eternals and therefore, according to Swedenborg, he must experience pain in his cold isolation which Ahania desires to allay through love. The drawing parallels another in *Vala* showing people worshipping a monumental phallus or, as we have come to know it, the 'Shivalingam'.

Had Blake been asked to re-title Milton's most famous work, he might have called it *Paradise Unseen.* At which thought, the last line of the Beatles' *Sgt Pepper's Lonely Hearts Club Band* sprang into this author's mind. Like John Lennon and Paul McCartney in their song 'A Day in the Life', Blake's Milton would *love to turn you on.*

TWENTY-TWO

The courage to suffer poverty and disgrace

1808–1810

Blake was 50, and he was struggling. As the year 1808 opened, Napoleon's forces were in Portugal, intent on destroying Portugal's trade with Great Britain. By the summer, Lieutenant General Arthur Wellesley, the future Duke of Wellington, would be in Portugal too, with an army 15,000 strong: the Peninsular War had begun.

In January, Blake finished a remarkable watercolour, *The Last Judgement*, for the Countess of Egremont of Petworth House, Sussex. He owed the commission to the generosity and interest of miniaturist Ozias Humphry (1742–1810), 'Portrait Painter in Crayons to the King' since 1792. Blake wrote several accounts of his painting (two for Humphry), but none does justice to the painting's extraordinary character (it is still held at Petworth by the National Trust).

Based on an earlier, simpler composition for *Blair's Grave*, Blake depicts the Last Judgement as a great swirling of monochromatic energy, with figures rising and falling, caught in their own self-willed or God-willed vortices. The detailing of the figures ranks Blake among the Masters of religious art, while its schematic originality puts the painting in a class of its own. Another remarkable thing is its size. It is astonishing how Blake succeeded in getting so much detail, so many figures, so much dimension into a work measuring no more than 20 x 15½ inches, but he did. Perhaps he felt he was competing with Humphry for astonishing effects in small.

The theology of the work bears close analysis: it is not orthodox. The essence of thought behind the design is Blake's belief that when an individual cast out error, a 'Last Judgement' was passed upon him. The Judgement then is not an *accusation*, as in the usual 'trial' concept: it is an exchange of energy, an acquisition of knowledge, and part of an eternal, not a temporal process. Jesus does not condemn; He is love and love seeks the welfare of the soul, but the individual must wage the Mental Fight, but for love, not from terror, though terror certainly awaits the one who ignores or attacks truth.

As if aware his conception deserved a bigger canvas, Blake set to work on *A Vision of the Last Judgement*, a work of seven feet by five feet – and Flaxman had advised Hayley that Blake should be discouraged from attempting large paintings! It is heartbreaking that this work, which Blake strove with, on and off, for years, has, like his only other large-scale painting *The Ancient Britons,* disappeared. Had the paintings survived, perception of Blake's artistic significance would most certainly have been enhanced, and people might see why he compared himself, without qualification, to Michelangelo and Raphael.

In the spring, Blake exhibited at a Royal Academy exhibition (drawing and miniature room) at Somerset House for the first time in nine years. Works exhibited were *Christ in the Sepulchre guided by Angels, Jacob's Dream* and *The Last Judgement,* possibly one of Blake's detailed drawings of the subject.

Perhaps the exhibition caught the eye of Abraham Raimbach, who was making prints for Hayley's Cowper translation of Latin poems project. When on 4 May, Raimbach suggested to Flaxman that Blake would do them better, Flaxman replied that he was not at that time having 'intercourse with Mr Blake'.

Then, at last, *Blair's Grave* was published, with designs by Blake.[1]

Reviewed in *The Examiner* on 7 August 1808 by Robert Hunt, brother of the journal's editor and publisher Leigh Hunt (1784–1859), Blake's work was attacked without mercy. Accused of impossibilities, the artist had apparently exceeded Art's proper limits; didn't Blake know the spiritual world was beyond depiction? Bentley observed that *The Examiner* had been attacking Methodism, and Blake was identified as an Enthusiast or Methodist. In 1809 Blake defended himself in the pages of his *Descriptive Catalogue*. People who blamed him for representing spirits with real bodies should think of Minerva and Apollo; their statues were representations of spiritual existences to the perishable organ of sight.

On 28 August, Leigh Hunt joined in, attacking what he called 'The Ancient & Redoubtable Institution of Quacks' whose 'Painting Officers' included Sir Francis Bourgeois, Copley, Craig and 'Blake', while among quack poets were Wordsworth and Walter Scott. Hunt was only 24, trying to make a name with the kind of smart-aleck satire of which inexperienced and egocentric youth is eminently capable. Hunt, incidentally, authored the verses 'Abou Ben Adhem' (*May His Tribe Increase*), wonderfully parodied by the BBC's *Not the 9 o'clock News* satire team in 1980.

In November, the *Anti-Jacobin Review* weighed in with *its* attack on Blake, while the *Scots Magazine* showed more generosity, to its credit.

Blake decided to take the bull by the horns and give the public an opportunity to judge his work for itself. In his forthcoming exhibition's *Descriptive Catalogue* (1809) he asserted that the Royal Academy would not show his 'frescos', being addicted to Venetian art and oil painting: 'Mr. B. appeals to the Public, from the judgement of those narrow blinking eyes, that have too long governed art in a dark corner.'[2]

On 19 December 1808, Blake informed Cumberland that despite the latter's having found Blake a buyer for his printed and illuminated works, he had no time for printing, being fully engaged in designing and painting. He was working for Butts, and he was working for his exhibition, to be held at his brother James's house, his birthplace: 1st floor, Broad Street.

The exhibition and its *Descriptive Catalogue* were as much a running polemic as they were self-defence and brazen promotion. Blake repeats his opposition to Venetian and Flemish art – the cult of shadows, oils, *chiaroscuro* – on moral and spiritual grounds. As he saw it, these incursions were dominating artists, rendering them afraid of trusting their own imaginations: 'like walking in another man's style, or speaking or looking in another man's style and manner, unappropriate and repugnant to your own individual character; tormenting the true Artist, till he leaves the Florentine [Raphael and Michelangelo], and adopts the Venetian practice, or does as Mr. B. has done, has the courage to suffer poverty and disgrace, till he ultimately conquers'.[3]

Blake's then was an *alternative* exhibition, and as such was largely ignored by the art community, who behaved as a pack. Anyone who paid the substantial two shillings and sixpence for the ticket and catalogue could see, above a Carnaby Market hosiery shop, nine 'frescos' and seven coloured drawings.

The frescos were *The Spiritual Form of Nelson guiding Leviathan*, *The Spiritual Form of Pitt guiding Behemoth* (Pitt had died in 1806), *The Canterbury Pilgrims, from Chaucer*, *The Bard, from Gray*, *The Ancient Britons*, *A Subject from Shakspeare* (the Spirit of Shakespeare), and *The Goats* (from a 'Missionary Voyage' tale of goats stripping vine leaves from 'savage girls').

The drawings exhibited were *The Spiritual Preceptor* (from Swedenborg's visions), *Satan calling up his Legions, from Milton*, *The Brahmins* (Mr Wilkin translating the Bhagavad-Gita), *The Body of Abel found by Adam and Eve*, *Cain fleeing away*, *Soldiers casting Lots for Christ's Garment*, *Jacob's Ladder*, *Angels hovering over the Body of Jesus in the Sepulchre*, *Ruth* and *The Penance of Jane Shore* (executed 20 years earlier).

Needless to say, Blake's comments throughout are informative and seriously eccentric, but beyond the eccentric manner one discerns first-class knowledge and insight. His comments on antique Britain for *The Ancient Britons* regarding the 'awakening of Arthur from sleep' are illuminating and inspiring. We cannot but lament the loss of this enormous painting of naked Britons: the Beautiful, the Strong and the Ugly, which Blake likens to three aspects of the fourfold nature of Man, the fourth being the Son of God.

Blake's comments on Swedenborg show he had assimilated the visionary without the rancour he felt during the days of the New Church's founding. He relates Swedenborg's vision of how 'The Learned, who strive to ascend into Heaven by means of learning, appear to Children like dead horses, when repelled by the celestial spheres. The works of this visionary are well worth the attention of Painters and Poets; they are foundations for grand things [...] O Artist! you may disbelieve all this, but it shall be at your own peril.'[4]

Detailed descriptions of Chaucer's intentions and his characters make clear what was lost to the British public when they were offered Cromek's alternative visionless vision. Such also was the conclusion of Samuel Taylor Coleridge's friend Charles Lamb (1775–1834) when he read Blake's account of Chaucer after Crabb Robinson gave him a copy of the *Descriptive Catalogue*.

Blake relates the eternal characters of the Pilgrims to the ancient Gods of Phoenicia: 'These Gods are visions of the eternal attributes, or divine names, which when erected into gods, become destructive to humanity. They ought to be the servants, and not the masters of man, or of society. They ought to be made to sacrifice to Man, and not man compelled to sacrifice to them; for when separated from man or humanity, who is Jesus the Saviour, the vine of eternity, they are thieves and rebels, they are destroyers.'[5]

Remarkably, Crabb Robinson left an account of his visit to the exhibition in his *Reminiscences*:

I went to see an exhibition of Blake's original paintings in Carnaby Market, at a hosier's, Blake's brother. These paintings filled several rooms of an ordinary dwelling-house, and for the sight a half-crown was demanded of the visitor, for which he had a catalogue. This catalogue I possess, and it is a very curious exposure of the state of the artist's mind. I wished to send it to Germany and to give a copy to Lamb and others, so I took four, and giving 10s., bargained that I should be at liberty to go again. 'Free! as long as you live,' said the brother, astonished at such a liberality, which he had never experienced before, nor I dare say did afterwards. Lamb was delighted with the catalogue, especially with the description of a painting afterwards engraved [the Canterbury Pilgrims], and connected with which is an anecdote that, unexplained, would reflect discredit on a most amiable and excellent man, but which Flaxman considered to have been not the wilful act of Stodart. It was after the friends of Blake had circulated a subscription paper for an engraving of his Canterbury Pilgrims, that Stodart was made a party to an engraving of a painting of the same subject by himself. Stodart's work is well known, Blake's is known by very few. Lamb preferred it greatly to Stodart's, and declared that Blake's description was the finest criticism he had ever read of Chaucer's poem.

In this catalogue Blake writes of himself in the most outrageous language – says, 'This artist defies all competition in colouring' – that none can beat him, for none can beat the Holy Ghost – that he and Raphael and Michael Angelo were under divine influence – while Corregio and Titian worshipped a lascivious and therefore cruel deity – Reubens a proud devil, etc. etc. He declared, speaking of colour, Titian's men to be of leather and his women of chalk, and ascribed his own perfection in colouring to the advantage he enjoyed in seeing daily the primitive men walking in their native nakedness in the mountains of Wales. There were about thirty oil-paintings, the colouring excessively dark and high, the veins black, and the colour of the primitive men very like that of the Red Indians. In his estimation they would probably be the primitive men. Many of his designs were unconscious imitations. This appears also in his published works – the designs of Blair's Grave, which Fuseli and Schiavonetti highly extolled – and in his designs to illustrate Job, published after his death for the benefit of his widow.[6]

The Ancient Britons, measuring 10 feet by 14, elicited Robinson's praise when he wrote about it in 1811 for the German publication *Vaterlädisches Museum:* 'His greatest and most perfect work is entitled "The Ancient Britons". It is founded on that strange survival of Welsh bardic lore which Owen gives thus under the name of Triads [...]'.[7] 'Owen', according to poet Robert Southey (1774–1843), was:

My old acquaintance William Owen, now Owen Pugh[e], [(1759–1835), Welsh antiquarian and Welsh-English dictionary writer], who became rich [...] found everything which he wished to find in the Bardic system, and there he found Blake's notions, and thus Blake and his wife were persuaded that his dreams were old patriarchal truths, long forgotten, and now re-revealed. They told me this, and I, who well knew the muddy nature of Owen's head, knew what his opinion upon such a subject was worth. I came away from the visit with so sad a feeling that I never repeated it.

The exhibition of his [Blake's] pictures, which I saw at his brother's house near Golden-square, produced a like melancholy expression. The colouring of all was as if it had consisted merely of black and red ink in all intermixture. [...] In others you perceived that nothing but madness had prevented him from being the sublimest painter of this or any other country.[8]

The above was written on 8 May 1830 to Southey's wife-to-be, Caroline Bowles, when Southey's impressions had become jaundiced by other unpleasant associations he held in his mind about Blake and Owen.[9] In

1847, Southey called *The Ancient Britons* 'one of his worst pictures, – which is saying much'.[10] By contrast, the artist Seymour Kirkup (1788–1880), who remembered the odd sight of Blake during this period with spectacles upside down at the Academy (so he could see pictures hung on high), called *The Ancient Britons* Blake's 'best work'. Kirkup was an Academy student, won a medal. As a youth he thought Blake was mad. Butts introduced this jeweller's son to Blake and 'his excellent old wife', and it is thanks to Kirkup that we have Kate's comment made to him: 'I have very little of Mr Blake's company, he is always in Paradise.' *The Ancient Britons*, so Kirkup wrote, made 'so great an impression on me that I made a drawing of it fifty years afterwards, which I gave to Swinburne'.[11] Like the original work, it too has disappeared.

On 17 September, Leigh Hunt savaged the exhibition in *The Examiner.* Using a pointing hand as an editorial symbol to sign his work, Hunt called *The Ancient Britons* 'a complete caricature', and declared Blake mad. The degree of pain Hunt caused Blake is evinced by the number of times an entity called 'Hand' would appear in his next epic poem, *Jerusalem*, along with magistrates and soldiers from the trial of 1804. These were all accusers, and Blake believed the spirit of accusation was Satan's. The hand that pointed was that of the Accuser: Blake's spiritual opposition manifested once more in human form.

His bitterness erupted in lines of rough verse in his *Notebook:*

> The Examiner whose very name is Hunt
> Calld Death a Madman trembling for the affront
> Like trembling Hare sits on his weakly paper
> On which he used to dance & sport & caper

Blake's *Notebook* also contains notes for a 'Public Address' (1809–10), which he never gave. It might have been intended for the 'Chalcographic Society' for engravers on copper, formed in 1802 and dominated by his old fellow apprentice James Parker, for such an audience appears in the *Notebook*. Blake defended and asserted his art and on page 18 gave his view of politics:

> I am really sorry to see my Countrymen trouble themselves about Politics. If Men were Wise the Most arbitrary Princes could not hurt them[.] If they are not Wise the Freest Government is compelld to be

a Tyranny[.] Princes appear to me to be Fools Houses of Commons & Houses of Lords appear to me to be fools they seem to me to be something Else besides Human Life[.][12]

What Human Life was really all about, Blake the prophet would adumbrate in the 100 exhausting plates of *Jersualem, the Emanation of the Giant Albion*, with which he busied himself during 1810 and throughout the next decade.

TWENTY-THREE

Obscurum per obscurius

1811–1819

A year before embarking on her notorious affair with Lord Byron, Lady Caroline Lamb (1785–1828), wife to the Hon. William Lamb, opened her townhouse for a party. It was the evening of 24 July 1811. England had been ruled by the Prince Regent since February, while the Prince's father went into seclusion and deeper insanity at Windsor. Among Lady Caroline's guests were Crabb Robinson and Robert Southey, of whom Robinson wrote in his diary: 'Southey had been with Blake & admired both his designs & his poetic talents at the same time that he held him for a decided madman. Blake, he says, spoke of his visions with the diffidence that is usual with such people & did not seem to expect that he should be believed. He [Blake] shewed S[outhey] a perfectly mad poem called Jerusalem. Oxford Street is in Jerusalem.'[1]

In what form Southey saw Blake's *Jerusalem* is unknown. It is usually held that the text was not complete until 1815 (on account of the poem's reference to the Treaty of Paris of that year), while most of the etching is thought to have been done between 1815 and 1820, in which latter year Blake's friend Thomas Griffiths Wainwright (later tried for serial murder) announced in the *London Magazine*'s September issue that he would examine *Jerusalem*'s gargantuan contents in due course. Wainwright's review never appeared, but Southey had found reference to Oxford Street and that would have taken him well into an epic that requires a full day's hard reading.

307

> There is in Albion a Gate of precious stones and gold
> Seen only by Emanations, by vegetations viewless,
> Bending across the road of Oxford Street; it from Hyde Park
> To Tyburns deathful shades, admits the wandering souls ...

If Southey had been reading consecutively, his eyes would have had to wander through more than 30 plates before arriving at Oxford Street in *Jerusalem's* second chapter.

Oxford Street *is* in Blake's Jerusalem: just one more incision scoring the earthly body of Albion, for *Jerusalem* gathers up every village and borough of London, and quite a few pubs, farms, streets and outlying towns before its spiritual suction draws into its psychic scope the whole territory and history of Great Britain and Ireland, sucked in, traversed as though by air, and shown to be the body on earth of Albion, the giant man, Man as spiritual idea, who has lost contact with his emanation 'Jerusalem' who is *Liberty*, spiritual liberty, the source of all freedoms. 'Jerusalem, thy sister calls!' The epic is a prophetic cry from the disturbed heart and mind of William Blake, now one of the 'poor', like the apostles, dervishes or despised prophets of old, reduced to sinew of simplicity, a force of God. 'Wake Up Great Britain and know why thou wert Great!' beats the theme.

Blake says he's giving us the end of a golden string. We must wind it into a ball. The ball will lead us in at heaven's gate, built in Jerusalem's wall. Remember that 'Jerusalem' in the poem is 'a city, yet a woman'. And note that the 'golden ball' verses were probably inspired by the final verse of Andrew Marvell's 'To his Coy Mistress':

> Let us roll all our strength, and all
> Our sweetness, up into one ball;
> And tear our pleasures with rough strife
> Thorough the iron gates of life.

Did Southey see any of the etchings? They are without parallel in English literature and art. From the huge megaliths, bigger than Stonehenge, to the Tantric lovers in orgasmic embrace, from Los wielding his mighty hammer, that is clearly a phallus and testes, pounding away like the great drum that used to accompany village fertility festivals until the Churches banned them, the poem is filled with the most intense anguish and the most extreme ecstasies. It could be called 'Welcome to my Nightmare', for the spiritual being of Albion is shown torn apart, flayed alive, staked out, crucified. And why? Is it because the sons of Albion have rejected the Bard, William Blake? For Blake in this poem has discovered *who he really is* and what he must do: he's not just Will the poet, painter, engraver, artist – no, he has discovered what *Art* is:

> I rest not from my great task!
> To open the Eternal Worlds, to open the immortal Eyes
> Of Man inwards into the Worlds of Thought, into Eternity
> Ever expanding in the Bosom of God, the Human Imagination.

Into the 'furnaces of affliction' described by Blake loom and lurk the persistent figures of his tormentors: 'Scofield' (former Sergeant Scolfield, with the emphasis perhaps on 'Scof' as in 'scoffer'), 'Kox' (Private Cock of the Dragoons), 'Coban' (probably an anagram for Francis *Bacon*), 'Kwantok' (Quantock, one of the Chichester magistrates), Peachey (another magistrate), 'Hand' (Hunt) and 'Hyle' (Greek for *matter,* probably 'Hayley'). They're like a gang of robbers stealing their way across England, ever-repeated in history: the shadow types that oppress, frustrate and murder in every age; and yet, they are the Sons of Albion; they also are called. Their fall from truth mirrors the vortex into which the Sons of Albion have sunk, forgetting their primitive dignity. Recovering that primitive dignity is one of the whirling themes that thunder and blaze through the poem, which, by the way, would have challenged Hollywood's best animators to giddy but deeply satisfying limits and limitlessness.

> The Vegetative Universe, opens like a flower from the Earths center:
> In which is Eternity. It expands in Stars to the Mundane Shell
> And there it meets Eternity again, both within and without,
> And the abstract Voids between the Stars are the Satanic Wheels.

Yes, Blake unravels a hidden mystery, a mystery also of the origins of religion. On Plate 27 of chapter 1 he makes an address 'To the Jews': *can it be true?* he asks, 'Was Britain the Primitive Seat of the Patriarchal Religion?' If it was, then the title page is true: Jerusalem is Albion's Emanation. 'Ye are united O ye Inhabitants of Earth in One Religion. The Religion of Jesus: the most Ancient, the Eternal: & the Everlasting Gospel'.

The entire world's destiny is somehow deeply involved with what happens in Britain. Britain is a spiritual pulse-centre, an *omphalos* for the globe: 'All things Begin & End in Albions Ancient Druid Rocky Shore.'

Blake informs his imaginary Jewish audience that their ancestors did indeed derive from Abraham, Heber, Shem and Noah. These men, declares Blake, were *Druids*. Their temples were the patriarchal pillars and oak groves described in the Bible, such as are found throughout the Earth. Blake received his idea of the Druids from antiquarian William Stukeley's book on Stonehenge, of course. This was respectable history, at the time, based in part on the *Annals* of Roman historian Cornelius Tacitus. Tacitus described an annihilation of Druids on Anglesey by a Roman army, justified as retaliation for the Druids' human sacrifices that even the Romans found intolerable. The idea then that the sacrifice of Isaac by Abraham in Genesis in patriarchal times was Druidic was a natural one to make, for the prophets of Israel, heeding the 'Poetic Genius', raged against human sacrifices, groves and pillars of nature-worship. Blake's view, then, was a simple fusion of scripture and history.

He reminds 'the Jews' of their kabbalistic tradition 'that Man anciently contain in his mighty limbs all things in Heaven & Earth: this you received from the Druids.' Now, he says, 'the starry Heavens are fled from the mighty limbs of Albion.' This flaying of Albion's body, formerly covered with planets and constellations, is conveyed graphically in the etchings that accompany the text. What Blake means is that whereas once Man saw and felt himself and the cosmos *as one*, the stars and suns and planets being within him as well as without, and there was no alienation or 'objectivity'; now, through the rending of the fabric of psyche wrought by Reason and abstraction, Man has become a 'grovelling root outside of himself', alienated and alone, dependent on matter, blind to spirit and truth, aggressive and warlike, and given to sacrifices, laws, oppressions, cruelties and destruction of all that once adorned the jewelled palaces of the total universe.

The parent of the Druids, Blake says, was Albion the Ancient MAN, but he fell into chaotic sleep and his faculties divided, and from this fall the Elohim created Adam and the world. Blake then opens the poem into a vision of England where Jerusalem and Albion, restored one to another, restore the life of the world: a vision of peace and love and colour and brightness, tenderness in children, fidelity in marriage, honesty in work, which is then shown to fall into gore and war as Jerusalem falls.

Blake winds up the chapter with an intriguing statement: 'If Humility is Christianity; you O Jews are the true Christians.' Perhaps inspired by heretical Rabbi Jacob Frank, Blake dreams of the impossible: 'The Return of Israel is a Return to mental Sacrifice & War. Take up the Cross O Israel & follow Jesus.' One might say they have, all the way to Jerusalem.

> What is Above is Within, for every-thing in Eternity is translucent:
> The Circumference is Within: Without, is formed the Selfish Center
> And the Circumference still expands going forward to Eternity.
> And the Center has Eternal States! These States we now explore.

All nations will at last come to Jerusalem.

The Everlasting Gospel

Jerusalem was the last major written work Blake published. Originals are exceptionally rare; nine original copies only are extant. One further copy known to have once existed has disappeared. Perhaps Blake felt he had said enough; perhaps he despaired of finding a public in his lifetime. He worked for the spirits with an eye on posterity. But for the biographer, there is very little meat to chew for the second decade of the 19th century. Blake in his fifties seems to have lived in great obscurity at subsistence level in South Molton Street. How he survived is a mystery, for while he and Kate lived exceptionally frugally, rent wanted paying, and Blake appears to have done very little engraving work. He probably had some discrete assistance, thanks to Providence.

And slowly, Blake's poetry came to the notice of a new generation of 'romantic' writers, generally as suspicious of 'Enlightenment' rationalism and as eager to excite the imagination as Blake had been when, at his most erudite, his voice had echoed in a distant wilderness.

On 24 May 1812 Crabb Robinson read some of Blake's poems to William Wordsworth, whose reputation as a poet of 'new sensibility' grew stronger as his enthusiasm for political liberty declined. According to Robinson, Wordsworth 'was pleased with some of them & considered Blake as having the elements of poetry a thousand times more than either Byron or Scott, but Scott he thinks superior to Campbell.'[2] Thomas Campbell (1777–1844) was a Scottish poet who in 1812 lectured on poetry at the Royal Institution. To whom is Campbell now familiar?

When Blake annotated his own copies of Wordsworth's Preface to *The Excursion, being a portion of The Recluse, A Poem* (1814) and the 1815 edition of Wordsworth's *Poems,* he took issue with what he called Wordsworth's worship of Nature, which for Blake made the poet an 'atheist': 'I see in Wordsworth the Natural Man rising up against the Spiritual Man Continually & then he is No poet but a Heathen Philosopher at Enmity against all true Poetry or Inspiration.'[3] Blake may have appeared spiritually wild in 1815, but the Church could do with him now! Not that many would realize it, in my experience.

Ralph Churton's Diary, 25 March 1815:

Alas! Buonaparte is, beyond doubt, again in Paris by the treachery of the army [Marshal Ney had betrayed Louis XVIII]. O Father of mercies, for Jesus Christ's sake, pardon a sinful world & restore peace & order![4]

During the crisis of Napoleon's sudden return from exile on the isle of Elba, George Cumberland's sons George and Sydney visited Mr and Mrs Blake. On 21 April, George reported what he had found to his father:

We call upon Blake yesterday evening[,] found him & his wife drinking Tea, durtyer than ever[;] however he received us well & shewed his large drawing in Water Colors of the last Judgement[;] he has been laboring at it till it is nearly black as your Hat [Tatham reckoned it was about six feet long and five wide but spoiled by overwork] – the only lights are those of a *Hellish Purple* – his time is now intirely taken up with Etching & Engraving – [...] Blake says he is fearful they will make too great a Man of Napoleon and enable him to come to this Country – Mrs B. says that if this Country does go to War our K—g ought to loose his head – [5]

While Napoleon amassed a new army and marched north towards Brussels to divide Wellington from allied Prussian forces led by Prince Blücher, Blake exchanged letters with Josiah Wedgwood the younger, son of the founder of the Etruria pottery in north Staffordshire. Wedgwood wrote on 29 July approving a drawing Blake had made of a terrine, which could now be engraved. The work was for the Wedgwood sales catalogue – not very auspicious work, but it paid the rent. Blake was still doing drawings for Wedgwood in September, before which time, the world shook again – as Ralph Churton's diary records:

23rd June [1815]. Banbury [Oxfordshire]. Important victory of the Duke of Wellington near Nivelles, 150 Cannon taken & 60 in the night by Prince Blucher in pursuit [of French forces]; but with heavy loss of Officers etc. 18th the decisive day in a battle [Waterloo] from 10 till 7, & fighting on 16th and 17th . D.G. [Thanks be to God][6]

27 June 1815. Banbury. Buonaparte, it is said, has abdicated. May he never reign nor disturb the world again![7]

And that appeared to be the end of the French Revolution's bitter legacy.

Blake pops up again two and a half years later on Tuesday 20 January 1818 as a guest at one of Lady Caroline Lamb's parties. The author Lady Charlotte Bury (1775–1861) kept a diary and Blake appears in it like a figure from another world:

I dined at Lady C. L—'s. She had collected a strange party of artists and literati and one or two fine folks, who were very ill assorted with the rest of the company, and appeared neither to give nor receive pleasure from the society among whom they were mingled. Sir T. Lawrence [the great portraitist], next whom I sat at dinner, is as courtly as ever. His conversation is agreeable, but I never feel as if he was saying what he really thought. ...

Besides Sir T., there was also present of this profession Mrs. M[ee]., the miniature painter, a modest, pleasing person; like the pictures she executes, soft and sweet. Then there was another eccentric little artist, by name Blake; not a regular professional painter, but one of those persons who follow the art for its own sweet sake, and derive their happiness from its pursuit. He appeared to me to be full of beautiful imaginations and genius; but how far the execution of his designs is equal to the conceptions of his mental vision, I know not, never having seen them. *Main-d'œuvre* is frequently wanting where the mind is most powerful. Mr. Blake appears unlearned in all that concerns this world, and, from what he said, I should fear he is one of those whose feelings are far superior to his situation in life. He looks care-worn and subdued; but his countenance radiated as he spoke of his favourite pursuit, and he appeared gratified by talking to a person who comprehended his feelings. I can easily imagine that he seldom meets with any one who enters into his views; for they are peculiar, and exalted above the common level of received opinions. I could not help contrasting this humble artist with the great and powerful Sir Thomas Lawrence, and thinking that the one was fully if not more worthy of the distinction and the fame to which the other has attained, but from which he is far removed. Mr. Blake, however, though he may have as much right, from talent and merit, to the advantages of which Sir Thomas is possessed, evidently lacks that worldly wisdom and that grace of manner which make a man gain an eminence in his profession, and succeed in society. Every word he uttered spoke the perfect simplicity of his mind, and his total ignorance of all worldly matters. He told me that Lady C— L— had been very kind to him. 'Ah!' said he, 'there is a deal of kindness in that lady.' I agreed with him, and though it was impossible not to laugh at the strange manner in which she had arranged this party, I could not help admiring the goodness of heart and discrimination of talent which had made her patronise this unknown artist. Sir T. Lawrence looked at me several times whilst I was talking with Mr. B., and I saw his lips curl with a sneer, as if he despised me for conversing with so insignificant a person. [Lawrence was an admirer of Blake and bought some of his works]. It was very evident Sir Thomas did not like the company he found himself in, though he was too well-bred and too prudent to hazard a remark upon the subject.

The literati were also of various degrees of eminence, beginning with Lord B—, and ending with —. The grandees were Lord L—, who appreciates talent, and therefore not so ill assorted with the party as was Mrs. G— and Lady C—, who did nothing but yawn the whole evening, and Mrs A—, who all looked with evident contempt upon the surrounding company.

As Bentley observed, summer 1818 brought a turning-point in Blake's life. Cumberland's son George introduced the 60-year-old Blake to 26-year-old John Linnell (1792–1882), landscape artist, engraver and Royal Academy medals winner in drawing, painting and modelling. Linnell decided very quickly that he wanted to help Blake. In June he brought Blake his portrait of James Upton, a Baptist preacher, for Blake to engrave.

Linnell also introduced Blake to a man who would venerate him, John Varley (1778–1842), noted watercolourist and astrologer.

Around this time, Blake was introduced to Samuel Taylor Coleridge, with whose idealist mind Blake had much in common. The introduction probably came from Charles Augustus Tulk (1786–1849), whose father had been a founder of the New Church back in 1789, when Blake and his wife attended the Eastcheap Swedenborgian conference. The Swedenborg-inspired Tulk, a longtime acquaintance of Flaxman, appears to have known Blake since 1816; he may have assisted him financially.

Tulk first met Coleridge at Littlehampton in September 1817 and, to discover what Coleridge thought of Blake's poetry, sent him a copy of *Songs of Innocence*, which Coleridge returned with a commentary on 12 February 1818. Coleridge greatly appreciated the poems, and while inevitably critical instantly recognized Blake's poetic stature, his striking and attractive 'audacity'.

Tulk took Coleridge to Blake's rooms to see the large painting of the *Vision of the Last Judgement*, which inspired streams of Coleridgean eloquence. It seems likely Tulk wrote an article called 'The Inventions of William Blake, Painter and Poet' which appeared in 1830 in the *London University Magazine*. In a footnote to the piece the author described how 'Blake and Coleridge, when in company, seemed like congenial beings of another sphere, breathing for a while on our earth; which may be easily perceived from the similarity of thought pervading their works.' Coleridge understood that the seat of spiritually vital religious belief was the heart-enlivened imagination.

Around this time, Blake worked on a didactic poem based on the expression, the 'everlasting gospel', carried by an angel to every person on Earth in Revelation 14:6. The poem survived, scattered as nine sections in Blake's *Notebook* with three further sections in loose papers. Assembled, the verses illuminate Blake's wizened take on the figure of Jesus, lampooning what he considered a false image purveyed by the Churches. Whether Blake ever considered this suitable for the general public in his or our age I cannot tell, for:

> The Vision of Christ that thou dost see
> Is my Visions Greatest Enemy
> Thine has a great hook nose like thine
> Mine has a snub nose like mine
> Thine is the Friend of All Mankind
> Mine speaks in parables to the Blind
> Thine loves the same world that mine hates
> Thy Heaven doors are my Hell Gates

And there's plenty more where that came from, as Blake cast a question mark over future images of a meek, mild, pale, romantic Jesus – suitable for Victorian Sunday Schools – and a Catholicized sexless man-god with his heart organ all over his chest. Blake's Jesus has balls.

Blake had developed a rather cynical and wry humour about the world in general, as brilliant men will in middle age, and one can no longer be sure if he wasn't occasionally pulling John Varley's leg in the matter of the so-called 'Visionary Heads'.

Varley was very impressed by Blake's visionary abilities and wished them demonstrated in a way Blake found amenable. The idea was to get figures of history to come and sit before Blake, who would draw them, usually in the dead of night. Varley, according to Samuel Palmer, probably thought the persons were objectively present, in the manner of spiritist séances, but while Blake was sometimes impressed by the apparently independent movements of his visionary sitters, a look at the drawings, whether of William Wallace, Edward III, Richard the Lionheart, the 'man who built the Pyramids', Voltaire, Cleopatra or many another figure of history (Blake did over 40 drawings for Varley in 1819), reveals them as portraits *illustrating* what Blake saw vividly in his imagination: 'through' not 'with' the eye. Now, this ability may have been so strong that he could touch timeless zones of spiritual awareness, accessing states of vision that transcended time, but the figures are clearly not photographic portraits. They are in Blake's style and, more or less, as he wanted to see them. Varley, however, took it that Blake's mysticism was miraculous. Blake knew better; he had developed a faculty most lose in childhood, along with their innocence – all of which, however, is not to concede entirely the thought that Blake may sometimes have taken his 'sitters' for real visitants from other realms, expressing themselves through the limitations of his pencil.

TWENTY-FOUR

A New Kind of Man

1820–1827

It was probably through John Varley that Blake got to know the young artist Francis Oliver Finch, a watercolorist, and one of the group of so-called 'Ancients' whose youthful devotion to the old man Blake lightened his last years considerably and whose confidence 'freed him up' to experiment with his infinite palette.

The son of a Cheapside merchant, born while Blake was living at Felpham (1802), Finch, fatherless, was apprenticed aged 12 to Varley for five years, a friend having paid the £200 premium. Finch's artistic talent came to the attention of Lord Northcliffe, and Finch was encouraged to specialize in romantic landscapes, intimate country scenes and old buildings in rural settings. One can well imagine, therefore, the wonder with which Finch greeted Blake's execution of a commission from Linnell's doctor, Robert John Thornton MD, in 1821.

The third edition of Thornton's *Pastorals of Vergil*, intended for schools, was adorned by Blake's profoundly affecting woodcuts. Blake made 17 blocks to convey intense scenes of Nature seen through, not with, the eye. His vision of tranquil dells, sheep huddled in their pen, the stars about a barn, country folk dancing freely, philosophers liberally expounding over simple meals and wine, shepherds at dawn and dusk, contemplatives in deep delvèd earth or by gently flowing stream, utterly captivated Finch and the friends he made through their common, or uncommon, love of Blake. Finch told Gilchrist he considered Blake 'a new kind of man', a wholly original kind of man who had produced a new art and a new poetry. For Finch and his friends, Blake was indeed the

Bard. There was little trace of 'Orc' in the young men who beat a path to Blake's rooms; they were sincere, religious boys, but their interest was sufficient to convince Blake there was a new world coming.

The influence of Blake's Pastorals can be seen in many works by 'the Ancients', most particularly in Samuel Palmer's most cherished works, such as his early 'The valley thick with corn' (1825), executed with pen and dark brown ink and brush with sepia mixed with gum on paper. It can be seen today at the Ashmolean, Oxford. These images take us back into a late 16th- and 17th-century Rosicrucianist setting when Nature brimmed with magick, when Izaak Walton, the 'Compleat Angler', recommended 'Study to be Quiet' by a flowing stream as he fished for God's bounty, or German alchemist Heinrich Khunrath sought 'Christ the Stone' within the green pumping core of the German countryside: 'while ye my contemporaries were idly dozing, I was watching and at work, meditating earnestly day and night on what I had seen and learned, sitting, standing, recumbent, by sunshine, by moonshine, by banks, in meadows, streams, woods, and mountains.' (Khunrath's 'Confession', *Amphitheatre of Eternal Wisdom,* 1595). There was divine light in the hidden nature. They sought Nature's transmutation into sequestered spirit, by power of vision and alchemy. Like Blake, they saw the sun not as a guinea-piece but as the multitude of the Heavenly Host singing 'Glory, Glory, Glory to the Lord God Almighty'. That is why Palmer, Finch, Calvert, Richmond and, for a season, Tatham (the Judas of the group), called themselves 'the Ancients'. They were spiritually inspired by something intense, religious and great, obscured by the creeping ivy of time and living in the past forever, yet reachable and capable of being brought like a grail of wonder into the materialist world of 19th-century commercial London to transform it. They held to the sacramental meaning of Nature, believing that imagination may (in Coleridge's words) 'disembody the soul of fact', and they believed Blake shared their vision at its root.

To see Blake's Pastorals, you would think so, but Blake was not quite so dewy-eyed about the natural world as romantics are supposed to be, and he was not fond of landscapes (though he admired Constable's as being visionary); he saw Nature's terrors also, for he understood Nature as fallen and in need of redemption, yet knew that in the *unus mundus,* in the complete vision, the Earth and stars were one with the spiritual Man, and the sensual world held secret paths to God which is Man, for we are in Him as He is in Us; so he believed, and so he lived.

They were romantics and they loved their country – above all, the country. Palmer would even get Blake out of his London safety zone to visit Palmer's old grandfather at Shoreham in Kent. They explored an old ruin, felt and smelt the wet grass, and the field and the dew, and the fern and the moss, and Blake showed signs of clairvoyance. The Ancients held Blake in honour as a prophet, and their worship of him has descended to us today in the reverence in which many men and women hold William Blake, for he had become, through trial and suffering, and poverty and embrace of spiritual life and Providence with a Will, a saint, a witness of the true holy life: a life not simply of withdrawal but of divine creation, of act and thought in act.

In 1821, Mr and Mrs Blake moved from South Molton Street to 3 Fountain Court, The Strand, a building kept by Kate's sister's husband, Mr Baines. Fountain Court was next door to Beaufort Buildings where Blake had learned drawing as a boy from Mr Pars, and where, incidentally, Ralph Churton had spent his honeymoon, at number 11, with his bride Mary in 1796. Churton knew well the reputation of the Fleet Street–Strand area. He wrote of it on 16 March 1820 to Bowyer Nichols (1779–1863), printer and editor of the influential, conservative *Gentleman's Magazine*, recently transplaced west to Parliament Street:

> In Fleet Street there are Printers, *radicals* or not radicals, in every court
> and corner; but in Westminster, and the best street in Westminster – not
> a printer, I ween [hope], to be found within a shilling coach fare.[1]

While Blake associated printers with liberty, Churton saw the trade as one frequently tarnished by radical hot-heads. Indeed, *The Examiner*, whence Leigh Hunt launched his attack on Blake in 1808, was based in Beaufort Buildings; Blake called it a 'nest of villains'. Churton would have agreed, for in 1813 *The Examiner* swung its journalistic cannon onto the Prince Regent, an attack for which Leigh Hunt and his brother received two years in Surrey Gaol. One wonders if Blake regarded the sentence as just.

Blake, 'radical or not radical', struggled on. In 1822, his straitened circumstances came to the Royal Academy's attention. On the recommendation of William Collins and Abraham Cooper, Blake received a gift of £25. Mrs Blake doubtless appreciated it. Kate had become accustomed to putting an empty plate before her husband, instead of his supper, as a silent sign to nudge him back into paid work.

On 25 March 1823, at the age of 65, Blake was commissioned by stalwart John Linnell to make a series of engravings from the Book of Job, a subject Blake had already treated in paint for Thomas Butts. Linnell paid Blake £100 for the designs and the copyright. Published in March 1826, the work would become, among the *cognoscenti* of an age Blake would not live to see, his most widely appreciated visual accomplishment.

Job

Blake had every reason to identify himself personally with the biblical figure whose faith in the justice of God is more than severely tested by the Almighty's prosecution counsel, called the 'Satan' or the 'Adversary', and by Blake, the 'Accuser'. Satan, answering the LORD's boast of his servant Job being 'a perfect and an upright man', accuses Job before the Lord of being so only on account of the good things in his life. 'Take them away,' says Satan, and Job will 'curse thee to thy face'. They have a kind of wager on it. The Lord backs Job, and Satan will do everything to strip Job of the last shred of personal dignity, to show that Job is only good because blessed.

We all know the phrase 'the patience of Job'; the biblical Job has very little of it. He is astounded and tries to discover what he has done to merit his 'misfortune'. Friends arrive to tell him that since God is just, he must be guilty of something, at some level, but Job denies it. Job's 'patience' consists in his persistent faith that the God of all creation will do right, though for himself he can see no end to his afflictions, no bottom to his wretchedness. At the story's dénouement, the Lord, satisfied that Job will not, as Satan insisted, curse him, appears to Job in a visionary epiphany, showing Job complexities of creation so overwhelmingly awesome as to render him conscious that he can never fathom the mysterious ways of the Lord. As George Bernard Shaw joked, it is no answer to the problem of innocent suffering to ask a man if he can make a hippopotamus! But Job is not necessarily an attempt to *justify* the ways of God to man; it is an affirmation of God's just rule even in the face of incomprehensible circumstances and pain.

Now, Blake was not the kind of man to leave the Bible as it appeared to orthodox reading. Blake's *Job* is not only a work of the highest artistic ability, an inimitable demonstration of magisterial conception and technique, and therefore greatly influential on artists: *Job* also stands as an independent commentary on its subject – a Blakean essay.

The first thing to notice is that the face of the Lord mirrors Job's own spiritual state. When the story begins, we see Job, smug in his self-righteousness, a servant of the letter, not the spirit, of the law. The instruments of joy, musical instruments, are all hung up on a tree, the strings unplucked. Likewise Job's wife is ignored. When Blake gives bread to the poor man, we see him give it with his left hand. In his right, he retains half the loaf. He only appears to be good.

The symbolism of right and left is maintained. Right stands for the eternal, the spiritual, and left for the finite and material. Job's error appears as Satan, and when Satan smites Job we see that he stands on Job's right leg. Spiritual suffering will follow physical suffering. Job has made foolish practices attractive to his sons by repressing them. Job is the source of the thought of accusation that flies to smite them. When messengers arrive, their left feet are put forward: material destruction is coming. We may also note how a Gothic cathedral (living form) is replaced, as the tumults begin, with a Druidic altar. Job is falling apart, his 'zoas' are in disorder: this is his fall. Satan brings four arrows down on Job. Four of his senses have been smitten and Satan is smiting the fifth: touch and sex. The road to heaven is closed. Job is truly wretched, an outcast from himself. He has not made the only sacrifice that matters: his self. He has offered the letter of the law, not the spirit, which he has denied to himself and others. His inner 'Urizen' has taken over, and this is reflected in the image of the 'Lord' as Job's crisis deepens and darkens.

When Eliphaz comes to preach the legal justice of the Lord, we see the Lord bound in his own Law. Job is now subject to the Law and suffers accordingly: blindness is his sight and deafness his hearing; he is a grovelling root outside of himself. But there is a chink in the cavern.

Job's 'comforter' Elihu arrives, angry with Job for not submitting to Urizen, 'the starry king'. 'Opposition is true Friendship', Blake had written many years before. And by opposing Job, Elihu makes his friend realize there is hope in resistance to the encroaching images of disaster. He gathers strength of spirit, and thereby imbibes the Poetic Genius, whereupon God comes to him in a whirlwind. God shows Job the Leviathan and the Behemoth that Blake's visionary forms of Pitt and Nelson had raised from the deeps. Finally Job's error is cast out in a 'Last Judgement', for Job has embraced truth at last and all is restored to him. In the final image of Job with his family, we see the instruments of joy have been taken off the tree (of nature) and are enjoyed to the glory of the Glory.

It takes a certain kind of genius to rewrite the Bible without changing a word of it!

Blake had that genius. Indeed, Blake's ability to transfigure his sources rather reminds me of Orson Welles's telling of Franz Kafka's *The Trial* in Welles's splendid movie of 1962. Kafka created a nightmare bureaucratic world in which the innocent 'Joseph K' is accused and victimized. The actor Anthony Perkins, believing 'K' a wholly innocent victim, was at first dismayed by Welles's advice to him on how to play the part: 'He's guilty as hell!' K's smug self-satisfaction is his spiritual error. Blake saw Job likewise.

Linnell had a genius for keeping Blake occupied and entertained. In November 1821, for example, he took Blake and Varley to a box at the West London Theatre in Tottenham Street. They sat down to enjoy a production of John Dryden's and Nat Lee's *Oedipus*, mis-presented as being the work of Sophocles. Seeing the imposture, the press pounced, but the men enjoyed themselves. Linnell wrote to the young baronet Edward Denny about the evening (Linnell was painting Denny's and his family's portraits). Denny would become a great *aficionado* of Blake; Linnell had introduced them to one another in 1819.

In November 1826, after *Job* was published, Sir Edward Denny wrote to Linnell: 'what shall I say, what *can* I say of the book of Job – I can only say that it is a *great* work – and tho' I cannot venture to pass my humble comments upon any thing so truly sublime – I do indeed feel its exquisite beauty and marvellous grandeur – It is a privilege to possess such a work and still greater to be able to feel it – it is, I think the most perfect thing I have seen from the hands of Mr Blake, and if his Dante is superior, he will, I may almost say, outdo himself – I hope indeed he may complete this valuable work…'[2]

Sir Thomas Lawrence had paid five guineas for his copy of *Job* on 29 April 1826. On 20 June 1827, two months before Blake's death, King George IV ordered *his* copy through Sir William Knighton and Dr Robert Gooch. Linnell received 10 guineas for the King's copy by Messrs. Budd & Calkin of Pall Mall. *Job* today resides at Windsor Castle Library.

Sir Edward Denny had good reason for hoping to see 'his Dante'. Shortly after Blake's 67th birthday, Linnell commissioned Blake for a series of drawings from Dante's *Divina Commedia*. Linnell's first payment to Blake of £3 for this work was made on 21 December 1824. Shortly before, Blake had been introduced to Samuel Palmer; Linnell had brought Palmer to Fountain Court on 9 October. Quite a number of pilgrims now came to the home of *Jerusalem*. Jerusalem was in the Strand.

As Palmer and Richmond would convey to Gilchrist more than 30 years later, Blake's *presence* made Fountain Court a portal to heaven, ever expanding. Blake was a liberated soul, a *jivanmukta*, and liberated souls impart something of the vision of heaven to those who come into genuine contact with them.

The liberated soul was lame in bed from a scalded leg when Palmer first arrived with Linnell. Recollecting the golden moment years later, Palmer said Blake was working, sitting up like an 'Antique Patriarch' or a 'dying Michelangelo', the sheets covered with books. He was working on a folio of fine Dutch watercolour paper, measuring 25 x 14½ inches. Palmer saw 'the sublimest designs' for Blake's *Dante*. Blake told the 19-year-old that he began them in fear and trembling. Palmer said: 'O! I have enough of fear and trembling.' 'Then,' said Blake, 'you'll do.'

'He designed them (100 I think),' Palmer told Gilchrist in a letter of 23 August 1855, 'during a fortnight's illness in bed!' Palmer had more to say: 'Moving apart, in a sphere above the attraction of worldly honours, he did not accept greatness, but confer it. He ennobled poverty, and by his conversation and the influence of his genius, made two small rooms in Fountain Court more attractive than the threshold of princes.'[3]

Whenever Palmer and his friends visited Blake, the physical evidence of the unfinished *Dante* was visible. The folio was still open on his bed when he died on 12 August 1827.

Dante

Blake made 102 designs in various states of completion. To produce the finished luminous paintings, he would begin with a pencil sketching, then add definition with pen and ink, and with ink and brush, then apply broad colours with a wash, then work over the whole design adding small amounts of colour as the colour beneath had dried, rather in the manner, as Milton Klonsky has observed, of Cézanne.

Blake taught himself some Italian and used both a 1564 Venetian version with notes by Cristoforo Landino and the Henry Cary 1814 English translation. He got to know Cary and they doubtless discussed Dante's work.

In the end, Blake executed seven engravings, six remaining unfinished. 'The Circle of the Lustful: Francesca da Rimini' he completed on the largest plate mark he had ever attempted: 13½ x 21 inches. However, more than the copper plate expanded as he worked on. Blake's style grew as he gained inner freedom and projected his inner state in the scale, ambition and liberty of his designs. He was going 'all the way' and must have known it, his gathering illnesses – jaundice, piles, agues – adding to the urgency.

Again, Blake put his own mark on Dante's account of *Inferno*, *Purgatorio* and *Paradiso*, for he profoundly disagreed with the Florentine poet's literary conception of a God who accepted that part of the joy of heaven's citizens would be to watch the torments of sinners in hell. Blake told Crabb Robinson that Dante was really just a 'politician' who had learnt in heaven to repent his cruelties and vanities. So Blake's *Dante* is a critical work as well as an incomplete artistic masterpiece.

We find that God is portrayed in the unmistakable form of Old Nobodaddy, a slumped-over Urizen: blind tyrant. It has been said that our conceptions of God mirror our own limitations. Blake had gone beyond the material, and found a more than material God and a more than material Man. Hell was for the earth-bound. And to be bound to earth is hell.

Blake's hellish torments then are not permanent tortures but 'states' through which the soul passes towards true freedom. The state of mind creates the hell: witness Hitler and Stalin and others of that God-forsaking brood, whose heaven is destruction and whose hell is self-sacrifice: people who won't let go, and so won't let others be free.

In 1825, the world's first publicly subscribed railway opened, in England between Stockton and Darlington, puffing and rattling away on rails of iron. Sadly, we do not have Blake's thoughts on the matter, but one may suppose that he would not have shared the shareholder's euphoria. He would not have been content with the idea of the Canterbury Pilgrims approaching the shrine of St Thomas on an iron road that cramped their individualities into regulation-size containers, measured for profit. The cloth should be cut for the size of the man, and one law for the lion and the ox is repression.

Blake liked to walk, when he could. He would walk with young Palmer to see Linnell's family at their Hampstead farmhouse, though Blake always said that his body instinctively gave him trouble when he ventured north. Linnell's children anticipated his visits with excitement. Blake could get on their level and play with them. He loved happy people more than miserable thinkers, slaves to Urizen.

He was invited to the Aders's dinners in Euston Square and, as we know, became subject to Crabb Robinson's rather sly, adversarial questioning. Blake was known to say ridiculous things to people he thought ridiculous, but as Palmer and Linnell both maintained, Blake could always give a rational explanation of things that could be rationally explained. Palmer found some of his religious views unnerving at times, and in later life wondered about Blake's overall orthodoxy, suspecting he may have imbibed too much from the 'bad company' of Joseph Johnson's literary dinners and the circle of political radicals; but Blake has turned out to be more radical than any of them, for everyone accepts that a workman is worth his wages, but Blake would say a workman is worth considerably more, if he but knew it.

In 1826, Blake began complaining of shivering fits. He seems to have suffered from gall bladder malfunction – such would account for the jaundice and stomach pains. In July, the misery of piles afflicted him. When Crabb Robinson enquired of him how he had received the news of Flaxman's death on 7 December, Blake simply said he had expected to go before him, and said no more, keeping his personal thoughts to himself.

In February 1827, Linnell suggested that Mr and Mrs Blake move for their health to his house at Cirencester Place, but Blake, typically, would not be moved. He had found his rock, and as long as it supported him, he accepted it.

On 12 April, he wrote to Cumberland, who had enquired whether he had more poetry to offer. Blake said the last work he had produced was called *Jerusalem,* in 1820. He meant that there would be no more. 'I have been very near the gates of death,' he told Cumberland, and had returned a feeble old man, but not in the spirit and life: in that he felt he grew stronger every day, as 'this foolish body decays'. Now Flaxman was dead, 'we must all soon follow,' each to his eternal house where each reigns as king and priest forever.

No longer daring 'to count on futurity', he went on with Dante. He went on with Dante through the hells, the purgatory and, at last, to Paradise, which he knew was for children like him.

Richmond told Palmer that their friend died 'in a most glorious manner' on Sunday 12 August 1827. His body, used and done with, was buried in Bunhill Fields, Finsbury, according to the rites of the Church of England whose sister, Jerusalem, called.

Endnotes

INTRODUCTION, pp.xxvii–xxxix

1 Marsha Keith Schuchard and Keri Davies, 'Recovering the Lost Moravian History of William Blake's Family', *Blake, An Illustrated Quarterly*, 38/1 (summer 2004), University of Rochester, New York, pp.36–43 (henceforth SCHUCHARD-DAVIS).

CHAPTER ONE, pp.1–10

1 *The Complete Poetry & Prose of William Blake*, ed. David V Erdman, commentary Harold Bloom, Anchor Books, revised edn, 1988 (henceforth abbreviated to *CPP*), 'Annotations to Thornton', p.669. I have added punctuation for purposes of comprehension; Blake's punctuation, or lack of it, was idiosyncratic.

2 GE Bentley, Jr, *Blake Records*, 2nd edn, Yale University Press, 2004 (henceforth abbreviated to *BR*), p.752.

3 *The Letters of William Blake, with related documents*, ed. Geoffrey Keynes, Kt; Clarendon Press, Oxford, 1980 (henceforth abbreviated to *LETTERS*), 'Letter from George Richmond to Samuel Palmer', Wednesday, 15 August 1827, p.171.

4 *BR*, p.625.

5 *BR*, pp.654–55.

6 *BR*, pp.682–3.

CHAPTER TWO, pp. 11–25

1 Moravian Church Archive (henceforth *MCA*), C/36/11/6 (Helpers Conference Minute Book. vol.VI: 6 June 1748–6 January 1766), unnumbered pages for 'Wednesday Nov: 20th 1751', quoted in Dr Keri Davies, Nottingham Trent University's paper, 'The Lost Moravian History of William Blake's Family: Snapshots from the Archive'; www. academia.edu/713215; (henceforth referred to as K DAVIES).

2 *MCA* C/36/7/5 (Congregation Diary. vol.V: 1 January 1751–31 December 1751), p.80. Also recorded in C/36/1/2 (Register of Deaths & Burials: Burials and Deaths: 1742–July 1951), fol. 12v: 'Thomas Armitage, M. [ie Married Brother] departed Nov. 19. 1751, was buried the 23d ibid. [ie at Bloomsbury]'; original text quoted in K DAVIES.

3 Margaret Ruth Lowery, *Windows of the Morning: a Critical Study of William Blake's Poetical Sketches,* 1783. Yale Studies in English, 93 (Yale University Press, New Haven, 1940).

4 Marsha Keith Schuchard and Keri Davies, 'Recovering the Lost Moravian History of William Blake's Family', *Blake, An Illustrated Quarterly*, 38/1 (summer 2004), University of Rochester, New York, pp.36–43 (henceforth SCHUCHARD-DAVIS).

5 SCHUCHARD-DAVIS, p.38.

6 *MCA* C/36/7/3.

7   *MCA* C/36/14/2 (Labourers Conference Minute Book: 10 January 1744–23 January 1751), unnumbered pages for 'March 12th 1749', K DAVIES, p.13.

8   *MCA* C/36/14/2 (Labourers Conference Minute Book: 10 January 1744–23 January 1751), unnumbered pages for 'Monday 13th August 1750'. K DAVIES, p.14.

9   *MCA* C/36/2/159. Catherine's letter has no date but Keri Davies considers it is probably 14 November 1750, like her husband's. K DAVIES, p.20.

10   *MCA* C/36/2/158. K DAVIES, p.21.

11   *MCA* C/36/7/5 (Congregation Diary. vol.V: 1 January 1751–31 December 1751), p.10. Also recorded in C/36/1/2 (Register of Deaths & Burials: Burials and Deaths: 1742–July 1751), fol. 10v: 'Thomas, Son of Thomas and Catharine Armitage, departed Febr. 1751, and buried March 1. at Bloomsbury'. K DAVIES, p.15.

12   *MCA* C/36/11/6 (Helpers Conference Minute Book. vol.VI: 6 June 1748–6 January 1766), unnumbered pages for 'Thursday Sep: 12: 1751'. K DAVIES, p.15.

13   *MCA* C/36/7/5 (Congregation Diary. vol.V: 1 January 1751–31 December 1751), p.61. K DAVIES, p.16.

14   *MCA* C/36/11/6 (Helpers Conference Minute Book. vol.VI: 6 June 1748–6 January 1766), unnumbered pages for 'Wednesday. Decr 4th 1751'. K DAVIES, p.17.

15   *MCA* C/36/11/6 (Helpers Conference Minute Book). The note to this effect marks Catherine Armitage's last appearance in the Archive. K DAVIES, p.17.

16   *MCA* C/36/5/1 (Church Book No. 1), p.45. K DAVIES, p.23.

17   K DAVIES, p.23.

CHAPTER THREE, pp. 27–36

1   *Diary, Reminiscences, and Correspondence of Henry Crabb Robinson, Barrister-at-Law, FSA. Selected and Edited by Thomas Sadler, PhD.* vol.2, XI, Macmillan, London,1869, pp.301ff.

2   Ibid., XIII, p.323.

3   Gilchrist, *The Life of William Blake*, ed. Ruthven Todd, Everyman's Library, Dent, London,1982, p.317.

4   *Nollekens and his Times: comprehending a Life of that Celebrated Sculptor; and memoirs of several contemporary Artists, from the time of Roubiliac, Hogarth and Reynolds, to that of Fuseli, Flaxman, and Blake,* Henry Colburn, London,1828.

5   'The Family History' series, 6 vols, John Murray, London, 1829–31.

6   JC Strange, MS Journal (1859–61), in *BR*, pp.707–32.

7   Ibid., p.728.

8   Ibid., p.729.

CHAPTER FOUR, pp.37–52

1   *BR*, p.2.

2   *An Exposition, or the True State, of matters objected in England, of the People known by the Name of Unitas Fratrum,* J Robinson, Ludgate Street, London,1755, pp.29–30.

3   Henry Meyer, *Child Nature and Nurture according to Nicolaus Ludwig von Zinzendorf,* Abingdon, New York, 1928.

4   *The Life of Mr John Cennick ... written by himself.* London, sold by J Lewis and Mr [James]

Hutton (bookseller of Little Wild St), 2nd edn, 1745, p.24. I am grateful to Marsha Keith Schuchard's *William Blake's Sexual Path to Spiritual Vision*, Inner Traditions, 2008, pp.125–6, for alerting me to the significance of the *Pia Desideria* and its connection to John Cennick.

5 *PIA DESIDERIA or Divine Addresses, In Three Books. Illustrated with XLVII. Copper-Plates. Written in Latine by Herm. Hugo. Englished by EDM. ARWAKER, MA, LONDON, Printed by JL for Henry Bonwicke at the Red Lion in St Paul's Churchyard MDCXC.*

6 *BR*, p.699.

7 Ray Coleman, *John Winston Lennon*, vol.1, *1940–1966*, Sidgwick & Jackson, London, 1984, p.39.

8 This theme was explored in *John Lennon: A Journey in the Life*, a 100-minute TV music-drama I researched for BBC Everyman in 1985, starring Bernard Hill as Lennon, and directed by Ken Howard, produced with the approval of Yoko Ono Lennon. In the course of the production, director Ken Howard interviewed John's 'Aunt Mimi' by phone; Mary Elizabeth 'Mimi' Smith vouched for the 'God' story related by Coleman.

9 *BR*, p.661. Quotations from Tatham's manuscript that follow in the text are from *BR*, pp.661–4.

10 *Blake, Coleridge, Wordsworth, Lamb, ETC. Being Selections from the Remains of Henry Crabb Robinson*, ed. Edith J Morley, Manchester University Press, 1922; 'Reminiscences of Blake', p.26.

11 See my book *The Missing Family of Jesus*, Watkins, London, 2010.

12 *Blake, Coleridge, Wordsworth, Lamb, ETC. Being Selections from the Remains of Henry Crabb Robinson*, ed. Edith J Morley, Manchester University Press, 1922; 'Reminiscences of Blake', p.26.

CHAPTER FIVE, pp. 53–62

1 Dr Richard Chandler (1738–1810), friend and correspondent of Archdeacon Ralph Churton FSA (1754–1831); Churton wrote a *Memoir of Dr Richard Chandler* for his new edition of Chandler's *Travels in Asia Minor and Greece* (with notes by Nicholas Revett), Oxford, 1825.

2 Allan Cunningham, from *Lives of the Most Eminent British Painters ... &c.* (1830), in *BR*, p.627.

3 *BR*, p.665.

4 *BR*, p.729.

5 Ibid.

CHAPTER SIX, pp.63–75

1 *BR*, p.15.

2 'Contemplation'; *CPP*, p.442.

3 Malkin, *A Father's Memoirs; BR*, p.563.

4 *BR*, p.15.

5 *BR*, p.16.

6 'A Discovery of a rare document on Masonic Origins – Stukeley and the Mysteries', *Freemasonry Today*, Autumn 1998, p.22ff.

7 A 'James Blakes', subsequently 'Blake', is listed as a member of Ancients' Lodge No. 38,

meeting at the Feathers, Oxford Road (later Street), London, from December 1757 to June 1759. Then, with 12 other members of this same lodge he transferred to become a member of Ancients' Lodge No. 24, meeting at its formation in 1753 at the Edinburgh Castle, Marsh Street, then later at the Bull Inn, Bristol, and he is listed as making subscription payments in this lodge from December 1759 to December 1761 when payments cease. It is believed that this lodge had ceased meeting by 1763–4. This might indicate that these members travelled to Bristol in relation to their occupations but no details are provided at this date for occupations – it is unclear whether this 'James Blake' relocated to Bristol. I am indebted to Susan A Snell BA, Archivist and Records Manager, The Library and Museum of Freemasonry, Freemasons Hall, for this information and information regarding James Basire's lease of 31 Great Queen Street.

8 Piloo Nanavutti, 'Blake and the Gnostic Legends'; *The Aligargh Journal of English Studies,* 1976, vol.1, no. 2, India, Aligargh Muslim University, pp.168–90.

CHAPTER SEVEN, pp. 77–93

1 British Library, 'Figures from a Greek Vase, after d'Hancarville: The Apotheosis of Bacchus'; BL 1867-10-12-207. 'Figures from a Greek Vase, after d'Hancarville, A Bacchic Mystery'; BL 1867-10-12-208.

2 *BR*, p.21; British Library Add. MSS 36,492, ff. 350–51.

CHAPTER EIGHT, pp.95–106

1 Art Institute, Chicago.

2 *BR*, p.633.

3 See *The Red Shoes* ballet sequence (1948) and the 'madness' sequence in *Black Narcissus* (1949), devised by producer-directors Michael Powell (1905–1990) and Emeric Pressburger (1902–1988) and their team.

4 *BR*, p.28.

5 *BR*, p.29.

6 *LETTERS,* p.3; John Flaxman to William Hayley, 26 April 1784.

7 *BR*, pp.40–1.

8 *BR*, p.32.

9 *BR*, pp. 39–40.

10 *CPP*, p.633.

CHAPTER NINE, pp.107–119

1 Martin Butlin, *The Paintings and Drawings of William Blake, Text,* Yale University Press, 1981, pp.57–65.

2 *BR*, p.500; from *The Reminiscences of Alexander Dyce*, ed. Prof. RJ Schrader, 1972, pp.134–5.

3 *BR*, p.500; entry in commonplace book for Wednesday, 30 December 1829.

4 *CCP*, p.449.

5 Marsha Keith Schuchard, *William Blake's Sexual Path to Spiritual Vision*, Inner Traditions, Vermont, 2008, pp.128–31.

6   London, printed for EG for Michael Sparke and Edward Forrest, 1638.

7   *LETTERS*, pp.19–20; Blake to John Flaxman, 12 September 1800.

CHAPTER TEN, pp.121–134

1   Printed by Fletcher & Hanwell, Oxford, 1795.

2   Letter: Richard Gough to Ralph Churton, 8 March 1797, *Churton Papers*, letters B33 to D79.

3   Colleague of Ralph Churton: George Buckly Bower, entered Brasenose College, 1764; Fellow, 1769; Rector of Great Billing, Northamptonshire, 1787; d.1800.

4   *Churton Papers*; transcripts 1799–1801.

CHAPTER ELEVEN, pp.135–158

1   'Minutes of a General Conference of the members of the New Church Signified by the New Jerusalem in the Revelation [of St John the Divine]', 13–17 April 1789; *BR*, p.50 (footnote).

2   Folder: 'Letters of Richard Heber and Richard Chandler to Ralph Churton'; *Churton Papers.*

3   Third Degree Emulation Ritual, p.183. See Tobias Churton, p.39 *Freemasonry: The Reality*, 2nd edn, Lewis Masonic, Hersham, 2009. We have no manuscripts for this Charge, as written, before the 19th century. It is arguable that its composition was not uninfluenced by Masonic Swedenborgians, who produced a distinct 'Swedenborgian Rite' at Avignon in 1773 which fell into disuse, but was temporarily revived in the 1870s and more recently in Italy as the 'Ancient Noachide Rite'. See RA Gilbert, 'Chaos out of Order: The Rise and Fall of the Swedenborgian Rite', Grand Lodge of British Columbia and Yukon AF & AM, 1995.

4   Jacob Duché to M Hopkinson, 5 May 1785, quoted in Clarke Garrett, 'Swedenborg and the Mystical Enlightenment in Late Eighteenth-Century England,'*Journal of the History of Ideas,* January 1984, pp.72–3.

5   *BR*, p.50.

6   Marsha Keith Schuchard, *Why Mrs Blake Cried: William Blake and the Sexual Basis of Spiritual Vision,* Century, London, 2006.

7   Martin Madan, *Thelypthora,* J Dodsley, London, 1780–81, II, 336; III, 273–9. Marsha Keith Schuchard suggested that Blake derived the name of the descending soul 'Thel' from Madan's title (*phthora* is Greek for 'corruption').

8   Alexander Gilchrist, *The Life of William Blake*, Dent, Everyman Paperback, London, 1982, ch. XXXIV, pp.314–15.

9   Ibid., p.327.

10 Algernon Charles Swinburne, *William Blake: A Critical Essay*, London, 1868.

11 Edwin John Ellis and William Butler Yeats, *The Works of William Blake*, I, London, 1893.

12 Gilchrist, *Life of William Blake*, p.332.

13 *Blake, Coleridge, Wordsworth, Lamb, ETC. Being Selections from the Remains of Henry Crabb Robinson,* ed. Edith J Morley, Manchester University Press, 1922; 'Reminiscences of

Blake', p.13.

14   Ibid., p.5.

15   Ibid., p.6.

16   *LETTERS,* Plate III.

17   *CPP,* pp.469–70 (from Blake's *Notebook,* Rossetti Ms. British Library; undated).

18   *CPP,* p.473 (from Blake's *Notebook,* Rossetti Ms. British Library; undated).

CHAPTER TWELVE, pp.159–178

1   Quoted in Rufus M Jones, *Spiritual Refomers in the 16th and 17th centuries,* Beacon Press, Boston, 1959, p.159.

2   *De Vita et Scriptis,* para. 11, quoted in Désirée Hirst, *Hidden Riches, Traditional Symbolism from the Renaissance to Blake,* Eyre & Spottiswoode, 1964.

3   Account of Dr Tobias Kober, quoted by JJ Stoudt, *Sunrise to Eternity,* p.191.

4   Closing paragraph: *Of Heaven and Hell; A Dialogue between Junius, a Scholar, and Theophorus, His Master,* from *The Works of Jacob Behmen,* 4 vols, ed. G Ward and T Langcake, trans. William Law, London, 1764–81.

5   Désirée Hirst, *Hidden Riches,* p.89.

6   *An Apology and Reply upon Esaiah Stiefel,* Englished by John Sparrow, London, 1651, no.16, p.90.

7   *Forty Questions of the Soul,* London, 1655, no.11, p.12.

8   Böhme, *Sämtliche Schriften,* vol.16, ed. WE Peuckert, Frommann, Stuttgart, 1957, p.233.

9   *Mysterium Magnum,* London, 1654, ch.18, no.2.

10   Quoted by Evelyn Underhill, *Mysticism: A Study in the Nature and Development of Man's Spiritual Consciousness,* 2nd edn, London, 1912, p.142.

11   *Of the Election of Grace,* Englished by John Sparrow, London, 1655, ch.VI, no. 29.

12   Dr Stoudt, *Sunrise to Eternity,* pp.264–6, on the *Mysterium Magnum.*

13   Kathleen Raine, *Blake and Antiquity,* Routledge & Kegan Paul, London,1979, p.75.

14   Quoted in Evelyn Underhill, *Mysticism: A Study in the Nature and Development of Man's Spiritual Consciousness,* 2nd edn, London, 1912.

15   From 'The Proverbs of Hell' (*Marriage of Heaven and Hell*).

16   The oldest known English Freemasonic catechism is Sloane Ms.3329 (British Library). It has been dated to *c.*1700 or a little earlier. There is every good reason to think it was in use at least until the take-over of an earlier Accepted Free-masonry body or bodies by a Whig and Newton-oriented 'Grand Lodge', a process that began its course *c.*1716–1723. The questioner in the catechism asks: 'How high is your Lodge?' The answer is given: 'Without foots, yards or inches it reaches to heaven.' Blake's references to a 'bound' and a 'roof' to 'accepted brethren' called 'free' suggests that this earlier infinite, heavenly conception of the Lodge has been attacked. Likewise, the conception of a 'Blazing Star', a biblical conception, suffers re-interpretation as a glorification of Geometry in the Grand Lodge system. Blake would have recognized the 'Great Architect' image as 'Urizen' or 'Old Nobodaddy'. The question and answer regarding the Lodge's height have disappeared from Masonic catechisms known after the union of the Grand Lodge and the Antients in 1813, after which

time we know of the contents of English Masonic ceremonies. It is possible Blake found himself in sympathy with continental High Grade Masonic systems based in part on the writings of Böhme, as well as Paracelsus, Pasqually, Dom Pernety and Swedenborg.

CHAPTER THIRTEEN, pp.179–189

1 Information on Astley's circus from Trevor Harris, 'The Masonic Benefit Society', *Freemasonry Today*, Spring 2000.
2 John Jackson, *A Treatise on Wood Engraving, Historical and Practical,* Charles Knight, London, 1839.
3 Kathleen Raine, *Blake and Antiquity*, Routledge & Kegan Paul, London, 1979, pp.34ff.
4 *The original letter belonged to Sir* Geoffrey Keynes but has disappeared, according to GE Bentley, Jr (*BR*).
5 *BR*, pp.59–60.
6 Martin Butlin, *The Paintings and Drawings of William Blake, Plates,* Yale University Press, 1981, plates 284–91.
7 *LETTERS*, p.4.
8 GE Bentley, Jr, *BR*, p.61.
9 *The Journal of John Gabriel Stedman 1744–1797*, ed. Stanbury Thompson, London, 1962.

CHAPTER FOURTEEN, pp.191–207

1 Rev. Ralph Churton (1754–1831), *Reminiscences*, folder; *Churton Papers*.
2 Printed by T Bensley, for J Edwards, Pall Mall, and T Payne, Mews Gate, 1798.
3 *CPP*, p.554, Notes on 'A Vision of the Last Judgement'; 'For the Year 1810 Additions to Blake's Catalogue of Pictures &c.' From Blake's *Notebook*, notes for an exhibition that never happened. But note the date: 1810. Blake's view of possibilities for a utopian society may have changed dramatically 1792–1810 owing to his bitter experience of the Terror and war, and his maturing of thought.
4 801 CPP, *Notebook*, p. 63.
5 From Blake's *Vala*, or *The Four Zoas* (begun *c*.1797).

CHAPTER FIFTEEN, pp.209–220

1 Thomas Mathias, *The Pursuits of Literature, A Satirical Poem in Four Dialogues*, 7th edn, revised, printed for T Becket, Pall Mall, London,1798 (first edn 1794), p.6.
2 See *Of Errors and of Truth, or Men recalled to the universal principle of Science,* 1775.
3 Yale Centre for British Art, Copy A, 1795.
4 Piloo Nanavutti, 'Blake and the Gnostic Legends', *The Aligargh Journal of English Studies*, ed. Ansari, I, 2, Aligargh Muslim University, 1976, p.174.
5 'Theletos' from the Greek *Thelema* = Will.

CHAPTER SIXTEEN, pp.221–239

1 *LETTERS*, p.65; Blake to Thomas Butts, 16 August 1803.
2 Thomas James Mathias, *The Pursuits of Literature, A Satirical Poem in four Dialogues, with Notes,* 7th edn, printed for T Becket, Pall Mall, London, 1798 (first edn 1794).

3   *BR*, pp.64–5.

4   *BR*, p.80.

5   Franz Hartmann, *Paracelsus, Life and Prophecies*, Kessinger Legacy Reprints, US, undated, p.41.

6   The discovery of a femur of what was probably a megalosaurus was reported and engraved in Dr Robert Plot's *Natural History of Oxfordshire* (1676). It was thought to be the bone of an animal, or possibly a giant, as referred to in Genesis 6. In 1763 R Brookes, writing about strange stones, observed its similarity to a pair of testicles and called it '*Scrotum humanum*'. Blake perhaps joined the two ideas and created an idea of 'Urizens army of horrors' – reptilized men, or corrupted beings, associated with the 'Giants' of Genesis.

7   *Cf* Blake on the Genesis 1 creation story in the context of Wordsworth's 'Nature worship', reported by Crabb Robinson from a meeting with Blake on 24 January 1826: 'For Nature is the work of the Devil. On my obtaining from him [Blake] the declaration that the Bible was the work of God, I [Robinson] referred to the commencement of Genesis "In the beginning God created the Heaven & the Earth." But I gained nothing by this, for I was triumphantly told that this God was not Jehovah ["Jahveh"], but the Elohim, & the doctrine of the Gnostics repeated with sufficient consistency to silence one so unlearned as myself.' Quoted in *Blake, Coleridge, Wordsworth, Lamb, ETC. Being Selections from the Remains of Henry Crabb Robinson*, ed. Edith J Morley, Manchester University Press, 1922; 'Reminiscences of Blake', p.23.

8   From the 'Epilogue' to the revised version of *For Children: The Gates of Paradise* (still dated 1793), reissued at an unknown date between 1806 and 1818 as *For the Sexes: The Gates of Paradise*, with four new pages of text and extended inscriptions. The 'Epilogue' concludes by asserting that, though 'The Accuser' is still worshipped as 'Jehovah' or 'Jesus', the figure is still Lucifer, the 'Son of Morn in weary Nights decline/ The lost Travellers Dream under the Hill'.

CHAPTER SEVENTEEN, pp.241–246

1   *LETTERS*, p.5; Blake to Cumberland, 6 December 1795.

2   Kathleen Raine, *Blake and Antiquity*, Routledge & Kegan Paul, London, 1979, pp.22–3.

3   *Fable of Cupid and Psyche*, trans. Thomas Taylor, 8vo, London, 1795. Taylor's complete 11-book *Metamorphosis, or The Golden Ass* did not appear until 1822.

4   Joseph Farington, RA (1747–1821), Fellow of the Society of Antiquaries, born in Leigh, Lancashire, son of William Farington, rector of Warrington and vicar of Leigh. Joseph Farington's brother Robert, who attended Brasenose College from 1777, was a friend, pupil and correspondent of Rev. Ralph Churton. Farington took on Churton's job and rooms as Junior Bursar when Churton was granted the living at Middleton Cheney in 1792. Churton received an interesting request from Farington, which Churton answered on 17 June 1797: 'Letter to Mr Farington (Mountebank asked leave to exhibit. No).' Farington was either painting himself while studying for his doctorate in divinity (awarded 1803) under Churton or, perhaps, was desirous of leaving his duties to attend a London exhibition; his brother Joseph being the Royal Academician. Robert Farington appears in Joseph Farington's famous Diary (vol. 5, ch. LXX), 11 September 1809: 'To meet by

Brother Robert at Salisbury and with him to proceed on a tour to Devonshire and Cornwall.' Robert Farington became vicar of St George in the East, London (a Brasenose living) in 1802, succeeded there in 1842 by Ralph Churton's son, Henry Burgess Whitaker Churton (1810–1891).

5   *BR*, p.69.

6   *BR*, p.70.

7   *The Farington Diary, by Joseph Farington RA*, ed. James Grieg, Vol. One, 1793–1802, 3rd edn, Hutchinson, London, pp.151–2.

8   On 5 April 1797, Sigismund Bacstrom, Swedish Mason, kabbalist and scholar of alchemy, initiated Blake's friend Alexander Tilloch (1759–1825) into his Rosicrucian Brotherhood. By a curious coincidence, this event occurred on the same day that Blake signed a testimonial (along with William Sharp, James Basire, and Writing Engraver WS Blake), among other engravers, supporting Tilloch's invention of an unforgeable Bank of England note. The engravers testified that Tilloch's specimen resisted forging by engravers' skills. Tilloch gave his address as 'Cary-street'. There were two streets of this name, one in Holborn, near Chancery Lane, the other, by Foster Lane, Cheapside, just north of St Paul's Cathedral. According to Adam McClean's article on Bacstrom (*Hermetic Journal,* No. 6, 1979), Bacstrom himself was admitted into a Rosy Cross Order on the island of Mauritius by the Comte de Chazal on 12 September 1794: 'When Bacstrom settled in London, one of his more important pupils was the Scotsman Alexander Tilloch, the editor of the *Philosophical Magazine,* which concentrated on papers and articles of early scientific research.

'In 1980 I discovered Tilloch's own copy of his admission document to Bacstrom's Rosicrucian Society, which is signed by Bacstrom, in the Ferguson Collection at Glasgow University Library. I decided to print this admission document in its entirety as it gives a valuable insight into the type of organisation and principles which Bacstrom worked within. It is likely, considering the possible Comte de St Cermain connection, that this was the kind of *Societas Roseae Crucis* which was operating throughout the eighteenth century.' The Society's principles would have been attractive to Blake, including the stipulation that women (unlike in regular Masonry) could be admitted, as there were no specific genders in heaven. (See www.levity.com/alchemy/bacstrm1)

CHAPTER EIGHTEEN, pp.247–261

1   *BR*, p.77.

2   1797 is the date on the first fair copy.

3   WB Yeats and EJ Ellis, *The Works of William Blake*, 1893.

4   Kathleen Raine, *Blake and Antiquity*, Routledge & Kegan Paul, London, 1978, p.24.

5   Blake's words were taken by Van Morrison for his 'Let the Slave (Incorporating the Price of Experience)' track on the *Sense of Wonder* album (1985).

6   *Churton Papers*, 'Ralph Churton, Private Journal 1793–1800'.

7   *BR*, p.80.

8   *BR*, p.96.

9   Robert Essick and Morton Paley, '"Dear Generous Cumberland": A newly discovered Letter & Poem by William Blake'; *Blake an Illustrated Quarterly* 32, 1998, pp.4–5. Blake sent

the letter from Felpham, Sussex, to Cumberland on 1 September 1800, adding: 'how canst thou Expect any thing but Envy in Londons accursed walls'. Perhaps Blake fancied bringing something of 'Sophis' to rural Felpham, as Hayley had made of Eartham Hall a sanctuary of repose for the poet William Cowper.

10   For an account of d'Olivet, see Tobias Churton, *The Invisible History of the Rosicrucians*, Inner Traditions, Vermont, 2008.

11   Martin Butlin, *The Paintings & Drawings of William Blake, Text*, Yale University Press, 1981. p.332.

12   *BR*, p.81.

13   When in 1800 Archdeacon Ralph Churton began researching his *Life of Dean Nowell* (Oxford, 1809), with engravings by James Basire, Blake's engraving master's son), Churton corresponded with Charles Townley's close friend, antiquarian Thomas Dunham Whitaker FSA, Rector of Holme (d. 2 January 1822). Whitaker (*Churton Papers*, 'Letters to Ralph Churton 1800–06') wrote from Holme, 3 September 1806: 'I will give Basire directions about it [the funding of the engraving by Townley's relative Mr Alexander Nowell, descendant of Churton's biographical subject] whenever you inform me that it is likely to be wanted.' Whitaker investigated the 'Townley Papers' on Churton's behalf; the Nowells and Townleys had long been related. Whitaker secured the artist Read to make a drawing of Dean Nowell for the engraving and dealt with Basire (*Churton Papers*, Whitaker to Churton, 14 February 1806). Townley had considered Basire for Blundell's engraving task. Charles Townley died 3 January 1805. Whitaker to Churton, 14 February 1806: 'I have the melancholy satisfaction of learning that a beautiful Monument to the Memory of Mr Charles Townley is now nearly finished by Nollekens [Joseph Nollekens, 1737–1823]. It is really more than I expected & had it not been ordered in the first Moments of Grief or Gratitude would never have been ordered at all.'

    Whitaker inspected Charles Townley's manuscripts shortly after Townley died: 'This search has been a melancholy Task, – the Volume in which the Evidences relating to the Family is contained being locked up in Mr Townley's own Dressing Room, where there are still left too many Remains of the Deceased Owner (even his Medicines) not to excite painful Feelings in those who loved him. [...] The Museum [Statuary, in Park St] is to be moved [...] to Townley [Lancashire] where it will be lost as a national Object.' (*Churton Papers*, 'Letters Whitaker to R.C. 1800–06'; Holme, 25 April 1805). The collection was eventually bought for the British Museum by parliamentary dispensation – and £30,000. It consisted of more than 300 marbles, terracottas, bronzes and other artefacts. Nolleken's bust of Townley was to be sold abroad when it was purchased for Towneley Hall, Burnley, Lancs.; it was returned to Townley's ancestral residence in 2008.

14   *LETTERS*, p.16; Blake to Hayley, 6 May 1800.

15   *LETTERS*, p. 16; Hayley to Blake, July 1800.

16   *LETTERS*, p.17; Blake to Cumberland, 2 July 1800.

17   Ibid.

18   *Letters of Lady Hesketh to the Rev John Johnson L.L.D. Edited by Catharine Bodham Johnson (née Donne)*, Jarrold & Sons, 1901, London, p.111.

19 Ibid., p.115.

20 *BR*, p.95.

21 *LETTERS*, p.23; Blake to Flaxman, 21 September 1800.

22 *BR*, p.95.

23 *LETTERS*, p.23; Blake to Flaxman, 21 September 1800.

24 *LETTERS*, p.25; Butts to Blake, 23 September 1800.

25 *LETTERS*, p.27–30; Blake to Butts, 2 October 1800.

26 *Churton Papers,* Letters to Ralph Churton B33–D.79; Letter from Henry Addington to Ralph Churton, Woodley, 6 November 1800.

CHAPTER NINETEEN, pp.263–276

1 *BR*, p.104.

2 *BR*, p.105.

3 *Churton Papers,* 'R.C. Private Journal 1793–1800', 20 November 1797.

4 *BR*, p.110.

5 *Churton Papers,* 'R.C. Private Journal 1801–1806', 3 October 1801.

6 *CPP*, p.500.

7 *CPP*, p.635ff.

8 *Churton Papers,* 'Letters Ralph Churton to Thomas Townson Churton, 382–400', 13 October 1814. The 'William' referred to is Ralph Churton's son, William Ralph (1801–1828), brother to Thomas Townson Churton (1798–1865).

9 *BR*, p.140.

10 *Religious Enthusiasm considered; in Eight Sermons, preached before the University of Oxford, in the year MDCCCII, at the lecture founded by John Bampton MA, Canon of Salisbury*, Oxford, 1803, pp.37–44.

11 *LETTERS*, pp.41–2; Blake to Butts, 22 November 1801.

12 *The Triumphs of Temper, A Poem by William Hayley in Six Cantos*, printed by J Seagrave, Chichester, for T Cadell & W Davies, The Strand, London, 1803.

13 *LETTERS*, pp.47–8; Blake to Butts, 10 January 1802.

14 Ibid. The willingness to have his works outside the 'cold galleries of fashion' undoubtedly has a bearing on his decision to exhibit at his brother's shop in Broad Street in 1809–10. Blake worked for a spiritual audience, and for posterity. He would, I think, have agreed that Christianity is a 'divine life', not a 'divine science'.

15 *LETTERS*, p.50; Blake to James Blake, 30 January 1803.

16 *LETTERS*, pp.56–8; Blake to Butts, 6 July 1803.

17 *BR*, p.150.

18 *Churton Papers,* 'R.C. Private Journal 1801–1806', 11 March 1803.

19 *LETTERS*, pp.57–8; Blake to Butts, 6 July 1803.

20 Ibid.

21 *Churton Papers,* 'R.C. Private Journal 1801–1806', 14 July 1803.

22 *LETTERS*, p.60; Hayley to Flaxman, 7 August 1803.

23 *LETTERS*, p.62, 'Scofield's [sic] information and complaint', 15 August 1803.

24 *Churton Papers,* 'RC [ditto] Private Journal 1801–1806', 7 September 1803.

25 *LETTERS*, p.68; Blake to Hayley, 7 October 1803.

26 *LETTERS*, p.70; Blake to Hayley, 26 October 1803.

27 *BR*, p.174; Lady Hesketh to William Hayley, 27 November 1803.

28 It is worth mentioning that a portrait of Lady Hesketh's relative, Peter Leopold Nassau Cowper, 5th Earl Cowper, is attributed to John Hoppner RA, who we know held Blake's art in contempt. The portrait belonged to the Cowper family until sold. According to records at *Bonhams* (art dealers), a portrait of Lord Cowper was recorded in the sale of John Hoppner's unfinished works on 31 May 1823, lot 29. Hoppner was a painter of the wealthy and powerful. His German mother had been a Royal attendant, and Hoppner was frequently visited by the Prince of Wales. His style deliberately echoed that of Reynolds, whom Blake, of course, despised.

CHAPTER TWENTY, pp.277–284

1 *Churton Papers,* 'Letters of Ralph Churton to John Brickdale Blakeway', 5 April 1804.

2 *BR*, p.183.

3 See endnote 28, Chapter Nineteen.

4 *BR*, pp.183–4.

5 *BR*, p.180.

6 *BR*, p.184.

7 Ibid. Hayley's *Memoirs* are dated 1823; the 3rd Duke of Richmond had died in 1806; self-censorship was politic in the circumstances.

8 *BR*, p.190.

9 Ibid.

10 *LETTERS*, p.91; Blake to Hayley, 28 May 1804. 'Our poor George': the King had another attack of his old complaint in February (porphyria?). Prime Minister Addington feared another onset of madness but the Lord Chancellor Lord Eldon protected the King from the restraining methods of 'mad doctors', the Willis brothers, and from Addington's misplaced faith in them. George did not lose his mind but he was getting old. A side-effect of the ailment was cataracts. George was losing sight in his right eye, finding it difficult to read; he was still convalescing in May when he decisively prevented a Pitt-Fox coalition government after the Addington's Commons defeat of 25 April 1804. Throughout this time, the Prince of Wales treated his father with a haughty arrogance reserved for the mentally ill; rumours of madness, or permanent indisposition, persisted.

11 *BR*, p.195.

12 *LETTERS*, p.98; Blake to Hayley, 7 August 1804.

13 *LETTERS*, p.101; Blake to Hayley, 23 October 1804.

14 *BR*, p.197.

15 *LETTERS*, pp.104–5; Blake to Hayley, 18 December 1804.

16 *BR*, p.206; Hesketh to Hayley, 1 September 1805.

17 *BR*, p. 204; Hesketh to Hayley, 27 July 1805.

18 Ibid.; Hesketh to Johnny Johnson, 31 July 1805.

19 *BR*, p.205; Hayley to Hesketh, 3 August 1805.

CHAPTER TWENTY-ONE, pp.285–298

1 See note 28, Chapter Nineteen.

2 *Churton Papers*, 'R.C. Private Journal 1801–1806', 21 October 1805.

3 British Library Add. MSS 39, 780, f.92; *BR*, p.220.

4 *LETTERS*, pp.120–1; Blake to Hayley, 11 December 1805.

5 The Arundel Marbles are now part of the collection of the Ashmolean Museum, Oxford.

6 *LETTERS*, p.122; Blake to Richard Phillips, June 1806.

7 *BR*, pp.229–30.

8 *BR*, p.227.

9 *LETTERS*, p.127; Cromek to Blake, May 1807.

10 *LETTERS*, p.125; Cromek to James Montgomery, 17 April 1807.

11 *LETTERS*, p.126; Cromek to James Montgomery, 17 April 1807.

12 *LETTERS*, pp.128–9; Cromek to Blake, May 1807.

13 Anna Eliza Bray, *Life of Stothard RA*, John Murray, London, 1851, pp.142–3.

14 *CPP*, p.508.

15 British Library Add. MSS 36, 519H, f.336; *BR*, p.246.

16 Swedenborg *Spiritual Diary* (1758), section 5107; trans. Bush, Smithson and Buss (1883–9) at www.sacred-texts.com

CHAPTER TWENTY-TWO, pp.299–306

1 Published by RH Cromek with Cadell & Davies; J Johnson, T Payne, 1808. There were 89 subscriptions.

2 *A DESCRIPTIVE CATALOGUE of PICTURES, Poetical and Historical Inventions* [...] *London, Printed by D.N. Shury, 7, Berwick-Street, Soho, for J. Blake, 28 Broad-Street, Golden-Square. 1809.* pp.iii–iv.

3 Ibid. p.56.

4 Ibid., p.53.

5 Ibid., p.22.

6 *Diary, Reminiscences, and Correspondence of Henry Crabb Robinson, Barrister-at-Law, F.S.A. Selected and Edited by Thomas Sadler, Ph.D.* Vol.2, XI, Macmillan, London, 1869.

7 *BR*, p.598.

8 *BR*, p.531, from *The Correspondence of Robert Southey with Caroline Bowles* (1881), pp.193–4.

9 Owen had joined Joanna Southcott's millenarian cult and had become an elder. Southey also associated Blake in his mind with prophetess Southcott (who believed she would give birth to the Messiah) and the radical prophet of Anglo-Israelism, Richard Brothers (1757–1824), and his sometime radical millenarian revolutionary followers William Bryan and John Wright who both had links with the Avignon *illuminés*. Brothers was arrested for treason in 1795, having prophesied the death of the King (he had also prophesied Louis XVI's death, correctly). Sent to an asylum and released in 1806, he spent the rest of his life designing flags and plans for his 'New Jerusalem', of which he believed himself prince. On 30 January 1815,

Crabb Robinson visited Flaxman who told him about Sharpe the engraver: 'who seems the ready dupe of any & every religious fanatic & imposter who offers himself'. Sharpe 'tho' deceived by Brothers became a warm partisan of Joanna Southcoat [*sic* after 1795] – He endeavoured to make a convert of Blake the engraver, but as Flaxman judiciously observed, such men as Blake are not fond of playing the second fiddle – Hence Blake himself a seer of visions & a dreamer of dreams would not do homage to a rival claimant of the privilege of prophecy.' Blake was talking to Flaxman again at this period (1815); *BR*, pp.319–20.

Southey had got to know the millenarians in the 1790s when he shared radical ideas with his friend Coleridge and wrote about them in *Letters from England* (1808) under the pseudonym Don Manuel Alvarez Espriella. He was the only mainstream writer who had inside knowledge of millenarian radical culture and personal knowledge of the protagonists. The thought of it all embarrassed him in later life, when hostile critic William Hazlitt pilloried him for having exchanged 'Liberty' for 'Legitimacy'. Southey had come to see Britain's susceptibility to revolutionary creeds and the possible violent results and was determined to expose dangerous ideologues. Blake, by association then, was tinged with Southey's suspicion of madness linked to revolutionary religious enthusiasm and fanaticism.

10 *BR*, p.307.

11 *BR*, pp.294–5; Seymour Kirkup to Lord Houghton, 25 March 1870.

12 *CPP*, p.580.

CHAPTER TWENTY-THREE, pp.307–317

1 *Blake, Coleridge, Wordsworth, Lamb, ETC. Being Selections from the Remains of Henry Crabb Robinson,* ed. Edith J Morley, Manchester University Press, 1922, p.1.

2 Ibid.

3 *CPP*, p.665.

4 *Churton Papers,* 'Journal of Ralph Churton 1807–1827'.

5 *BR*, p.320.

6 Ibid.

7 Ibid.

8 Quoted in Mona Wilson, *The Life of William Blake,* London, Granada, 1971, pp.314–16. Wilson dates the occasion to 20 January 1820, but according to Bentley (*BR*), there is an error in the dating of Lady Bury's diary. Bentley argues convincingly for 1818.

CHAPTER TWENTY-FOUR, pp.319–328

1 *Churton Papers,* 'Letters from Ralph Churton to John Nichols 1784–1820 inc.', letter to John Bowyer Nichols (son of printer John Nichols), 16 March 1820.

2 *LETTERS,* p.165; Sir Edward Denny to John Linnell, 26 November 1826.

3 Letter Palmer to Alexander Gilchrist, 23 August 1855, quoted in Milton Klonsky, *Blake's Dante,* Sidgwick & Jackson, London, 1980, p.6.

Bibliography

Ackroyd, Peter, *Blake*, Vintage, 1996.

Agrippa, Heinrich Cornelius, *Three Books of Occult Philosophy* (English version, 1651), reprint: Chthonios Books, Hastings, 1986.

Anderson, Rev. James, *Constitutions of Free-masons*, Kessinger Reprints (undated), originally: London, 1723.

Bentley, Jr, GE, *Blake Records*, 2nd edn, Yale University Press, 2004.

The Stranger from Paradise: A Biography of William Blake, Yale University Press, 2003.

Blake, William, *The Complete Poetry & Prose of William Blake*, ed. David V Erdman, commentary by Harold Bloom, Anchor Books, New York, revised edn 1988.

The Notebook of William Blake: A Photographic and Typographic Facsimile, ed. David V Erdman, with Donald K Moore), Clarendon Press, Oxford, 1973.

Böhme, Jacob, *Mysterium Magnum*, London, 1654.

Of the Election of Grace, Englished by John Sparrow, London, 1655.

Of Heaven and Hell; A Dialogue between Junius, a Scholar, and Theophorus, His Master, from *The Works of Jacob Behmen*, 4 vols, ed. G Ward and T Langcake, trans. William Law, London, 1764–81.

Sämtliche Schriften, ed. WE Peuckert, vol.16, Frommann, Stuttgart, 1957.

Brettingham, Matthew; Hamilton, Gavin; Revett, Nicholas; and Stuart, James, *The Antiquities of Athens and Other Monuments*, John Haberkorn, London, 1762.

Bryant, Jacob, *A New System, or an Analysis of Ancient Mythology: Wherein an Attempt is made to divest Tradition of Fable, and to Reduce the Truth to its Original Purity*, 3 vols, London 1774–76. Bürger, Gottfried Augustus, *Lenore*, trans. John Thomas Stanley, printed S Gosnall, 1796.

Butlin, Martin *The Paintings and Drawings of William Blake, Plates,* Yale University Press, 1981.

The Paintings and Drawings of William Blake, Text, Yale University Press, 1981.

Cennick, John, *The Life of Mr John Cennick … written by himself*, 2nd edn, sold by J Lewis and Mr [James] Hutton (bookseller of Little Wild St), London, 1745.

Chandler, Dr Richard; Pars, William; Revett, Nicholas, *Ionian Antiquities*, published with the permission of the Society of Dilettanti, printed by T Spilsbury and W Haskell, London, 1769.

Chandler, Dr Richard, *Travels in Asia Minor and Greece*, including *A Memoir of Dr Richard Chandler* by Archdeacon Ralph Churton FSA, and notes by Nicholas Revett, Oxford, 1825.

Churton, Archdeacon Ralph, *Life of Dean Nowell*, Oxford University Press, 1809.

Churton, Tobias, *Freemasonry: The Reality*, 2nd edn, Lewis Masonic, Hersham, 2009.

The Invisible History of the Rosicrucians, Inner Traditions, Vermont, 2008.

Comenius, *Orbis Sensualium Pictus* ('The Visible World in Pictures'), Nuremberg, 1658.

Cunningham, Allan, *Lives of the Most Eminent British Painters, Sculptors and Architects*, 6 vols, John Murray, 'The Family Library', London, 1830.

Darwin, Erasmus, *The Botanic Garden* (first part), London, Joseph Johnson, 1791.

Gilchrist, Alexander, *The Life of William Blake*, ed. Ruthven Todd, Everyman's Library, Dent, London, 1982 (first edn 1863).

Gough, Richard, *Sepulchral Monuments of Great Britain, applied to illustrate the history of families, manners, habits and arts at the different periods from the Norman Conquest to the Seventeenth Century*, 2 vols, London, printed by J Nichols, 1786–96.

Guyon, Madame (Jeanne-Marie Bouvier de la Motte Guyon), *L'Âme Amante de son Dieu, representée dans les Emblèmes de Hermannus Hugo*, Paris, 1790.

Hanegraaf, WJ (ed.), *Dictionary of Gnosis and Western Esotericism*, EJ Brill, Leiden, 2006.

Hartmann, Franz, *Paracelsus, Life and Prophecies,* Kessinger Legacy Reprints, US, undated.

Hayley, William, *An Essay On Sculpture – in a Series of Epistles to John Flaxman Esq. R.A.*, T Cadell Jr & W Davies, The Strand, London, 1800.

The Triumphs of Temper, A Poem by William Hayley in Six Cantos, printed by J Seagrave, Chichester, for T Cadell & W Davies, The Strand, London, 1803.

Hirst, Désirée, *Hidden Riches, Traditional Symbolism from the Renaissance to Blake*, Eyre & Spottiswoode, London, 1964.

Hugo, Herman, *PIA DESIDERIA* ['Pious Desires'], *or Divine Addresses, In Three Books. Illustrated with XLVII. Copper-Plates. Written in Latine by Herm. Hugo. Englished by EDM. ARWAKER, M.A, LONDON, Printed by J.L. for Henry Bonwicke at the Red Lion in St Paul's Churchyard MDCXC* (1690).

Jackson, John, *A Treatise on Wood Engraving, Historical and Practical*, Charles Knight, London, 1839.

Johnson, Catharine (ed.), *Letters of Lady Hesketh to the Rev John Johnson L.L.D. Edited by Catharine Bodham Johnson (née Donne)*, Jarrold & Sons, London, 1901.

Jones, Rufus M, *Spiritual Reformers in the 16th and 17th centuries,* Beacon Press, Boston, 1959.

Keynes, Sir Geoffrey (ed.), *Blake: Complete Writings*, Oxford University Press, Oxford and New York, 2nd revised edn, 1966.

The Letters of William Blake, with related documents, 3rd edn, Clarendon Press, Oxford, 1980.

Klonsky, Milton, *Blake's Dante*, Sidgwick & Jackson, London, 1980.

Knight, Richard Payne, *Account of the remains of the worship of Priapus*, 1786.

Lardner, Nathaniel, *The History of the Heretics of the two first centuries after Christ*, Joseph Johnson, London, 1780.

Lowery, Margaret Ruth, *Windows of the Morning: a Critical Study of William Blake's Poetical Sketches, 1783*, Yale Studies in English, 93, Yale University Press, New Haven, 1940.

Madan, Martin, *Thelyphthora: Or a Treatise on Female Ruin*, J Dodsley, London, 1780.

Malkin, Benjamin Heath, *A Father's Memoirs of His Child*, Longman, Hurst, Rees and Orme, London, 1806.

Mathias, Thomas James, *The Pursuits of Literature, A Satirical Poem in Four Dialogues*, 7th edn, 'Printed for T Becket, Pall Mall' (London), 1798.

Meyer, Henry, *Child Nature and Nurture according to Nicolaus Ludwig von Zinzendorf*, Abingdon, New York, 1928.

Morley, Edith J (ed.), *Blake, Coleridge, Wordsworth, Lamb, ETC. Being Selections from the Remains of Henry Crabb Robinson*, Manchester University Press, 1922.

Mosheim, JL, *Ecclesiastical History Ancient & Modern*, 6 vols, trans. Archibald Maclaine, T Cadell, London, 1782.

Nott, George Frederick, *Religious Enthusiasm considered; in Eight Sermons, preached before the University of Oxford, in the year MDCCCII, at the lecture founded by John Bampton MA, Canon of Salisbury*, Oxford University Press, 1803.

Paley, Morton D (ed.), *William Blake, Jerusalem, The Emanation of the Giant Albion*, The William Blake Trust, Tate Gallery, London, 1991.

Priestley, Joseph, *An History of the Corruptions of Christianity*, 2 vols, Joseph Johnson, Birmingham, 1782.

Raine, Kathleen, *Blake and Antiquity*, Routledge & Kegan Paul, London, 1979.
  Blake and Tradition, 2 vols, Princeton University Press, 1968.

Rimius, Henry, *A Candid Narrative of the Rise and Progress of the Herrnhutters*, A Linde, London, 1753.
  A Solemn Call on Count Zinzendorf, 'Printed for A. Linde', London, 1754.

Rimius, Henry (ed.), *A Pastoral letter against Fanaticism, Addressed to the Mennonites of Friesland, by Mr John Stinstra*, 'Printed for A. Linde, Stationer to His Majesty', London, 1753.

Sadler, Thomas (ed.), *Diary, reminiscences, and Correspondence of Henry Crabb Robinson, Barrister-at-Law, F.S.A. Selected and Edited by Thomas Sadler, PhD.* Vol.2, Macmillan, London, 1869.

Schuchard, Marsha Keith, *William Blake's Sexual Path to Spiritual Vision*, Inner Traditions, Rochester, Vermont, 2008; formerly published as *Why Mrs Blake Cried: William Blake and the Sexual Basis of Spiritual Vision*, Century, London, 2006.

Smith, John Thomas, *Nollekens and his Times: comprehending a Life of that Celebrated Sculptor; and memoirs of several contemporary Artists, from the time of Roubiliac, Hogarth and Reynolds, to that of Fuseli, Flaxman, and Blake*, vol.2, Henry Colburn, London, 1828.

Stoudt, JJ, *Sunrise to Eternity: A Study in Jacob Boehme's Life and Thought*, University of Pennsylvania Press, Philadelphia, 1957.

St Martin, Louis Claude de, *Des Erreurs et de la Vérité (Of Errors and of Truth, or Men recalled to the universal principle of Science)*, Paris, 1775.

Studley, Rev. Peter, *The Looking-Glass of Schism* (pamphlet), Shrewsbury, 1633.

Stukeley, William, *Stonehenge, a Temple Restor'd to the British Druids*, London, 1740.

Swinburne, Algernon Charles, *William Blake: A Critical Essay*, London, JC Hotten, 1868.

Taylor, Thomas, *Dissertation on the Eleusinian and Bacchic Mysteries*, J Weitstein, Amsterdam, 1790.

Taylor, Thomas (trans.), *Concerning the Beautiful, or a paraphrased translation from the Greek of Plotinus, Ennead I, Book 6*, printed for the author, London, 1787.

    Fable of Cupid and Psyche, translated from …Apuleius, printed for the author, London, 1795.

    Five Books of Plotinus, London, 1794.

    The Phaedrus of Plato, London, 1792.

Thompson, Stanbury (ed.), *The Journal of John Gabriel Stedman 1744–1797*, Mitre Press, London, 1962.

Underhill, Evelyn, *Mysticism: A Study in the Nature and Development of Man's Spiritual Consciousness,* EP Dutton & Co., New York, 1911.

Wilkins, Rt Rev. John, *Mathematical and Philosophical Works*, printed for J Nicholson, London, 1708.

    Principles and Duties of Natural Religion, 2 vols, 8th edn, printed for J Nicholson, London, 1722.

Wilson, Mona, *The Life of William Blake,* Granada, London, 1971.

Wollstonecraft, Mary, *Original Stories from Real Life: with Conversations, Calculated to Regulate the Affections and Form the Mind to Truth and Goodness*, J Johnson, London, 1791.

Wright, Thomas, *The Life of William Blake*, 2 vols, T Wright, Olney, 1929.

Yeats, William Butler, and Ellis, Edwin John (ed.), *The Works of William Blake, Poetic Symbolic and Critical*, 3 vols, B Quaritch, London, 1893

Yeats, WB (ed), *The Poems of William Blake*, Routledge & Kegan Paul, London, 1979.

Zinzendorf, Count Nicolaus, *An Exposition, or the True State, of matters objected in England, of the People known by the Name of Unitas Fratrum*, J Robinson, Ludgate Street, London, 1755.

Papers and Articles Consulted

The Churton Papers, transcribed and edited by Victor Churton (1927–2007), including the diaries and correspondence of Archdeacon Ralph Churton (1754–1831).

Dr Keri Davies, Nottingham Trent University, paper entitled 'The Lost Moravian History of William Blake's Family: Snapshots from the Archive', www. academia.edu/713215.

Marsha Keith Schuchard and Keri Davies, 'Recovering the Lost Moravian History of William Blake's Family', *Blake, An Illustrated Quarterly*, 38/1 (Summer 2004), University of Rochester, New York, pp.36–43.

David Haycock, 'A Discovery of a rare document on Masonic Origins – Stukeley and the Mysteries', *Freemasonry Today*, Autumn 1998.

Piloo Nanavutti, 'Blake and the Gnostic Legends', *The Aligargh Journal of English Studies*, Vol. 1, 1976, No. 2, India, Aligargh Muslim University, pp.168–90.

Clarke Garrett, 'Swedenborg and the Mystical Enlightenment in Late Eighteenth-Century England', *Journal of the History of Ideas*, January 1984.

Trevor Harris, 'The Masonic Benefit Society', *Freemasonry Today*, Spring 2000.

Robert N Essick and Morton D Paley: 'Dear Generous Cumberland: A newly discovered Letter & Poem by William Blake'; *Blake, An Illustrated Quarterly* 32 (1998), University of Rochester, New York, pp.4–13.

Index

The abbreviation WB refers to William Blake.

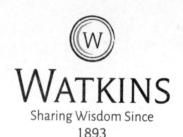

WATKINS
Sharing Wisdom Since
1893

The story of Watkins Publishing dates back to March 1893, when John M. Watkins, a scholar of esotericism, overheard his friend and teacher Madame Blavatsky lamenting the fact that there was nowhere in London to buy books on mysticism, occultism or metaphysics. At that moment Watkins was born, soon to become the home of many of the leading lights of spiritual literature, including Carl Jung, Rudolf Steiner, Alice Bailey and Chögyam Trungpa.

Today our passion for vigorous questioning is still resolute. With over 350 titles on our list, Watkins Publishing reflects the development of spiritual thinking and new science over the past 120 years. We remain at the cutting edge, committed to publishing books that change lives.

DISCOVER MORE ...

Read our blog

Watch and listen to
our authors in action

Sign up to
our mailing list

JOIN IN THE CONVERSATION

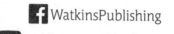 WatkinsPublishing   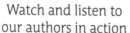@watkinswisdom

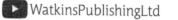 WatkinsPublishingLtd   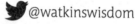+watkinspublishing1893

Our books celebrate conscious, passionate, wise and happy living.
Be part of the community by visiting

www.watkinspublishing.com